# *PERSPECTIVES ON LOSS*

**SERIES IN DEATH, DYING, AND BEREAVEMENT**
ROBERT A. NEIMEYER, CONSULTING EDITOR

Nord—*Multiple AIDS-Related Loss:A Handbook for Understanding and Surviving a Perpetual Fall*
Harvey—*Perspectives on Loss:A Sourcebook*

*FORMERLY*

**SERIES IN DEATH EDUCATION, AGING, AND HEALTH CARE**
HANNELORE WASS, CONSULTING EDITOR



Bard—*Medical Ethics in Practice*
Benoliel—*Death Education for the Health Professional*
Bertman—*Facing Death: Images, Insights, and Interventions*
Brammer—*How to Cope with Life Transitions: The Challenge of Personal Change*
Cleiren—*Bereavement and Adaptation: A Comparative Study of the Aftermath of Death*
Corless, Pittman-Lindeman—*AIDS: Principles, Practices, and Politics, Abridged Edition*
Corless, Pittman-Lindeman—*AIDS: Principles, Practices, and Politics, Reference Edition*
Curran—*Adolescent Suicidal Behavior*
Davidson—*The Hospice: Development and Administration, Second Edition*
Davidson, Linnolla—*Risk Factors in Youth Suicide*
Degner, Beaton—*Life-Death Decision in Health Care*
Doka—*AIDS, Fear, and Society: Challenging the Dreaded Disease*
Doty—*Communication and Assertion Skills for Older Persons*
Epting, Neimeyer—*Personal Meanings of Death: Applications of Personal Construct Theory to Clinical Practice*
Haber—*Health Care for an Aging Society: Cost-Conscious Community Care and Self-Care Approaches*
Hughes—*Bereavement and Support: Healing in a Group Environment*
Irish, Lundquist, Nelsen—*Ethnic Variations in Dying, Death, and Grief: Diversity in Universality*
Klass, Silverman, Nickman—*Continuing Bonds: New Understandings of Grief*
Lair—*Counseling the Terminally Ill: Sharing the Journey*
Leenaars, Neimeyer, Maltsberger—*Treatment of Suicidal People*
Leenaars, Wenckstern—*Suicide Prevention in Schools*
Leng—*Psychological Care in Old Age*
Leviton—*Horrendous Death and Health: Toward Action*
Leviton—*Horrendous Death, Health, and Well-Being*
Lindeman, Corby, Downing, Sanborn—*Alzheimer's Day Care: A Basic Guide*
Lund—*Older Bereaved Spouses: Research with Practical Applications*
Neimeyer—*Death Anxiety Handbook: Research, Instrumentation, and Application*
Papadatou, Papdatos—*Children and Death*
Prunkl, Berry—*Death Week: Exploring the Dying Process*
Riker, Myers—*Retirement Counseling: A Practical Guide for Action*
Samarel—*Caring for Life and Death*
Sherron, Lumsden—*Introduction to Educational Gerontology, Third Edition*
Stillion—*Death and the Sexes: An Examination of Differential Longevity, Attitudes, Behaviors, and Coping Skills*
Stillion, McDowell—*Suicide Across the Life Span—Premature Exits*
Vachon—*Occupational Stress in the Care of the Critically Ill, the Dying, and the Bereaved*
Wass, Corr—*Childhood and Death*
Wass, Corr—*Helping Children Cope with Death: Guidelines and Resources, Second Edition*
Wass, Corr, Pacholski, Forfar—*Death Education II: An Annotated Resource Guide*
Wass, Neimeyer—*Dying: Facing the Facts, Third Edition*
Weenolsen—*Transcendence of Loss over the Life Span*
Werth—*Rational Suicide? Implications for Mental Health Professionals*

# *PERSPECTIVES ON LOSS: A Sourcebook*

*Edited by*
**John H. Harvey**
University of Iowa

| | | |
|---|---|---|
| **USA** | Publishing Office: | BRUNNER/MAZEL<br>*A member of the Taylor & Francis Group*<br>325 Chestnut Street<br>Philadelphia, PA 19106<br>Tel: (215) 625-8900<br>Fax: (215) 625-2940 |
| | Distribution Center: | BRUNNER/MAZEL<br>*A member of the Taylor & Francis Group*<br>1900 Frost Road, Suite 101<br>Bristol, PA 19007-1598<br>Tel: (215) 785-5800<br>Fax: (215) 785-5515 |
| **UK** | | BRUNNER/MAZEL<br>*A member of the Taylor & Francis Group*<br>1 Gunpowder Square<br>London EC4A 3DE<br>Tel: +44 171 583 0490<br>Fax: +44 171 583 0581 |

**PERSPECTIVES ON LOSS: A Sourcebook**



1 2 3 4 5 6 7 8 9 0

Printed by Edwards Brothers, 1998.

A CIP catalog record for this book is available from the British Library.
∞ The paper in this publication meets the requirements of the ANSI Standard Z39.48-1984 (Permanence of Paper)

**Library of Congress Cataloging-in-Publication Data**

Perspectives on loss : a sourcebook / edited by John H. Harvey.
p. cm.—(Death, dying, and bereavement)
Includes bibliographical references and index.

1. Loss (Psychology). 2. Grief. 3. Bereavement—Psychological aspects. I. Harvey, John H., 1943– . II. Series: Series in death, dying, and bereavement.
BF575.D35P47 1998
152.4—dc21 98-4026
CIP

ISBN 0-87630-909-0 (hardcover)
ISBN 0-87630-910-4 (paper)
ISSN 1091-5427

# Dedication

*Give sorrow words:*
*The grief that does not speak*
*Whispers the o'er-fraught heart,*
*And bids it break.*
—William Shakespeare, *Macbeth*

This volume is dedicated to Viktor Frankl, the late champion of our quest to find meaning, who died in September 1997, and to all other survivors like him who have faced great sorrow with words and deeds that reflect the highest qualities of compassion, courage, and hope.

# Contents

*Contributors* xv
*Acknowledgments* xxiii
*Preface* xxv

*I*
*THEORETICAL PERSPECTIVES*

1 **New Directions in Loss Research**
*Eric D. Miller and Julie Omarzu* 3

What Is Loss? 3
Moving Beyond Traditional Definitions of Loss 6
Loss Research at a Crossroads 12
Conclusion and Goals 16
References 17

2 **Blockades to Finding Meaning and Control** 21
*Suzanne C. Thompson*

Strategies for Finding Meaning 22
Strategies for Reestablishing Control 23
Blockades to Finding Meaning and Control 24
Cognitive Work 25
Adopting New Perspectives 27
Goals: Identification and Disengagement 29
Conclusion 31
References 31

3 **Disillusionment and the Creation of Values: From Traumatic Losses to Existential Gains** 35
*Ronnie Janoff-Bulman and Michael Berg*

Shattered Assumptions: Understanding the Loss of Illusions Post-Trauma 36
Confronting a Meaningless, Malevolent Universe 39
Creating a Meaningful Life: The Role of Loss in Value Creation and Appreciation 41
References 44

4 **Exploring Loss through Autoethnographic Inquiry: Autoethnographic Stories, Co-Constructed Narratives, and Interactive Interviews** 49
*Carolyn Ellis*

Autoethnographic Stories: Coping with Love, Loss, and Chronic Illness 51
Co-Constructed Narratives: Deciding about Abortion 55
Interactive Interviews: Experiencing Bulimia 56
Research and Lived Experience 58
References 59

5 **A Case for Hope in Pain, Loss, and Suffering** 63
*C. R. Synder*

It Hurts 63
Pain, Loss, and Suffering 63
A Theory of Hope 65
Here Comes the Pain 67
The Pain Stays 68
Hopelessness Got Us into This, So Can Hope Get Us Out? 71
From Pills to Psychology: Putting Pain in Perspective 76
References 77

6 **Trauma and Grief: A Comparative Analysis** 81
*Margaret Stroebe, Hank Schut, and Wolfgang Stroebe*

The Phenomena: Trauma and Bereavement 82
Stress Response Syndromes and Grief Manifestations 84
Models of Coping 88
Conclusions 94
References 94

*II*
*LOSSES WITHIN CLOSE RELATIONSHIPS*

7 **The Dissolution of Close Relationships** 99
*Susan Sprecher and Beverly Fehr*

Types of Relationship Dissolution 99
Why Relationships End 102
The Process and Aftermath of Relationship Endings 105
Conclusion 108
References 108

8 **Fatal Attractions: Contradictions in Intimate Relationships** **113**
*Diane H. Felmlee*

Relationship Beginnings and Endings **114**
Theoretical Issues **114**
Research Findings **117**
Contradictory Themes **119**
Discussion **121**
Future Research **123**
References **123**

9 **Loss in the Experience of Multiracial Couples** **125**
*Paul C. Rosenblatt and Carolyn Y. Tubbs*

The Study **126**
Who Are We to Say People Have Experienced Loss? **126**
The Losses to African-Americans Resulting from Racism **127**
The Losses to Multiracial Couples Resulting from Racism **128**
The Loss to Whites from Racism **131**
The Value of Taking Multiple Perspectives in Grief Research **134**
Racism and Loss **134**
The Importance of Macrosystemic Process **135**
Reference **135**

10 **Curbing Loss in Illness and Disability: A Relationship Perspective** **137**
*Renee F. Lyons and Michael J. L. Sullivan*

Dealing with Relationship Loss and Change **139**
The Increased Need for Quality Relationships **141**
Addressing Specific Relationship Challenges **143**
Determinants of Relationship Adaptation **147**
A Final Word on Loss **150**
References **150**

11 **Passion Lost and Found** **153**
*Michael R. Cunningham, Anita P. Barbee, and Perri B. Druen*

Passion and Love **153**
Biology, Evolution, and Passion **155**
The More or Less Passionate Receiver **156**
The Object of Passion **158**
Structural Interaction Effects **160**
Passion Gone Awry **161**
Solutions to Passion's Decline **162**
References **164**

## III
## LOSSES FACED BY SURVIVORS AND CARETAKERS

**12 Implications of Communal Relationships Theory for Understanding Loss among Family Caregivers** **173**
*Gail M. Williamson and David R. Shaffer*

The Caregiving Role and Psychological Well-Being **173**
Loss as a Component of Caregiver Well-Being **174**
The Theory of Communal Relationships and Its Implications for Caregiver Burden and Depressed Affect **175**
Loss as a Contributor to Caregiver Depressed Affect **179**
Preliminary Tests of the Model **181**
Concluding Comments and Implications **183**
References **184**

**13 Brain Injury: A Tapestry of Loss** **189**
*Kathleen Chwalisz*

Losses Sustained by Persons with Brain Injuries **190**
Caregiver Loss **192**
Interventions with Caregivers: Confronting Loss **195**
Implications of Loss for Survivors of Brain Injury **199**
References **199**

**14 Loss Experienced in Chronic Pain and Illness** **201**
*Patricia Kelley*

Personal Loss **202**
Interpersonal Loss **204**
Concrete Losses **206**
Re-Storying One's Life **207**
Conclusions **209**
References **209**

**15 When a Loss is Due to Suicide: Unique Aspects of Bereavement** **213**
*Lillian M. Range*

Stigma **213**
Blame **214**
A Search for Meaning **214**
Being Misunderstood **215**
Limitations in Suicidal Bereavement **216**
Research Recommendations **217**
Conclusion **218**
References **218**

**16 Mental Health Professionals' Responses to Loss and Trauma of Holocaust Survivors** 221
*Zahava Solomon, Anca Ram, and Yuval Neria*

Turning a Deaf Ear 222
Lack of Knowledge 223
Prevailing Social Attitudes 224
Countertransference 226
References 228

**17 Breaking the Cycle of Genocidal Violence: Healing and Reconciliation** 231
*Ervin Staub*

The Effects of Violence on Groups and Their Members 231
Healing from Violence against One's Group 232
Self-Healing 234
Reconciliation 235
Conclusions 237
References 238

*IV*
*LOSSES RELATED TO SOCIAL IDENTITY*

**18 The Experience of Loss in Sport** 241
*David Lavallee, J. Robert Grove, Sandy Gordon, and Ian W. Ford*

Coping with Loss 242
Athletic Injury 242
Performance Slumps 244
Retirement from Sport 247
Athletic Identity: A Synthesizing Construct 248
References 250

**19 What Is Lost by Not Losing: Losses Related to Body Weight** 253
*Carol T. Miller*

Body Weight and Perceived Control 253
Losses Related to Perceived Control 254
Lost Opportunities 256
Psychological Outcomes 259
For Every Loss, Is There a Gain? 261
References 264

**20 Homelessness and Loss: Conceptual and Research Considerations** 269
*Gary A. Morse*

Becoming and Being Homeless 270
Associated Aspects of Loss 272
Secondary Loss 275
Recovery 276
Conclusion 277
References 278

**21 Coping with Threat from Intimate Sources: How Self-Protection Relates to Loss for Women** 281
*Paula S. Nurius and Jan E. Gaylord*

What Are We Talking about and Why Is It Important? 281
Assumptive Worlds and Self-Concept: Cognitive Mechanisms Linking Threat to Loss 283
Between a Rock and a Hard Place: The Bind of Choosing among Losses? 285
Complications in Coping When Threat Is from Intimate Sources 286
Conclusion 289
References 290

**22 Loss of Collective Identity: Self-Sacrifice, Beauty Contests, and Magical Practices** 293
*Aurora Liiceanu*

Elana Ceausescu Syndrome 295
Rituals and Beliefs 296
Lost in Models 300
References 301

**23 Job Loss: Hard Times and Eroded Identity** 303
*Richard H. Price, Daniel S. Friedland, and Amiram D. Vinokur*

Documenting the Impact of Job Loss on Individuals and Families 304
Historical Perspectives on Job Loss: Jahoda and Bakke 305
Moving from the Past to the Present: Focusing in on Economic Hardship and Identity in Job Loss Research 306
Risk Groups and Event Resolution 310
References 312

## V
## SYNTHESIZING COMMENTARIES ON LOSS THEORY AND RESEARCH

**24 Why There Must Be a Psychology of Loss** **319**
*John H. Harvey and Ann L. Weber*

The Case for a Psychology of Loss 319
An Implicit Assumptive Base 320
Reverberating Losses, Self-Schemas, and Self-Identity 322
A Language, Rhetoric, and Culture of Loss 323
The Dialectic of Loss and Growth: The Value of Confronting Loss 325
Can We Ever Really Achieve Resolution? 327
Conclusion 328
References 328

**25 Can There Be a Psychology of Loss?** **331**
*Robert A. Neimeyer*

A Bridge Too Far? 331
Grand Unifying Theory 332
Common Factors Model 333
Application of General Theories 334
Multidisciplinary Cross-Fertilization 335
The Social Embeddedness of Loss 336
Meaning Reconstruction 337
Therapeutic Implications 339
Conclusion 340
References 340

**26 Issues in the Study of Loss and Grief** **343**
*Robert S. Weiss*

The Conceptualization of Loss and Consequent Distress 343
Freud, Lindemann, Bowlby, and Fundamental Issues in the Study of Grief 344
Is Grief Universal? 346
Do Responses to Loss Assume the Form of a Progression of Stages? 348
Is Grief Work Necessary if People are to Return to Normal Functioning after Loss? 349
Research on Loss 350
References 351

*Index* **353**

# *Contributors*

**Anita P. Barbee**
Associate Research Professor in the Kent School of Social Work at the University of Louisville, Kentucky. Recipient of the 1997 International Network on Personal Relationship's Gerald Miller Early Career Award for her experimental studies on interactive coping in close relationships. She has published in various journals and is on the editorial boards of *Journal of Social and Personal Relationships and Motivation and Emotion.*

**Michael B. Berg**
Received his M.S. in personality and social psychology from the University of Massachusetts, Amherst, where he is presently completing his Ph.D.

**Kathleen Chwalisz**
Associate Professor of Counseling Psychology in the Department of Psychology at Southern Illinois University. She is a licensed psychologist currently providing group-based interventions for caregivers of people with brain injuries and other illnesses and injuries. She also conducts research on caregiver burden issues and interventions.

**Michael R. Cunningham**
Professor in the Department of Psychology at the University of Louisville. He investigates social and evolutionary motives in several domains of prosocial behavior such as honesty, helping, relationship initiation and maintenance. He has developed the facialmetric system for evaluating physical attractiveness, described in his 1990 and 1995 *Journal of Personality and Social Psychology* articles. He serves on the editorial boards of *Journal of Personality and Motivation and Emotion.*

**Perri B. Druen**
Assistant Professor in the Department of Psychology at York College, Pennsylvania. She conducts research in the areas of deception, mate selection processes, and personality in close relationships. She has published in the Journal of Social Issues, *Journal of Personality and Social Psychology, and Journal of Nonverbal Behavior.*

**Carolyn Ellis**
Professor of Communication and Sociology at the University of South Florida. She is the author of *Final Negotiations: A Story of Love, Loss, and Chronic Illness* and coeditor of *Composing Ethnography: Alternative Forms of Qualitative Writing.* In

her current work on illness, relationships, emotions, and stigma, she seeks to write evocative texts that remind readers of the complexity of their social worlds.

**Beverly Fehr**
Associate Professor of Psychology at the University of Winnipeg. She has published in the areas of emotion and close relationships, including research on conceptions of love and commitment, anger scripts, and the facial expression of emotion. Her current research is focused on anger scripts in close relationships and on interaction patterns underlying relationship expectations in friendship and marriage.

**Diane H. Felmlee**
Professor in the Sociology Department at the University of California, Davis. Her research interests include social psychology, social relationships, and gender inequality. She has recently published articles in *Personal Relationships* (1998), and in *Sex Roles* (1994). She is currently examining the processes involved in fatal attraction in a sample of married and divorced couples, and studying the effects of social networks on students' relationships and college performance.

**Ian W. Ford**
A PhD candidate in Sport and Exercise Psychology within the Department of Human Movement at the University of Western Australia. His research focuses on the psychosocial aspects of sport injury, with a particular emphasis on the role of social support during rehabilitation.

**Daniel S. Friedland**
Doctoral student in Organizational Psychology at the University of Michigan. His research is focused in two areas: well-being, in relation to social roles and identity, and the implementation of social innovations in organizations.

**Jan E. Gaylord**
Doctoral student in the Department of Social Welfare at the University of Washington, where she received her MSW in 1993. Her primary research interests are in the areas of women's health, social-cognitive factors that influence risk perception and health behavior, and the influence of social, cultural, and contextual factors on health related decision making.

**Sandy Gordon**
Senior Lecturer in Sport and Exercise Psychology within the Department of Human Movement at the University of Western Australia. He conducts research in the areas of sport injuries, exercise promotion, career transitions in sport, and mental skills training.

**J. Robert Grove**
Associate Professor of Sport and Exercise Psychology within the Department of Human Movement at the University of Western Australia. His current research interests include attributions and expectancies in sport, coping processes, psychological aspects of exercise, and personality influences on sport behavior.

**John H. Harvey**
Professor of Psychology at the University of Iowa. He is a social psychologist and previously was on the faculties at Vanderbilt, Ohio State, and Texas Tech Universities. In 1983, he was the Founding Editor of the *Journal of Social and Clinical Psychology,* and from 1995 has been the Founding Editor of the *Journal of Personal & Interpersonal Loss.* He also has been Editor of *Contemporary Psychology* (1992–1998). In 1998, he was a Fulbright Research Scholar, studying loss among women in Romania. He is the author or editor of several books, including the most recent *Embracing Their Memory: Loss and the Social Psychology of Story-Telling.*

**Ronnie Janoff-Bulman**
Professor of Psychology at the University of Massachusetts, Amherst. Her present research interests include the motivational bases of perspective-taking and the psychological processes underlying value creation. Among her publications is *Shattered Assumptions: Towards a New Psychology of Trauma.*

**Patricia Kelley**
Professor and Director of the School of Social Work at the University of Iowa. Her area of teaching and research interest is in clinical social work practice with individuals and families. She is licensed as an independent social worker in Iowa, Board Certified as a Diplomate in Clinical Social Work, and is a clinical member and approved supervisor for the American Association For Marriage and Family Therapy. Her recent work has been on the use of narrative approaches in work with vulnerable populations.

**David Lavallee**
Lecturer in Sport and Exercise Science within the School of Leisure and Sports Studies at Leeds Metropolitan University. His research interests are in the areas of developmental psychology, counseling athletes, and retirement from sport. He received his PhD in Sport and Exercise Psychology from the University of Western Australia.

**Aurora Liiceanu**
Professor at the International Faculty of Human Sciences, Senior Researcher at the Institute of Psychology at the Romanian Academy, Assistant Director of the Society for Education in Contraception and Sexuality (Romania), and a full member of the European Association of Experimental Social Psychology. She was named International Woman of the Year in 1992 and was a guest professor at L'Ecole des Hautes Etudes en Sciences Sociales (Paris) in 1994. She is author of *The Story of a Witch: An Anthropological Approach.*

**Renee F. Lyons**
Professor in the School of Health and Human Performance at Dalhousie University, with cross appointment in the Department of Psychology. She is also Director of the Atlantic Health Promotion Research Center, a collaborative effort by the Faculties of Medicine Dentistry and Health Professions to enhance research and health policy in Atlantic Canada. She has authored several articles and chapters on relationship

processes in chronic illness and disability, and was the principle author for *Relationships in Chronic Illness and Disability.*

**Carol T. Miller**
Professor of Psychology at the University of Vermont, Burlington. She received her PhD in Social Psychology from Purdue University in 1979. Her research focuses on how people who are the targets of stereotyping and prejudice cope with the reaction others have to them.

**Eric D. Miller**
Doctoral candidate in the personality and social psychology program at the University of Iowa. He is assistant editor and reviewer for the *Journal of Personal and Interpersonal Loss* and conducts research that examines the impact of imagining loss on relationship satisfaction and the role of spirituality in coping with major loss.

**Gary A. Morse**
Executive Director of Community Alternatives: Innovations in Behavioral Care, and Adjunct Professor of Psychology and Gerontology at the University of Missouri-St. Louis. He is the Principal Investigator of a current project supported by the National Institute of Mental Health to develop and study effective methods of helping homeless people with serious mental disorders and co-occurring substance abuse disorders.

**Robert A. Neimeyer**
Professor at the Department of Psychology, University of Memphis, where he also maintains an active clinical practice. He has conducted extensive research on the topics of death attitudes and suicide intervention. He has published 14 books and has authored over 200 articles and book chapters. He is currently conducting research on personal reactions of counselors who work with death and loss, and on the evaluation of suicide counseling skills. He is the Editor of *Death Studies,* Series Editor for the Taylor & Francis Series on Death, Dying, and Bereavement, and served as President of the Association for Death Education and Counseling (1996–1997).

**Yuval Neria**
Clinical Psychologist and Faculty Member at Tel Aviv University, Israel, The Bob Shapell School of Social Work. He received his MS in Psychology from Hebrew University and his PhD in Psychology from the University of Haifa. He is the author of several articles and book chapters relating to the issues of vulnerability and resiliency under traumatic stress.

**Paula S. Nurius**
Professor and Director of the Doctoral Program at the University of Washington School of Social Work. Her current research focuses on factors that influence women's appraisal of and coping responses to risk from counterintuitive and complex sources such as threat of harm from partners, acquaintances, and symbolically threatening health and social conditions. Recent publications include *Social Cognition and Individual Change, and Practicing Constructivism.*

**Julie Omarzu**
Doctoral candidate in the personality and social psychology program at the University of Iowa. She is an editorial associate and reviewer for the journal *Contemporary Psychology* and the coauthor of a book chapter to be published in C. E. Walker's Foundations of Clinical Psychology.

**Richard H. Price**
Professor of Psychology and Senior Research Scientist at the Institute for Social Research, University of Michigan, where he also serves as Director of the Michigan Prevention Research Center. He has written a number of books and scientific articles on prevention research and is a recipient of the Lela Roland Award for prevention research and the Distinguished Contribution Award from the Society for Community Research and Action. His research interests are in work, life transitions, and mental health.

**Anca Ram**
Psychiatrist working at the Pediatric Psychosomatic Unit at Sheba Medical Center in Tel-Hashomer, Israel. She spent several years at the National Institute of Mental Health in Bethesda, Maryland, where she was involved in basic and clinical research concerning the molecular basis of psychiatric diseases. She has extensive clinical experience in psychiatric disorders and psychopathologies in children, adolescents, and adults.

**Lillian M. Range**
Professor of Psychology at the University of Southern Mississippi. She is the author of the chapter "Suicide and Life-Threatening Behavior in Childhood" in C. A. Corr and D. Corr (Eds.), *Helping Children Cope With Death and Bereavement.*

**Paul C. Rosenblatt**
Professor of Family Social Science at the University of Minnesota. His book *Multiracial Couples: Black and White Voices,* co-authored with Terri Karis and Richard Powell, won an award from the Gustavus Myers Center for the Study of Human Rights as an outstanding book on the Subject of Human Rights in North America. His research focuses on family systems, loss and families, and multiracial/multicultural families.

**Hank Schut**
Adjunct Director of the Psychology and Health Research Institute, The Netherlands; and Lecturer in Social Organizational Psychology at Utrecht University. He is the author of *Individuele Rouwbegleiding* (Individual Grief Counseling) with Jos de Keijser, and of many articles in the area of bereavement and therapy. He runs training courses on bereavement for funeral directors and medical practitioners, and is on the Board of Directors of the Dutch National Association for Bereaved.

**David R. Shaffer**
Professor and Chair of the Social Psychology Program at the University of Georgia. He has published more than 75 articles investigating various topics in social psy-

chology such as self-disclosure, attitudes and attitude change, prosocial behavior, and psycholegal issues. He is author of three major textbooks in the field of Human Development: *Developmental Psychology* (4th ed.), *Life-Span Human Development* (2nd ed., with C. K. Sigelman), and *Social and Personality Development* (3rd ed.), all with Brooks/Cole Publishing.

**C. R. Snyder**
Professor of Psychology at the University of Kansas. Since 1975, he has been the Director of the Clinical Psychology Program at Kansas. He is the Editor of the *Journal of Social and Clinical Psychology* and a Fellow in APA divisions 2, 8, 12, and 38.

**Zahava Solomon**
Professor of Psychiatric Epidemiology and Social Work at the Tel-Aviv University and the Head of the Adler Research Center for Child Welfare and Protection. She is internationally known for her research in traumatic stress, and especially on the psychological sequelae of combat stress reactions, war captivity, and the Holocaust. She is the author of two books on psychic trauma related issues: *Combat Stress Reaction: The Enduring Toll of War* and *Coping With War-Induced Stress: The Gulf War and the Israeli Response.*

**Susan Sprecher**
Professor of Sociology at Illinois State University. She teaches in the areas of marriage and the family, human sexuality, and social psychology. Her current research interests are in attraction, equity and exchange, sexuality in close relationships, and the breakup of relationships.

**Ervin Staub**
Professor of Psychology at the University of Massachusetts, Amherst. His primary areas of work are on the determinants and development of helping behavior and altruism, and on harmdoing, aggression, and violence in individuals and groups. He has authored several books on these topics such as *The Roots of Evil: The Origins of Genocide and Other Group Violence.* Among his awards is the Otto Lineberg Intercultural and International Prize from the Society for the Psychological Study of Social Issues.

**Margaret Stroebe**
Lecturer of Clinical and Health Psychology at the University of Utrecht, The Netherlands. With W. Stroebe, she has published *Bereavement and Health: The Psychological and Physical Consequences of Partner Loss* and has edited the *Handbook of Bereavement.* Her current interests in bereavement include interactive patterns of coping, theoretical approaches to grief and grieving, and assessment and efficacy of bereavement intervention.

**Wolfgang Stroebe**
Professor of Social, Organizational, and Health Psychology at the University of Utrecht, The Netherlands; and Scientific Director of the Research Institute for Psychology

and Health. He is the author of scholarly books, chapters, and articles on topics in social- and health psychology, and editor of the *European Review of Social Psychology,* with Miles Hewstone. His current research interests span bereavement, attitude change, and eating disorders.

**Michael J. L. Sullivan**
Associate Professor with the Clinical Program of the Department of Psychology at Dalhousie University, Halifax, Nova Scotia. He is also practicing Clinical Psychologist and Director of Fenwick Psychological Services, where he specializes in the treatment of marital dysfunction and persistent pain disorders. Dr. Sullivan's research is funded by the Social Sciences and Humanities Research Council of Canada.

**Suzanne C. Thompson**
Professor of Psychology at Pomona College in Claremont, California. She has published extensively on perceptions of control and coping with chronic illness. Her current research focuses on illusions of control and how they affect health protective behaviors.

**Carolyn Y. Tubbs**
Faculty member in the Department of Family Social Sciences at the University of Minnesota. She is also a family therapist who has worked with a variety of clients in various settings. Her research interests include the application of postmodern thought to clinical practice and supervision, the transformative power of language, and the development of clinical competence in novice clinicians.

**Amiram D. Vinokur**
Senior Research Scientist at the Institute for Social Research, University of Michigan, and an Associate Director of the Michigan Prevention Research Center, funded by the National Institute of Mental Health. His research focuses on determinants and consequences of stress in the areas of health, work, and unemployment, and on the roles of social support and social undermining in the stress and coping process.

**Ann L. Weber**
Professor of Psychology at the University of North Carolina at Asheville. A social psychologist, she is co-author with Zimbardo of *Introductory Psychology* and co-author with Harvey and Orbuch of *Interpersonal Accounts: A Social Psychology Perspective.* She is coeditor with Harvey and Orbuch of *Attributions, Accounts, and Close Relationships.* She is a member of the Society of Experimental Social Psychology, and is on the Editorial Boards of several journals.

**Robert S. Weiss**
Senior Fellow of the Institute of Gerontology, University of Massachusetts; Emeritus Professor of Sociology, University of Massachusetts; and a Lecturer in Sociology, Harvard Medical School. He has studied issues of loss and grief for thirty-five years, much of that time as a member of Harvard Medical School's Laboratory of Community Psychiatry. His books include *Recovery from Bereavement* (with Colin M. Parkes) and *Marital Separation.*

**Gail M. Williamson**
Associate Professor and Chair of the Life-Span Developmental Psychology program at the University of Georgia. She is presently the principal investigator on a newly funded grant from the National Institute on Aging for a multi-site longitudinal project investigating mental health and quality of care in medically compromised older adults and their family caregivers. She has served on the editorial boards of *Journal of Gerontology, Psychology and Aging* and *Contemporary Psychology,* and has published several chapters in edited volumes.

# *Acknowledgments*

I would like to thank a number of people who have been most helpful and encouraging in this work, both on the present volume and on the *Journal of Personal and Interpersonal Loss*. They include: Taylor & Francis Editor-in-Chief Mac Fancher; former Taylor & Francis Senior Acquisitions Editor Elaine Pirrone; Bernadette Capelle, Associate Acquisitions Editor; Alison Howson of Taylor & Francis; Robert Neimeyer, who generously reviewed the original proposals for the volume and journal; Daniel Perlman, who reviewed and made insightful inputs about the entire manuscript; C. R. Snyder, a contributor to this volume who greatly encouraged its development; my colleagues at the University of Iowa, Eric Miller and Julia Omarzu, for their fine help in reviewing the chapters for this volume; the scores of contributors to this volume and the journal, who by virtue of presenting their work have placed their faith in this enterprise; the hundreds of students at the University of Iowa who have taken my undergraduate course entitled "Loss and Trauma," and who by their writing and speaking have reported eloquently on the details and pain of loss that occur even among the young. Finally, I thank Pamela Harvey, Precious Memory, and Red Dukes, our "little fury men," for their unwavering support of me and my work.

*John H. Harvey*

# Preface

## BACKGROUND FOR PRESENT VOLUME

This volume is entitled a "sourcebook" because it is intended to stimulate ideas and research on the newly constituted field of psychological aspects of loss. It is designed to collect in a single volume the writings of a set of distinguished scholars representing psychology and related fields to address their ideas on the dimensions of loss. I am familiar with the concept of a "sourcebook" from the invaluable volume *Theories of Cognitive Consistency: A Sourcebook,* edited by Robert P. Abelson, Elliot Aronson, William J. McGuire, Ted M. Newcomb, Milton J. Rosenberg, and Percy H. Tannenbaum, published in 1968 by Rand McNally. This book brought together the various concepts of cognitive consistency that had been developing over the preceding decade.

Similarly, the present "soucebook" seeks to bring together many strands of work on loss that have emerged in the last several years. As such, the volume complements my work with Taylor & Francis Publishers in creating and beginning in 1996 the *Journal of Personal & Interpersonal Loss (JPIL).* In the opening editorial and commentary (Harvey, 1996, *JPIL, 1*(1), iii–ix), I present a case for a broadly construed field of loss dealing with both personal losses (such as aging) and interpersonal losses (such as divorce). I argue there, as do Harvey and Weber in Chapter 24 of the present volume, that a field entitled the psychology of loss would be a conceptually defensible development and would complement other fields such as death and dying, traumatology, and stress and coping. We also contend that psychology as a discipline (and some related disciplines too, as represented in this volume) has been remiss in its explicit recognition of and theoretical and empirical work on loss.

Losses are pervasive in our lives, but they sometimes unfold in subtle ways. For example, a speaker in my loss and trauma class at the University of Iowa, who was an activity director at a residential center for the frail elderly, noted that the diversity of losses these individuals experience goes far beyond that of simply being close to death or having friends die regularly around them. She pointed to the gradual losses of vision, hearing, taste, perspiration regulation, mental capacity and flexibility, sexual activity, and hope as some of the most debilitating losses faced by the frail elderly. The readers of this volume, as well as *JPIL* and related works on this so-called psychology of loss, will be the judges of this development.

## ORGANIZATION OF THE PRESENT VOLUME

The introductory chapter in the volume is by my graduate student colleagues at the University of Iowa, Eric Miller and Julia Omarzu. They provide an introduction to the loss topic based on their own analysis of the field and on their work with me in research and in reviewing manuscripts in the early years of *JPIL*. Along with Chapter 24 by Harvey and Weber, the introductory chapter discusses the definition of major loss and the salience of the topic of loss and trauma in the general public in the late 1990s. Miller and Omarzu also note some basic goals of this volume and directions for the field in general.

The chapters and authors in this volume were chosen so as to represent some of the most interesting current work on different types of loss and adaptation in the whole of the social and behavioral sciences. I do not believe that any current volume reveals as much breadth on the topic of major loss phenomena, covered by scholars with active research programs, as is provided in the current volume. Also, in both the introductory and the final sections, authors provide general comments regarding basic principles and conceptual issues in the study of loss and trauma.

The array of loss topics reflected in this volume, while representative, is still quite incomplete. Not only is it incomplete in terms of types of loss represented, it is also incomplete in its coverage of issues. As was noted by Neimeyer in Chapter 25, one major issue not well covered is that of application. I do believe, however, that many of the chapters have considerable heuristic value for practitioners and that providing the conceptual and logical foundation for an expanded study of major loss is a first step before we will have a lot to offer to practitioners.

Neimeyer raises one other issue that should be noted at the outset. He appropriately points to the possibility that this new field of work on loss may involve a "bridge too far" in its breadth. Are there, for example, basic ideas that will help us span such a diversity of phenomena? I believe that the bridge is in the erection stage and needs a lot of thought and work before it will be sturdy. Many foundational ideas and useful research approaches are displayed here. Hopefully, you the reader will be educated and stimulated by these contributions to provide your own critique of our construction work to date.

*John H. Harvey*
Spring 1998

# I

# *THEORETICAL PERSPECTIVES*

# 1

# *New Directions in Loss Research*

***Eric D. Miller and Julie Omarzu***
*University of Iowa*

Most of us experience losses during our lives. Perhaps we even experience relatively minor, ephemeral losses on a daily basis. We might not get the grade we had hoped for on a certain exam, or perhaps a friend rebuffed us at a social event. Usually, upon reflection, we decide that these losses are relatively minor in our lives. We can usually tell someone what major losses we have experienced in life: for instance the death of a sibling, the loss of a romantic relationship, a severe illness experienced by a close friend, and the loss of self-esteem due to harassment at work. These are just a few "major" losses we could mention. Why are they considered major? Perhaps it is because these losses have never really "left" our consciousness. Perhaps we think about them daily; maybe we could, and do, even talk about them at a moment's notice. Maybe they have changed us, for better or worse—but they have greatly affected our lives. Although we may not necessarily have control over whether these loss events occur, we can control how we respond to them.

This chapter (and this sourcebook) attempts to thoughtfully examine the nature of loss in a thorough, scientific manner. However, as the previous paragraph illustrates, loss is not just an academic matter to be dispassionately studied. Loss events can be the most personal and emotional happenings that humans experience. This point should never be underemphasized. As a matter of fact, it is the ultimate reason *why* loss needs to be studied from an academic and scientific perspective.

## WHAT IS LOSS?

*"Loss is nothing else but change, and change is Nature's delight."*

—Marcus Aurelius

**The origin of the word "loss."** One relatively objective way to understand what exactly is meant by "loss" can be achieved by briefly considering the origin and history of this word. According to *The Barnhart Concise Dictionary of Etymology* (1995), the word *loss,* found in Old English form, was probably first used before 1200 and was synonymous with death and destruction. The word *loss* was also probably influenced by the word *lose,* which originally meant "to be deprived of"

(p. 443). The term *loss* suggests that we no longer have someone or something that we used to have.

**Loss as defined by college students.** An innovative way to understand what precisely is meant by *loss* is to simply ask laypeople how they would define this term. To this end, Miller et al. (1996) randomly divided students enrolled in a class titled "Loss and Trauma," at The University of Iowa, into two experimental conditions. (This was done on the first day of class.) These two conditions involved the following variations: 74 college students wrote for five minutes regarding a recent major loss experience (defined by the subject); a second group of 74 students wrote for five minutes about a recent joyful experience (defined by the subject). For the purposes of this chapter, we shall only discuss the responses of students who wrote about a recent major loss experience.

Among the questions posed to the students in the "loss" condition were the following two open-ended questions: "Please list in order the first thoughts or images that come to your mind when you think of *loss*," and "How many major losses have you experienced in life to date? Please briefly identify each with two or three words or phrases."

Table 1 lists all of the words, thoughts, or images that students associated with the term *loss*. After examining these terms, it becomes clear that most students tend to view loss as a negative occurrence. In particular, the nine most frequently listed terms appear to have clear negative connotations. Moreover, very few terms tend to overtly convey a sense that loss is or can be a positive event (i.e., associated with psychological growth). Another intriguing finding is that nearly half of all terms provided were stated only once by the entire sample; this may further suggest that loss is an event that affects individuals in very idiosyncratic ways.

Nearly 60% of the students ($N = 44$) associated the term *loss* with *death*; this term was, in fact, the most common word associated with loss. This theme is also quite prevalent in the descriptive data from Table 2. Table 2 lists all of the types of major losses that college students experienced in life to date. The 74 students who responded to this question listed a total of 171 loss events. Of these 171 loss events, 131 events (76.6%) were loss events involving death. It appears that the term *loss* serves as a memory prime for the term *death*. However, this study was conducted on the first day of class; it is possible that in the final weeks of the class their answers may have provided more variation.

**Is loss research synonymous with the study of death?** Based on the responses from the study described above, one might be tempted to answer this question affirmatively. Clearly, though, death is only one form or type of loss that a person can experience.

Loss can take many different forms. Harvey (1996a) offers a sampling of the many different types of losses that we may endure, including loss of biological parents early or late in life due to death, loss of health because of disease or injury, loss of home because of poverty, loss of contact with friends because of one party moving, loss of peace of mind, war-time trauma, and victimization due to domestic abuse or crime. Surely, the chapters in this sourcebook also present many other intriguing and interesting types of losses. Ultimately, Harvey (1996b) suggests that a major loss is an event involving a significant diminution in one's resources. Moreover, as Rando (1988) posits, there are two basic types of losses:

*Table 1.* Frequency (f) of college students' reports of words, thoughts, or images associated with the term "*loss*"

| Term | f | Term | f |
|---|---|---|---|
| Death | 44 | Abortion | 1 |
| Sadness | 37 | Anxiety | 1 |
| Emptiness | 24 | Ashamed | 1 |
| Loneliness | 22 | Blood | 1 |
| Grief | 17 | Cemeteries | 1 |
| Cry | 13 | Challenging | 1 |
| Depression | 12 | Childhood | 1 |
| Pain | 12 | Class | 1 |
| Scared | 12 | Cold | 1 |
| Friends | 11 | Community | 1 |
| Love | 10 | Crazy | 1 |
| Anger | 9 | Cubs | 1 |
| Fear | 9 | Despair | 1 |
| Confusion | 8 | Determined | 1 |
| Hurt | 8 | Dissolution | 1 |
| Black/gray | 6 | Distance | 1 |
| Family | 6 | Distraught | 1 |
| Stress | 6 | Failure | 1 |
| Divorce | 5 | Family | 1 |
| Heartache | 5 | Fear of future | 1 |
| Sorrow | 5 | Fears | 1 |
| Breakups | 4 | February | 1 |
| Denial | 4 | Harvey | 1 |
| Father | 4 | Hospitals | 1 |
| Funeral | 4 | Human being | 1 |
| Helpless | 4 | Importance | 1 |
| Memories | 4 | Light | 1 |
| Relationship | 4 | Lose personal items | 1 |
| Shock | 4 | Lost | 1 |
| Grandpa | 3 | Misfortune | 1 |
| Guilt | 3 | Mother | 1 |
| Moving | 3 | Negative | 1 |
| Permanent | 3 | Nervous | 1 |
| Regret | 3 | Never | 1 |
| Trauma | 3 | Old age | 1 |
| Upset | 3 | Ones left behind | 1 |
| Acceptance | 2 | Overwhelmed | 1 |
| Car accident(s) | 2 | Pay last respects | 1 |
| Disappointment | 2 | Pets | 1 |
| Gone/no more | 2 | Pressure | 1 |
| Guns/knife | 2 | Proud | 1 |
| Happiness | 2 | Remote | 1 |
| Illness | 2 | Roses | 1 |
| Money | 2 | Status | 1 |
| Peace | 2 | Strength | 1 |
| Separation | 2 | Surprise | 1 |
| Suffering | 2 | Tired | 1 |
| Support | 2 | Tomorrow | 1 |
| Tragedy | 2 | Train wreck | 1 |
| Turmoil | 2 | Worry | 1 |
| Uncle | 2 | | |

Note: $N = 74$.

*Table 2.* Frequency (f) of college students' reports of types of major losses experienced in life to date

| Loss event | f | Loss event | f |
|---|---|---|---|
| Death (of): | | Parents' divorce | 10 |
| Grandparent | 44 | Relationship breakup | 9 |
| Friend | 32 | Moving (away) | 4 |
| Pet | 12 | Illness | 2 |
| Aunt | 10 | Job loss | 2 |
| Uncle | 9 | Partner moves away | 2 |
| Cousin | 7 | Sexual assault | 2 |
| Father | 5 | Termination of pregnancy | 2 |
| Great-grandparent | 5 | Burglary | 1 |
| Father-in-law | 1 | Husband/military leave | 1 |
| Mother | 1 | Loss of innocence | 1 |
| Boy/girlfriend | 1 | Rape | 1 |
| Nonspecified | 4 | Loss of security | 1 |
| | | Loss of self-confidence | 1 |
| | | Loss of skill | 1 |

Note: $N = 74$.

physical losses, where something tangible has been made unavailable (e.g., death of a spouse), and symbolic losses, where there are abstract changes in one's psychological experiences of social interactions (e.g., losing status as a result of job demotion).

Yet, the question still remains: why are the terms *loss* and *death* often used interchangeably? To be sure, the majority of studies pertaining to loss tend to focus on death. Solomon, Greenberg, and Pyszczynski's (1991) terror management theory suggests why death is the ultimate form of loss. In short, the authors argue that thinking about one's death creates the potential for terror, since we may feel as though we are living meaningless lives. But perhaps there is an even simpler reason why death is the ultimate form of loss. Although all losses have the potential to cause pain and suffering, death is a special and unique form of loss. We can recover our sense of self-worth; we can receive organ transplants or artificial limbs; we can even remarry the same person whom we divorced. Death is probably the only type of loss that can never be recovered: death is loss forever.

## MOVING BEYOND TRADITIONAL DEFINITIONS OF LOSS

**Why loss is an important topic to study.** As we suggested from the outset of this chapter, the ultimate reason why loss is such an important topic to study is that it can truly have a dramatic, everlasting impact on the lives of people. Actually, we would argue that no one really is immune to the experience of loss.

Although some people seemingly withstand transitions and tragedies better than others, it would be difficult for any one of us to pass through life without experiencing a major loss or upheaval of some kind. Death robs us of people we love. Illness or disability may cause us to lose treasured abilities or force us to abandon some dreams. Social changes cost us jobs, friendships, or social status. Loss is an everyday, common event. As such, it has an impact on human emotion, cognition, and behavior that merits concentrated study on the part of social and behavioral scientists. Without an understanding of how people cope with and perceive loss experiences, we cannot hope to completely understand human nature.

Harvey and Weber (in Chapter 24 of this volume) provide many more thoughtful reasons why there must be a psychology of loss, and they discuss how loss has been represented in contemporary society. We would like to briefly extend that discussion by providing some recent anecdotes of how the topic of loss now pervades (American) popular culture.

To be sure, the importance of loss events can be most easily seen in the prevalence of loss themes and images in popular culture. Funerals are among our most powerful social and religious ceremonies. Kübler-Ross' (1969) "stages-of-grieving" model has become common knowledge in our society. Support groups abound for almost every type of loss experience imaginable, from death of a child to unemployment.

Loss clearly was a major theme in the 1996 U.S. Presidential election. Many were moved by Vice President Al Gore's tribute to his deceased sister at the Democratic National Convention; likewise, many were moved by the life-long ability of Republican standard-bearer, Bob Dole, to overcome his personal war injuries. Although President Clinton was ultimately reelected, many consider that "The Comeback Kid" may not have won had it not been for a major crisis, namely, the Oklahoma City bombing (Mitchell, 1996). On a related topic, Celente (1997) forecasts that the Oklahoma City bombing is only the beginning of a new wave of horrific terrorism that will sweep across the United States. Clearly, the psychological consequences of terrorism are still understudied.

The themes of loss can easily be found in contemporary music and movies. For instance, the song "One Sweet Day," by Mariah Carey and Boyz II Men—which is ranked as one of the longest-running "Number 1" pop single in "Hot 100" history, according to *Billboard* magazine (Bronson, 1996)—deals with the hope that deceased friends have found peace in the afterlife. In addition, many of the recent Academy Award-winning Best Pictures have had loss as central plot themes. In a recent column, Goodman (1996) suggested that the classic film *It's a Wonderful Life* has more relevance today than it did when it was released in 1946, due to the harsh realities of contemporary American life. If nothing else, Americans were inundated with the theme of loss via the ongoing O. J. Simpson saga.

These examples from popular culture are not intended to serve merely as provocative stories. Rather, they show that the theme of loss is strongly embedded within contemporary American culture and society. This is another reason why it is essential to conduct loss research.

**The study of loss is not yet a fully recognized academic discipline.** How do people cope with different types of losses? What makes up the experience of loss? Do different kinds of loss events produce similar emotions and behaviors? What is happening when someone talks about "recovering" from a loss; what has changed?

Why are some people more affected than others, and how can we help them? Is there a way to satisfactorily explain the loss experience so that we may better understand it and grow from it? While these questions have been examined by researchers, none has been definitively answered.

We contend that, at this point, the current literature in most loss research topics is largely disjointed, disorganized, and descriptive. It is a given that loss researchers must be fully aware of all developments in their respective areas of research. Moreover, we are not simply arguing that more loss research needs to be done. Rather, we suggest that too much loss research has been conducted that has not been grounded in a larger theoretical context. In addition, there needs to be more overall integration in the area if it is to be recognized as its own independent discipline.

This point can be dramatically illustrated by considering the paltry amount of research that developmental psychologists have conducted about how children cope with the death or illness of a parent. Siegel et al. (1992) note that while this topic has been considered in the clinical literature, most of the studies have been descriptive. Issel, Ersek, and Lewis (1990) add that "virtually no research has focused on the impact of a parent's chronic physical illness on school-age children. Consequently, the effects of parental illness such as cancer on school-age children are poorly understood and warrant empirical investigation" (p. 5). Not only is it puzzling that this topic has been largely ignored, but it is just as surprising that developmental researchers have not made vigorous attempts to link this topic with the larger theoretical models of attachment (Bowlby, 1969, 1980), internal working models (Bretherton, 1985; Main, Kaplan, & Cassidy, 1985), and the emotional security hypothesis (Cummings & Davies, 1994).

In sum, we maintain that unless loss research is placed within pre-existing or newly developed theoretical models, this area will continue to be disjointed.

**Previous models of loss and how they differ from what we are discussing.** Much early loss research was derived from Freud's (1957) psychoanalytic theory. According to this theory, when infants receive nourishment and comfort from a parent, they have great difficulty perceiving the source of these positive feelings as separate from themselves (as cited in Singer, 1984). As they develop emotionally and learn to separate themselves from their parents, they sometimes internalize aspects of their parents and of other important people around them. When this happens, the child does not fully separate from these others but continues to view them as extensions of him- or herself. Losing a parent (or close other) can feel like losing oneself. According to psychoanalytic theory, it is only through "grief work," which explores these early connections of childhood and infancy, that a loss can be successfully resolved. Relatedly, Lindemann (1944) was the first grief researcher to contend that the bereaved must complete the process of "grief work" by detaching oneself from memories and thoughts of the deceased.

Psychoanalytic theory focuses on the individual emotional response to loss. It pays little or no attention to larger social forces or interactions with others. It also does not apply well to losses other than those of bereavement, such as those stemming from illnesses or social situations.

Somewhat similar to the psychoanalytic view of loss is Bowlby's (1969) attachment theory. Attachment theory is based on the premise that children form different types of bonds with their parents, depending on the reliability and nurturing abilities of the parents. These bonds become attachment "styles" that children carry with them into adulthood. Ultimately, attachment style affects how an individual interacts and develops relationships with other adults. Parenting styles that are characterized by ambivalence or neglect can result in children who may grow up to be anxious about relationships and have difficulty establishing intimacy or coping with separation and loss. This poor or unstable attachment style is presumed to cause prolonged or debilitating grief reactions in the case of a loss event (Middleton, Raphael, Martinek, & Misso, 1993). During childhood, according to Bowlby (1980), if a child's primary caregiver or attachment figure dies, it is essential for the child to promptly secure emotional ties with another adult.

Thus, both of these models assume that intense or prolonged grief is pathological in nature, stemming from flaws in emotional development during childhood. This point of view treats loss as a transient state that demands recovery in order to be "normal" or healthy. Naturally then, clinicians turned to examining how best to facilitate this recovery. From these investigations came various stages-of-grieving models. Among the most well known of these models is that of Kübler-Ross (1969), whose stages of grief include denial, anger, bargaining, depression, and acceptance. The idea behind these models is that an individual experiencing loss or bereavement must successfully "pass through" the stages, eventually reaching the "acceptance" or recovery stage. Perhaps not coincidentally, the idea of passing successfully through stages echoes the psychoanalytic model of individual emotional development, which inspired the first theories of grief and loss.

We contend that these above-mentioned models are flawed because they imply that "unhealthy" grief is inherently associated with pathology. Loss is an event that forever alters the shape and outlook of one's life. Thus, we should not view loss as an event that one must "get over" as quickly as possible (e.g., Silverman & Klaas, 1996). To this end, Rosenblatt (1993) describes loss as a disruption in social reality that affects self-definition. He emphasizes loss as a reaction to various social transitions. As we mature and our lives change, we enter new social contexts and leave others. A sense of loss may stem from these changes. This situational perspective also stresses the importance of cultural expectations in determining how individuals express loss.

The view of how people deal with major losses appears to be in transition. The idea of grief as a disease from which one "recovers" is subsiding in favor of a view which accepts loss as an expected part of life, producing permanent change. We are gradually turning away from the pathological theories of loss and focusing more on feelings of loss which result from the interaction between social situations and individual perception.

This newer perspective accepts that individuals who suffer a loss may never completely return to their pre-loss state and concedes that this may not even be an optimal goal. Instead, the aim is to survive the loss, come to terms with the changes, and integrate oneself into a new social context or identity. These evolving theoretical changes require that any new theory or definition of loss acknowledge social context, influence, identity, and attributions.

**Social psychology and loss theory.** In our view, social psychologists should be more active in the development of theories pertinent to the psychology of loss.

The topic of loss has natural links to the field of social psychology. Loss research would thus benefit from the attention of experts in social behavior and cognition.

Consider Allport's (1968) classic definition of social psychology as: "an attempt to understand and explain how the thoughts, feelings, and behavior of individuals are influenced by the actual, imagined, or implied presence of others" (p. 3). According to Rando (1988), we experience symbolic losses as direct consequences of social interactions. Clearly, these losses would be consistent with the essence of social psychology as described by Allport (1968). Rando's (1988) other category of loss, physical losses, does not appear to mesh with Allport's definition of social psychology as easily as symbolic losses do. There are some types of physical losses, such as the death of one's spouse, where the individual will obviously be "influenced by the . . . imagined or implied presence of others." While some other physical losses (e.g., a stolen car, a work-related injury) may not necessarily appear to conform to Allport's definition, we argue that, in fact, they are related to this definition. For example, if one's car is stolen, one may begin to feel as though all humans are "bad." Even if one suffers a self-inflicted serious injury, the individual may, for instance, begin to feel anxious about how he or she will be perceived by others. In short, we posit that both symbolic and physical losses have direct and obvious ties with mainstream social psychological research.

Social psychologists, however, have certainly been involved in the study of stress and coping. The largest body of social psychological literature that directly relates to loss theory is, in fact, research into the social psychology of stress and coping. Numerous studies, over several decades, have been conducted on the effects of various stressors on human performance and mood. The majority of this work has focused on physical or environmental stressors, such as noise (Glass & Singer, 1972), crowding (Heller, Groff, & Solomon, 1977), or electric shock (Geer, Davison, & Gatchel, 1970). The aim of much of this research has been to demonstrate that environmental stress reduces attentional capacity, which is often experimentally measured by poor performance on paper-and-pencil tasks. While this research demonstrates that certain types of stress can erode judgment and mental abilities, it is not directly related to the emotional or social experience of loss, which can occur independently of any stressful environmental conditions. The coping research also tends toward the examination of temporary stressful conditions—which can be easily simulated in a laboratory—rather than permanent changes in social condition.

As social psychologists became more involved in the area of health psychology, their stress research expanded to include more social events, including those of loss. Most dramatic have been the studies linking bereavement with higher mortality rates, which often find that the loss of a spouse or partner can increase one's risk of illness or premature death (Stroebe & Stroebe, 1993). These studies inspired researchers to investigate the effects of other types of stressors on health and wellness but did not begin a rush of studies into the effects of other types of loss events. We now are learning more about the effects of "stress" on overall health, but we still have little understanding about the mechanisms that specifically cause this "stress" link between bereavement and mortality rates, because we have not fully studied the experience of the loss.

Another branch of social/health psychology research that touches on loss explores the attitudes and coping abilities of those who are diagnosed with serious illnesses (e.g., Shontz, 1975). Contracting an illness can certainly be construed as a loss event (loss of health, physical strength, perhaps life expectancy); thus this work does specifically investigate some effects of loss. The majority of this research, however, focuses on the effects of coping skills and psychological adjustment on the eventual progress of the disease, not the effect of the experience of disease on coping and adjustment.

Social psychologists have tended to classify many different types of experiences under the heading of "stressors." These include environmental stressors (cold, noise, shock), cognitive stressors (doing math problems in one's head), and social stressors (important exams, blind dates). Expressing a negative mood has been operationalized as stress in at least one study into stress and health (Cohen et al., 1995). Combinations of stressors, such as social and physical stressors, are often treated as one big source of "stress," with loss events also treated as general "stressors."

Although social psychologists certainly do not regard all types of stressors as equivalent, there is not much research which clarifies differences between different classes of stressors. Thus, social psychological studies into loss are often "issue-driven" (Stroebe, Stroebe, & Hansson, 1993) studies of stress: studies on coping with a specific type of loss, rather than studies providing a larger theoretical viewpoint of loss. Several contributors to this volume attempt to correct this trend by presenting their theoretical models of loss.

*Regardless, we argue that mainstream social psychology has not, by and large, fully incorporated the study of loss.* This point becomes rather evident when one examines some of the prominent social psychology textbooks. For instance, Myers' (1996) superb textbook, *Social Psychology*, does not mention the topic of loss whatsoever. We can only speculate on why loss has not been a salient topic for most social psychologists. Perhaps the main reason is that social psychologists may have considered loss to be an innately clinical phenomenon. Social psychologists in general appear resistant to the idea of loss as a particular type of social stress that can be examined as its own subfield. Part of this resistance may be due to previous associations between loss, grief, and psychoanalytic theory. Another factor may be the connotation of loss as primarily involved with individual emotional responses. The plethora of "self-help" books marketed to assist people in dealing with grief also may serve to diminish the importance of loss as a scientific area of study and to emphasize its individualistic and clinical nature. Since social psychologists prefer to focus on situational factors, the strong relationship of loss research with more individual, clinical approaches may keep them focused on the broader stress and coping models. But while the study of loss certainly has clear clinical applications, social psychologists must also consider how their field relates to the study of loss.

We also offer two other reasons why researchers and scholars, in general, may feel somewhat intimidated by this field. As we will discuss below, in order to conduct rigorous studies in the area of loss, one must employ methodological procedures that can be time-consuming and complex. Likewise, since general theoretical models of loss are relatively scarce, researchers may feel reluctant to enter this line of research. Also, due to the emotional nature of this topic, some researchers may feel uneasy about studying it.

## LOSS RESEARCH AT A CROSSROADS

As we stand on the brink of a new century of psychological research, we argue that psychologists and other academics face many critical choices about how to conduct loss research. Therefore, it is essential to reflect on the current nature and status of loss research. Certainly this sourcebook, along with the newly established *Journal of Personal and Interpersonal Loss* (Harvey, 1996a), helps to bring into focus certain issues that are pertinent to this field.

However, we argue that there are several questions that loss researchers must consider—and ultimately answer—if this field is to flourish in the next century and beyond. To be sure, there is a plethora of such questions. Due to the brevity of this chapter, we will discuss the seven most urgent questions (in our view) that need to be addressed.

**Can we define loss in a way that is broad enough to encompass a variety of phenomena but that still provides limits?** Overall, this sourcebook was designed to emphasize social psychological perspectives on loss research and to hopefully inspire debate on general theories regarding the global experience of loss. To that end, we offer our own definition of loss. *Loss is produced by an event which is perceived to be negative by the individuals involved and results in long-term changes to one's social situations, relationships, or cognitions.* Thus, there is an interaction between the person's perceptions and attributions and the situational context.

This definition of loss borrows from previous theorists, and is extremely broad, covering much more than the traditional grief and bereavement research. Changes in residence, employment, social/economic status, or family relationships can, by this definition, all be viewed as potential loss experiences. Additionally, experiences which produce negative changes in one's thoughts about oneself, such as a lowering of self-esteem, decreased feelings of personal safety, or fears about the future, can also be considered loss events—if such thoughts persist over the long-term.

The definition is also limiting in important ways, however. Loss experiences, as so defined, do not stem from brief traumatic events, unless the events produce significant long-term change. Thus a frightening but superficial injury will most likely not produce a sense of loss. Pain or trauma in themselves do not equal loss; there must be an accompanying social or cognitive change that is perceived to be mainly negative.

Ambivalent experiences (positive and negative changes occurring together), such as getting married or having a child, may or may not be considered loss events, depending on the perceptions and reactions of the individuals involved. This "gray area" deserves further scrutiny in research. Both acute trauma and ambivalent life stressors are important psychological topics deserving of attention; by our definition, they are not automatically topics of loss.

**What are the implications of multiple and subsequent losses?** We contend that the occurrence of either multiple or subsequent losses can greatly impact how one defines and perceives loss experiences, and how well one copes with such events. We argue that, all too often, researchers have conceptualized loss as an experience with single, as opposed to multiple, consequences. However, Ellis (1995) poignantly illustrates how a single event can lead to several different losses. Ellis (1995) describes how the terminal illness of her romantic partner caused an entire series of losses, ranging from loss of self-esteem to loss in their ability to be intimate with each other. In addition, Walsh and McGoldrick (1991) cite 14 factors that, when present, may complicate how one deals with loss; these factors include the sociopolitical and historical context of death. In short, we contend that a single loss event may actually cause an individual to experience several disparate losses.

We have just discussed the concept of multiple losses as the consequences of one event. However, how does an individual define, perceive, and cope with multiple loss experiences over the course of one's lifespan? The topic of losses and challenges throughout the lifespan certainly has received some attention from many prominent scholars (e.g., Erikson, 1968; Levinson et al. 1978; Viorst, 1986; Harvey, 1996b). While these previously mentioned schlolars have documentated that we do, in fact, endure many losses over our lifespans, we contend that little is known about the processes of how previous losses affect general coping with subsequent losses. For example, suppose the best friend of a 19 year old died in a drunk driving accident and then, 10 years later, the wife of this same hypothetical person experiences a miscarriage: how might the previous loss affect how this individual copes with his wife's miscarriage? Unfortunately, at this point, no definitive answer can be offered. We postulate that individuals may use previous losses as yardsticks by which they may be able to "measure" their current level of grieving; however, how such processes may operate is still unknown.

**Should we study loss from a single, general theoretical framework, or develop a taxonomic system?** Harvey (1996b) cogently posits that there are many similarities between categories of losses. Since the field of loss research currently is so fragmented, it would be helpful if we could conceptualize loss in a single, general theoretical framework. For instance, Sprecher and Fehr (in Chapter 7 of this volume) posit that it is entirely possible that the termination of a friendship can be just as painful as the dissolution of a marriage. Yet, as these authors note, virtually no research has compared the levels of distress experienced as a result of different types of relationship breakups. We contend that if we are to study general models of loss, then we must actively test whether the psychological reactions to different loss events are relatively similar. Obviously, certain loss events will be more stressful than others (e.g., Holmes & Rahe, 1967) or more negative than others (e.g., Sarason, Johnson, & Siegel, 1978). The question is whether the underlying processes of differing losses are the same. For instance, suppose "Person A" considered the death of his pet dog to be a major loss, and "Person B" considered her failure to find employment to be a major loss. Would the general, fundamental reactions of Person A and Person B to these "major" losses be similar? If so, then a general model of loss would be a viable option to pursue.

Conversely, we must consider the opposite alternative: is it most appropriate to study loss by developing a taxonomic system? To illustrate what is meant by this, consider how some have proposed the development of a taxonomic system for psychotherapy research. For instance, Paul (1969) has suggested that clinical researchers need to consider the "ultimate question" with respect to psychotherapy: "What treatment, by whom, is most effective for the individual with that specific problem, under what set of circumstances?" (p. 44). Another example of a taxonomic system that has more palpable applications to loss research is Moos' (1982) crisis theory. This theory discusses three major factors that may influence how people adjust to a crisis, such as an illness: illness-related factors, background and personal factors, and physical and social environmental factors. By developing a taxonomic model for the study of loss, this necessarily implies that loss can only be understood at the microlevel. For example, in order to predict whether someone will be depressed after a loss, we would need to know specific factors, such as the type of loss experienced, whether the loss was anticipated or not, the individual's pre-loss personality, and the quality of the individual's social support.

A taxonomic-type model of loss has great appeal, especially after reviewing the plethora of studies which suggest that there may be many interesting interactive effects that should be considered in loss research. A prime example is Parkes and Weiss' (1983) finding that bereaved spouses who had low-conflict marriages, in comparison to bereaved spouses who had high-conflict marriages, showed poorer emotional, physical, and social adjustment in the short term; however, in the long term, the reverse pattern was found.

Inevitably, we believe that it is essential to have a taxonomic approach to the study of loss. Such an approach will not cause the field to become further disjointed; rather, it can cause the field to become better organized. Ironically, the only way by which we can determine the degree to which general models of loss are appropriate is to devise taxonomic systems. For instance, if we find that individual caregivers' reactions to their loved one's condition—regardless of the specific condition—are relatively similar, then this is one factor that can be held constant. Since there are so many disparate forms of loss, we should strive to make the study of loss as parsimonious as possible. Thus, the ideal goal would be to devise general models of loss, but such models can only be achieved through the initial development of taxonomic systems.

**To what degree do pre-loss personological variables predict post-loss psychological functioning?** The answer to this question can have tremendous implications for loss research. It is widely assumed that certain pre-existing characterological traits may influence whether one is more likely to become depressed (Watson, Clark, & Harkness, 1994) or to suffer from heart disease (Rosenman, Brand, Sholtz, & Friedman, 1976) and even cancer (Morris, 1980). Likewise, Wortman and Silver (1989) discuss several studies that suggest that those who are most bereaved shortly after losing a spouse are also likely to be those most bereaved years after the loss episode.

We argue that it is crucial to collect data from individuals before *and* after they have experienced major losses. Many researchers may find such an endeavor to be daunting. Obviously, since many forms of loss happen suddenly and unexpectedly, it would be very difficult to collect pre-loss data. It is worth noting that some researchers (e.g., Cohen & Roth, 1984) have collected pre- and post-loss data from women who had voluntary abortions. However, some researchers (e.g.,

Adler, 1992) argue that in the short term, women may not necessarily view abortion as a form of loss, but rather as a way to reduce distress.

In any event, a new methodology needs to be developed: one that allows researchers to monitor individuals, on a regular basis, until and after a major loss event occurs. This type of methodology could finally reveal the degree to which pre-loss variables (e.g., personality and demographic variables) predict post-loss functioning. If it were found that pre-loss variables accounted for the greatest amount of variance, in terms of predicting post-loss functioning, such a finding would suggest that loss is a relatively unexciting psychological phenomenon to study. Moreover, such a finding could then highlight the importance of personality–health research in studying loss.

**Do stage models still make sense?** Many researchers have proposed "stage models" of coping with loss. Perhaps the most prominent model was suggested by Kübler-Ross (1969), in which she described how terminally ill patients adjust to dying. Another well-known model was proposed by Harper-Neeld (1990), in order to help those who recently lost a spouse. Wortman and Silver (1989), in a well cited and respected article, vehemently argue against the rationale of such stage models. In short, they argue that it is foolish to believe that everyone will experience and cope with loss in the same exact fashion; moreover, they add that, for some individuals, the grieving process associated with a particular loss may never end.

However, Stroebe, Van Den Bout, and Schut (1994) contend that Wortman and Silver (1989) have inaccurately characterized stage models. They criticize Wortman and Silver (1989) by noting that: "Researchers acknowledge individual differences in the time course of grief, and would therefore be reluctant to make precise statements about the duration of grief. . . . It is generally accepted that a few bereaved people continue to suffer intensely for much longer than the majority, and a great deal of research effort has been invested into . . . understanding . . . bereavement complications" (p. 198).

We believe that there must be a resolution to the question of whether loss can be studied in distinct stages. Wortman and Silver's (1989) point about the role of individual differences in studying loss is extremely well taken. Further, the implications of Wortman and Silver's (1989) thesis are quite profound. Once again, we are faced with the question of whether loss is an important event to study. If we assume that stage models are invalid due to individual differences, then the phenomenon that becomes of interest is the personality–health interface. If we assume that loss is, in fact, an interesting event, then we must necessarily assume that there are some similar stages or processes that all individuals may experience, albeit at different points in time.

Closer analyses of Wortman and Silver's (1989) and Stroebe et al.'s (1994) theses show that there actually may be some consensus between these two intellectual camps. Both theoretical models seem to suggest that some individuals may experience grief in a process that begins with sorrow and ends with some form of recovery. Such thinking would be entirely consistent with Lewin's (1990) very influential formula for behavior, that is, that behavior is a function of the person and the environment. Thus, we proffer that there may be several different universal grief processes or stages. However, the particular stage that a person may endure will be largely dependent on their personological characteristics.

**Can loss actually cause a fundamental change in an adult's personality?** Costa and McCrae (1991) present much empirical evidence which suggests that, overall, the personality of adults remains relatively stable, especially after age 30. However, Costa and McCrae (1991) offer some caveats to this grand finding. In particular, they note that: "Personality may change as a result of catastrophic stressors . . ." and "longitudinal studies that include both pre- and post-measures are needed here" (p. 198). Moreover, Harvey and Weber (in Chapter 24 of this volume) argue that losses can alter one's self-identity or self-schema.

This question is truly provocative, since most researchers (to date) have only considered personality variables as predictors of post-loss functioning. Very little research has considered whether loss is predictive of personality change. One important exception is Rohde, Lewinsohn, and Seeley's (1990) research on the scar hypothesis: there is some evidence that an episode of depression may create a relatively permanent residual deficit that continues to foster depression. In sum, we believe that we must carefully determine whether and how an individual's personality and identity may change after a loss.

**What are the most important post-loss psychological variables to study, and how should they be operationalized and measured?** This question attempts to consider what ought to be the ultimate goals or functions of loss research. When a loss occurs, what precisely are we trying to find out? We presume that most loss researchers are interested in "psychological adjustment," but how should this be conceptualized?

In order to make this line of research more coherent and organized, loss researchers should contemplate which psychological factors are most essential to consider while attempting to predict psychological adjustment. Clearly, depression (e.g., Beck, 1967) remains one of the most important outcome measures that are used. However, there are several other dependent variables that researchers have used in loss research, such as the search for meaning (e.g., Thompson, 1991), spirituality (e.g., Ellison & Smith, 1991), the role of self-blame attributions (e.g., Janoff-Bulman, 1992), hardiness (e.g., Kobasa, 1979), positive illusions (e.g., Taylor & Brown, 1988), internal/external control beliefs (e.g., Stroebe & Stroebe, 1992), hope (e.g., Snyder, in Chapter 5 of this volume), and coping patterns (e.g., Dunkel-Schetter, Feinstein, Taylor, & Falke, 1992). However, many of these concepts are very controversial or are still poorly understood.

Marshall, Wortman, Vickers, Kusulas, and Hervig (1994) found that most health-relevant dimensions appear to be complex mixtures of broad personality dimensions, such as the five-factor model of personality (Costa & McCrae, 1991). Consequently, it would be very beneficial to aggregate redundant measures or concepts wherever possible. In sum, loss researchers should use or develop empirically sound instruments so that we can clearly understand which constructs are the most important outcome measures to study in loss research.

## CONCLUSION AND GOALS

It is our hope that this chapter has caused the reader to re-examine his or her previous ideas about the topic of loss. First, we hope that we have broadened the definition of what it means to endure a loss. Second, we hope that we have provided compelling arguments for why loss needs to be studied, especially since it has previously not been fully examined by mainstream academic psychology, particularly social psychology. Most importantly, we have suggested seven critical questions that loss researchers must consider if this line of research is to thrive into the next century. There certainly is much research that needs to be done in this amorphous field. The question is: are enough researchers ready to meet this most challenging and fascinating endeavor?

This chapter was designed to serve as a broad overview of the field of loss, so that the reader may better appreciate the diverse topics that will be discussed in subsequent chapters. Not only should this sourcebook expose the reader to various forms of loss (which previously he or she may not necessarily have even thought of as a type of loss), but it should also serve as a springboard for the development of further research and theoretical work. This sourcebook also features social psychological perspectives on loss research, which will hopefully inspire debate on general theories regarding the global experience of loss. If this sourcebook inspires the reader to think more deeply about the nature of loss, then it will have served its primary purpose.

## REFERENCES

Adler, N. E. (1992). Abortion: A case of crisis and loss? An examination of empirical evidence. In L. Montada, S.-H. Filipp & M. J. Lerner (Eds.), *Life crises and experiences of loss in adulthood* (pp. 65–79). Hillsdale, NJ: Lawrence Erlbaum.

Allport, G. W. (1968). The historical background of modern social psychology. In G. Lindzey & E. Aronson (Eds.), *The handbook of social psychology: Vol. I* (2nd ed., pp. 1–80). Reading, MA: Addison-Wesley.

Barnhart, R. K. (Ed.). (1995). *The Barnhart concise dictionary of etymology* (1st ed.). New York: Harper Collins.

Beck, A. T. (1967). *Depression: Clinical, experimental and theoretical aspects.* New York: Harper & Row.

Bowlby, J. (1969). *Attachment and loss: Vol. 1. Attachment.* New York: Basic Books.

Bowlby, J. (1980). *Attachment and loss: Vol. 3. Loss.* New York: Basic Books.

Bretherton, I. (1985). Attachment theory: Retrospect and prospect. In I. Bretherton & E. Waters (Eds.), *Growing points in attachment theory and research* (Monographs of the Society for Research in Child Development No. 50, pp. 3–35).

Bronson, F. (1996, December 28). The year in charts. *Billboard, 108,* YE-8, YE-10, YE-21–YE-22.

Celente, G. (1997). *Trends 2000: How to prepare for and profit from the changes of the 21st century.* New York: Warner Books.

Cohen, L., & Roth, S. (1984). Coping with abortion. *Journal of Human Stress, 10,* 140–145.

Cohen, S., Doyle, W. J., Skoner, D. P., Fireman, P., Gwalthey, J. M., & Newsom, J. T. (1995). State and trait negative affect as predictors of objective and subjective symptoms of respiratory viral infections. *Journal of Personality and Social Psychology, 68,* 159–169.

Costa, P. T., & McCrae, R. R. (1991). Trait psychology comes of age. *Nebraska Symposium on Motivation, 39,* 169–204.

Cummings, E. M., & Davies, P. T. (1994). The impact of parents on their children: An emotional security hypothesis. In R. Vasta (Ed.), *Annals of child development. Vol. 10* (pp. 167–208). Bristol, PA: Kingsley.

Dunkel-Schetter, C., Feinstein, L. G., Taylor, S. E., & Falke, R. L. (1992). Patterns of coping with cancer. *Health Psychology, 11,* 79–87.

Ellis, C. (1995). *Final negotiations: A story of love, loss, and chronic illness.* Philadelphia: Temple University Press.

Ellison, C. W., & Smith, J. (1991). Toward an integrative measure of health and well-being. *Journal of Psychology and Theology, 19,* 35–48.

Erikson, E. H. (1968). *Identity: Youth and crisis.* New York: Norton.

Freud, S. (1957). Mourning and melancholia. In J. Strachey (Ed. & Trans.), *The standard edition of the complete psychological works of Sigmund Freud. Vol. 14* (pp. 239–260). New York: Norton.

Geer, J. H., Davison, G. C., & Gatchel, R. I. (1970). Reduction of stress in humans through nonveridical perceived control of aversive stimulation. *Journal of Personality and Social Psychology, 16,* 731–738.

Glass, D. C., & Singer, J. E. (1972). Behavioral aftereffects of noise. *American Scientist, 60,* 457–465.

Goodman, E. (1996, December 25). Story of a decent dreamer. *The Cedar Rapids Gazette,* p. A2.

Harper-Neeld, E. (1990). *Seven choices: Taking the steps to new life after losing someone you love.* New York: Delta.

Harvey, J. H. (1996a). Editorial and commentary: On creating the "Journal of Personal and Interpersonal Loss" and the nature of loss. *Journal of Personal and Interpersonal Loss, 1,* iii–ix.

Harvey, J. H. (1996b). *Embracing their memory: Loss and the social psychology of storytelling.* Needham Heights, MA: Allyn & Bacon.

Heller, J. F., Groff, B. D., & Solomon, S. H. (1977). Toward an understanding of crowding: The role of physical interaction. *Journal of Personality and Social Psychology, 35,* 183–190.

Holmes, T. H., & Rahe, R. H. (1967). The social readjustment rating scale. *Journal of Psychosomatic Research, 11,* 213–218.

Issel, L. M., Ersek, M., Lewis, F. M. (1990). How children cope with mother's breast cancer. *Oncology Nursing Forum, 17,* 5–12.

Janoff-Bulman, R. (1992). *Shattered assumptions: Towards a new psychology of trauma.* New York: The Free Press.

Kobasa, S. C. (1979). Stressful life events, personality, and health: An inquiry into hardiness. *Journal of Personality and Social Psychology, 37,* 1–11.

Kübler-Ross, E. (1969). *On death and dying.* New York: Macmillan.

Levinson, D. J., Darrow, C. N., Klein, E. B., Levinson, M. H., McKee, B. (1978). *The seasons of a man's life.* New York: Ballantine Books.

Lewin, K. (1990). Behavior and development as a function of the total situation. In A. G. Halberstadt & S. L. Ellyson (Eds.), *Social psychology readings: A century of research* (pp. 20–28). New York: McGraw-Hill.

Lindemann, E. (1944). Symptomatology and management of acute grief. *American Journal of Psychiatry, 101,* 141–148.

Main, M., Kaplan, N., & Cassidy, J. (1985). Security in infancy, childhood, and adulthood: A move to the level of representation. In I. Bretherton & E. Waters (Eds.), *Growing points in attachment theory and research* (Monographs of the Society for Research in Child Development No. 50, pp. 66–104).

Marshall, G. N., Wortman, C. B., Vickers, R. R., Jr., Kusulas, J. W., & Hervig, L. K. (1994). The five-factor model of personality as a framework for personality-health research. *Journal of Personality and Social Psychology, 67,* 278–286.

Middleton, W., Raphael, B., Martinek, N., & Misson, V. (1993). Pathological grief reactions. In M. S. Stroebe, W. Stroebe, & R. O. Hansson (Eds.), *Handbook of bereavement* (pp. 44–60). New York: Cambridge University Press.

Miller, E. D., Porth, M. F., Clementson, L. K., Courtin, E. S., Medow, L. R., & Harvey, J. H. (1996). *Influence of writing about loss or joy on mood.* Unpublished raw data.

Mitchell, A. (1996, November 7). Stung by defeats in '94, Clinton regrouped and co-opted G.O.P. strategies. *The New York Times,* pp. B1, B5.

Moos, R. H. (1982). Coping with acute health crises. In T. Millon, C. Green, & R. Meagher (Eds.), *Handbook of clinical health psychology* (pp. 129–151). New York: Wiley.

Morris, T. A. (1980). "Type C" for cancer? Low trait anxiety in the pathogenesis of breast cancer. *Cancer Detection and Prevention, 3,* 102.

Myers, D. G. (1996). *Social psychology* (5th ed.). New York: McGraw-Hill.

Parkes, C. M., & Weiss, R. S. (1983). *Recovery from bereavement.* New York: Basic Books.

Paul, G. L. (1969). Behavior modification research: Design and tactics. In C. M. Franks (Ed.), *Behavior therapy: Appraisal and status* (pp. 29–62). New York: McGraw-Hill.

Rando, T. A. (1988). *Grieving: How to go on living when someone you love dies.* Lexington, MA: Lexington Books.

Rohde, L., Lewinsohn, P. M., & Seeley, J. R. (1990). Are people changed by the experience of having an episode of depression? A further test of the scar hypothesis. *Journal of Abnormal Psychology, 99,* 264–271.

Rosenblatt, P. C. (1993). Grief: The social context of private feelings. In M. S. Stroebe, W. Stroebe, & R. O. Hansson (Eds.), *Handbook of bereavement* (pp. 102–111). New York: Cambridge University Press.

Rosenman, R. H., Brand, R. J., Sholtz, R. I., & Friedman, M. (1976). Multivariate prediction of coronary heart disease during 8.5 year follow-up in the Western Collaborative Group Study. *American Journal of Cardiology, 37,* 903–910.

Sarason, I. G., Johnson, J. H., & Siegel, J. M. (1978). Assessing the impact of life changes: Development of the Life Experiences Survey. *Journal of Consulting and Clinical Psychology, 46,* 932–946.

Shontz, F. C. (1975). *The psychological aspects of physical illness and disability.* New York: Macmillan.

Siegel, K., Mesagno, F. P., Karus, D., Christ, G., Banks, K., Moynihan, R. (1992). Psychosocial adjustment of children with a terminally ill parent. *Journal of the American Academy of Child and Adolecent Psychiatry, 31,* 327–333.

Silverman, P. R., & Klass, D. (1996). Introduction: What's the problem? In

D. Klaas, P. R. Silverman, & S. L. Nickman (Eds.), *Continuing bonds: New understandings of grief* (pp. 3–27). Washington, D.C.: Taylor & Francis.

Singer, J. L. (1984). *The human personality.* Orlando, FL: Harcourt Brace Jovanovich.

Solomon, S., Greenberg, J., & Pyszczynski, T. (1991). A terror management theory of social behavior: The psychological functions of self-esteem and cultural world-views. In M. P. Zanna (Ed.), *Advances in Experimental Social Psychology. Vol. 24* (pp. 93–139). San Diego, CA: Academic Press.

Stroebe, W., & Stroebe, M. S. (1992). Bereavement and health: Process of adjusting to the loss of a partner. In L. Montada, S.-H. Filipp, & M. J. Lerner (Eds.), *Life crises and experiences of loss in adulthood* (pp. 3–22). Hillsdale, NJ: Erlbaum.

Stroebe, M. S., & Stroebe, W. (1993). The mortality of bereavement: A review. In M. S. Stroebe, W. Stroebe, & R. O. Hansson (Eds.), *Handbook of bereavement* (pp. 175–195). New York: Cambridge University Press.

Stroebe, M. S., Stroebe, W., & Hansson, R. O. (1993). Bereavement research and theory. In M. S. Stroebe, W. Stroebe, & R. O. Hansson (Eds.), *Handbook of bereavement* (pp. 3–22). New York: Cambridge University Press.

Stroebe, M., Van Den Bout, J., & Schut, H. (1994). Myths and misconceptions about bereavement: The opening of a debate. *Omega, 29,* 187–203.

Taylor, S. E., & Brown, J. D. (1988). Illusion and well-being: A social psychological perspective on mental health. *Psychological Bulletin, 103,* 193–210.

Thompson, S. C. (1991). The search for meaning following a stroke. *Basic and Applied Social Psychology,12,* 81–96.

Viorst, J. (1986). *Necessary losses.* New York: Fawcett.

Walsh, F., & McGoldrick, M. (1991). Loss and the family: A systematic perspective. In F. Walsh and M. McGoldrick (Eds.), *Living beyond loss: Death in the family* (pp. 1–29). New York: Norton.

Watson, D., Clark, L. A., & Harkness, A. R. (1994). Structures of personality and their relevance to psychopathology. *Journal of Abnormal Psychology, 103,* 18–31.

Wortman, C. B., & Silver, R. C. (1989). The myths of coping with loss. *Journal of Consulting and Clinical Psychology, 57,* 349–357.

# 2

# *Blockades to Finding Meaning and Control*

***Suzanne C. Thompson***
*Pomona College*

*When we think of loss we think of the loss, through death, of people we love. But loss is a far more encompassing theme in our life. For we lose not only through death, but also by leaving and being left, by changing and letting go and moving on. And our losses include not only our separations and departures from those we love, but our . . . losses of romantic dreams, impossible expectations, illusions of freedom and power, illusions of safety—and the loss of our own younger self.*

—(Viorst, 1986, p. 2)

Loss is part of the human condition and an unavoidable fixture of life. The inevitability of major loss, however, does not mean that many of us are well prepared to handle this type of stress. Significant losses in life are likely to engender overwhelming negative emotions, disruption in everyday life, and long-term problems in resolving the loss. In addition to the trauma of losing something or someone we cherish, major loss experiences have these profound psychological effects because they shatter adaptive assumptions that had previously given structure and meaning to life (Janoff-Bulman & Freize, 1983; Taylor, 1983). These assumptions include the perception that one has some control over protecting oneself from harm and that life has meaning and purpose. The loss of these important beliefs may leave one vulnerable to depression, anxiety, and feelings of helplessness. Successful coping with the event includes the restoration of a sense of meaning and control.

The benefits derived from finding meaning and having a sense of control following a serious loss are extensively documented. Accident victims (Bulman & Wortman, 1977), incest survivors (Silver, Boon, & Stones, 1983), those whose homes were lost or damaged by a fire (Thompson, 1985), mothers with an infant in intensive care (Affleck, Tennen, & Gershman, 1985), stroke patients and their caregivers (Thompson, 1991a; Thompson, Bundek, & Sobolew-Shubin, 1990), cancer patients (Thompson & Pitts, 1993), and bereaved individuals (McIntosh, Silver, & Wortman, 1993; Schwartzberg & Janoff-Bulman, 1991) cope better with the event if they report that they have found meaning in their experiences. A sense of control is also an important part of coping with a traumatic situation. As one pain patient relates, "just the fact you know you have some control makes a whole lot of difference in how you view yourself and your situation" (Filips, 1995, p. D4). Perceived control is related to better coping for a variety of groups under stress, including patients with coronary heart disease (Taylor, Helgeson, Reed, & Skokan, 1991), cancer patients (Taylor, Lichtman, & Wood, 1984; Thompson, Sobolew-Shubin, Galbraith, Schwankovsky, & Cruzen, 1993), HIV-positive men (Thompson, Nanni, & Levine, 1994), and HIV-positive male inmates (Thompson, Collins, Newcomb, & Hunt, 1996).

Despite the advantages associated with recovering a sense of meaning and control in the aftermath of a significant loss, it may not be easy to do so. Although most studies in this area do not report how many of the participants have restored adaptive assumptions, the few studies that have examined this topic indicate that many people have not been able to reestablish a strong sense of meaning and control following trauma or loss. For example, half of the stroke patients in one study and slightly more than half of their family-member caregivers reported that they had not been able to find meaning in their experience with stroke (Thompson, 1991a). Fifty percent of bereaved college students stated that they had never been able to find a satisfying answer to the question of why their parent had died (Schwartzberg & Janoff-Bulman, 1991), and 32% of women who had miscarried saw no positive effects to their experience (Tunaley, Slade, & Duncan, 1993). More than half of the mothers with an infant in intensive care had not found an answer to the question of why this had happened and about one quarter did not feel that any benefit had come from the experience (Affleck & Tennen, 1991). Even when the search for meaning has taken place over a much longer period of time, many individuals may be unable to come to a satisfactory resolution. Over half of the survivors of incest that had taken place an average of 20 years previous to the interview were unable to make any sense of their experience (Silver et al., 1983). In a study of women who had been sexually assaulted in the prior two years, Scheppele and Bart (1983) found that 23% of the women had an extreme fear reaction characterized by low feelings of control over future victimization. For another 32% of the women, the fear response was less extreme, but the loss of control still generalized to situations other than that in which the attack took place. These figures suggest that often a third to a half of those who have experienced a major loss do not find meaning or regain a sense of control following the experience. Moreover, one study of long-term survivors of victimization found that many victims have less positive assumptions than those who have not had a major trauma, even 10 to 15 years after the victimization (Janoff-Bulman, 1989).

Given the clear advantages associated with restoring adaptive assumptions of meaning and control after a major loss, why do so many individuals fail to do so? To answer that question, we need to consider how people find meaning and how they restore a sense of control after a traumatic loss.

## STRATEGIES FOR FINDING MEANING

Finding meaning following a serious loss can be accomplished in several ways. According to the life scheme model, one strategy to restore adaptive assumptions involves changing one's life scheme or the cognitive representation of one's life so that it is not inconsistent with the traumatic experience (Thompson & Janigian, 1988). This can be done through reordering priorities, changing to goals that can be reached despite the adversity, or adapting one's self-image in a positive way that incorporates loss, for example, seeing oneself as a "coper" or "survivor." A second strategy to restore assumptions is to change one's perception of the stressful event through reinterpretation of the event using positive focus, changing perspective, or making social comparisons to others who are worse off. This approach makes the event seem less negative and, therefore, less of a challenge to useful assumptions of meaning and control (Thompson & Janigian, 1988).

As predicted by cognitive models of coping (e.g., Janoff-Bulman & Freize, 1983; Taylor, 1983; Thompson & Janigian, 1988), the strategies of changing to reachable goals, positive interpretation, and making downward comparisons are associated with the ability to find meaning and with better psychological outcomes. For example, cancer patients who reported changing to goals that were more internal and less materialistic following their diagnosis had a stronger sense of meaning than those who did not (Thompson & Pitts, 1993). Stroke patients and their family caregivers who stated that the stroke helped them appreciate life and their spouses more and that they had grown from the experience were more likely to have found meaning in their experiences with the stroke (Thompson, 1991a). In addition, downward comparison has been associated with better coping for breast cancer patients (Taylor, Wood, & Lichtman, 1983), for mothers of infants in newborn intensive care units (Affleck, Tennen, Pfeiffer, Fifield, & Rowe, 1987), and for adults undergoing bone marrow transplantation (Ersek, 1992). Thus there is evidence that changing one's goals, interpreting the event, or comparing oneself to those who are worse off are ways to find meaning in a traumatic experience.

## STRATEGIES FOR REESTABLISHING CONTROL

A number of studies have investigated ways in which individuals might find a sense of control in aversive situations that do not seem to offer many opportunities for obtaining desired outcomes. One strategy is to use acceptance to help maintain an overall sense of control. Rothbaum, Weisz, and Snyder (1982) made the distinction between primary control, which is the perception that one can get desired outcomes through one's own action, and secondary control, which involves accepting the situation as it is and adjusting to it. By accepting some outcomes, people's overall sense of control is enhanced because they avoid feelings of helplessness regarding those outcomes and can concentrate their efforts in areas that may be more conducive to influence. Through the judicious use of primary and secondary control, individuals can maintain an overall sense of control and have better psychological outcomes even in circumstances of low personal control (Heckhausen & Schulz, 1995). In support of these ideas, it has been found that secondary control serves a back-up function for perceptions of primary control. Men with HIV who did not feel that they could exercise primary control over events in their daily lives were not depressed if they had higher perceptions of secondary control (Thompson et al. 1994). Similar results have been found with late midlife adults regarding their control over age-related appearance changes (Thompson, Thomas, Rickabaugh, & Tantamjarik, 1996). Thus accepting some negative outcomes may help protect individuals from feelings of helplessness in circumstances that offer restricted options for real control.

A second strategy for maintaining a sense of control is to heighten awareness of areas in which one's attempts to exercise control have been successful. According to Langer's model of mindlessness (Langer, Blank, & Chanowitz, 1978), perceptions of control are stronger if individuals are aware of their experience of exercising control. For example, those who act mindlessly might effect desired change, but this success would not feed into stronger perceptions of control. Thus what one focuses on and is aware of when judging one's sense of control can affect the final judgment. Perlmuter and Langer (1982) describe a technique designed to increase people's awareness of their decision-making control by having individuals monitor several regular daily behaviors such as their choice of breakfast beverage, shirt color, or TV programs. Presumably, feelings of control can be enhanced by focusing on areas of successful influence.

Five ways of restoring a sense that life is meaningful and that one has some control over desired outcomes following a major loss have been discussed: changing to reachable goals, making positive reinterpretations, engaging in downward comparisons, accepting some outcomes, and focusing on areas of higher perceived control. These are not the only ways that adaptive assumptions can be restored, but they are among the most common and the ones most studied by researchers.

## BLOCKADES TO FINDING MEANING AND CONTROL

To understand how people fail to find meaning and control following a loss, we need to understand what might keep them from using these techniques. The circumstances or type of loss and characteristics of the person experiencing the loss will be discussed as possible reasons for difficulty in finding meaning and control following a loss.

### Situational Factors

The most obvious influence on how easy it is to find meaning and control in the aftermath of a loss is the seriousness and extent of the loss. As one would expect, those who have suffered a more serious loss find it more difficult to find meaning and to recapture a sense of mastery. For example, cancer patients (Thompson & Pitts, 1993), stroke survivors (Thompson, 1991a), and stroke caregivers (Thompson et al., 1990) report they have found less meaning in the experience if their loss is greater (poorer physical functioning on the part of the patient). Lower physical functioning was also associated with lower feelings of control for cancer patients (Thompson et al., 1993), although there was no relationship between number of symptoms and primary control for men with HIV (Thompson et al., 1994). It should be noted, however, that severity of loss is, at best, a weak predictor of having difficulties in finding meaning and control, accounting for an average of

9% of the variance in these variables in the five studies cited above. Furthermore, when severity is controlled for, there is still a strong relationship between restoring assumptions and adaptive coping.

A second situational factor that might make it difficult to restore assumptions is the type of loss. There is some evidence that unexpected loss, misfortune perpetrated by trusted others, and loss in a situation where one had exerted control make coping particularly difficult. For example, Smith, Range, and Ulmer (1991–1992) found that individuals who were mourning a suicide or accident found less meaning in the death than did those bereaved by other causes. Assault from family members such as that experienced by incest victims may be particularly difficult to resolve (Silver et al., 1983). These types of losses may be especially strong challenges to beliefs in meaning and control.

Undoubtedly, severity of loss and circumstances of the loss can affect how easy or difficult it is to cope with a serious loss. Yet, what is striking is the variability of response among individuals who have experienced objectively very similar losses. Furthermore, one must be impressed with some individuals' adaptability in being able to see a meaningful life with some degree of control even in very adverse circumstances. It appears that no matter how poor the situation is relative to that of others, some dimension for downward comparison can be found (Affleck & Tennen, 1991; Taylor, 1983), some aspect of the situation can be controlled, if only one's attitude toward the lack of control (Frankl, 1963), some reason for hope and optimism can be identified. This suggests that there are personal factors that influence the ability to restore adaptive assumptions.

### Personal Factors

There are some similarities in the five approaches that impart a sense of meaning or control. First, these techniques involve some cognitive work. Giving up goals and identifying new ones, finding a positive perspective, and accepting some outcomes all involve attention to the loss and its ramifications and, perhaps, intense thinking about the issue and discussing it with others. They are not likely to be accomplished through denial or avoidance of the loss. In fact, Harvey, Orbuch, Weber, Merbach, and Alt (1992) suggest that it may take as long as 200 hours of cognitive-emotional work to come to some closure about the loss of a close, personal relationship that had lasted about a year. Second, many of these ways of finding meaning and control involve adopting a new way of seeing the situation, and therefore may require the ability to change views and to try out new perspectives. Third, some of these strategies require the ability to let go of some goals and embrace others. Thus, some flexibility in goal identification is required. We will now consider each of these three common themes in finding meaning and control.

## COGNITIVE WORK

Being willing and able to perform the cognitive-emotional work that is necessary to reestablish adaptive assumptions following a traumatic experience requires the strength to deal with emotional pain, rather than engaging in avoidance or denial, and is greatly helped by opportunities to talk about the loss with others.

### Approach to Dealing with Emotionally Painful Material

There is no question that it is a painful process to make sense of a major loss and begin to come to some resolution. There is much to be considered: Why did it happen? Why to me? Could it have been avoided? Who is to blame? What are the many ramifications of this loss for all areas of my present and future life? Will I recover from this? All of this can arouse feelings of sadness, anger, self-blame, regret, and despair. Not surprisingly, the first response is often one of avoidance, and then gradually, people may allow themselves to become aware of the full impact of the loss.

In general, research has found that escapism and avoidance can be associated with successful coping in the short-term, but when long-term outcomes are considered, attention to the problem emerges as a more effective strategy (Suls & Fletcher, 1985). For example, mothers with infants in newborn intensive care who used an "escapist" coping style (e.g., wishful thinking, avoiding social contacts, and distraction behaviors) had greater long-term distress than those who did not (Affleck & Tennen, 1991).

The fear of being overwhelmed by negative emotions and the intense pain of considering difficult questions may be too much for some individuals, so that they avoid thinking and talking about the loss or deny its effects even after the initial shock. Thus individuals who generally use repression of negative emotions (Byrne, 1964) or avoidant coping styles (Holahan & Moos, 1986) may not engage in the cognitive work that can help to make sense out of an event and restore adaptive assumptions.

### Opportunities to Talk to Others about the Loss

An important component to doing the cognitive-emotional work that is necessary to recover from a traumatic loss is the chance to vent or discuss one's reaction and feelings. This seems to help people begin to make sense out of their experience, receive validation for their thoughts and feelings, explore alternative ways of understanding their situation, and let go of their negative emotions. One study found that rescue workers who worked at a serious airline crash overwhelmingly endorsed the value of talking with others to help cope with their experience (Smith, Rippenkroeger, Wehrle, & Harvey, 1991). Just having someone who was willing to listen was mentioned as a supportive and helpful action in studies of men with AIDS and adult diabetic patients (Dunkel-Schetter, Blasband, Feinstein, & Herbert, 1992). Silver and Wortman (1980) conclude that opportunties for the free expression of feelings can have a number of benefits for those dealing with undesirable life events.

A number of factors could be obstacles to talking about one's experience for those who might want to. Wortman and Dunkel-Schetter (1979) suggest that potential support people may avoid open communication with survivors of trauma or loss because of their own fears or due to the mistaken notion that it would be upsetting rather than helpful to discuss the traumatic event. Victims themselves may feel that their own reactions and feelings are extreme and inappropriate, making it difficult to share these thoughts with others (Silver & Wortman, 1980). It can be particularily difficult to communicate with others about victimizations that are stigmatized. For example, people with AIDS and their families may be reluctant to reveal the disease to others for fear of harsh judgment or ostracization.

The availability of opportunities to vent one's reactions to a traumatic experience is also influenced by the social resources and personality of the victim. Connell and D'Augelli (1990) found that adults who were more affiliative, nurturing, and willing to seek support had larger support networks and received more support from others. In addition, people need to know how to use their support network, so that it remains available to them and they do not overburden any one individual. As one young adult with cancer puts it, "I save all my dumping for (the college psychiatrist). I'm very conscious of not wanting to dump my problems on my friends all the time—they think they should be able to help, and sometimes they can't" (Fay, 1983, p. 269).

In summary, individuals who tend to repress difficult material rather than dealing with it directly and those who have fewer opportunities to vent or are less skilled at seeking and maintaining supportive contacts may not be able to do the cognitive work that helps in the search for meaning and control.

## ADOPTING NEW PERSPECTIVES

Many of the ways of restoring control and meaning following a major loss involve finding an adaptive perspective for viewing the situation. This may include identifying and focusing on benefits from the situation, putting the event in the context of worse situations, making comparisons to others who are worse off, or taking a different temporal perspective on the situation, e.g., focusing on the long run (Thompson, 1985). There are a number of reasons why people may find it difficult to explore more adaptive perspectives for viewing an event and its consequences. This paper will focus on two of them: the belief that positive thinking involves self-delusion and an inability to be open to new ways of looking at a phenomenon.

### Positive Interpretation and Reality

Some people may resist the use of positive interpretation and find it difficult to restore adaptive assumptions because these strategies may seem to involve "positive thinking," which has a bad reputation. We associate it with being a pollyanna, with self-delusion, and with pop philosophical thinking such as espoused by Norman Vincent Peale or Dale Carnegie. It appears to be an affront to Western civilization's emphasis on rational thinking and living a life based on reality. As one reviewer of a book on the life stories of AIDS patients wrote, "I'm really tired of hearing about what a great gift AIDS has been, that we've learned so much and that transformation, Shirley MacLaine stuff. What we've supposedly 'learned' is hardly worth our loss of thousands. This is a sophisticated bliss-ninny form of denial of the horror and tragedy of AIDS!" (Perow, 1990, p. 147).

It is not just popular culture that has viewed these techniques as being used at the expense of denying reality, deluding oneself, and distorting one's experience. For example, Bearison and Pacific (1984), in their analysis of the basis for psychological meaning among children with cancer and their families, characterize the search for meaning as involving "mutual pretense" and a "conspiracy of pretense," implying that it is only at the cost of distorting reality that children with a serious disease and their parents find meaning in the event.

In support of this view, Colvin and Block (1994) argue that the hallmark of good mental health is being in touch with reality and developing a self-image that is an honest assessment of one's abilities and attributes. Illusions and unrealistic self-enhancement, they maintain, are impediments to psychological health that promise short-term benefits at the expense of long-term disadvantages.

In order to reconcile these negative views of positive interpretation with the view that finding a positive focus is an important part of coping with a serious loss, it is important to acknowledge that for many of the types of judgments involved in finding meaning and control, there is no correct, "rational" assessment of the situation that can be distinguished from an inaccurate, self-delusional judgment. Comparative judgments, by their nature, are influenced by one's comparison frame and attentional focus. An individual who adopts a comparison frame that leads to more positive emotions and a more adaptive response is no less rational or self-delusional than someone who uses a comparison frame that leads to more negative emotions and more difficulty in coping with the loss. In fact, the argument could be made that, given the greater adaptiveness of using positive reinterpretation, positive focus techniques are more "rational" than negative interpretations.

The general point that positive focus techniques do not necessarily involve self-delusion or irrational thought is not to say that there are not ways of viewing a situation that could be characterized as delusional or involving denial. This is illustrated by making a distinction between the facts of a situation, on the one hand, and how one interprets or reacts to the facts on the other. Whether or not the facts of a situation exist, for example, a diagnosis of cancer, death of one's spouse, or rejection by a lover, is not a question of perspective or interpretation. To deny that these events have occurred would constitute denial and self-delusion. However, how one chooses to view the facts by focusing on the possibility of controlling the cancer rather than the uncontrollable aspects, comparing the circumstances of a loved one's death to worse alternatives, or by attending to the benefits of being out of the relationship does not constitute denial or delusion. It is a question of which perspective to take on the same set of facts. The extent to which individuals believe that any positive view of a basically undesirable situation is self-delusional, however, will make it more difficult to restore a sense of meaning and control.

## Rigidity in World Views and Beliefs

In addition to the view that using positive interpretation techniques is a form of self-delusion, other beliefs may make it problematic to find meaning and control because they do not facilitate adopting a positive perspective. At the broadest philosophical level, nihilistic, pan-determinist, or reductionist approaches to life are at odds with the ideas of choice and of basic meaningfulness in life (Fabry, 1988). Other, less encompassing, belief systems may also have implications for the ability to maintain control and meaning. Ellis has proposed that many individuals engage in irrational thinking, characterized by the belief that happiness and self-worth are dependent only on certain attainments, the attitude that one cannot control one's emotional responses, a tendency to catastrophize (focus on the worst possible interpretation), and the avoidance of difficult or painful situations (Ellis & Harper, 1975). These types of beliefs are particularly relevant to the search for meaning and control because irrational thinking leads one to avoid the necessary cognitive work and to focus on negative rather than positive interpretations, and contributes to a lack of flexibility in identifying alternative goals. In support of the idea that irrational thinking reduces the likelihood of engaging in the cognitive work and perspective-taking that helps individuals to find meaning, Thompson and Pitts (1993) found that cancer patients who more strongly endorsed irrational beliefs were less likely to report that they had found meaning in their experience with cancer. On the other hand, optimistic thinkers as measured by the Life Orientation Test (Scheier & Carver, 1985) had stronger feelings of meaning. It seems likely that the restoration of adaptive assumptions is difficult to do if one's world views indicate that people do not have a choice in how to view their situation, that happiness and self-worth are independent of attaining certain goals, that the most negative interpretations are the only valid ones, and that painful deliberation should be avoided.

## GOALS: IDENTIFICATION AND DISENGAGEMENT

Being invested in important goals serves a number of functions related to finding meaning and control. The identification and pursuit of goals, as well as the perception that one is making progress toward attaining one's goals, give a sense of purpose and meaning to life. As one author states, "when it comes right down to specifying what makes their lives meaningful, people turn to the incentives in their lives—the personal relationships, job goals, recreational activities, inner experiences, and simple daily pleasures that people spend most of the time pursuing and enjoying" (Klinger, 1977, p. 9).

Goals also serve a central role in the perception that one has control in life. The ability to specify one's goals, to identify paths to reach them, and to disengage from unreachable goals is part of the process of feeling a sense of control (Thompson, 1991b). It is difficult to have a sense that one's own actions can achieve desired outcomes unless there is a fairly good sense of what those desired outcomes might be.

One reason why a major loss can undermine the sense that life is meaningful is that the goals associated with the lost object or attribute are no longer attainable. For example, an illness or physical disability may render a career or athletic goal impossible, and the loss of a loved one eliminates goals that are related to or dependent on the relationship such as being a good husband, experiencing intimacy, or the success of a common business venture.

Another reason why a loss can undermine feelings of meaning and control has to do with the process of dealing with unattainable incentives. According to Klinger's (1975, 1977) theory of incentive relationships, when progress toward a goal is frustrated, an incentive/disengagement cycle occurs. This involves invigoration and aggression phases in which the goal is actively sought and takes on increased value. The depression phase takes place when people begin to give up the goal and grieve for its loss. Finally, recovery is reached when disengagement from the goal and the identification of other attractive aims is achieved. Because the blocked incentive becomes more attractive and other goals lose their appeal during the phases of invigoration and aggression, more mundane everyday goals that had given direction and satisfaction to life may lose their value. Thus one would expect that for some time following a major loss, it will be difficult for other goals unrelated to the loss to serve as a source of meaningfulness.

Finding satisfying alternative goals when a loss prevents the attainment of previous aims in life is dependent on disengaging from former goals and identifying new incentives and possible sources of satisfaction. Disengagement from previous goals that are now unrealistic or impossible to achieve and the identification of new goals are likely to be affected by several characteristics of the person who experienced the loss. First, the types of beliefs described in the previous section that block the search for a positive interpretation also make it difficult to disengage from former goals. For example, the irrational belief that happiness and self-worth are dependent on achieving only certain goals leads to a rigidity in goal definition. People with this style of thinking will find it difficult to let go of the goals such as career success or the approval of valued others that to them seem like the only route to feeling good about themselves. Second, an individual who has a greater diversity of goals will find it easier to disengage from a particular goal that is now unlikely to be reached and will have alternative goals that already have incentive value. Although the value of alternative goals may be reduced in the invigoration phase following goal blockage, those who have not put "all their eggs" into one goal basket will have a better chance of retaining incentives in other areas that still function to give life meaning. Third, disengaging from a goal is likely to involve the acceptance of not having that goal now or in the future.

Not a great deal is known about how people come to accept an undesirable situation and make peace with the idea of not reaching a desired goal, but several studies have found that acceptance of a difficult situation is associated with a stronger sense of primary control (Thompson, Collins, et al., 1996; Thompson et al., 1994; Thompson, Thomas, et al., 1996). That is, individuals who feel that they can attain their desired outcomes, in general, are also more likely to state that they accept an undesirable situation, perhaps because a sense of being able to attain other goals compensates for a loss in one area. Acceptance also involves seeing value in one's current situation. The same positive interpretation strategies that put the loss in a less negative perspective may function to help people give up former goals. For example, finding positive aspects of one's situation without a particular goal may make accepting the loss of that goal easier.

In summary, attachment to new goals that can structure and give meaning to life and promote a sense of control is an important part of the recovery process.

Individuals who cannot disengage from now unreachable goals and identify and find value in new incentives will find it difficult to restore positive assumptions.

## CONCLUSION

Finding meaning and control following a serious loss is accomplished through changing goals, making positive interpretations, engaging in helpful comparisons, accepting outcomes, and focusing on areas of higher control. Although features of the loss may make it more difficult to use these techniques to find meaning and restore a sense of control, there is considerable evidence that personal dispositions and world views make a major contribution to the likelihood that adaptive assumptions will be restored. In particular, the ability to engage in cognitive work, to change views and adopt new perspectives, and to be flexible in goal identification are necessary personal dispositions for restoring assumptions. Those individuals who use avoidance and denial to deal with difficult emotional material, who are not skilled at recruiting social support, who find it difficult to adopt a positive perspective, who have rigid world views, and who are not skilled at engaging new goals will be at a disadvantage in finding meaning and control in their experience with loss. Education about the coping process that debunks common misconceptions of coping, therapy to help people find more adaptive perceptions and beliefs, and help in identifying a variety of opportunities for venting may make it easier for individuals to cope with traumatic life experiences.

## REFERENCES

Affleck, G., & Tennen, H. (1991). The effect of newborn intensive care on parents' psychological well-being. *Children's Health Care, 20,* 6–14.

Affleck, G., Tennen, H., & Gershman, K. (1985). Cognitive adaptations to high-risk infants: The search for mastery, meaning, and protection from future harm. *American Journal of Mental Deficiency, 89,* 653–656.

Affleck, G., Tennen, H., Pfeiffer, C., Fifield, C., & Rowe, J. (1987). Downward comparison and coping with serious medical problems. *American Journal of Orthopsychiatry, 57,* 570–578.

Bearison, D. J., & Pacific, C. (1984). Psychological studies of children who have cancer. *Journal of Applied Developmental Psychology, 5,* 263–280.

Bulman, R. J., & Wortman, C. B. (1977). Attributions of blame and coping in the "real world": Severe accident victims react to their lot. *Journal of Personality and Social Psychology, 35,* 351–363.

Byrne, D. (1964). Repression-sensatization as a dimension of personality. In B. A. Maher (Ed.), *Progress in experimental personality research. Vol. i* (pp. 169–220). New York: Academic Press.

Colvin, C. R., & Block, J. (1994). Do positive illusions foster mental health? An examination of the Taylor and Brown formulation. *Psychological Bulletin, 116,* 3–20.

Connell, C. M., & D'Augelli, A. R. (1990). The contribution of personality characteristics to the relationship between social support and perceived physical health. *Health Psychology, 9,* 192–207.

Dunkel-Schetter, C., Blasband, D. E., Feinstein, L. G., & Herbert, T. B. (1992). Elements of supportive interactions: When are attempts to help effective? In S. Spacapan & S. Oskamp (Eds.), *Helping and being helped. Naturalistic studies* (pp. 83–114). Newbury Park, CA: Sage.

Ellis, A., & Harper, R. A. (1975). *A new guide to rational living.* North Hollywood, CA: Wilshire Books.

Ersek, M. (1992). The process of maintaining hope in adults undergoing bone marrow transplantation for leukemia. *Oncology Nursing Forum, 19,* 883–889.

Fabry, J. (1988). Dilemmas of today—Logotherapy proposals. *International Forum for Logotherapy, 11,* 5–12.

Fay, M. (1983). *A mortal condition.* New York: Coward-McCann.

Filips, J. (1995). Transcending pain. *The Oregonian,* pp. D1, D4.

Frankl, V. E. (1963). *Man's search for meaning.* New York: Pocket Books.

Harvey, J. H., Orbuch, R. L., Weber, A. L., Merbach, N., & Alt, R. (1992). House of pain and hope: Accounts of loss. *Death Studies, 16,* 99–124.

Heckhausen, J., & Schulz, R. (1995). A life-span theory of control. *Psychological Review, 102,* 284–304.

Holahan, C. J., & Moos, R. H. (1986). Personality, coping, and family resources in stress resistance: A longitudinal analysis. *Journal of Personality and Social Psychology, 51,* 389–395.

Janoff-Bulman, R. (1989). Assumptive worlds and the stress of traumatic events: Applications of the schema construct. *Social Cognition, 7,* 113–136

Janoff-Bulman, R., & Frieze, I. H. (1983). A theoretical perspective for understanding reactions to victimization. *Journal of Social Issues, 39,* 1–17.

Klinger, E. (1975). Consequences of commitment to and disengagement from incentives. *Psychological Review, 82,* 1–25.

Klinger, E. (1977). *Meaning and void.* Minneapolis, MN: University of Minnesota Press.

Langer, E. J., Blank, A., & Chanowitz, B. (1978). The mindlessness of ostensibly thoughtful action: The role of "placebic" information in interpersonal interaction. *Journal of Personality and Social Psychology, 36,* 635–642.

McIntosh, D. N., Silver, R. C., & Wortman, C. B. (1993). Religion's role in adjustment to a negative life event: Coping with the loss of a child. *Journal of Personality and Social Psychology, 65,* 812–821.

Perlmuter, L. C., & Langer, E. J. (1982). The effects of behavioral monitoring on the perception of control. *Clinical Gerontologist, 1,* 37–43.

Perow, S. (1990). *Dancing against the darkness.* Lexington, MA: D.C. Heath and Co.

Rothbaum, F., Weisz, J. R., & Snyder, S. S. (1982). Changing the world and changing the self: A two-process model of perceived control. *Journal of Personality and Social Psychology, 42,* 5–27.

Scheier, M. F., & Carver, C. S. (1985). Optimism, coping, and health: Assessment and implications of generalized outcome expectancies. *Health Psychology, 4,* 219–247.

Scheppele, K. L., & Bart, P. B. (1983). Through women's eyes: Defining danger in the wake of sexual assault. *Journal of Social Issues, 39*(2), 63–81.

Schwartzberg, S. S., & Janoff-Bulman, R. (1991). Grief and the search for meaning: Exploring the assumptive worlds of bereaved college students. *Journal of Social and Clinical Psychology, 10,* 270–288.

Silver, R. L., Boon, C., & Stones, M. H. (1983). Searching for meaning in misfortune: Making sense of incest. *Journal of Social Issues, 39,* 81–101.

Silver, R. L., & Wortman, C.B., (1980). Coping with undesirable life events. In J. Garber & M. E. P. Seligman (Eds.), *Human helplessness* (pp. 279–340). New York: Academic Press.

Smith, P. C., Range, L. M., & Ulmer, A. (1991–1992). Belief in afterlife as a buffer in suicidal and other bereavement. *Omega, 24,* 217–225.

Smith, D., Rippenkroeger, A., Wehrle, S., & Harvey, J. (1991). As cited in J. H. Harvey, R. L. Orbuch, A. L. Weber, N. Merbach, & R. Alt (1992). House of pain and hope: Accounts of loss. *Death Studies, 16,* 99–124.

Suls, J., & Fletcher, B. (1985). The relative efficacy of avoidant and nonavoidant coping strategies: A meta-analysis. *Health Psychology, 4,* 249–288.

Taylor, S. E. (1983). Adjustment to threatening events: A theory of cognitive adaptation. *American Psychologist, 38,* 1161–1173.

Taylor, S. E., Helgeson, V. S., Reed, G. M., & Skokan, L. A. (1991). Self-generated feelings of control and adjustment to physical illness. *Journal of Social Issues, 47*(4), 91–109.

Taylor, S. E., Lichtman, R. R., & Wood, J. V. (1984). Attributions, beliefs about control, and adjustment to breast cancer. *Journal of Personality and Social Psychology, 46,* 489–502.

Taylor, S. E., Wood, J. V., & Lichtman, R. R. (1983). It could be worse: Selective evaluation as a response to victimization. *Journal of Social Issues, 39,* 19–40.

Thompson, S. C. (1985). Finding positive meaning in a stressful event and coping. *Basic and Applied Social Psychology, 6,* 279–295

Thompson, S. C. (1991a). The search for meaning following a stroke. *Basic and Applied Social Psychology, 12,* 81–96.

Thompson, S. C. (1991b). Intervening to enhance perceptions of control. In C. R. Snyder & D. Forsyth (Eds.), *Handbook of social and clinical psychology* (pp. 607–623). New York: Pergamon Press.

Thompson, S. C., Bundek, N. I., & Sobolew-Shubin, A., (1990). The caregivers of stroke patients: An investigation of factors associated with depression. *Journal of Applied Social Psychology, 20,* 115–129.

Thompson, S. C., Collins, M. A., Newcomb, M. D., & Hunt, W. (1996). On fighting versus accepting stressful circumstances: Primary and secondary control among HIV-positive men in prison. *Journal of Personality and Social Psychology, 70,* 1307–1317.

Thompson, S. C., & Janigian, A. (1988). Life schemes: A framework for understanding the search for meaning. *Journal of Social and Clinical Psychology, 7,* 260–280.

Thompson, S. C., Nanni, C., & Levine, A. (1994). Primary versus secondary and disease versus consequence-related control in HIV-positive men. *Journal of Personality and Social Psychology, 64,* 540–547.

Thompson, S. C., & Pitts, J. (1993). Factors that are related to a person's ability to find meaning following a diagnosis of cancer. *Journal of Psychosocial Oncology, 11,* 1–21.

Thompson, S. C., Sobolew-Shubin, A., Galbraith, M. E., Schwankovsky, L., & Cruzen, D. (1993). Maintaining perceptions of control: Finding perceived control in low-control circumstances. *Journal of Personality and Social Psychology, 64,* 293–304.

Thompson, S. C., Thomas, C., Rickabaugh, C., Tantamjarik, P., Otsuki, T., Pan, D., Garcia, B. F., & Sinar, E. (in press). *Primary and secondary control over age-related changes in physical appearance.* Manuscript under review.

Tunaley, J. R., Slade, P., & Duncan, S. B. (1993). Cognitive processes in psychological adaptation to miscarriage: A preliminary report. *Psychology and Health, 8,* 369–381.

Viorst, J. (1986). *Necessary losses.* New York: Ballantine Books.

Wortman, C. B., & Dunkel-Schetter, C. (1979). Interpersonal relationships and cancer: A theoretical analysis. *Journal of Social Issues, 35,* 120–155.

# 3

# *Disillusionment and the Creation of Value: From Traumatic Losses to Existential Gains*

**Ronnie Janoff-Bulman and Michael Berg**
*University of Massachusetts, Amherst*

*The world isn't as it was. It doesn't make sense, and*
*I feel stripped of all security. It's terrifying to think*
*that disaster could strike again at any moment*
*and destroy my life or the lives of those I love.*

*Everything is different now. I really live life now;*
*I'm not just existing. I appreciate the important things.*
*I can't say I'm happy for what happened, but*
*my life is far richer and fuller now.*

These dramatically different words are both responses of individuals who experienced a traumatic event in adulthood. For one survivor the victimization is associated with losses, whereas for the other it is associated with gains. It would be a simple matter to dismiss these differences by attributing them to the nature of the traumatic events or the different coping abilities of the survivors. Yet, based on years of work with trauma victims, it has become increasingly clear that the two quotes could readily have come from the same person (Janoff-Bulman, 1985, 1992; also see, e.g., Collins, Taylor, & Skokan, 1990; Lehman et al., 1993; Tedeschi & Calhoun, 1996).

Survivors commonly experience the terror of a shattered, malevolent world as well as the gratification of a deeper, more meaningful existence. They move from perceiving a meaningless universe to creating a meaningful life, and this journey involves a potent and disturbing process of disillusionment. It is not simply that some trauma survivors cope well and perceive benefits *in spite of* their losses, but rather that the creation of value and meaning occurs *because* of their losses, particularly the loss of deeply held illusions. In the end, survivors often feel both more vulnerable and more appreciative, two states that are fundamentally linked.

## SHATTERED ASSUMPTIONS: UNDERSTANDING THE LOSS OF ILLUSIONS POST-TRAUMA

When we think of losses, we typically consider negative, perceptible changes in external circumstances: loss of loved family members or friends, physical health, important jobs, valued possessions (see, e.g., Harvey, Orbuch, Weber, Merbach, & Alt, 1992; Harvey, Weber, & Orbuch, 1990). The loss of illusions is relatively easy to overlook, for it is intangible, internal, and therefore imperceptible to others. Yet, research with survivors of traumatic events, including life-threatening diseases, the untimely death of loved ones, rape and other crimes, and debilitating accidents, suggests the pivotal role of disillusionment in the aftermath of victimization. At the very core of our psyches are fundamental assumptions that are shattered by the traumatic experience (Janoff-Bulman, 1985, 1992; also see Epstein, 1991; McCann & Pearlman, 1990). The assumptions are recognized for what they were: illusions that cannot account for the tragic victimization.

The phrase heard most often during 20 years of working with victims was "I never thought it could happen to me!" In the aftermath of traumatic events, survivors powerfully recognize the extent to which they had taken for granted their own sense of safety and invulnerability. We might ask why victims are so shocked; after all, don't we all know that "bad things happen"? We certainly acknowledge that a large number of people are in car accidents, get cancer, or are victims of crime. Why, then, is disbelief virtually a universal response to victimization? Somehow, we know that bad things happen, but deep in our psyches and deep in our guts we don't believe they will happen to us (see, e.g., Lifton, 1967; Perloff, 1983; Weinstein, 1989). We feel protected, but often are unaware of this feeling until we are victimized. At the core of our cognitive-emotional system are fundamental assumptions about the world and ourselves that provide us with this sense of safety and relative invulnerability (see Bowlby, 1969, on working models; Epstein, 1973, on theories of reality; Parkes, 1975, on assumptive worlds). What are these assumptions that enable us to believe in the continuity of a secure existence?

### Fundamental Assumptions and Invulnerability

At least three of these assumptions, which typically go unquestioned and unchallenged, involve views of ourselves, the world, and the relation between the two. More specifically, at the very deepest levels of our psyche, we assume that we are worthy, the world is benevolent, and what happens to us "makes sense" (Janoff-Bulman, 1985, 1992). We believe that we are good, decent, capable people. By discounting the importance of domains in which we don't excel and selectively seeing ourselves as responsible for desirable outcomes, we maintain our positively biased self-perceptions. These positive self-evaluations are apparent in the skewed distributions consistently found by researchers of self-esteem (Greenwald, 1980; Taylor, 1990; Taylor & Brown, 1988).

We also maintain a basic belief in the benevolence of the world, or, more precisely, our world of people and events. We assume what happens to us will be positive—that events are good and people are kind and caring, at least the events and people that touch our lives. We know that hatred, disease, and ill-fortune exist, but psychologically we manage to keep them at a distance by distinguishing between the world at large and our own world. Maya Angelou captures this assumption in explaining her choice of a title for her book of poetry, *Just Give Me a Cool Drink of Water 'fore I Diiie* (Angelou, 1971). She notes her fascination with people's "unconscious innocence," illustrated by the belief that even a murderer would have enough compassion to give us a "cool drink of water" before killing us (Weller, 1973).

A third assumption that resides at the core of our inner world—that the world is meaningful—is particularly important, for it entails our tacit understanding of the "workings of the universe" (Janoff-Bulman & Frantz, in press). When viewed from the perspective of fundamental assumptions, a "meaningful" world is one in which there is a contingency between people and their outcomes. In other words, the relationship between people and what happens to them "makes sense." It is the selective incidence of events that is of concern; we are interested not simply in why cancer or rape occur, but rather why cancer and rape strike particular people. A meaningful world is one that provides an answer not only to "Why?" but also to "Why me?" or "Why him or her?"

Just as events in science are comprehensible if they fit certain accepted physical laws or theories, so in our daily lives outcomes are comprehensible if they fit accepted social laws or theories. Among the Azande of the Sudan, for example, witchcraft provides a meaningful explanation for the death of a child whose boat was overturned by a hippo. The child's parents know the physical cause of death (i.e., drowning), but they invoke witchcraft and the belief that a witch or sorcerer brought together the paths of the hippo and their son to answer "Why him?" (Gluckman, 1944). For the Azande parents, the child's death was not a random occurrence.

In Western culture, our most accepted theories of person–outcome contingency are, broadly conceived, those of justice and control (for a more complete discussion, see Janoff-Bulman, 1992; Janoff-Bulman & Frantz, 1997). Justice accounts for a person's outcomes through a consideration of the individual's character and moral attributes; people get what they deserve, and personal outcomes are essentially viewed as rewards and punishments (Lerner, 1980). Person–outcome contingencies also make sense to us through a consideration of people's actions and behaviors; by assuming that we can behaviorally control our outcomes (see, e.g., Henslin, 1967; Langer, 1975; Wortman, 1975), we believe that by taking the proper precautions (e.g., exercising, eating right, walking in safe areas, staying alert while driving), we can prevent misfortune.

Together, our assumptions of a benevolent, meaningful world and a worthy self afford us tremendous comfort. Given our fundamental beliefs in a world that makes sense, as long as we are good people who engage in the right behaviors, we will be protected from misfortune. Our world will continue to be a benevolent one. These assumptions are taken for granted, as is the sense of relative invulnerability they produce and sustain. Yet victims all too readily discover that these comfortable assumptions are illusions, and the process of disillusionment is an extraordinarily painful one in the immediate aftermath of traumatic victimization.

## Fundamental Assumptions and the Nature of Illusions

Understanding the sense in which our fundamental assumptions are illusions can provide important clues to survivors' long-term adjustment. The term "illusion" connotes falseness or some lack of correspondence with reality, yet determining what is real is a path laden with dead ends and pitfalls; the ontological status of any belief may be unknowable. Our fundamental assumptions are not illusions in the sense that they are simply wishes (Freud, 1927), lacking any substantial correspondence with reality, like the pipe dreams held by the piteous patrons of Harry Hope's bar in *The Iceman Cometh* (O'Neill, 1946). They are, nevertheless, false conceptions, because they go too far; our fundamental assumptions are illusions because they are overgeneralizations. Derived from our real interactions in the world, they are generally true, but not always.

We commonly use the term "illusion" to refer to a category of perceptual events that provides a good illustration of illusion-as-overgeneralization. Two well-known visual "tricks" are the Muller-Lyer, or arrow illusion, and the Ponzo, or railroad track illusion; in both cases, line segments of identical length are perceived as different. Now, in neither instance are we simply seeing what we want to see, but rather, in both, we are responding to depth cues (e.g., converging lines) in the picture. In general, these cues accurately suggest depth and distance in the real world, but these perceptual principles are inappropriately applied in the case of the Muller-Lyer and Ponzo illusions. The visual rules are not wrong, for they are generally accurate in describing reality. Instead, the illusions are instances of overgeneralization or overapplication of principles that generally—but not always—serve us well.

Our fundamental assumptions, too, are overgeneralizations: positive views of our world and ourselves that are overapplied. It is not their positive valence, but their overextension, that accounts for their illusory nature. From a preponderance of positive experiences, we generalize to abstract theories that often, but not always, correspond to reality. Our fundamental assumptions originate in our earliest experiences (see, e.g., Bowlby, 1969; Fairbairn, 1952; Winnecott, 1965). Interactions with a responsive caregiver, or caregivers, provide the basis for preverbal representations of the world and the self. By responding to the child's cries, for example, a caregiver provides the earliest basis for perceiving a person–outcome contingency and a benevolent other; the seed is also planted for the infant to perceive the self as worthy of such care. In these early social interactions, then, the child begins to develop a representation of the world as benevolent and meaningful, and of the self as worthy. To develop positive representations, the caregiving need not be excellent or maximally responsive, but simply "good enough" (Winnecott, 1965). As Stern (1985) notes, by the age of seven months, infants construct high-level generalizations about the self and others. These typically positive generalizations are the preverbal foundation for our fundamental assumptions.

Although these representations may be revised over time, assimilation processes are generally more powerful than accommodation processes (Piaget, 1952). By providing the lens through which we process and interpret new information, our pre-existing schemas, or assumptions, maximize the possibility of self-verification; information that does not fit can be ignored, forgotten, underestimated in significance, or massaged so as to be assimilated. Our own behaviors are apt to produce outcomes that confirm rather than disconfirm our assumptions (see, e.g., Rosenthal, 1974; Snyder & Swann, 1978). By the time we reach adulthood, our fundamental assumptions are our most abstract, general schemas, residing at the very foundation

tion of our cognitive-emotional systems. Here they are typically insulated from direct behavioral challenges, which are more apt to address our narrower, more specific assumptions about ourselves and our environment (for a more detailed discussion of these issues, see Janoff-Bulman, 1989). Deeply embedded and protected at the core of our inner world, our fundamental assumptions provide us with the trust, confidence, and positive motivation to go on each day.

Our generalized beliefs in a benevolent and meaningful world and in our self-worth are not wholly inaccurate. Certainly, the world—*our* world—is benevolent and meaningful, and we are worthy, decent human beings. Yet our fundamental assumptions are overgeneralizations, and as such they are in part false; they are exaggerations more than outright lies.

## CONFRONTING A MEANINGLESS, MALEVOLENT UNIVERSE

Traumatic life events strike at the core of our inner world and shatter our deepest assumptions (Janoff-Bulman, 1985, 1992; also see Epstein, 1991; McCann & Pearlman, 1990). Extreme negative experiences in adulthood force survivors to recognize the extent to which they had taken for granted positive, security-inducing views of the world and themselves. The very assumptions that had provided psychological stability and coherence in a complex world are recognized for what they are: illusions that are inadequate reflections of reality. With the very foundation of their inner worlds in a state of massive upheaval, survivors experience psychological disintegration. Traumatic life events radically crack the earlier complacency provided by comforting assumptions, and survivors experience the terror of their own vulnerability.

Abrupt, painful disillusionment characterizes the internal change induced by traumatic life events. This is not the stuff of "normal" change, which is apt to be gradual and strike less deeply. Most change we experience is incremental, as in physical growth or the acquisition of knowledge and skills. In science, these are the "additive adjustments to theory" discussed by Kuhn (1962) in explicating the course of "normal science." Disillusionment itself may be a part of "normal" lifespan development (see, e.g., Gould, 1978; Viorst, 1986), but in this case typically involves gradual transitions that proceed incrementally so as to preclude an overwhelming attack on the cognitive-emotional system. Following traumatic life events, disillusionment is powerfully accelerated, and confrontation with mortality and fragility is direct and sudden. What otherwise might take a lifetime to complete is prematurely thrust upon the survivor in one fell swoop. The attack on survivors' illusions is profound, parallelling Kuhn's (1962) "scientific revolution," a massive crisis that occurs when anomalous scientific data cannot be assimilated and a new paradigm is needed. Similarly, the potent, menacing data of a traumatic experience also cannot be assimilated, and survivors are stripped of their illusions.

Existence is now perceived as frightening; old securities and certainties are gone. Survivors can no longer assume that their own self-worth or precautionary behaviors will protect them, for arbitrariness and randomness characterize the workings of the universe. The terror of their own fragility is overwhelming; their own injury and annihilation seem all too possible and imaginable. Survivors are profoundly aware that bad things can happen to them and to those they love. The world no longer makes sense; there is no comprehensible person–outcome contingency, and therefore no guarantee of safety and protection. Ernest Becker powerfully describes this state in writing that it is terrifying and devastating "to see the world as it really is . . . it makes *routine, automatic, secure, self-confident activity impossible*. . . . It places a trembling animal at the mercy of the entire cosmos and the problem of meaning of it" (Becker, 1973, p. 26).

Survivors are essentially thrown into an existential crisis, in which there seems to be no hope for universal safety, no cure for anxiety, and no end to suffering; this is the world of absurdity described by Existentialists (see, e.g., Sartre, 1964, 1966; also see Barrett, 1962). Survivors feel helpless in the face of an uncaring, incomprehensible universe; their world no longer makes sense, and their vulnerability has been glaringly exposed.

In the aftermath of victimization, coping involves rebuilding the inner world of the survivor. This process is framed by two extreme possibilities: re-embracing the old, comfortable assumptions or accepting the new, frightening self- and worldviews. The old assumptions, though psychologically appealing for their solace, are now seen as illusory and naive; the negative assumptions implied by the victimization, however, are extraordinarily disturbing, though seemingly more valid given the survivor's traumatic experience. Having come face-to-face with their own mortality and fragility, survivors generally cannot wholly embrace their old assumptions. Nevertheless, they are motivated to not wholly accept the new ones either; to live in such a malevolent, meaningless world would entail constant hyperarousal and intense anxiety.

Not surprising, early attempts at coping and rebuilding assumptions often involve efforts to reestablish some semblance of a meaningful universe, one in which there is a comprehensible person–outcome contingency. Thus, in the aftermath of victimization, there is considerable self-blame, far beyond any blameworthiness of the survivors (for a review, see Janoff-Bulman & Lang-Gunn, 1989). By blaming themselves, survivors are able to minimize the perceived randomness of the world and their sense of helplessness. Based on work with crime victims, for example, researchers note that survivors often seem eager to take responsibility for what happened by faulting themselves for some behavior (Bard & Sangrey, 1979; Medea & Thompson, 1974). Survivors of life-threatening diseases blame themselves for not taking good enough care of themselves—eating poorly, not exercising, putting themselves under too much stress (e.g., Bard & Dyk, 1956; Taylor, 1983). Survivors replay their victimization, looking for their own contributions to the outcome. It is not that they are actually to blame, but rather that in this way they can begin to minimize the threatening, meaningless implications of their traumatic experience. Further, by going through the motions of daily living—by engaging in small actions that have expected outcomes (e.g., buying needed goods, keeping an appointment, driving to a chosen destination, making a phone call)—survivors are able to see that at least some parts of their world are not random. By taking action, survivors begin to reestablish a sense of outcome control and a belief in person–outcome contingencies.

Other motivated cognitive strategies (Janoff-Bulman, 1992), such as downward social comparisons (Taylor, 1983; Taylor, Wood, & Lichtman, 1983; Wills, 1981), enable survivors to minimize the malevolence of their victimization. By comparing with real or hypothetical others who are worse off, they see their experience as cause for some reassurance rather than simply despair. Further, social support by others, if available, provides strong evidence that the world is not wholly malevolent; caring others allow survivors to directly experience benevolence and to see themselves, over time, as worthy individuals, thereby reenacting the process of building assumptions during the survivor's earliest childhood interactions.

Over time, most survivors reestablish an assumptive world that is not wholly threatening. They cope and adjust, some in a matter of weeks and others in a matter of years. They do not recover in the sense of returning to who they were before their traumatic victimization. Just as physical diseases are biologically encoded and leave a physiological memory of the illness (e.g., antibodies), traumatic experiences are psychologically encoded and leave their mark on the inner world of survivors (Janoff-Bulman, 1992). Their fundamental assumptions have changed; survivors do not simply get over their experience and embrace their earlier assumptions. Rather, their self- and world-views allow for the possibility of misfortune. Research with very varied victim populations has found that even years after their traumatic events, survivors' views of the world and themselves are more negative than those of nonsurvivors; victims perceive the world as less benevolent, less meaningful (in terms of person–outcome contingency), and themselves as less worthy (for a review, see Janoff-Bulman, 1992). Their assumptions, however, could not be characterized as negative and pessimistic; rather, they are again positive, but not absolutely so. The early overgeneralization and overapplication of positive assumptions are now corrected. Survivors generally recognize that the world is good, they are good, and the world makes sense—but not always. Yet the powerful impact of disillusionment remains, for their representations of themselves and the world now allow for the real possibility of misfortune and disaster.

## CREATING A MEANINGFUL LIFE: THE ROLE OF LOSS IN VALUE CREATION AND APPRECIATION

> *It was previously a question of finding out whether or not life had to have a meaning to be lived. It now becomes clear, on the contrary, that it will be lived all the better if it has no meaning.*
>
> —Albert Camus

For survivors, the world is no longer unquestionably safe and secure. The real possibility of tragedy and loss remains etched in their inner worlds, and it is this remnant of the traumatic victimization that frequently fosters a significant transformation in their lives. Survivors begin to engage in a different kind of meaning-making, that of finding, or more accurately, creating, value in their own lives.

There are two primary understandings of meaning: comprehensibility and significance (Janoff-Bulman & Frantz, 1997). The first entails questions about whether something "makes sense," which characterizes victims' post-trauma concerns about the workings of the universe, particularly the relationship between people and their outcomes. The second involves questions about value and worth; and it is in this sense that survivors over time (and for many this may be a very long time) construct meaning. Ultimately they move from their early response that "the world is meaningless" to "my life is full of meaning," a transition from terror to gratification. Yet, it is the very awareness that dread dwells next door, that tragedy could strike at any time, that promotes a new realization of value and appreciation in their lives.

Traumatic life events lead to a new "valuation" or reevaluation of living. With life having been stripped to its essentials in the shape of human mortality and fragility, survivors consider their lives and what is important. They cease looking for meaning "out there" and recognize their ability to create their own meaning close to home. Typically, this involves a newfound appreciation of their lives, or aspects of their lives, and a consequent reordering of priorities (e.g., Affleck, Tennen, & Gershman, 1985; Collins et al., 1990; Janoff-Bulman, 1985, 1992; Lehman et al., 1993; Schwartzberg, 1996; Silver & Wortman, 1980; Taylor, 1983; Taylor, Lichtman, & Wood, 1984; Tedeschi & Calhoun, 1996; Thompson, 1985; Thompson & Janigian, 1988). It is not unusual to hear statements such as the following: "Now I'm alive; before I was just existing"; "I never really appreciated what I had until now"; "My life is far richer and fuller these days"; "Now I spend more time on the important things in my life."

Now that survivors know all too well that randomness does operate and tragedy could happen at any time, we might expect a far different turn of events; the insignificance of the human condition, with its inherent fragility and puny role on the world stage might preclude any perception of value in human existence. Yet it is precisely this new, jarring awareness of our finitude and physical limitations that provides the catalyst for seeking value. Because life can end at any time, it cannot be taken for granted; because undesirable outcomes can occur when least expected, people must decide what matters and make choices. As Existentialists such as Sartre (1964, 1966) have asserted, in the face of dread and absurdity, we must create our own values out of nothingness. Concentration camp survivor Frankl (1978) has similarly argued that meaning must be personally discovered and involves our attitude towards life, which, even after great suffering, is an act of will and determination. Ultimately, we do not have control over what happens to us in terms of life's outcomes, but we have considerable control over our own choices and what matters to us in our lives. Our choices become the basis for our commitments (Brickman, 1987), and it is here that meaning and fulfillment lie.

For survivors who have painfully experienced disillusionment, the malevolence and meaninglessness of the universe is acknowledged in the new assumptive world. If these negative views are wholly embraced and therefore overwhelm the survivor's new assumptive world, the result will be profound anxiety and despair. By focusing only on loss, people cannot see past the negative to anything positive. By maintaining the possibility of loss—not overgeneralizing, but including the possibility of tragedy—people can experience gains. The rebuilt inner world of most survivors incorporates the possibility of trauma without being overwhelmed by it, and the negative beliefs thereby function as a potent, available touchstone against which the ongoing stream of life's activities is compared. Daily experiences are now perceived and evaluated within the context of a new framework, one that includes their own past victimization. (For various perspectives on this contrast effect see, e.g., Brickman, Coates, & Janoff-Bulman, 1978, and Helson, 1964, on adaptation level theory; Kahneman & Miller, 1986, on norm theory; Kahneman & Tversky, 1982, and Taylor & Schneider, 1989, on simulation processes; and Kahneman & Tversky, 1973, on anchoring and adjustment processes.)

A uniformly positive assumptive world, as exists pre-victimization and pre-disillusionment, is not as likely to provide the backdrop and sustenance for a life filled with value and appreciation. Most of us take our lives, or important parts of our lives, for granted, and appreciation is clearly not a necessary consequence of good fortune. This is the gist of Emily's sorrowful realization in *Our Town* (Wilder, 1975). After she is given the opportunity to witness daily life in Grover's Corners after her death, Emily remarks through her tears, "I didn't realize. So all that was going on and we never noticed? . . . Oh, earth, you're too wonderful for anybody to realize you" (p. 138). Another deceased character tells her, "Yes, now you know. Now you know! That's what it was to be alive. To move about in a cloud of ignorance. . . . To spend and waste time as though you had a million years" (pp. 139–140).

It is likely that neither uniformly positive assumptions nor uniformly negative assumptions are conducive to the development of appreciation and valuing of our lives. In fact, work on commitment by Brickman (1987) compellingly argues that value creation necessarily involves both a positive and a negative element (also consider psychoanalytic work on the significance of ambivalence in our lives). Singer (1996), too, claims that we create meaning by undergoing a dialectic between the positive and negative, doubt and motivation. Applied to survivors' sense of appreciation and value over time, the co-existence of positive (i.e., my outcomes are generally benevolent and make sense) and negative (i.e., bad things can happen to me and those I love) elements creates the psychological climate for appreciation, meaning, and commitment. Anxiety and doubt associated with the known possibility of loss remain, but now function so as to focus our attention on the amazing fact of existence rather than nonexistence, the wonder of life rather than the absolute terror of annihilation.

Accessible and easily imagined in the form of the survivor's victimization (e.g., Kahneman & Tversky, 1973), the trauma-induced realization of possible loss and tragedy resides alongside the survivor's more positive rebuilt assumptions. Survivors know that all is transient and ultimately insecure, and yet it is this very awareness that leads them to value life; life is worth living and noticing. The survivor's life, and particular chosen components, become appreciated and worthy of considerable investment because they are no longer taken for granted. It is not surprising, then, that recent research investigating changes reported in a general population over the course of a year found that the perception of positive change, in terms of greater appreciation of life, better relationships with others, and increased personal strengths, was strongest for those who experienced severe trauma (Tedeschi & Calhoun, 1996). These authors conclude that "there is emerging evidence that more intense experiences with trauma may produce greater benefits" (p. 464).

Survivors no longer operate on "automatic." Dual-process models in psychology have made it very clear that in the interests of conserving mental energy, we do a great deal automatically; yet, we are "motivated tacticians" who engage in thoughtful, effortful processing when we are sufficiently interested in the interaction or outcome (Fiske & Taylor, 1991). Survivors are motivated to live life differently: to pay attention and begin to live as if each day counts. They consciously notice what is around them and make choices about what is important to them, whether close family and friends, a social cause, spiritual devotion, or natural beauty, and these choices become the basis for action and the commitment of time and effort. It is in the very process of choosing and acting that humans create value (Brickman, 1987). Survivors profoundly feel this new sense of commitment and value in their lives, as well as a feeling that they are engaged in meaningful, worthwhile, fulfilling activities.

This process of meaning-making and the creation of value ultimately transforms the traumatic victimization for many survivors. Their experience is no longer wholly horrible, but now has redemptive and instrumental worth. The victimization is regarded as a teacher, providing important lessons and benefits (for a review, see Janoff-Bulman, 1992). This transformation of the traumatic experience is actually not a coping process or strategy, as has generally been claimed by researchers. Rather, the transformation is an outcome—the outcome of a long process of rebuilding that again allows the survivor to perceive the world and the self positively, but nevertheless incorporates the trauma within the new assumptive world. As they continue to acknowledge a threatening universe and the possibility of loss, survivors create value in their newly appreciated lives.

Survivors simultaneously recognize that there are positive and negative changes that have resulted from their victimization. It is not simply that some report great benefits and others grave disadvantages, but rather that the same people often report both. Survivors acknowledge both the anxiety and uneasiness that follow from their awareness of vulnerability as well as the gratification and appreciation that follow from their realization that life is special. It is knowing the possibility of loss that promotes the gains of victimization, and that of disillusionment that creates a newfound commitment to living fully.

## REFERENCES

Affleck, G., Tennen, H., & Gershman, K. (1985). Cognitive adaptations to high-risk infants: The search for mastery, meaning, and protection from future harm. *American Journal of Mental Deficiency, 89,* 653–656.

Angelou, M. (1971). *Just give me a cool drink of water 'fore I diiie.* New York: Random House.

Bard, M., & Dyk, R. B. (1956). The psychodynamic significance of beliefs regarding the cause of serious illness. *Psychoanalytic Review, 43,* 146–162.

Bard, M., & Sangrey, D. (1979). *The crime victim's book.* New York: Basic Books.

Barrett, W. (1962). *Irrational man: A study in existential philosophy.* Garden City, NY: Doubleday.

Becker, E. (1973). *The denial of death.* New York: Free Press.

Bowlby, J. (1969). *Attachment and loss. Vol. 1: Attachment.* London: Hogarth.

Brickman, P. (1987). *Commitment, conflict, and caring.* Englewood Cliffs, NJ: Prentice-Hall.

Brickman, P., Coates, D., & Janoff-Bulman, R. (1978). Lottery winners and accident victims: Is happiness relative? *Journal of Personality and Social Psychology, 36,* 917–927.

Collins, R. L., Taylor, S. E., & Skokan, L. A. (1990). A better world or a shattered vision: Changes in life perspectives following victimization. *Social Cognition, 8,* 263–285.

Epstein, S. (1973). The self-concept revisited, or a theory of a theory. *American Psychologist, 28,* 404–416.

Epstein, S. (1991). The self-concept, the traumatic neurosis, and the structure of personality. In D. Ozer, J. M. Healy Jr., & A. J. Stewart (Eds.), *Perspectives on personality. Vol. 3.* London: Jessica Kingsley.

Fairbairn, W. R. D. (1952). *An object-relations theory of the personality.* New York: Basic Books.

Fiske, S. T., & Taylor, S. E. (1991). *Social cognition.* New York: McGraw-Hill.

Frankl, V. E. (1978). *Man's search for meaning: An introduction to logotherapy.* New York: Washington Square Press.

Freud, S. (1927). *The future of an illusion.* Garden City, NY: Doubleday.

Gluckman, M. (1944). The logic of African science and witchcraft: An appreciation of Evans-Pritchard's "Witchcraft Oracles and Magic among the Azande" of the Sudan. *The Rhodes-Livingstone Institute Journal,* June 1944, 61–71.

Gould, R. (1978). *Transformations.* New York: Simon & Schuster.

Greenwald, A. G. (1980). The totalitarian ego: Fabrication and revision of personal history. *American Psychologist, 35,* 603–618.

Harvey, J. H., Orbuch, T. L., Weber, A. L., Merbach, N., & Alt, R. (1992). House of pain and hope: Accounts of loss. *Death Studies, 16,* 1–26.

Harvey, J. H., Weber, A. L., & Orbuch, T. L. (1990). *Interpersonal accounts: A social psychological perspective.* Oxford, UK: Blackwell.

Helson, H. (1964). *Adaptation level theory: An experimental and systematic approach to behavior.* New York: Harper.

Henslin, J. M. (1967). Craps and magic. *American Journal of Sociology, 73,* 316–330.

Janoff-Bulman, R. (1985). The aftermath of victimization: Rebuilding shattered assumptions. In C. Figley (Ed.), *Trauma and its wake: The study and treatment of post-traumatic stress disorder.* New York: Brunner/Mazel.

Janoff-Bulman, R. (1989). The benefits of illusions, the threat of disillusionment, and the limitations of accuracy. *Journal of Social and Clinical Psychology, 8,* 158–175.

Janoff-Bulman, R. (1992). *Shattered assumptions: Towards a new psychology of trauma.* New York: Free Press.

Janoff-Bulman, R., & Frantz, C. M. (1997). The impact of trauma on meaning: From meaningless world to meaningful life. In M. Power & C. Brewin (Eds.), *The transformation of meaning in psychological therapies.* London: John Wiley.

Janoff-Bulman, R., & Lang-Gunn, L. (1989). Coping with disease and accidents: The role of self-blame attributions. In L. Y. Abramson (Ed.), *Social-personal inference in clinical psychology.* New York: Guilford.

Kahneman, D., & Miller, D. T. (1986). Norm theory: Comparing reality to its alternatives. *Psychological Review, 93,* 136–153.

Kahneman, D., & Tversky, A. (1973). On the psychology of prediction. *Psychological Review, 80,* 237–251.

Kahneman, D., & Tversky, A. (1982). The simulation heuristic. In D. Kahneman, P. Slovic, and A. Tversky (Eds.), *Judgment under uncertainty: Heuristics and biases.* New York: Cambridge University Press.

Kuhn, T. S. (1962). *The structure of scientific revolutions.* Chicago: The University of Chicago Press.

Langer, E. J. (1975). The illusion of control. *Journal of Personality and Social Psychology, 32,* 311–328.

Lehman, D. R., Davis, C. G., DeLongis, A., Wortman, C. B., Bluck, S., Mandel, D. R., & Ellard, J. (1993). Positive and negative life changes following bereavement and their relations to adjustment. *Journal of Social and Clinical Psychology, 12,* 90–112.

Lerner, M. J. (1980). *The belief in a just world.* New York: Plenum.

Lifton, R. J. (1967). *Death in life: Survivors of Hiroshima.* New York: Simon and Schuster.

McCann, I. L., & Pearlman, L. A. (1990). *Psychological trauma and the adult survivor: Theory, therapy, and transformation.* New York: Brunner/Mazel.

Medea, A., & Thompson, K. (1974). *Against rape.* New York: Farrar, Straus, & Giroux.

O'Neill, E. (1946). *The iceman cometh.* New York: Random House.

Parkes, C. M. (1975). What becomes of redundant world models? A contribution to the study of adaptation to change. *British Journal of Medical Psychology, 48,* 131–137.

Perloff, L. S. (1983). Perceptions of vulnerability to victimization. *Journal of Social Issues, 39,* 41–62.

Piaget, J. (1952). *The origins of intelligence in children.* New York: International Universities Press.

Rosenthal, R. (1974). *On the social psychology of the self-fulfilling prophecy: Further evidence of Pygmalion effects and their mediating mechanisms.* New York: MSS Modular Publications (Module 53).

Sartre, J. P. (1964). *Nausea.* Norfolk, CT: New Directions, 1964.

Sartre, J. P. (1966). *Being and nothingness: A phenomenological study of ontology*. New York: Washington Square Press.

Schwartzberg, S. S. (1996). *A crisis of meaning: How gay men are making sense of AIDS.* New York: Oxford University Press.

Silver, R. L., & Wortman, C. B. (1980). Coping with undesirable life events. In J. Garber & M. E. P. Seligman (Eds.), *Human helplessness: Theory and application.* New York: Academic Press.

Singer, I. (1996). *The creation of value.* Baltimore: The Johns Hopkins University Press.

Snyder, M. L., & Swann, W. B., Jr. (1978). Hypothesis-testing processes in social interaction. *Journal of Personality and Social Psychology, 36,* 1202–1212.

Stern, D. N. (1985). *The interpersonal world of the infant: A view from psychoanalysis and developmental psychology.* New York: Basic Books.

Taylor, S. E. (1983). Adjustment to threatening events: A theory of cognitive adaptation. *American Psychologist, 38,* 1161–1173.

Taylor, S. E. (1990). *Positive illusions: Creative self-deception and the healthy mind.* New York: Basic Books.

Taylor, S. E., & Brown, J. D. (1988). Illusion and well-being: A social-psychological perspective on mental health. *Psychological Bulletin, 103,* 193–210.

Taylor, S. E., Lichtman, R. R., & Wood, J. V. (1984). Attributions, beliefs about control, and adjustment to breast cancer. *Journal of Personality and Social Psychology, 46,* 489–582.

Taylor, S. E., & Schneider, S. K. (1989). Coping and the simulation of events. *Social Cognition, 7,* 176–196.

Taylor, S. E., Wood, J. V., & Lichtman, R. R. (1983). It could be worse: Selective evaluation as a response to victimization. *Journal of Social Issues, 39*(2), 19–40.

Tedeschi, R. G., & Calhoun, L. G. (1996). The posttraumatic growth inventory: Measuring the positive legacy of trauma. *Journal of Traumatic Stress, 9,* 455–471.

Thompson, S. C. (1985). Finding positive meaning in a stressful event and coping. *Basic and Applied Social Psychology, 12,* 81–96.

Thompson, S. C., & Janigian, A. S. (1988). Life schemes: A framework for understanding the search for meaning. *Journal of Social and Clinical Psychology, 7,* 260–280.

Viorst, J. (1986). *Necessary losses.* New York: Simon & Schuster.

Weinstein, N. D. (1989). Optimistic biases about personal risks. *Science, 246,* 1232–1233.

Weller, S. (1973). Work in progress: Maya Angelou. *Intellectual Digest,* June 1973, 11–12, 14.

Wilder, T. (1975). *Our town.* New York: Avon Books.

Wills, T. A. (1981). Downward comparison principles in social psychology. *Psychological Bulletin, 90,* 245–271.

Winnecott, D. W. (1965). *The maturational process and the facilitating environment.* New York: International Universities Press.

Wortman, C. B. (1975). Some determinants of perceived control. *Journal of Personality and Social Psychology, 31,* 282–294.

# 4

# *Exploring Loss through Autoethnographic Inquiry: Autoethnographic Stories, Co-Constructed Narratives, and Interactive Interviews*

**Carolyn Ellis**
*University of South Florida*

This chapter describes autobiographical and ethnographic practices of writing and research applied to the study of meaning-making and emotional life experiences. I refer to this work as autoethnographic inquiry, a term introduced by Hayano in 1979. Autoethnography connects the ethnographic impulse, or the "gaze outward" at worlds beyond our own, to the autobiographical impulse, or the "gaze inward" for a story of self (Neumann, 1996, p. 173). Through describing concrete and intimate details of a particular life lived, autoethnographies also show social processes, conceptualizations, and ways of life experienced more generally by groups of people living in similar circumstances (Reed-Danahay, 1995).

Autoethnography blurs distinctions between social science and literature, the personal and the social, the individual and culture, self and other, and researcher and subject. Here authors occupy dual interactive roles of researcher and research participant; when others participate, authority is shared to the extent feasible. Autoethnography emphasizes what is heard and felt as much as what is seen. The focus is on emotional and bodily knowledge, as well as cognitive perception; knowledge comes through direct participation as well as observation; recognition involves the interplay between observer and observed; and understanding requires a reflection inward as well as observation outward (Jackson, 1989, pp. 6–8; for exemplars, see Ellis and Bochner, 1996).

Much autoethnographic work falls under the broad rubric of loss narratives, also referred to as illness narratives (Frank, 1993) or personal disaster narratives (Mairs, 1994; for exemplars, see Ellis, 1993; Frank, 1991; Murphy, 1987; Paget, 1993; Ronai, 1995; Zola, 1982). Since storytelling helps humans make sense of epiphanies (Denzin, 1989), often autoethnographers are drawn to experiences of loss out of which such existential crises arise. An experience of loss shatters the meaningful world people have assembled for themselves. Often, we have a strong desire to

Thanks to Arthur Bochner, John Harvey, Laurel Richardson, and Lisa Tillmann-Healy for encouragement and helpful remarks on earlier versions of this paper.

understand, manage, and recover by creating an account that makes sense of loss and puts the pieces back together. As Harvey and his associates argue (Harvey, 1996, p. 10), recovery from loss is contingent on the private experience of formulating an account and imagining the telling of the story, and the public experience of sharing it with others (see, also, Bochner, Ellis, & Tillmann-Healy, 1997).

Working from an orientation that blends the practices and emphases of social science with the aesthetic sensibility and expressive forms of art (Benson, 1993, p. xi), my colleagues and I seek to tell stories that show our experiences as lived intimately and deeply; that represent the uniqueness of our losses, yet connect them to the losses of others so that they might be used as points of comparison or lessons in living; that may offer guidance in figuring out how to live; that encourage tellers and readers to re-story their experience and themselves as survivors while acknowledging the pain of loss; and that help all of us—writers, readers, and participants in the studies—to understand and cope with our own losses, heal wounds, create meaning, and move ahead with our lives. These stories are produced in the tension that occurs between our desires to move beyond yet work through, withdraw from yet remember, more fully and deeply the important losses in our lives.

This chapter focuses on three autoethnographic approaches, autoethnographic storytelling, co-constructing narratives, and interactive interviewing, that reflect our philosophical stance toward research. Autoethnographic stories are known also as first-person accounts, personal narratives, impressionist tales, and feminist ethnographies. They often start with personal experiences of researchers; however, they also may come from personal experiences of participants encouraged by researchers to tell their stories. Sometimes the researcher's story is integrated with or told alongside participants' stories (e.g., Behar, 1993; Brown, 1991). The personal story is told within and moves through the layers of the social, from relationships to family outward to culture. In this orientation, the inner workings of the self are investigated and presented in concrete action, thoughts, and feelings; developed and problematized relationally through dialogue; shown processually in vivid scenes and dramatic plot; and contextualized by history, social structure, and culture, which themselves often operate as unstated subtexts that are dialectically revealed through action, thought, and language. As Bochner (1997, p. 349) says, "there is nothing as theoretical as a good story."

Good storytelling also is important in co-constructed narratives, which refer to tales jointly constructed by relational partners about an epiphanal event in their lives. These stories show dyads engaged in the specific, concrete, and unique details of daily living. They cope with the untidy ambiguities, ambivalences, and contradictions of relationship life and try to make sense of their local situations. This type of research focuses on the interactional sequences by which interpretations of lived experiences are constructed, coordinated, and solidified into stories. The local narratives that are jointly produced thus display couples in the process of "doing" their relationships, trying to turn fragmented, vague, or disjointed events into intelligible, coherent accounts. Ideally, participants might include two researchers who have a relationship outside the research process, a researcher and a partner, or a researcher who serves as coordinator and moderator for the joint construction by another relational pair.

Interactive interviews are produced in a similarly collaborative communicative process. They take place in a small group setting in which both participants and researchers are accorded space to share their stories in the context of their developing relationships. The feelings, insights, and stories that researchers bring to the interactive session are as important as those of other participants; the understandings that emerge among all parties during interaction—what they learn together—is as compelling as the stories each brings to the session. Ideally, all participants should have some history together or be willing to work to develop a strong affiliation. It is helpful for researchers as well as co-participants to have personal experience with the topic under investigation; if that is not the case, the researcher should be willing to take on the role and lived experience of other participants in this regard.

In this chapter, I focus on the process of writing my first autoethnographic project, a personal story, that began my journey into this kind of research. The goals and procedures I discuss in detail here also pertain to the co-constructed narratives and interactive interviews I introduce after this section. I describe briefly two co-authored works that use co-constructed narratives and interactive interviewing to make the texts emotional, multivoiced, processual, and interactive. Given that one of the main purposes of these texts is to evoke readers' identification and experiences linked to the topics being discussed, I hope that the brief methodological and theoretical treatments given here will inspire readers to examine the complete narrative texts of these projects.

## AUTOETHNOGRAPHIC STORIES: COPING WITH LOVE, LOSS, AND CHRONIC ILLNESS[1]

In *Final Negotiations: A Story of Love, Loss, and Chronic Illness* (Ellis, 1995), I tell a personal story of my nine-year intimate relationship with a chronically ill partner, Gene Weinstein, a sociologist who died in 1985 from emphysema. Taking the form of a story within a story, the central narrative gives a detailed account of negotiating the complexities of romantic attachment, living with chronic illness, and coping with the loss of a loved one. The framing story chronicles my endeavor to write as a sociologist about this intimate and emotional experience.

My goal was to write a personal narrative that would candidly portray the events that took place and bring readers into what it felt like to go through the experience. Thus, I revealed my flaws and bad decisions as well as my strengths and good judgments; my disappointments as well as my celebrations. I intended to write a book about personal loss that would provide companionship (Mairs, 1994) for others in similar circumstances and contribute a new form for emphasizing process and concrete expression to the study of close relationships, illness, and loss.

Told from an autobiographical perspective, the narrative emphasizes the complexity of my feelings, thoughts, and coping strategies, moving from negotiating

[1]Earlier versions of portions of this section have appeared in Ellis (1996, 1997).

attachment to managing stability and change, and, finally, to coping with loss. *Final Negotiations* concentrates on the interplay of Gene's deteriorating condition and our relationship. The repeated plateaus of the illness provide structure for the chaotic and disruptive nature of the disease process; the renegotiation of changing roles and redefinition of love throughout the illness provide relational thematic representation of the paradoxical and ambivalent emotions and actions of our moment-to-moment experiences. The story presents enacted episodes of the dialectics of close relationships; that is, it shows in descriptive detail and dialogue how the contradictory pulls of private and public life, adventure and security, instrumentality and affection, independence and interdependence, and expressiveness and protectiveness are played out in ordinary and extraordinary circumstances (Bochner, 1984). The relationship narrative shows the ambiguous and complex aspects of my connection to Gene as we interacted in our day-to-day lives, confronted epiphanies, managed attachment and loss, and struggled to make our life together meaningful.

It took nine years to write and rewrite *Final Negotiations,* to work out satisfactorily a version of what this relationship had been and had meant to me, and to tell a story that cohered with both what I remembered and what my life had become (Crites, 1971). Writing about this relationship was so difficult that I kept notes on the writing process in the same way I had kept fieldnotes on the actual relationship and illness process. These notes eventually became the basis for telling how I transformed ethnographic fieldwork into a story that I hoped would speak therapeutically to a mass audience and sociologically to an academic one (Ellis, 1995, Part V).

The goal of writing sociology as an intimate conversation about the intricacies of feeling, relating, and working grew out of my awareness of the deficiencies of traditional social science research for dealing with day-to-day realities of chronic illness and relational process. From the beginning, I violated many taken-for-granted conventions of social science research and writing: making myself the object of my research breached the separation of subject and researcher (Jackson, 1989); writing about one relationship violated the traditional idea of generalizability across cases and focused instead on generalization within a case (Geertz, 1973); the episodic portrayal of the ebb and flow of relationship experience dramatized the motion of connected lives across the curve of time and thus resisted the standard practice of portraying behavior as a "snapshot"; and the disclosure of normally hidden details of private life highlighted emotional experience and thus challenged the rational actor model of social performance.

As I wrote and rewrote, I moved closer to telling an evocative and dramatic story and farther away from writing a realist ethnography that tried to represent accurately every event as it had actually occurred. I *showed* interaction so that the reader might participate more fully in the emotional process, not merely observe the resolution. This meant moving from generalizing about a kind of event that took place repeatedly to showing one event in particular, such as a hospital stay, often through condensing a number of scenes into evocative composites.

I began to concentrate more on being true to the feelings that seemed to apply in each situation I described, rather than on getting all the "facts" in the exact order and time sequence. Gradually I moved away from trying to make my tale a mirror representation of chronologically ordered events and toward telling a story, where events and feelings cohered, where questions of meaning and interpretation were emphasized, and where readers could grasp the main points and feel what I had felt.

Along the way, more canons of social science research were called into question as I began to understand research and scholarly writing as a possible means of healing and to experience the benefits of being emotionally involved with what I studied. I began to advocate writing social science as creative nonfiction with scene setting, dialogue, and unfolding dramatic action; showing details instead of telling abstractly; and evoking readers' experiences and feelings in addition to analytic closure as appropriate goals of research.

Although I continued to be committed to writing a truthful account, my means of achieving this goal—systematic introspection (Ellis, 1991) and writing from the heart as well as the head—meant my project differed considerably from the "truth" of most social science. Nevertheless, my aim was to tell a story that cohered with the details of personal experience I had recorded in my notes, the recollections of others, and the way I remembered (Krieger, 1984). I tried to tell a story that was "faithful to the facts" and stayed as close as possible to what happened (Richardson, 1992). My concern was that the story be both horizontally coherent—that the events were cohesive enough to warrant their meaningfulness—and vertically coherent—that the episodes were warranted by an honest depiction of the feelings and thoughts of the characters (Rosenwald, 1992, p. 285).

The first version of the text poured out of me uncensored. It seemed important to get it "all" down and contextualized, so that I might have some sense of "what had been." I wrote with the confidence that I could delete anything anytime. The notes that I kept during the eight months prior to Gene's death and for two years afterward guided my writing. I interacted constantly with them to recall the way events had happened and how I had felt, adding remembered details. Additionally, interviews with family and friends; physicians' records and nurses' notes; tape recordings of conversations; and diaries, calendars, and travelogues, all helped me systematically recollect our relationship prior to the note taking. I also called on my memory of many sociologically oriented conversations about our relationship and illness process that Gene and I had had throughout the years.

Over time I allowed myself more dramatic license to tell an evocative story, since it was clearly not so much the "facts" that I wanted to redeem, but rather an articulation of the significance and meaning of my experiences. I became less concerned with "historical truth" and more involved with "narrative truth," which Spence (1982) describes as "the criterion we use to decide when a certain experience has been captured to our satisfaction." It is "what we have in mind when we say that such and such is a good story, that a given explanation carries conviction, that one solution to a mystery must be true" (p. 28). Narrative truth seeks to keep the past alive in the present. Through narrative we learn to understand the meanings and significance of the past as incomplete, tentative, and revisable according to contingencies of present life circumstances and our projection of our lives into the future (Bochner et al., 1997). I wanted to incorporate alternative versions of what had happened as well as the revised senses of my self that were generated with each reflection on the experience (Rosenwald, 1992, p. 275). As Merleau-Ponty

(1964) says, I tried "to give the past not a survival, which is the hypocritical form of forgetfulness, but a new life, which is the noble form of memory" (p. 59).

My hope was that readers would learn from my candor and vulnerability. Necessarily, the disclosures had to include betrayals, uncertainties, and self-doubt, including doubt about what I had written. I wanted readers to trust that I had started with what I didn't know and discovered what I did know through the process of writing (Richardson, 1994). I never pretended to have it all worked out, nor to suggest that the finished product disclosed the "bare truth." In fact, I felt a commitment to camouflage details that might negatively impact others' lives. Thus, while attempting to keep meaning intact, I changed occasional particulars, concealed a few identities, and created composite characters when necessary. I worked constantly to reach a balance between candid writing and good sense, between portraying life as intimately as I could and protecting my presentation of self, my current relationships with characters in the story, and my imagined and actual relationships with readers.

I was more intent on probing my psychic defenses and the emotional ambivalences and contradictions of this experience than on recovering each detail precisely as it had happened and declaring an outcome. I understood that my probing would be limited by what is possible to know and admit to oneself about oneself. But as Virginia Woolf (1953) states about Michel de Montaigne's essays, I attempted "to communicate a soul . . . to go down boldly and bring to light those hidden thoughts which are the most diseased; to conceal nothing; to pretend nothing" (p. 66).

To explore these psychological processes, I used a practice of "emotional recall," similar to the "method acting" of Lee Strasberg at the Actors' Studio (Bruner, 1986, p. 28). To give a convincing and authentic performance, the actor relives in detail a situation in which he or she previously felt the emotion to be enacted. I placed myself back into situations, conjuring up details until I was immersed in the event emotionally. Because recall increases when the emotional content at the time of retrieval resembles that of the experience to be retrieved (Bower, 1981), this process enhanced the recollection of more details.

The moves in and out of these emotional situations were painful, yet therapeutic. They allowed me to experience emotionality safely in my office, where a phone call or a click of the computer key often reminded me that I was not actually *in* this situation. If the emotionality became too intense, I could stop and return to current time, a safety valve I did not have while engulfed by the actual experience. Similar to the underlying premise of "re-evaluative counseling" (Scheff, 1972), this "safety" gave me confidence to explore each incident as fully as I could, and to pay attention to what was most upsetting and least resolved.

I concentrated on the singular, loud voice screaming inside my head or the raw fear gnarling within my gut. Then, embracing the multiplicity of selves that all human beings harbor, I tried to bring to my consciousness the contradictory and ambiguous thoughts and feelings that I also had felt. Whenever possible, I wrote down what the many competing voices in my head were saying. The experience was similar to a conference call in which I interacted with many speakers at once.

The plot of my story, its drama and suspense, invited readers to move with me through my defenses and toward deeper levels of examination (Lopate, 1994, pp.

xxv–xxvi). I wanted my story to "grasp" readers, pull them into its world, and persuade them that they were "in the reality of the story" (Parry, 1991, p. 42). In describing my experience, I wanted readers to feel I had penetrated their heads and hearts. At the same time, my text needed to be sufficiently open to permit readers to move back and forth between being in my story and being in theirs, where they could fill in or compare their experiences and provide their own sensitivities about what was going on. I hoped they would grapple with the ways they were unique and the ways we were similar, that they might feel the specificity of my situation, yet sense the unity of human experience as well (Lopate, 1994, p. xxiii). Along with Mairs (1994), I shared the sense that if "I do my job, the books I write vanish before your eyes," and I invited readers into "the house of my past," hoping the "threshold" crossed would lead them into their own homes (p. 120).

Within this open text, I felt that it was my responsibility, as a sociologist, not only to probe feelings but to try to make sense of the experiences, and to conceptualize how certain actions, even contradictory ones, fit together. Similar to the "grounded theory" approach (Glaser & Strauss, 1967), I looked for larger schemes within which these events might be contained. Sometimes I could explain situationally or historically why seemingly contradictory details had occurred. Often, features of culture, social structure, gender, and socialization had impacted my experience, and social conventions and commitments had narrowed my vision and understanding of myself (Rosenwald, 1992, pp. 276, 280). Without interrupting the plot of the relational and illness story, I tried to give readers enough clues about these macrosocial forces and patterns that they could see the impact and draw their own conclusions.

Sometimes, unlike grounded theory, I let contradictions and seemingly random events stand, willing to admit, after deep exploration, that no explanatory scheme or pattern was readily apparent. This contributed to my goal of making sure that lived experience did not get lost under the authority of abstract explanatory concepts. I hoped that this stance would resonate with readers who I assumed also had experienced at times a similar lack of resolution in or explanation for their thoughts and feelings. With this story, I tried to communicate that all of us must learn to live with contingency; to attempt to explain it away would be to live under an illusion (see Becker, 1994).

"As far as I'm concerned," states Mairs (1994), "my text is flawed not when it is ambiguous or even contradictory, but only when it leaves you no room for stories of your own. I keep my tale as wide open as I can" (p. 74). Coles (1989, p. 47) similarly suggests that "the beauty of a good story is its openness"—how the reader takes it in and uses it for herself. In light of that, I wanted my story to be judged by its narrative truth—by what consequences it had in and for the lives of others (Bochner et al., 1997).

## CO-CONSTRUCTED NARRATIVES: DECIDING ABOUT ABORTION

"Telling and Performing Personal Stories: The Constraints of Choice in Abortion" (Ellis and Bochner, 1992; see also, Bochner and Ellis, 1992) tells the story of a decision my partner Art and I had to make upon discovering only 10 weeks into our relationship that I was pregnant. After much agonizing, I had an abortion. This experience profoundly impacted our relationship and our personal lives.

For the next two months, we were numb, self-protective, and unable to express our thoughts and feelings about the abortion. When we finally broke through our resistance, we realized how much the experience had affected us and how deeply we had ventured into our private and submerged registers of emotion. We were startled to admit that we had not known how to feel about or interpret what was happening and wondered whether others who had experienced abortion had these feelings as well.

In the literature on abortion, details of the emotional and communicative processes of the experience were obscure, leaving readers without a sense of the complexity, confusion, and vacillation often associated with the lived experience of abortion. The emotional trauma seemed bleached of its most profound and stirring meanings. Most of the literature bypassed the conflicts in favor of political ideology or moral indignation.

Desiring to understand our own experience and to provide companionship to others who may have been similarly bruised by the ambivalence and contradictions associated with the constraint of making a choice, we decided to write a story about our experience. First, we independently constructed a detailed chronology of the emotions, events, decisions, and coping strategies that had taken place. After completing our individual accounts, we read each other's version and began to co-construct a single story of what had happened. We took notes on our discussions and asked others with whom we had consulted during the decision-making about the abortion to contribute to the narrative, thus producing a multivocal text.

This process led us to investigate the power and relativity of modes of description. For example, we commented on the graphic differences between Art's experience of grief and my experience of unworthiness, and on my repeated use of the term "baby" juxtaposed against Art's references to "fetus." These descriptive revelations led us to contemplate further the significance of frames: grief versus self-contempt, physical pain juxtaposed against emotional pain, and the experience-near female voice compared to the more distanced male voice.

We wrote our final story as a script that presented, in sequence, critical scenes in which we expressed our self-reflections, feelings, and analysis of the main events: the discovery and shock of the pregnancy, pre- and postdecision interactions, and the abortion procedure described side by side in both the female and male voice. Later we performed this narrative at a professional social science conference, which became a vital part of our attempt to cope with and bring closure to this experience.

## INTERACTIVE INTERVIEWS: EXPERIENCING BULIMIA

"Interactive Interviewing: Talking about Emotional Experience" (Ellis, Kiesinger, and Tillmann-Healy, 1997) describes a project about the embodiment and meanings of bulimia. The research was conducted by three researchers: Lisa Tillmann-Healy, a Ph.D. candidate; Christine Kiesinger, a recent Ph.D.; and me, a professor. Lisa and Christine have had direct personal experience with bulimia; I have not.

But we all share concerns about food and bodies that arise from women's immersion in cultural contradictions of thinness of bodies and abundance of food and commodities. Also, we share a desire to work within a methodological and theoretical orientation that privileges emotional and concrete details of everyday life and that critically interrogates traditional social science interviewing practices.

In this project, the three of us met approximately every three weeks from January through May 1996, taping and then transcribing our two-hour discussions about bulimia and how we might methodologically access important bodily, emotional, and interactive details of the experience. During that time, we also met once for dinner at a restaurant. Prior to this project, Christine and Lisa interviewed and wrote each other's stories and constructed their own autoethnographic accounts of bulimia (Kiesinger, 1995; Tillmann-Healy, 1996). Our final paper consisted of four stories, two written from transcripts of the dyadic interviews between Christine and Lisa, one from the interactive sessions in which all three of us participated, and the last from our dinner at Applebee's written as a narrative ethnography. These accounts tell the story of the development of our interactive interviewing project, with each story adding another textured layer to the approach.

Christine's story showed her attempt as a researcher to get past Lisa's controlled public face to access the "mess" underneath. Her reflections highlighted how her own struggles with bulimia impacted the questions she asked. For example, Christine explored fully Lisa's relationship with her dad because she had had an abusive relationship with her own father.

Lisa's narrative demonstrated the interactive nature of her research and how her story took on a new form as she interviewed Christine. That is, after hearing Christine's account of her disordered life, Lisa reassessed her own story and felt she no longer had a plausible account of her struggles with bulimia.

My story about our group discussions added reflections from the position of a participant who did not engage in the bulimic behaviors we were seeking to understand. I showed how, as an "outsider," I considered the problems and risks in this kind of interview situation, how I attempted to get inside a world I knew little about, and how Christine and Lisa moved me to consider my own relationship to my body and food.

The story of our dinner together showed the impact of bulimia on how we thought, felt, and related as we ate a meal. We revealed our concerns about sharing food, our rules for eating with others, the inner dialogues that occupied us during dinner, our obsession with the food in front of us, our concerns about how we were being perceived by others, and the similarities and differences in the eating experiences of women who do and do not have bulimia. We later integrated our multiple versions of what unfolded, basing our joint account on introspective fieldnotes each of us wrote immediately after the event, upon realizing the narrative possibilities this occasion provided.

This project provides multivoiced and multilayered accounts of the experience of bulimia. It also offers a reflexive chronicle of the process and value of interactive interviewing to access and understand emotionally sensitive topics connected to experiences of loss and identity, in this case, bulimia. We attempt to show how we managed discussions of such a sensitive topic and how we moved back and forth between expression and protection and between disclosure and restraint, always making the others' feelings our priority. In doing so, we raise questions about orthodox interviewing practices and the boundaries traditionally erected between therapy and research.

## RESEARCH AND LIVED EXPERIENCE

The strategies my colleagues and I have developed for accomplishing our research goals include procedures that reflect the ways people cope with intense experience and relate to close associates in everyday life. As researchers, we have tried to be true to the lived particulars of what happens in epiphanies rather than to the traditional social science research practices that categorize, generalize, and abstract about the experiences of others from short snippets of fieldnotes or forced-choice survey responses.

In living through epiphanies, such as a relationship embedded in chronic illness, most of us formulate and then tell our personal stories repeatedly, coordinating and changing them to fit with our sense of who we think we are, have been, and will be in the future. Each story we construct and tell subsequently impacts our identities (Bruner, 1986). We share stories to try to understand the lives we have led, to provide narrative order and coherence to the chaotic disorder and fragmented living that we experience in epiphanies, and to create a life we can live with and a world we can live in (Nin, 1976).

As reflected in co-constructed narratives of happenings such as unanticipated pregnancies, we negotiate and co-author with others multivoiced stories that sustain and are sustained through close relationships and cultural understandings. Partners participate in the creative activity of jointly producing stories about their relationships that attach meaning and significance to their lived experiences. Co-constructed narrative research is based on the assumption that all couples confront the sense-making problem of transforming "real" events into individual stories that can then be formed into collective stories to be performed publicly. Thus, the process of writing and performing a narrative account reproduces and underscores the practices of communication that are played out in the "real" world of interpersonal relationships.

As reflected in interactive interviews, we tell our stories to and listen to stories of others who are, have been, or will be in similar situations. We let our stories, such as those about eating and bodies, intermingle and impact each other, learning from what happens in our joint interaction. Our procedures bring the study of interpersonal communication closer to the ways in which long-term relationships are lived: as conversations where one person's disclosures and self-probing invite another's disclosures and self-probing; where an increasingly intimate and trusting context makes it possible to reveal more of ourselves and to probe deeper into another's feelings and thoughts; where listening to and asking questions about another's plight lead to greater understanding of one's own; and where the examination and comparison of experience offer new insights into both lives.

In all three cases, autoethnography represents our attempts to write open stories of varied experiences that provoke diverse readers to recall, imagine, feel, tell, and write about their own situations. This reflects our experience in the conversational realities of everyday discourse where we respond to others' stories with stories of our own and compare our lives to theirs in order to come to some understanding of how we might cope with our circumstances and live useful and ethical lives. We write in the discursive space between humanities and social science, hoping to connect the practices of social science to the living of life, contribute to a collective voice that lets many have a part, and make a positive difference in people's lives.

## REFERENCES

Becker, H. (1994). "FOR PER ACACIA": Conceptualizing coincidence. *The Sociological Quarterly, 35,* 183–194.

Behar, R. (1993). *Translated woman: Crossing the border with Esperanza's story.* Boston: Beacon.

Benson, P. (Ed.). (1993). *Anthropology and literature.* Urbana: University of Illinois Press.

Bochner, A. P. (1984). The functions of communication in interpersonal bonding. In C. Arnold & J. Bowers (Eds.), *Handbook of rhetorical and communication theory* (pp. 544–621). Boston: Allyn & Bacon.

Bochner, A. P. (1997). Storied lives: Recovering the moral importance of social theory. In J. S. Trent (Ed.), *At the helm in Speech Communication* (pp. 345–353). Boston, MA: Allyn & Bacon.

Bochner, A. P., & Ellis, C. (1992). Personal narrative as a social approach to interpersonal communication. *Communication Theory, 2,* 165–172.

Bochner, A. P., Ellis, C., & Tillmann-Healy, L. (1997). Relationships as stories. In S. Duck (Ed.), *Handbook of personal relationships* (2nd ed.). New York: John Wiley.

Bower, G. H. (1981). Mood and memory. *American Psychologist, 36,* 129–148.

Brown, K. M. (1991). *Mama Lola: A Vodoun priestess in Brooklyn.* Berkeley: University of California Press.

Bruner, E. (1986). Experience and its expressions. In V. Turner & E. Bruner (Eds.), *The anthropology of experience* (pp. 3–30). Urbana: University of Illinois Press.

Coles, R. (1989). *The call of stories: Teaching and the moral imagination.* Boston: Houghton Mifflin.

Crites, S. (1971). The narrative quality of experience. *Journal of the American Academy of Religion, 39,* 291–311.

Denzin, N. (1989). *Interpretive interactionism.* Newbury Park, CA: Sage.

Ellis, C. (1991). Sociological introspection and emotional experience. *Symbolic Interaction, 14,* 23–50.

Ellis, C. (1993). "There are survivors": Telling a story of sudden death. *Sociological Quarterly, 34,* 711–730

Ellis, C. (1995). *Final negotiations: A story of love, loss, and chronic illness.* Philadelphia: Temple University Press.

Ellis, C. (1996). On the demands of truthfulness in writing personal loss narratives. *Journal of Personal and Interpersonal Loss, 1,* 151–177.

Ellis, C. (1997). Evocative autoethnography: Writing emotionally about our lives. In W. Tierney & Y. Lincoln (Eds.), *Representation and the text: Re-framing the narrative voice* (pp. 116–139). New York: SUNY Press.

Ellis, C., & Bochner, A. P. (1992). Telling and performing personal stories: The constraints of choice in abortion. In C. Ellis & M. Flaherty (Eds.), *Investigating subjectivity: Research on lived experience* (pp. 79–101). Newbury Park, CA: Sage.

Ellis, C., & Bochner, A. P. (1996). *Composing ethnography: Alternative forms of qualitative writing.* Walnut Creek, CA: AltaMira.

Ellis, C., & Kiesinger, C., & Tillmann-Healy, L. (1997). Interactive interviewing: Talking about emotional experience. In R. Hertz (Ed.), *Reflexivity and voice* (pp. 119–149). Thousand Oaks, CA: Sage.

Frank, A. (1991). *At the will of the body: Reflections on illness.* Boston: Houghton Mifflin.

Frank, A. (1993). The rhetoric of self-change: Illness experience as narrative. *The Sociological Quarterly, 34,* 39–52.

Geertz, C. (1973). *The interpretation of cultures.* New York: Basic Books.

Glaser, B., and Strauss, A. (1967). *The discovery of grounded theory.* Chicago: Aldine.

Harvey, J. H. (1996). *Embracing their memory: Loss and the social psychology of story-telling.* Needham Heights, MA: Allyn and Bacon.

Hayano, D. (1979). Auto-ethnography: Paradigms, problems, and prospects. *Human Organization, 38,* 99–104.

Jackson, M. (1989). *Paths toward a clearing: Radical empiricism and ethnographic inquiry.* Bloomington: Indiana University Press.

Kiesinger, C. (1995). *Anorexic and bulimic lives: Making sense of food and eating.* Unpublished dissertation, University of South Florida.

Krieger, S. (1984). Fiction and social science. In N. Denzin (Ed.), *Studies in Symbolic Interaction. Vol. 12* (pp. 269–287). Greenwich, CT: JAI Press.

Lopate, P. (1994). *The art of the personal essay: An anthology from the classical era to the present.* New York: Anchor Books.

Mairs, N. (1994). *Voice lessons: On becoming a (woman) writer.* Boston: Beacon Press.

Merleau-Ponty, M. (1964). *Signs,* Translated by Richard C. McCreary. Evanston, IL: Northwestern University Press.

Murphy, R. (1987). *The body silent.* New York: Henry Holt.

Neumann, M. 1996. Collecting ourselves at the end of the century. In C. Ellis & A. Bochner (Eds.), *Composing ethnography: Alternative forms of qualitative writing* (pp. 172–198). Walnut Creek, CA: AltaMira.

Nin, A. (1976). *In favor of the sensitive man and other essays.* New York: Harcourt Brace Jovanovich.

Paget, M. A. (1993). Edited by M. L. DeVault. *A complex sorrow: Reflections on cancer and an abbreviated life.* Philadelphia: Temple University Press.

Parry, A. (1991). A universe of stories. *Family Process, 30,* 37–54.

Reed-Danahay, D. (1995). *Autobiographical schooling narratives and the ethnography of power in rural France.* Paper presented at American Anthropological Association meetings, Session on Auto/ethnography and Ethnos/biography, Washington, D.C.

Richardson, L. (1992). The consequences of poetic representation: Writing the other, rewriting the self. In C. Ellis & M. Flaherty (Eds.), *Investigating subjectivity: Research on lived experience* (pp. 125–137). Newbury Park, CA: Sage.

Richardson, L. (1994). Writing as a method of inquiry. In N. Denzin & Y. Lincoln (Eds.), *Handbook of qualitative research* (pp. 516–529). Thousand Oaks, CA: Sage.

Ronai, C. R. (1995). Multiple reflections of child sex abuse: An argument for a layered account. *Journal of Contemporary Ethnography, 23,* 395–426.

Rosenwald, G. (1992). Conclusion: Reflections on narrative understanding. In G. Rosenwald & R. Ochberg (Eds.), *Storied lives: The cultural politics of self-understanding* (pp. 265–289). New Haven, CT: Yale University Press.

Scheff, T. (1972). Re-evaluative counseling: Social implications. *Journal of Humanistic Psychology 12,* 58–71.

Spence, D. (1982). *Narrative truth and historical truth: Meaning and interpretation in psychoanalysis.* New York: W. W. Norton and Co.

Tillmann-Healy, L. (1996). A secret life in a culture of thinness: Reflections on body, food, and bulimia. In C. Ellis & A. Bochner (Eds.), *Composing ethnography: Alternative forms of qualitative writing* (pp. 76–108). Walnut Creek, CA: AltaMira.

Woolf, V. (1953). *The Common Reader.* New York: Harcourt Brace and World.

Zola, I. K. (1982). *Missing Pieces: A chronicle of living with a disability.* Philadelphia: Temple University Press.

# 5

# *A Case for Hope in Pain, Loss, and Suffering*

***C. R. Snyder***
*University of Kansas–Lawrence*

*"Pain is mandatory, but suffering is optional."*
—Actor Craig T. Nelson

## IT HURTS

Have you ever had a pressure, heartburn, and burning that lurks somewhere behind your sternum, letting you know that you have an unwanted visitor? You probably have had this, but it went away after several hours or, perhaps, a few days. I have experienced this constantly and with deep intensity for over four years now. Although I would be ecstatic if my pain were to go away, and would even gain some solace from knowing its source, I have learned important lessons because of this pain. During my several hospital stays and various medical procedures, I have had the privilege of knowing some remarkable patients whose pain did *not* produce a sense of loss or suffering. I also learned from other patients whose pain had thrown them into the catacombs of suffering. To all of these people, I owe the kernels of insight that fueled my present theory of pain, loss, suffering, and hope.

In the following chapter, I will weave a tale that is borne out of my personal pain and the research I have conducted over the past 10 years. More importantly, I will outline a theory that suggests that pain is not the most important part of this saga in terms of one's overall coping. On this latter point, I will argue that hope plays a critical role in whether pain causes a sense of loss and suffering.

## PAIN, LOSS, AND SUFFERING

Although the experience of pain varies between people, there is considerable theoretical agreement about what it is. Pain is a mentally registered signal of physical discomfort (see, for review, Skevington, 1995). Normally, we are not aware of our

I thank Sheryle Gallant, Ruth Leibowitz, Michael Rapoff, and Annette Stanton for their input on an earlier version of this chapter.

bodily sensations as we go about the matters of daily living. During a pain episode, however, this unpleasant perceptual experience is at the center of our mental awareness. Thus, our previous neutral or perhaps somewhat positive body perception is lost as physical pain looms in our consciousness. It is important to emphasize, even at this beginning stage, that "Pain is always a cerebral phenomenon" (Leriche, 1937, p. 40). This point is similar to the distinction made between raw sensation and the act of perception in which the mind interprets the sensation-based input (Snyder, 1994b). I draw this distinction to foreshadow my subsequent emphasis on the importance of mental processes in dealing with pain.

Pain immediately makes a person aware of the potential for an important loss: one's health. Usually taken for granted, our health is a cherished assumption as we go about the procurement of the many other daily goals (see Ware & Young, 1979, for corroboration of the value placed on health). Indeed, for most of us, good health means that we are feeling no pain. But, as we all know, accidents happen. Likewise, serious and not-so-serious diseases visit. And aging can lessen our seeming physical invulnerability even further. Whatever the source, we all experience temporary or more enduring losses to our health, and pain announces such losses. We could not sense that we have lost our health, of course, if we had not previously had good health. Losses reflect hoped-for goals that are temporarily or permanently removed from being potentially reachable (see Snyder, 1996), and this is especially the case when people undergo pain and illness and lose their "good health."

At this point, I would like to add another concept to our discussion, that of suffering (for reviews, see Cassell, 1991; Fordyce, 1988; Morris, 1991). Suffering is often confused with pain, but it is somewhat different and, in my estimation, much more important. Suffering is not merely a reaction to physical pain, but it reflects a larger psychological process in which pain is an important player.[1] Suffering reflects how one has dealt with the pain in the context of performing the usual tasks of life and, importantly, the degree to which the pain has resulted in a sense of loss. Thus, two people can have virtually identical physical pains, and yet their suffering may differ. For example, some people with physical pain may have relatively low suffering because they do not perceive that the pain has produced important losses, i.e., those cutting them off from pivotal goals. Conversely, other people with physical pain may experience very high suffering because the pain signals a sense of loss that has negatively permeated many, if not all aspects of their lives.

In summary, pain is a physical stimulus that is registered mentally and is appraised as producing a potential loss of health (and other goals); suffering is the barometer of the larger impact of the pain and the associated loss upon a person's functioning as a whole. This pain-loss-suffering process is modulated by yet

[1]Having drawn this distinction, however, I would hasten to add that pain and suffering do have some modest positive relationship, and that extreme pain is more likely to be related to higher suffering. Indeed, in the truly extreme forms, the magnitude of the pain may be sufficiently high so as to negatively impact all aspects of the person's life. In this latter instance of excruciating pain, therefore, suffering by necessity will result (unless very strong pain medications are employed). In most cases, including those of very profound pain, however, suffering is not inevitable. This latter type of pain is the focus in this chapter.

another process that is important to human functioning: hope. At this juncture, I would like to describe my theoretical model of hope, and build a case for how it can help to understand and potentially alleviate the typical pain-loss-suffering cycle.

## A THEORY OF HOPE

Hope is a pattern of thinking that involves a sense of agency and pathways for one's goals (Snyder, 1994a, 1994b, in press; Snyder, Harris, et al., 1991; Snyder, McDermott, Cook, & Rapoff, 1997; Snyder, Sympson, et al., 1996). More formally, we (Snyder, Harris, et al., 1991) have defined hope as "a reciprocally derived sense of successful (a) agency (goal-directed determination) and (b) pathways (planning of ways to meet goals)" (p. 571). Hopeful thinking may be trait-like in that it applies across differing goal situations (see Snyder, Harris, et al.), or state-like in that it applies to a given situation and a particular point in time (see Snyder, Sympson, et al., 1996). For our present purposes, the focus is on trait hope.[2]

### Goal Thoughts

The critical anchor in this definition is the goal, which is the desired endpoint of human actions. We focus on goal objects so that we can effectively respond to our environment. Shortly after birth, for example, we can differentially attend to the caregiver who delivers nourishment to us. Throughout the developmental sequence, and for the rest of our adult lives, we form goals that are the targets of our thinking and actions. In this regard, high-hope people usually can clearly conceptualize their goals, while low-hope people are more vague and ambiguous about their goals (Snyder, Harris, et al., 1991). As shown in the mind's eye of the person shown in Figure 1, the thoughts are aimed at goal endpoints.

### Pathway Thoughts

There are two important additional thoughts related to goals. A first goal-related process is what I call pathway thinking. Pathway thinking reflects the one or more routes that people attach to goals. Pathway thought taps the capacity to produce mental maps to reach goal destinations; typically there is at least one avenue that is the focus for the journey to any goal. As shown in Figure 1, in the mind of our example individual, the pathway thought leads to a particular conjured goal.

[2]Trait hope has correlated positively with optimism, positive affectivity, and problem-solving, and negatively with depression, negative affectivity, and anxiety. Although it shares variances with these other measures, trait hope has provided significant and unique predictive variance in regard to various coping indices with adults (Snyder, Harris, et al., 1991) and children (Snyder, Hoza, et al., 1997). Further, state hope has correlated positively with other indices of optimism, positive affectivity, and self-esteem, and negatively with negative affectivity and anxiety; likewise, state hope has provided unique variance over these other state indices in regard to predicting ongoing goal-related activities (Snyder, Sympson, et al., 1996).

*Figure 1.* Schematic of Hope, Including Agency and Pathway Thinking Toward Goals.

## Agency Thoughts

A second goal-related thought pertains to the individual's perceived ability to initiate and continue movement on the chosen pathway. This type of thinking, which I call agency, serves as a source of determination that energizes the individual to actually employ a pathway. Agentic thought thus provides the motivation to go after goals. As shown in Figure 1, the agency thinking is channeled though the pathway toward the goal.

## Putting Hope Together

These three components combine to form the cognitive motivational concept of hope. More specifically, hope is defined as a manner of thinking in which the protagonist has a goal, as well as the associated pathway to reach the goal and the agency to apply to that pathway. To have only agency or pathway thought alone does not suffice to produce hope. It takes both of these goal-related thought components to activate hope; accordingly, the protagonist in Figure 1 can be said to have hopeful thinking.

### Impediments

Because hope theory is predicated on goal pursuit thinking, anything that serves to block either pathway or agency thought can play an important role in coping. One premise of hope theory is that the unimpeded pursuit of goals results in positive emotions, whereas the encountering of blockages can result in negative feelings. On this point, research using correlational and causal designs shows that goal blockages yield negative emotional responses (Snyder, Sympson, et al., 1996).[3] Generally, however, it should be noted that high-hope people do not experience the same degree of negative emotional reactions when blocked as do low-hope people. One reason for this is that high- as compared to low-hope individuals can generate alternative paths, especially when the original one is blocked (Snyder, Harris, et al., 1991). On the other hand, low-hope people not only are unclear about their primary pathway to a goal, but become stymied when they encounter a blockage to that pathway. Furthermore, relative to low-hope persons, high-hope people perceive that they can and will employ both the primary and alternate routes to their goals, particularly when confronted with blockages. On this latter point, research reveals that higher- as compared to lower-hope children and adults have advantages in the normal goal pursuits of life (Snyder, 1994b; Snyder, Harris, et al.; Snyder, Hoza, et al., 1997; Snyder, Sympson, et al.), and that these advantages are particularly apparent when individuals encounter blockages to the goal pursuits (Barnum, Snyder, Rapoff, Mani, & Thompson, in press; Elliott, Witty, Herrick, & Hoffman, 1991; Irving, Snyder, & Crowson, in press; Sherwin, 1992; Snyder, 1994b, 1996; Snyder, Harris, et al.; Snyder, Hoza, et al., 1997; Snyder, Irving, & Anderson, 1991).

## HERE COMES THE PAIN

Because we typically take our health and painlessness for granted, we are not aware of these goals as we pursue other more captivating goals. We are not infallible, of course, and pain gives us a sudden signal that we have lost the healthy "no pain" serenity and, as such, must reorder our thoughts and activities. No longer being able to take "no pain" as a given, we are forced by pain to alter our goal priorities. Accordingly, the person experiencing pain adopts "no pain" as the primary goal on his or her mental agenda.

In the case of a pain caused by a physical strain or mild injury, the person attends to it by applying ice or heat, staying off the injured appendage, and so on. She or he may also lie down, rest, and take medication. We all know the routine related to this first level of response to pain.

[3]The hope theory premise that impeded goal pursuit results in negative emotions and lowered well-being is receiving support in other laboratories. More specifically, theory and research suggest that difficulties in the pursuit of meaningful goals undermines the development and maintenance of well-being (Diener, 1984; Emmons, 1986; Little, 1983; Omodei & Wearing, 1990; Palys & Little, 1983; Ruehlman & Wolchik, 1988) and that the perceived blockages or lack of progress toward important goals is the cause of reduced well-being rather than vice versa (Brunstein, 1993; Little, 1989).

If the pain is more severe, our protagonist probably talks with a nurse or goes to a physician. In turn, these experts at dealing with such matters attend to the source of the ill health and the pain as well. For pains reflecting more severe physical problems, we may have to visit or stay in a hospital, undergoing tests and treatments that can vary from the relatively minor to the more serious. These latter events truly set off the person's concerns about the pain also producing potential losses.

These steps at procuring the "no pain" goal are generally understood and followed by most people (Morris, 1991). Further, people who are in pain because of illness are excused from their other goal pursuits by their families, friends, and employers (see Snyder, Higgins, & Stucky, 1983). Finally, this scenario comes full circle when the acute pain is lessened because its source has been found and "fixed." Thus, the protagonists in these typical stories of pain again have no pain and, importantly, assume that they have regained good health. Such people then return to the goals pursued before the pain onset. This scenario describes acute pain, which lasts less than three to six months. However, not all pain goes away, as we shall explore next.

## THE PAIN STAYS

In the previous pain example, one that we have all been through probably one or more times, the protagonist may or may not experience a sense of loss and suffering. It will depend on the depth of the underlying injury or illness that produced the pain, as well as the duration of the pain. Let us suppose, however, that the pain is fairly intense and enduring for the person. Although acute pain can undermine hopeful thinking, it is chronic pain that more typically begins to block and deplete normal hope and goal-directed thinking processes. Pain produces two principal blockages and I explore these next.

### Pathway Blocks

One of the most powerful means by which pain can produce both a sense of loss and suffering is through the blocking of the normal pathway thinking that the person engaged in prior to the onset of the pain. As can be seen in the mind of a person experiencing pain in Figure 2, the pain literally serves as a blockage between the usual pathway thought and the goal toward which it is aimed. In this example, it needs to be emphasized that the blockage pertains to the "no pain" goal, as well as to the goal or goals that the person had before the onset of the pain. These latter usual life goals may relate to relationships, work, or any of the other arenas for important desired outcomes. As the pain continues, people become keenly aware of the routes that they *cannot* take to their usual goals because of the pain.

As can be seen by the pain burst that is portrayed in the pathway thinking of our protagonist in Figure 2, the perception is that she or he cannot use the typical avenue to the goal favored prior to the onset of pain. On this point, research consistently shows, with a variety of populations, that it is the perceived restriction

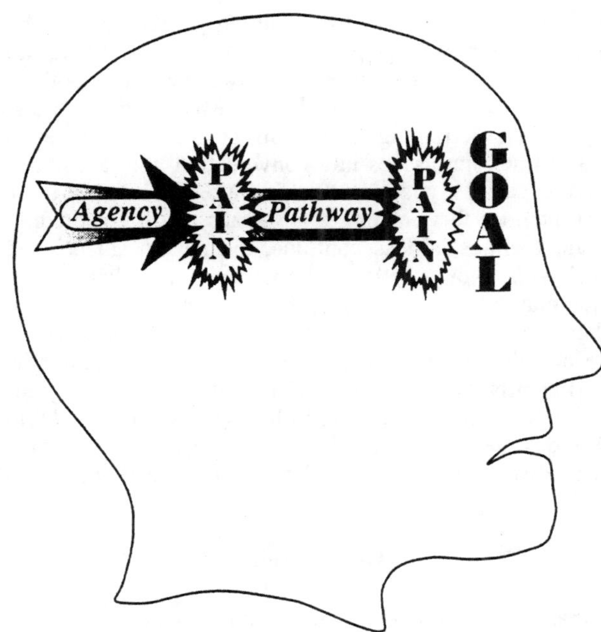


*Figure 2.* Schematic of Pain in the Context of Hope, Including the Blockages Produced by Pain on Agency and Pathway Thinking.

of routine pathways that triggers the sense of loss and suffering more generally (Ditto, Druley, Moore, Danks, & Smucker, 1996; Nieboer & Schulz, 1996; Williamson, 1996; Williamson & Schulz, 1992, 1995; Williamson, Schulz, Bridges, & Behan, 1994). Further, with samples of young and elderly adults, pain has been suspected of interfering with a person's capacity to pursue valued life goals (Ditto et al., 1996). From the perspective of hope theory, this repeated and profound blockage of normal pathway thinking produces the associated sense of loss relative to previous functioning, and it can lead to an even more pervasive sense of suffering.[4] Thus, pathway blockages that are more central and more prolonged, as well as those having greater impact upon more of the available pathways, should elicit more suffering.

When the pain continues to interrupt normal pathway thinking, the sense of overall loss is heightened. If one listens to the words of people experiencing chronic pain, for example, they frequently describe how the pain is getting in the way, not allowing them to take the usual routes to their goals. Once they are no longer able to engage in the accustomed routes, people miss them not only for their familiarity, but for the pleasures that they previously brought. In relationships, for ex-

[4]This theoretical hope perspective is similar to a recent theory of control in which it is suggested that the restriction of activity evokes depression (Heckhausen & Schulz, 1995).

ample, talking is a crucial vehicle for attaining shared goals. The person with severe and chronic pain, however, may find it difficult to attend to a loved one's words and to spend the time that is necessary to achieve good communication. Similarly, in the work setting, the pain may interfere with the person's ability to pay attention to matters pertaining to the correct use of machinery, or the person may not be able to track key issues in a conversation with a coworker. The possibilities for interference with pathway thinking are endless, but the common issue is that important avenues for reaching one's goals are interrupted.

If the pain and feelings of loss continue, the person suffers and the sense of well-being deteriorates. Not only does the person sense that the usual routes are blocked, but they may also begin to question that any routes will ever be available for reaching their goals. On this issue, the interference produced by severe and chronic pain, especially when accompanied by an identifiable illness, has been judged to be sufficiently conducive to suffering that the majority of people report that they would prefer to die rather than to live with such pain (Ditto et al., 1996). Unless the path blockage and loss produced by pain is dealt with in an appropriate manner, as I will discuss later in this chapter, a cycle of continued suffering is likely.

### Agency Blocks

The other impact of pain relates to the eventual blocking of agency thought. As shown by the pain burst at the tip of the agency arrow in Figure 2, pain also registers itself as a blockage of mental energy. In other words, the pain intercedes to rob us of the energy to initiate and sustain movement along our favored pathways (Jensen & Karoly, 1991; Jensen, Turner, Romano, & Karoly, 1991; Karoly & Ruehlman, 1996).

When experiencing pain, we are initially aroused with frustration and anger, especially if we perceive that something or someone is blocking us.[5] If the goal blockage is sustained over time, however, the anger and arousal subsides and people are often drained of mental energy.

From the experiential perspectives of persons with pain, a common complaint is that the pain is robbing them of their "energy." They mean by this not only a loss of physical energy, but a more fundamental loss involving a psychological lack of willfulness. The constant, unrelenting quality of the pain makes it difficult to apply oneself not only to the previously favored paths, but to any paths. Further, the pain gives voice to an internal "I can't" message that undermines the person's propensity to start or sustain action (Karoly & Ruehlman, 1996).

Particularly when this pain message continues unabated, people express regret about the loss of their previous energy. There is a poignant quality to such statements as "Why, I used to be able to . . ." and "The old zip is gone." Personally, I experienced pain as a roadblock that not only stopped me, but often drained me of whatever available energy that I might have on a given day. To make matters

[5]See Snyder (1994b) for a more detailed exposition of the similarities of hope theory to the frustration-aggression hypothesis as initially espoused by Dollard, Doob, Miller, Mowrer, and Sears (1939), and more recently examined by Berkowitz (1962) and Zillman (1979).

worse, this low-energy person was totally unlike the previous vision I had had of myself, and I felt a loss of core vitality.

Once a person has experienced loss due to the pain and its attendant blockage of agency thought, the possibility of suffering looms large. Without one's usual mental zest, the game of life loses its wonder and attraction. Lacking in mental vigor, one's usual goal pursuit activities are shut down (Karoly & Ruehlman, 1996).

### Double Pain

As shown in Figure 2, pain serves to block both pathway and agency thought. It would be bad enough if pain blocked just one, but in truth it acts on both pathway and agency thinking so as to intensify the sense of loss. Further, whenever we think about one of these two components (the blocked habitual pathway associated with an object, or the impeded agency), we often think of the other. As such, the pain blockages reverberate in our consciousness so as to compound the sense of loss and eventual suffering. Therefore, not only does the pain hurt in a physical sense, but it also registers as an unwanted reminder of how we are blocked in pathway and agency thoughts. In fact, I would suggest that the more important implications of pain for loss and suffering rest *not* upon the actual registering of the pain sensation, but upon the psychological interpretation of being blocked in both agency and pathway thoughts.

## HOPELESSNESS GOT US INTO THIS, SO CAN HOPE GET US OUT?

Hopeful thinking is tied inextricably to the processes of loss and suffering. The reason for this assertion is that hope involves a type of goal-directed thought, and when there are blockages to such thinking, hope may be undermined. Further, the person so blocked may experience a loss and, with repeated exposure to continuing blockages and perceived losses, hopelessness and suffering. Although there are many forces in life that can serve to block us and to yield a sense of loss, the major point of the present chapter is *that pain can be considered as an important source of blockage*. This is not meant to deny the importance of the pain sensation per se, but rather to shift our focus to the blockage properties of pain. What follows are suggestions for diminishing these perceived pain-induced blockages, and thereby lessening the sense of loss and suffering more generally.

Recent research suggests that optimistic and hopeful people have coping advantages when dealing with both psychological and physical problems (Scheier & Carver, 1992; Snyder, 1996, in press). Accordingly, we can learn from high-hope people about how they fight through the struggles of life, particularly when confronted with blockages. One misconception is that people who are higher in hope have lived lives of ease in which they have been free of impediments to their desires (Snyder, 1994b). On the contrary, they typically have been confronted by losses and blockages that are as numerous and large in magnitude as those encountered by other people. Based on these experiences, high-hope people have learned to think so as to anticipate and bounce back from such blockages and losses (Irving et al., in press; Snyder, 1994b). This observation echoes that made of resilient children (Cowen & Work, 1988; Garmezy, 1991; Rutter, 1994), who have often undergone severe hardships and losses, and yet remain positive and flexible so as to continue to achieve their goals.

In this section, I will use the components of hope theory—goal, pathway, and agency thinking—to explore how pain, loss, and suffering can be lessened.

## Goal Work

One of the major coping approaches of high-hope people is that they consider alternative goal objects when an original goal is truly lost (Snyder, 1994b, 1996). High-hope people establish goals in each of their life arenas (e.g., relationships, career, recreation, etc.) and often have differing goals within a particular arena. By having multiple goals, the high-hope person can switch to another goal without being overly demoralized by the loss of any one goal when that goal appears to be unobtainable.

Hoping involves knowing that our goal objects are not always attainable, and that we can turn to another goal as an outlet when one goal is truly curtailed. This is especially the case when unabating pain renders one goal impossible. To hope involves a replacing of the original lost object with another one. But, the pursuit of a replacement goal should not proceed too quickly. Grieving is natural when pain precludes the pursuit of a relished goal, and it takes time to mourn the loss of the previously attainable goal. With time, however, and with an understanding of the characteristics of one's pain, it is appropriate to entertain a substitute goal. With this new object increasingly capturing one's attention, hope can be renewed.

Perhaps a personal example would be useful at this point. I have loved to play baseball as a source of recreation for most of my life. When I ruptured my Achilles tendon in a game four years ago, I tried to return to the game as soon as possible. Unfortunately, not only did I have the pain from a stiff, albeit repaired, Achilles tendon, but I also had the chest pain I described previously. Much to my dismay, sudden movements such as lurching for a ball and accelerating to the next base, as well as other "jerky" movements required in baseball, all seemed to make my chest and leg pain even worse. I began to look for another goal that would give me pleasure, but without the extra pain. I switched to working with wood in my basement workshop, and painting my house inside and out (which is an almost never-ending task).

Physical injuries may leave people racked with pain and no longer able to undertake previously coveted activities. The person with a physical handicap who stubbornly refuses to give up a goal-related activity that truly is no longer tenable will almost surely experience increased pain and suffering. In this scenario, however, it is the hopeful person, not the person who clings to past expectations, who can find a new goal activity. By attaching one's thoughts to a substitute goal, a person becomes less focused on what cannot be done. Equally important, such a person spends more time thinking about what *can* be done. Pain seems smaller in the context of what one can rather than cannot do.

## Pathway Work

Assuming that the pain is of a sufficient magnitude that it is blocking one's usual route to a goal, there are several steps to alleviate this problem. First, people in profound pain may catastrophize and generalize, assuming that the pain will block all paths. Such thinking needs to be changed, or the sense of loss and suffering will grow needlessly. Instead of concluding that the pain will impede all paths, it is more helpful to conclude that you have information about the one or more paths that will not work. In other words, a person can use the pain linked to a given pathway as diagnostic feedback to aid in the search for another pathway where the pain may not intervene as readily. It is also important not to give up on finding routes that may be less painful, or perhaps even painless.

As a case on the aforementioned point, I once worked with a man who came to treatment because of a deepening depression. A highly successful university professor in his middle years, he was becoming increasingly debilitated because of arthritis. Since his undergraduate days, he had written enormous amounts by hand in yellow pads, and had even done this for the books he had authored. The arthritis had made writing by hand more and more difficult, however, to the point that he simply could no longer hold a pencil firmly without excruciating pain. He was very angry and sad about losing his long-cherished ability to write effortlessly by hand. At this point, I asked him what the goal was for all this handwriting. He answered that he wanted to be able to get his ideas into readable form. I suggested learning how to type. Never having done this, he initially balked at this possibility. Nevertheless, he began to practice typing. Unlike the holding of a pencil, typing did not produce as much pain. Eventually he became quite proficient at typing. Over time, he credited this new typing skill as playing a major role in helping him to arise from his depression.

Another pathway lesson for persons blocked by pain is to break a goal down into substeps. By taking smaller, incremental steps to a desired goal, the pain is not as likely to appear in major proportions. (The smaller steps also allow for some successes that are empowering, i.e., that provide an increase in agency.) This was a lesson that I had to learn when dealing with my own pain. I was previously accustomed to working for very long stretches of time, but I simply could not do this because of pain. If, however, I worked for shorter periods, resting in between, the pain did not mushroom as readily.

Shortening one's pathway thinking also has the advantage of preserving agentic thought. In this regard, I sometimes tell myself and my clients the following joke.

> *Question:* Do you know how to make God really laugh?
> *Answer:* Tell her your long-range plans.

Pain has less likelihood of getting us down if we live more for the moment.

Additionally, I would encourage persons with chronic pain to search for the nearest qualified psychologists who are trained to use cognitive behavior therapy for managing pain (Keefe, 1996; Keefe, Beaupre, & Gill, in press; Turk, Meichenbaum, & Genest, 1983). These programs are aimed expressly at teaching people new pathways for achieving better pain management. For more information for professionals and lay people, contact the pain management programs in nearby medical centers, or write the persons listed in the footnote.[6]

## Agency Work

Agentic thought is the fuel that enables us to pursue goals. Pain, as I have noted, depletes this reservoir of psychological energy, making it more likely that a person will become increasingly inactive. There are several antidotes to this process. First, there is what I call the "self voices" exercise. Based on our laboratory research, we have found that high-hope people tend to have an ongoing self-dialogue of affirming, energizing statements such as "I can," "I'll make it," and "I won't give up" (Snyder, LaPointe, Crowson, & Early, 1996). These inner voices serve as cheerleaders for the person being drained by pain, and I have used this with both my clients and myself to produce a mental jolt. (A caveat is warranted here, however, in that people should not be encouraged to work so hard as to increase the pain.)

There is another version of this exercise that I use when I am feeling a good deal of pain and I need to teach my undergraduate class. As I prepare to walk into the auditorium to face some 400 students, I imagine a giant slug (the slimy sidewalk mollusk) with a slash drawn through it. I call this my "slugbuster" logo (patterned after the *Ghostbusters* movie, whose "logo" was a circled ghost with a slash drawn through it), and it gives me a lift.

Another repercussion of recurring pain is that people do not feel like doing much, and as a result, they get into a cycle of engaging in fewer and fewer physical activities because these only seem to make the pain worse. In fact, however, exercise sustains one's overall agentic thought, and the key is to find a form that allows one to maintain physical stamina without making the pain worse. Finding an appropriate exercise regimen may take some time, but it is worth the search because exercise does not let the pain increase in its debilitating capacity. For many people with pain, swimming and walking provide minimal discomfort, while producing the desired aerobic lift. Not surprisingly, pain management programs routinely include some type of exercise regimen.

Pacing one's activities also makes it more likely that the pain will not overtake one's consciousness. Training in pacing is part of the cognitive behavior therapy programs for pain that I discussed in the previous section, "Pathway Work." One of the lessons learned from high-hope people, in this regard, is that they go at a reasoned pace in the pursuit of their goals, and accordingly are more likely to enjoy the process or journey. A frantic, time-oriented approach only makes the

[6]Training opportunities can be obtained through workshops held by the American Pain Society, the International Association for the Study of Pain, and the Association for the Advancement of Behavior Therapy. Information about training possibilities can be garnered by writing one of the following three experts: (1) Laurence A. Bradley, Ph.D., Division of Rheumatology, 429 Tinsley Harrison Tower, University of Alabama-Birmingham, Birmingham, AL 35294; (2) Francis J. Keefe, Ph.D., Pain Management Program, Box 3159, Duke University Medical Center, Durham, NC 27710; and (3) Dennis Turk, Ph.D., Center for Pain Evaluation/Pain Treatment Institute, Center for Sports Medicine and Rehabilitation, Daum Boulevard at Craig Street, Pittsburgh, PA 15213.

pain appear more detrimental to one's sense of agency. An important part of such pacing is to obtain a sufficient amount of rest so as to renew one's energy.

People in pain can also become tense and anxious, which only serves to further deplete mental energy. As such, pain management psychologists teach progressive relaxation exercises to decrease muscle tension, as well as distraction techniques so as to divert attention away from the pain (Keefe, 1996).

I also teach people to find humor in their ongoing plights. When a person can adopt an existential perspective about the sometimes ridiculous nature of life, then the edge is taken off the pain.[7] A particular line that my clients and I have found helpful is, "If you don't laugh at yourself, you have missed the biggest joke of all" (Snyder, 1994b, p. 228).

Additionally, when the pain appears to be especially debilitating, people often forget that they have coped successfully with this pain in the past, and that they have gotten through it. In other words, it is important to remember one's previous successful pain battles, and to draw some strength and vigor from such recollections.

Last, and somewhat counterintuitively, one's family can undermine the sense of agency in the person with chronic pain. This is accomplished by well-meaning family members who become overly solicitous and protective of the person, thereby reinforcing that person's feeling of being depleted of energy because of pain (Flor, Kerns, & Turk, 1987; Keefe, Gil, & Rose, 1986). As an extreme example of this phenomenon, I once worked with a woman who had come to call herself an "invalid" through the repeated behaviors on the part of her family to treat her thus. Imagine the degree to which one would be robbed of agency via the "invalid" label.[8] To stop this paradoxical and unfortunate cycle, family members need to be apprised of their role in further diminishing the agentic thoughts and actions of the person with chronic pain. Once this pattern is exposed and understood, the family and the person with chronic pain can embrace a manner of interacting that reinforces activity rather than inactivity.

## Hope and Pain Trilogy

In this section, I have discussed the establishment of new goals, and the means of producing alternative pathways and agentic thinking as if they are independent processes. In actuality, however, these three components of hopeful thought are related, and it may take only one to elicit the other two components. At times, for example, merely finding a substitute goal also will produce a flood of related

[7]For a review of the benefits of humor, read Cousins (1979).

[8]A vivid discussion of this issue of being an "invalid" is given in the Thomas Szasz book *The Theology of Medicine* (1977; see particularly chapter 2). On this point, Szasz (1977, p. 19) writes: "Language, the oldest but still the most reliable guide to a people's true sentiments, starkly reveals the intimate connection between illness and indignity. In English, we use the same word to describe an expired passport, and a person disabled by a disease. We call each of them *invalid.* To be an invalid, then, is to be an invalidated person, a human being stamped *not valid* by the invisible but invincible hand of popular opinion" (author's emphases). Although I have discussed the notions of protective familial and societal treatment and invalidism as promoting a loss of agency in the target person, it should be noted that these processes also produce reductions in the person's pathways thinking.

pathway thoughts, as well as a surge of energy to apply to those pathways. Likewise, a patient with pain may come up with a new pathway or skill, whereafter the appropriate goal and agency also will appear. Finally, an increase of mental energy, in and of itself, can enable the person to find an appropriate goal outlet and the related pathways to reach the goal. What is called for in coping with pain, therefore, may be a simple change in only one process (or area), and the other two hope-related components may follow naturally.

## FROM PILLS TO PSYCHOLOGY: PUTTING PAIN IN PERSPECTIVE

One approach that I have not emphasized in this chapter is the alleviation of pain through medication. Pain alleviation via analgesic medications deserves a discussion in and of itself, but I will not describe this approach in any detail because of present space constraints. It should be noted, however, that exciting advances are being made in pain treatment with drugs that previously have been used solely for psychological problems (e.g., tricyclic antidepressants, serotonin reuptake inhibitors, etc.) Additionally, opiates are increasingly being used to diminish pain, and the evidence overwhelmingly suggests that addiction is extremely rare when these controlled medications are used for pain (Cassell, 1991; Twillman, 1996). Further, selected physicians are becoming more involved in the treatment of pain per se. Based on my personal experience, and what I have observed about the effectiveness of such medically oriented treatment approaches, I believe that they offer an important vehicle for lessening the negative impact of pain. Indeed, I would encourage those who experience pain to cast off any stigma that they may have with regard to the taking of medications for pain.

Pain is a complex issue, and a multifaceted approach is warranted in order to diminish its negative impact. My focus has been on the psychological process of hope as a means of containing the debilitating aspects of pain. The thrust of this chapter has been to provide a theoretical framework for hope, and to illustrate how pain can intervene in this normal goal-directed process to produce a sense of loss and subsequent suffering for some, but not all, people. Pain can block a person's usual pathway thinking for goal pursuits, and it can impede the typical agentic thinking to go after goals. In these two major and often interrelated blockages, a more pervasive sense of loss develops, so that intense suffering also is likely.

An important point is that pain and suffering, while often related, are not synonymous. As actor Craig T. Nelson (cited at the beginning of this chapter) put it, "Pain is mandatory, but suffering is optional" (Caudill, 1995, p. 1). Indeed, just as we can understand the pain-loss-suffering sequence through the principles of hope theory, so too does this theory offer some clues about how to contain the pain so that it does not produce suffering. To maintain hope in the presence of pain means that we can put it in the background and bring the enjoyable goal pursuits of life to the front of our consciousness.[9] Based on present research, interactions with

[9]The notion that persons who successfully cope with pain do so because they are fully occupied with the matters of living is the conclusion reached by Fordyce (1988) in his classic paper on pain and suffering.

other patients, and my own experience with chronic pain, I would suggest that such pleasures are considerable.

## REFERENCES

Barnum, D. D., Snyder, C. R., Rapoff, M. A., Mani, M. M., & Thompson, R. (in press). Hope and social support in the psychological adjustment of children who have survived burn injuries and their matched controls. *Children's Health Care.*

Berkowitz, L. (1962). *Aggression: A social psychological analysis.* New York: McGraw-Hill.

Brunstein, J. C. (1993). Personal goals and subjective well-being: A longitudinal study. *Journal of Personality and Social Psychology, 65,* 1061–1070.

Cassell, E. J. (1991). *The nature of suffering and the goals of medicine.* New York: Oxford.

Caudill, M. A. (1995). *Managing pain before it manages you.* New York: Guilford Press.

Cousins, N. (1979). *Anatomy of an illness as perceived by the patient.* New York: Norton.

Cowen, E. L., & Work, W. C. (1988). Resilient children, psychological wellness, and primary prevention. *American Journal of Community Psychology, 16,* 591–607.

Diener, E. (1984). Subjective well-being. *Psychological Bulletin, 95,* 542–575.

Ditto, P. H., Druley, J. A., Moore, K. A., Danks, J. H., & Smucker, W. D. (1996). Fates worse than death: The role of valued life activities in health-state evaluations. *Health Psychology, 15,* 332–343.

Dollard, J., Doob, L. W., Miller, N. E., Mowrer, O., & Sears, R. (1939). *Frustration and aggression.* New Haven, CT: Yale University Press.

Elliott, T. R., Witty, T. E., Herrick, S., & Hoffman, J. T. (1991). Negotiating reality after physical loss: Hope, depression, and disability. *Journal of Personality and Social Psychology, 61,* 608–613.

Emmons, R. A. (1986). Personal strivings: An approach to personality and subjective well-being. *Journal of Personality and Social Psychology, 51,* 1058–1068.

Flor, H., Kerns, R. D., & Turk, D. C. (1987). The role of spouse reinforcement, perceived pain, and activity levels of chronic pain patients. *Journal of Psychosomatic Research, 31,* 251–259.

Fordyce, W. E. (1988). Pain and suffering. *American Psychologist, 43,* 276–283.

Garmezy, N. (1991). Resiliency and vulnerability to adverse developmental outcomes associated with poverty. *American Behavioral Scientist, 34,* 416–430.

Heckhausen, J., & Schulz, R. (1995). A life-span theory of control. *Psychological Review, 102,* 284–304.

Irving, L. M., Snyder, C. R., & Crowson, J. J., Jr. (in press). Hope and the negotiation of cancer facts by college females. *Journal of Personality.*

Jensen, M. P., & Karoly, P. (1991). Control beliefs, coping efforts, and adjustment to chronic pain. *Journal of Consulting and Clinical Psychology, 59,* 431–438.

Jensen, M. P., Turner, J. A., Romano, J. M., & Karoly, P. (1991). Coping with chronic pain: A critical review of the literature. *Pain, 47,* 249–283.

Karoly, P., & Ruehlman, L. S. (1996). Motivational implications of pain: Chronicity, psychosocial distress, and work construal in a national sample of adults. *Health Psychology, 15,* 383–390.

Keefe, F. J. (1996). Cognitive behavior therapy for managing pain. *The Clinical Psychologist, 49,* 4–5.

Keefe, F. J., Beaupre, P. M., & Gil, K. M. (in press). Group therapy for patients with chronic pain. In R. J. Gatchel & D. C. Turk (Eds.), *Psychological treatments for pain: A practitioner's handbook.* New York: Guilford.

Keefe, F. J., Gil, K. M., & Rose, S. C. (1986). Behavioral approaches in the multidisciplinary management of chronic pain: Programs and issues. *Clinical Psychology Review, 6,* 87–113.

Leriche, R. (1937). *The surgery of pain.* Translated by A. Young. London: Balliere, Tindall and Cox.

Little, B. R. (1983). Personal projects: A rationale and method for investigation. *Environment and Behavior, 15,* 273–309.

Little, B. R. (1989). Personal projects analysis: Trivial pursuits, magnificent obsessions, and the search for coherence. In D. M. Buss & N. Cantor (Eds.), *Personality psychology: Recent trends and emerging directions* (pp. 15–31). New York: Springer-Verlag.

Morris, D. B. (1991). *The culture of pain.* Berkeley, CA: University of California Press.

Nieboer, A. P., & Schulz, R. (1996, August). *Spousal caregiver's activity restriction and depression: A model for changes over time.* Paper presented at the American Psychological Association Convention, Toronto, ON, Canada.

Omodei, M. M., & Wearing, A. J. (1990). Need satisfaction and involvement in personal projects: Toward an integrative model of subjective well-being. *Journal of Personality and Social Psychology, 59,* 762–769.

Palys, T. S., & Little, B. R. (1983). Perceived life satisfaction and organization of personal projects systems. *Journal of Personality and Social Psychology, 44,* 1221–1230.

Ruehlman, L. S., & Wolchik, S. A. (1988). Personal goals and interpersonal support and hindrance as factors in psychological distress and well-being. *Journal of Personality and Social Psychology, 55,* 293–301.

Rutter, M. (1994). Resilience: Some conceptual considerations. *Contemporary Pediatrics, 11,* 36–48.

Scheier, M. F., & Carver, C. S. (1992). Effects of optimism on psychological and physical well-being: Theoretical overview and empirical update. *Cognitive Therapy and Research, 16,* 201–228.

Sherwin, E. D., Elliott, T. R., Rybarcysk, B. D., Frank, R. G., Hanson, S., & Hoffman, J. (1992). Negotiating the reality of care giving: Hope, burnout, and nursing. *Journal of Social and Clinical Psychology, 11,* 129–139.

Skevington, S. M. (1995). *Psychology of pain.* New York: Wiley.

Snyder, C. R. (1994a). Hope and optimism. In V. S. Ramachandren (Ed.), *Encyclopedia of human behavior, Volume 2* (pp. 535–542). San Diego, CA: Academic Press.

Snyder, C. R. (1994b). *The psychology of hope: You can get there from here.* New York: Free Press.

Snyder, C. R. (1996). To hope, to lose, and hope again. *Journal of Personal and Interpersonal Loss, 1,* 16.

Snyder, C. R. (in press). Hope. In H. S. Friedman (Ed.), *Encyclopedia of mental health.* San Diego, CA: Academic Press.

Snyder, C. R., Harris, C., Anderson, J. R., Holleran, S. A., Irving, L. M., Sigmon, S. T., Yoshinobu, L., Gibb, J., Langelle, C., & Harney, P. (1991). The will and the ways: Development and validation of an individual differences measure of hope. *Journal of Personality and Social Psychology, 60,* 570–585.

Snyder, C. R., Higgins, R. L., & Stucky, R. (1983). *Excuses: Masquerades in search of grace.* New York: Wiley-Interscience.

Snyder, C. R., Hoza, B., Pelham, W. E., Rapoff, M., Ware, L., Danovsky, M., Highberger, L., Rubinstein, H, & Stahl, K. (1997). The development and validation of the Children's Hope Scale. *Journal of Pediatric Psychology, 22*(3), 399–421.

Snyder, C. R., Irving, L. M., & Anderson, J. R. (1991). Hope and health. In C. R. Snyder & D. R. Forsyth (Eds.), *Handbook of social and clinical psychology: The health perspective* (pp. 285–305). Elmsford, NY: Pergamon Press.

Snyder, C. R., LaPointe, A. B., Crowson, J. J., Jr., & Early, S. (1996). *Voices in the mind: Preferences of high- and low-hope people for self-referential statements.* Unpublished manuscript, the University of Kansas-Lawrence.

Snyder, C. R., McDermott, D., Cook, W., & Rapoff, M. (1997). *Hope for the journey: Helping children through good times and bad.* Boulder, CO: Westview/HarperCollins.

Snyder, C. R.., Sympson, S. C., Ybasco, F. C., Borders, T. F., Babyak, M. A., & Higgins, R. L. (1996). Development and validation of the State Hope Scale. *Journal of Personality and Social Psychology, 2,* 321–335.

Szasz, T. (1977). *The theology of medicine.* New York: Syracuse University Press.

Turk, D. C., Meichenbaum, D., & Genest, M. (1983). *Pain and behavioral medicine: A cognitive-behavioral perspective.* New York: Guilford.

Twillman, R. (1996, October). *The management of pain.* Colloquium presented to the Health and Rehabilitation Proseminar of the Graduate Program in Clinical Psychology, Department of Psychology, University of Kansas, Lawrence, KS.

Ware, J. E., Jr., & Young, J. (1979). Issues in the conceptualization and measurement of value placed on health. In S. J. Mushkin & D. W. Dunlop (Eds.), *Health: What is it worth* (pp. 141–166). New York: Pergamon.

Williamson, G. M. (1996). *The centrality of restricted routine activities in psychosocial adjustment to illness and disability: Advances in the identification of contributing factors.* Paper presented at the American Psychological Association Convention, Toronto, ON, Canada.

Williamson, G. M., & Schulz, R. (1992). Pain, activity restriction, and symptoms of depression among community-residing elderly adults. *Journal of Gerontology, 47,* 367–372.

Williamson, G. M., & Schulz, R. (1995). Activity restriction mediates the association between pain and depressed affect: A study of younger and older adult cancer patients. *Psychology and Aging, 10,* 369–378.

Williamson, G. M., Schulz, R., Bridges, M., & Behan, A. (1994). Social and psychological factors in adjustment to limb amputation. *Journal of Social Behavior and Personality, 9,* 249–268.

Zillman, D. (1979). *Hostility and aggression.* Hillsdale, NJ: Erlbaum.

# 6

# Trauma and Grief: A Comparative Analysis

***Margaret Stroebe, Henk Schut, and Wolfgang Stroebe***
*Utrecht University, Utrecht, The Netherlands*

The expression in the English language "to come to grief" is synonymous with "to meet with disaster." One could infer, then, that bereavement is to be considered a disaster—a traumatic event. In fact, the studies of bereavement and trauma share a common origin in the seminal work of Sigmund Freud. It can be said that Freud's (1917) contribution "Mourning and Melancholia," providing, as it did, the first theoretical analysis of distinctions between normal and complicated forms of grieving, has shaped the development of the scientific study of bereavement up to the present day. Likewise, the evolution of his ideas about the relationship of traumatic events to the development of hysterical symptoms, most notably in his volume with Breuer *Studies in Hysteria* (Breuer & Freud, 1895/1937) and in his later work, influenced by World War I experiences with war victims, are still of relevance to trauma research (see Kleber & Brom, 1992).

It is even more curious to note that Freud's interest in the phenomena of both trauma and bereavement was stimulated to a very large extent by one single case, that of Anna O, a patient of Breuer. This young woman had been ill, suffering from symptoms that were hard to diagnose, for quite some time before the death of her father. She had seen him only rarely during her illness, and she apparently idolized him. His death, as Breuer described, was "the most severe psychic trauma which could have happened to her" (Breuer & Freud, 1895/1937, p. 17).

There are, then, good reasons to argue that the early origins of the fields of both bereavement and trauma are not only to be found in the work of one scholar, but in a single case study. Anna O. was utterly grief-stricken and, according to Freud's detailed analysis of this case, deeply traumatized as a consequence of the loss of her beloved father. There was no question, it seems, in Freud's mind, that loss was coupled with reactions relating to both grief and trauma.

Yet, despite this common history, which persisted through the 1940s, with Lindemann's (1944) classic analysis of symptomatology following traumatic bereavement, scientific investigations of bereavement and trauma have developed into relatively independent disciplines and have been treated differently with respect to scientific analysis. As will be elaborated below, trauma has been examined in the context of pathology, whereas bereavement has been treated as a normal human experience.

This chapter is a revised and extended version of an article that has appeared in the Dutch journal *Gedrag & Gezondheid.*

There are good reasons to argue that bereavement should be viewed within a general framework of stress response syndromes, that is, to study bereavement as a trauma. After all, bereavement represents a major stressful life event in most people's lives. Nevertheless, the question arises whether this approach provides an adequate explanation of ways of coping with bereavement. In order to evaluate this, one first needs to describe commonalities and distinctions between the phenomena of trauma and bereavement, to identify respective patterns of reactions, and to examine the contribution of theoretical formulations provided by each area. Examination is made of these three aspects—the phenomena, the manifestations, and the respective theoretical approaches—in this chapter. This should enable assessment of how each field can profit from knowledge acquired in the other discipline. The focal theme of this chapter is thus to explore ways that models of grief and trauma may grow through knowledge acquired in the other field.

The work of Mardi Horowitz on trauma (e.g. 1983, 1986) is distinctive not only as a major contribution to trauma research itself, but also as offering potential for application to the analysis of bereavement phenomena. Furthermore, examination of the *Diagnostic and Statistical Manual* (DSM-IV; American Psychiatric Association [APA], 1994) criteria for the disorder known as Post Traumatic Stress Disorder (PTSD) shows the influence of this particular perspective. This chapter's treatment of the trauma field, given the space limitations, will therefore focus on this theory. With respect to bereavement, a brief overview of traditional theorizing is first given in order to provide the necessary background to understanding our own approach, namely, the dual process model of coping with loss (Stroebe & Schut, 1995). This model is an extension of traditional approaches, which were found wanting in explanatory power.

There is a more general interest underlying the theme of this paper. Researchers must be aware and concerned about the possibility that the scientific process itself may have an impact on societal interpretation—in the case of trauma and of bereavement, by defining a phenomenon as either pathological or normal. Perhaps by bringing together the two scientific disciplines that analyse these related phenomena in such very different ways, we can reduce such polarization and provide more accurate representations of the two types of stressors and their psychological effects. One might say that we are using our two fields to make a comparative case study for reflection on the nature and consequences of the scientific endeavor itself.

## THE PHENOMENA: TRAUMA AND BEREAVEMENT

First, the basics: how do we define the two life events, trauma and bereavement, and their accompanying symptomatologies, and what are the commonalities and distinctions between them?

### Trauma

Trauma entails the personal experience of drastic, horrendous, unpleasant, shocking events. Examples of traumatic experiences range from war to natural disasters such as hurricanes or floods, to man-made atrocities such as concentration camp internment, to violence, including assault on oneself or one's loved ones.

Trauma can, but does not necessarily, lead to the development of characteristic disordered symptomatology, most commonly known as PTSD, a disorder which is included in both of the widely used classification systems, DSM-IV (APA, 1994) and the International Classification of Diseases (ICD-10; World Health Organization, 1994). The *essential feature of the experience* leading to the development of characteristic disordered symptomatology is described as "following exposure to an extreme traumatic stressor involving direct personal experience of an event that involves actual or threatened death or serious injury . . . *or learning about unexpected or violent death . . . or threat of death or injury experienced by a family member or other close associate*" (APA, 1994, p. 424).

## Bereavement

A bereavement can be defined as the situation of an individual who has recently experienced the loss of someone significant through that person's death. Some examples, as for trauma, come easily to mind: death of one's child, parent, spouse, sibling, or other person with whom one had a close, meaningful relationship. Others are less obvious, for example, in cases where a person suffers a loss that cannot be openly acknowledged, publicly mourned, or socially supported, such as in nontraditional love relationships (see Doka, 1989).

In contrast to PTSD, "bereavement" (i.e., the death of a loved one) is not classified in DSM-IV (APA, 1994) as a condition meriting recognition as a diagnostic category, but among "conditions that may be a focus for clinical attention" (so-called "V-codes"). It seems likely that this is a consequence of the general tendency to view bereavement as normal human experience. Nevertheless, there is strong pressure to create a category of pathological grief. It is beyond the scope of this chapter to go into this complex issue (see Horowitz, Bonanno, & Holen, 1993; Stroebe, van Son, Stroebe, Kleber, Schut, & van den Bout, unpublished manuscript).

## Trauma and Bereavement: Commonalities and Distinctions

What is the extent of overlap versus distinctiveness of the two phenomena? First we need to consider the nature of the two types of stressors. The first commonality is obvious: both trauma and bereavement are environmental stressors which have been shown to precipitate psychological disturbance in most and disorder in some individuals. The second derives from overlap of the two stressors: some bereavements (deaths) are traumatic, as in the case of a daughter raped and murdered. Some traumas are (also) bereavements: one's family wiped out in the holocaust.

Nevertheless, trauma and bereavement can be distinct phenomena. It is possible to experience trauma without bereavement: all members of a family survive an armed gun raid; and bereavement without trauma: the peaceful, expected death of a loved one who gradually slips away.

Second, distinctions in types of definition can be identified. It is noteworthy that trauma is typically defined in terms of the extremity of the life event; the enormity of the event itself is seen as critical to the degree of impact/outcome. To illustrate, it was formerly described, in DSM III-R (APA, 1980, p. 247), as an event "outside the range of usual human experiences (i.e., outside the range of such common experiences as simple bereavement . . .)". Bereavement, on the other hand, the "usual human experience" of the loss of a loved person, is defined in terms of the nature and closeness of the lost relationship, in addition to the extremity of the life event (sudden, traumatic bereavements are frequently considered to be the worst type). It will become evident that this makes an essential difference when the theoretical approaches to the two types of events are compared. We turn now to an examination of respective psychological reactions.

## STRESS RESPONSE SYNDROMES AND GRIEF MANIFESTATIONS

The terms trauma and bereavement refer to life events, following which individuals may become "traumatized" or "grief-stricken," in everyday language (specialists are cautious in their usage of such words). Both states incorporate psychological and/or physical patterns of reactions that prototypically (not inevitably) occur following the event, but which subside with time, and do not constitute, necessarily, negative health outcomes. These are referred to, respectively, as stress response syndromes (Horowitz, 1986) and manifestations of grief (Stroebe & Stroebe, 1987; Stroebe & Schut, 1994). These are outlined next.

### Stress Response Syndromes

Even normal manifestations following the experience of a traumatic event have been described as a "syndrome," and here Horowitz has been influential. In fact, knowledge about normal patterns of response largely derives from work on PTSD.

As mentioned above, the difference between normal and disordered reactions to trauma lies in the intensity and frequency rather than the type of reactions that occur: researchers regard them as lying on a continuum (van den Bout, Kleber, & Brom, 1991; Kleber & Brom, 1992, p. 190). For manifestations to become classified as a disorder they have to be more extreme: PTSD lasts much longer and gets blocked or aggravated. It is important to note that other pathological responses to traumatic events are possible (e.g., depressive reactions, anxiety disorders, dissociative reactions, and brief psychotic episodes).

Antithetical reactions of intrusion and denial are perhaps the most distinctive feature of trauma reactions to have been identified in contemporary scientific analyses. Horowitz (1986), on the one hand, identified *intrusion*, that is, compulsive reexperiencing of feelings and ideas to do with the event (sleep and dream disturbance, startle reactions, preoccupations, hypervigilance, inability to otherwise concentrate, searching behavior, review, and pangs of emotion). On the other hand, *avoidance* co-occurs, that is, denial and avoidance (including symptoms such as daze, evidence of disavowal, amnesia, selective inattention, frantic overactivity, inability to visualize memories, and numbing). These extreme deflections to "too much" or "too little" conscious experience may, according to Horowitz (Horowitz et al.,

1993), either be simultaneous manifestations or may show a sequence of phases, a conception which, though not always occurring, is basic to his model of coping.

It is probably true to say that Horowitz (see, e.g., 1986) sees the symptomatology of intrusion and denial as at the essence of psychological reactions following a traumatic event. However, also characteristic of PTSD responses are anxiety-provoking ideas, worry over loss of control, new phobias plus fear of repetition of the traumatic event, chronic tension, and hypervigilance (Horowitz, 1986).

## Grief Reactions

While Horowitz's approach to the identification of stress response symptomatology was through study of the minority of victims who suffer from PTSD, our analysis of the consequences of bereavement has been derived, for the most part, from nonclinical populations (cf. Stroebe & Stroebe, 1987). According to this, manifestations are dominated by negative affect, but also cover a wide range of *emotional, cognitive, behavioral, and physiological reactions* (these to some extent overlap). Affective manifestations include depressed mood, anxiety, guilt feelings, anger, anhedonia, and loneliness. Behavioral manifestations include agitation, fatigue, searching, crying, and social withdrawal. Cognitive manifestations include preoccupation with the deceased, lowered self-esteem, hopelessness, and retardation of thought and memory. Finally, physiological/somatic manifestations include loss of appetite, sleep disturbances, somatic complaints, and susceptibility to illness and disease. Not all of these symptoms appear in every bereaved person, nor at any one time across the duration of bereavement.

Included among the disorders for which bereaved people are at heightened risk are depression, anxiety disorders, somatic complaints, and infections (cf. Parkes, 1972/1996; Stroebe, Stroebe, & Hansson, 1993). DSM-IV (APA, 1994) states that as part of their reaction to loss, "some grieving individuals present with symptoms characteristic of a Major Depressive Episode" (p. 684), and yet, there are differences. Symptoms not characteristic of "normal" grief that also differentiate from a major depressive disorder were listed as: "(1) guilt about things other than actions taken by the survivor at the time of death; (2) thoughts of death other than the survivor feeling that he or she would be better off dead or should have died with the deceased person; (3) morbid preoccupation with worthlessness; (4) marked psychomotor retardation; (5) prolonged and marked functional impairment; and (6) hallucinatory experiences other than thinking that he or she hears the voice of, or transiently sees the image of, the deceased person" (APA, 1994, pp. 684–685).

There is further evidence from recent empirical work that indicates the need for a distinct category of complicated grief. Prigerson has identified a set of symptoms that are distinguishable from bereavement-related depression, and which are associated with enduring functional impairments (see, e.g., Prigerson et al., 1995). Symptoms of complicated grief included searching, yearning, preoccupation with thoughts of the deceased, crying, disbelief regarding the death, and lack of acceptance of the death. In Prigerson et al.'s (1995) analyses, the symptoms have much to do with the lost relationship and attachment to the deceased, but less with trauma symptomatology.

Despite such advances in understanding, it is nevertheless difficult to define "pathological grief." As a general guideline, one can say that pathological grief is a deviation from the (cultural) norm in the time course or intensity of specific or general symptoms of grief (cf. Stroebe & Schut, 1994). The deviation may occur with respect to the *timing* of specific or general symptomatology. There may be a blocking of certain thoughts and/or feelings; the bereaved person may also get stuck or "locked" with respect to one single aspect (e.g., guilt); something may have "gone wrong" in recovery; or there may be a "standing still" in the grief process.

## Commonalities and Distinctions between Traumatic Stress and Grief Responses

**Manifestations.** At first inspection, reactions following the two types of event look very different, and clearly, there are differences due to the very nature of each event: one cannot yearn for the deceased if there is no deceased. But one can yearn for a lost livelihood, or the use of one's limbs after spinal injury. There is also considerable overlap. Were we to apply Horowitz's categorization to non-traumatically bereaved persons, we would find much that would be an accurate description, and the same would be the case in applying the grief symptomatology categorization to nonbereavement trauma victims.

Furthermore, resemblance between reactions to the two events has been empirically shown. In a study conducted in the Netherlands, an evaluation was made of the proportion of conjugally bereaved persons who experienced post traumatic stress symptomatology. In this two-year longitudinal study, 50% of a bereaved sample met the criteria for PTSD at one of four data collection points, whereas 9% did so at all four points (Schut, de Keijser, van den Bout, & Dijkhuis, 1991).

Nevertheless, in each field, specific symptomatologies have been identified which reflect the scientific interpretation of each life event. In the trauma area, general patterns of symptoms (cognitions, memories, etc.) have been identified in relationship to the *stressfulness of the traumatic event itself and its aftermath.* Focus is on anxiety reactions. Bereavement research has concentrated on specific symptomatology due to *loss of an attachment figure.* Symptomatology (most centrally, depression) relates not only to the death event itself, but to life with the deceased. Trauma research has much to learn by considering aspects to do with the lost relationship, when this co-occurs, and bereavement has to include analysis of stressful components that are integral to bereavement.

**Intrusion-avoidance as symptom versus process**. An important difference in the scientific analyses of trauma and bereavement phenomena is that Horowitz analyzes intrusion-avoidance processes as *symptomatic* of traumatic reactions, whereas in the bereavement area, they have been regarded as *coping strategies*, and even as *coping styles*.

A fundamental difference has to do with the degree of *personal control* over intrusion-avoidance symptomatology that is experienced within the two types of loss. This concept, central to Horowitz's (1986) model of coping with trauma, and also of relevance to analyses of bereavement phenomena, will be discussed below.

**Comparative extremity of the impact of traumas and bereavements**. Since

Holmes and Rahe (1967) put loss of a loved one at the top of the list of stressful life events, bereavement has been repeatedly cited as the worst that can happen to one. Yet, as we saw, trauma and not bereavement is the life stressor that so far merits recognition as the precipitator of mental disorder in standard diagnostic classification manuals. Although one may be tempted to conclude that trauma, by its very definition, is generally more horrendous and impactful than bereavement, such conclusions must be drawn with great caution. In our view, discussion of the comparative severity of the impact of events in this context is not very fruitful.

**Determinants of adjustment to trauma and bereavement**. Just as both "bereavement" and "trauma" cover a myriad of different types of events, which impact variously on outcome, so, in both cases, do a number of scientifically identified additional factors act as determinants, including placement within other life events, the social and physical environmental context, the person's pre-existing personality structure and style(s) of coping (cf. Horowitz et al., 1993; Stroebe, Stroebe, & Hansson, 1993), to say nothing of trying to capture the fundamental but elusive "meaning of loss" factor, which is so intricately bound up with measures of adjustment that assessment is almost precluded.

**Detrimental health consequences following trauma and bereavement**. Both types of events have been shown quite conclusively to be associated with detrimental consequences to both psychological and physical health, and even with mortality (e.g., the early studies by Eitinger & Strom (1973) documenting excessive morbidity and mortality among Norwegian concentration camp survivors and Parkes (1972/1996) similarly, for bereaved husbands and wives). Recent reviews of outcome studies confirm these early results (see, e.g., Stroebe, Stroebe, & Hansson, 1993; Wilson & Raphael, 1993).

**Treatment of traumatic stress and grief reactions**. In cases where traumatic stress and grief reactions co-occur following exposure to a life event that is simultaneously traumatic and a bereavement, experts are of the opinion that it is *indeed necessary to deal with the traumatic component, which may block grief, before grieving for the lost person can be facilitated* (Raphael, Middleton, Martinek, & Misso, 1993). Nevertheless, in our view, there are unique components to bereavement adjustment that lead to different types of complication and that may also need specific intervention. Bereavement cannot simply be understood as a (less intense) traumatic event.

**Pathology**. Discussion of DSM categorization of the two phenomena (APA, 1994) indicated that there are also clear differences in views about what comprises pathology in each area. Reactions to traumatic life events are measured in terms of intensity of symptoms, reactions to bereavement (in addition) according to different types of complications. These bereavement complications have been linked to different types of attachment (Parkes, 1991). Although some researchers disagree (e.g., van den Bout et al., 1991), in our view pathological grief does not simply differ from normal grief in terms of intensity and duration of the symptoms. This, then, is in contrast to the type of complications assumed to follow traumatic events. However, each field has neglected the complications identified in the other. Given the overlap in the life experiences, this needs to be amended in both fields. Discussion of the theoretical models will make this clearer.

## MODELS OF COPING

### Stressor Life Events

Central to Horowitz's (1986) cognitive model is the analysis of regulatory control processes (active warding off or reexperiencing of aspects of the traumatic event) that occur if the situation (the trauma) cannot be altered. When this happens, ". . . the inner models or schemata must be revised so that they conform to the new reality" (Horowitz, 1979, p. 244). In the course of this processing, information (about the traumatic event) is regulated and reinterpreted. Beliefs and images about the self and others are reexamined, and new information is sought. Shifts in meanings and revision of the schemata take place. Associated emotions are repeatedly reduced or activated. Kleber and Brom (1992, p. 139) have succinctly described how these control processes operate:

> *Control processes work in such a way that the continuous representation of the event is inhibited or accelerated. Optimal control delays the intrusion and yields tolerable dosages of the new information and the emotions. This leads to an optimal alternation between denial and intrusion. . . . Thus completion can occur; inner models can adapt to reality.*

Following this model, too much control (denial or avoidance) prevents processing; with too little control (too much intrusion) one succumbs to continual rehearsal of the traumatic experience and excessive, fearful emotions.

Horowitz's observations (1986, p. 86) led him to view these stress response tendencies of intrusion and denial as occurring *in temporal phase*, which may overlap, vary in sequence, and be subject to individual differences. Abstracting a general stress response tendency, he described the following cognitive and emotional sequence: there is a phase of initial realization that a stressful event has occurred, often with a sharply accelerated expression of reactive emotion. This is followed by a phase of denial and numbness, which is succeeded by a mixed phase of denial and intrusive repetition in thought, emotion, and/or behavior. Then comes a phase of further ideational and emotional processing, working through, and acceptance (or stable defensive distortion), with a loss of either the denial or the peremptory recollection of the stress event. At the different phases, intense or prolonged experiences may become symptomatic with the following manifestations: overwhelmed reaction, panic or exhaustion, extreme avoidance, flooded states, psychosomatic responses, and character distortions (see Horowitz, 1986, p. 86 for a detailed account).

Those are the most relevant tenets of Horowitz's model with respect to the comparison with bereavement models. Next we describe what has been done in the latter field and begin to compare the two approaches.

### Bereavement

**Traditional models of coping with grief**. As in trauma research, models of coping with bereavement grew out of the psychoanalytic tradition. Central to traditional formulations has been the concept of "grief work." According to major theorists such as Freud (1917), Lindemann (1944), Parkes (1972/1996), Bowlby (1980), Raphael (Raphael & Nunn, 1988), in order to come to terms with the death of a loved one, one has to confront and work through the loss.

Thus, while Horowitz's model postulated "working through" as a phase of coping with trauma that succeeded intrusion and denial, in traditional analyses of coping with grief, this is not a phasal reaction but a strategy of coping that is associated with eventual recovery and adjustment. Also, in trauma research, denial processes have been recognized as necessary components, rather than impediments.

Also fundamental to traditional approaches to coping with bereavement have been conceptualizations of the grieving process in terms of *phases* or *tasks* (cf. Bowlby, 1980; Worden, 1982/1991). Again, the contrast with Horowitz's phasal conceptualization is evident. Formulations vary slightly from one researcher to another, but they typically postulate the following phases of grief (cf. Bowlby, 1980): (1) shock, associated with numbness and denial; (2) yearning and protest, as realization of the loss develops; (3) despair, accompanied by somatic and emotional upset and social withdrawal; (4) gradual recovery, marked by increased well-being and acceptance of loss. It is important to note that these should not be taken to imply a set, fixed, clear-cut, or prescriptive sequence.

Task models differ from the above in that there is more scope for variation both across time and between individuals, and in that more consideration is given to the griever as agentic in the recovery process (cf. Worden, 1982/1991). The tasks are: (1) accepting the reality of loss; (2) experiencing the pain of grief; (3) adjusting to an environment without the deceased; (4) and "relocating" the deceased emotionally and moving on with life.

So here, in contrast to Horowitz's model, denial is an initial reaction, not conceived of as periodically returning or fluctuating with intrusion. Apart from this, there is much similarity, including the symptomatology of fear, sadness, and rage (outcry) in the early stages of each coping process.

***Shortcomings of traditional models of coping with bereavement.*** We had a number of reasons to be dissatisfied with these traditional models of grief (Stroebe & Stroebe, 1991; Stroebe & Schut, 1995). In brief, these included the fact that: (1) they did not seem to be supported by our empirical results, neither in Germany nor here in the Netherlands; (2) they did not seem to reflect cross-cultural or historical differences in ways of coping with loss; (3) conceptualizations of "grief work" were indistinguishable from rumination processes or general negative affect.

Most important here, however, was the fact that denial processes were accorded a function in coming to terms with loss *only*, as noted above, in the initial phase, when reality is too painful and some dosage of realization necessary. Otherwise, emphasis has most certainly been on the dysfunctional consequences of denial, avoidance, suppression, and repression. This did not seem to reflect what was actually happening to bereaved people. Following analysis of our own data sets (Stroebe, Stroebe, & Schut, 1993; Stroebe & Stroebe, 1991), the analysis of denial processes that seemed to be needed was actually, in retrospect, more similar to Horowitz's formulation than to those of traditional grief models. In our view, analysis of coping with bereavement needed to include a finer-grained analysis of approach versus avoidance of thoughts and feelings connected with the loss of a loved one.

Rather than looking, as Horowitz did, primarily on the level of cognitive processing, we were initially guided by individual and subgroup differences that we observed between bereaved people, along what one might call the dimension of working through versus not working through grief. On the one hand, some people seemed to adopt a way of coping with grief by confronting it and going over details of the experience. On the other hand, some people seemed to avoid memories, distract themselves, and keep busy with other things, in an apparent effort to move on to new relationships and, it seemed, to try to put their loss behind them.

However, this was not the only shortcoming. Traditionally, following leads from both psychodynamic and attachment theory, focus has been on the tie or bond with the deceased, and on the lost relationship. Yet the bereavement experience incorporates much more than this. If we take a stress theory perspective, along the lines of Lazarus and Folkman (1984), it becomes clear that bereavement encompasses *secondary* stresses that need confrontation and that also impact on the course of adjustment and determine the ways that a person copes.

To summarize, it seemed to us that what was needed was not only (1) a more precise analysis of processes of coping with loss, but (2) a broadening of the perspective to include analysis of the differential tasks of grieving, not only those necessitated by the loss of the loved relationship directly, but also those that lead toward coping with the changes in the surrounding world consequent to the loss. With respect to the former interest, there is common ground between our theory and that of Horowitz for the trauma area, and there are possibilities for further integration of his cognitive, information-processing approach into our analysis. With respect to the latter, our differential task analysis may have something to offer the trauma field, as the following example illustrates. Consider items on the Impact of Event Scale, developed by Horowitz and his colleagues as a self-report instrument to measure the essential characteristics (intrusion-avoidance symptomatology) associated with stress disorders (Horowitz, Wilner, Kaltreider, & Alvarez, 1980). In the instructions and questionnaire items, reference is made throughout to "it," the traumatic event. Using this scale as a measure of approach-avoidance in bereavement is problematic: what is "it"? Adaptation necessitates specification of "the loved person" versus "circumstances surrounding the loss" or "the death event" or, also quite importantly, "the consequences of loss." The original scale also takes no account of confrontation-avoidance of current life stressors, from dealing with to avoiding financial trouble consequent to loss, to facing up to, versus retreat from, a society where one is the odd man (person) out.

**Development of the dual process model of coping with loss.** What evolved from these two types of concerns, on the one hand with coping phenomena, on the other with stressor definition, was our dual process model of coping with loss. It becomes evident that, in some ways, this model owes much to both the attachment approach, with its emphasis on the lost relationship, and stress theory, with its concentration on the demands imposed by stressful life events, and the resources that individuals bring to bear on such situations in order to cope. (See Figure 1.) The model, which is still at the stage of development and undergoing further em-

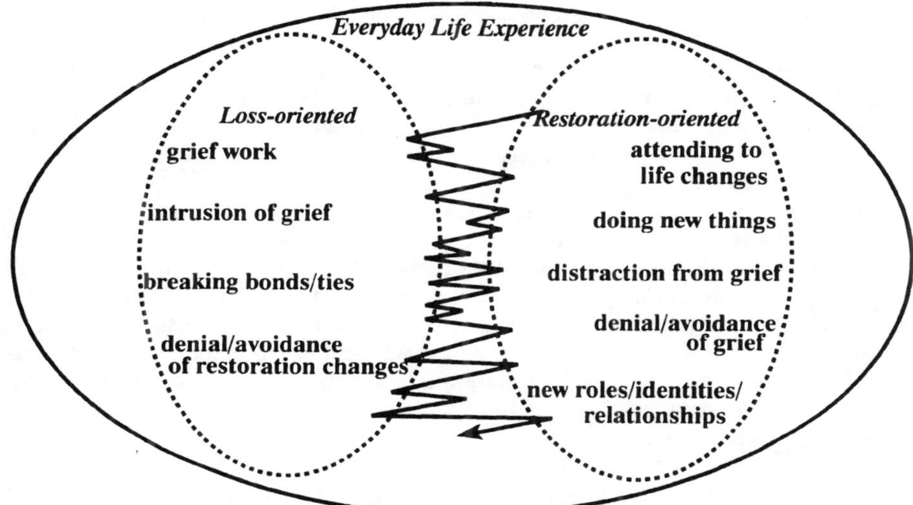


*Figure 1.* A Dual Process Model for Coping with Loss.

pirical examination, was formulated in the context of marital/partner bereavement. It may have potential application to other types of bereavement and loss, but, again, further research is necessary before such generalizations are made.

## Loss- and Restoration-Oriented Coping

This model incorporates two processes related to approach versus avoidance of grief, and approach versus avoidance of secondary stressors, which we call *loss-orientation* and *restoration-orientation.* So here already, our model differs from that of Horowitz: we have postulated two types of stressors that necessitate cognitive processing. The consequence is the possibility that *selective attention* occurs: rather than intrusion or avoidance of "it," in attending to the one, one avoids the other.

**Loss-orientation.** By loss-orientation we mean that a person is concentrating on, dealing with, and processing some aspect of the loss experience. Grief work falls within this dimension, as do rumination and yearning for the deceased, just thinking or talking about him or her, looking at photos, and imagining how he or she would react. Facing up to loss or crying over the death would also be part of this process. Confrontation with one's emotional reactions to the loss of the loved person and focusing on the personal meaning of what has happened are central features of loss orientation. There can also be a resistance to change (to restoration), reflected in a clinging to the past. It may be hard to accept that the old roles and routines have gone forever, and nostalgia may predominate.

In loss-orientation, it is, then, the lost relationship that is the focus of attention.

In our view, this aspect is what attachment theorists such as Bowlby (1980) have focused on.

**Restoration-orientation**. By contrast, the process less familiar, and certainly less explicit, in bereavement research and counselling, is that of restoration-orientation. When a loved one dies, not only do we grieve for him or her, we also have to adjust to substantial changes that are secondary consequences of loss. In the case of spousal bereavement, these may include attending to tasks that the deceased had previously undertaken, such as finances or the cooking. In focusing on these, one is not (or not directly) focusing on the emotional impact of the loss of the loved one. It incorporates learning to do things alone—learning to go places as a single person, not as part of a couple (and this, perhaps more than anything, may force confrontation again with the fact of loss). It means establishing new routines, fulfilling new roles, developing a new identity, and adjusting to an environment without the deceased; these are the things that we mean by "restoration." Perhaps stress/trauma perspectives have more to offer with respect to analysis of this type of orientation.

A number of points need to be made clear. (1) For most people, whatever the positive or negative consequences of either strategy, it is necessary to do both, that is, to cope with loss and with restoration concerns, since there have been massive changes within both spheres, following the death of a loved one. (2) The model accommodates individual differences: people differ in their patterns of coping on the loss-restoration dimension. For Horowitz, personality factors contribute to the magnitude of PTSD *symptomatology* (whether one does or does not develop the disorder), whereas for us, individual differences can be seen to impact on the *coping process* directly. The most obvious example is sex differences, where men are more restoration- and women more loss-oriented (Stroebe, Schut, & Stroebe, 1995). (3) The model is not limited to intrapersonal processes, as Horowitz's is; it enables analysis of interpersonal variables in facilitation versus hindrance of the grieving process. If, for example, one bereaved person is loss-oriented and a second is restoration-oriented, there may only be facilitation to the extent that oscillation is promoted. This would be concordant. Other concordant and discordant patterns can be derived. (4) In claiming that there is restoration-orientation, we are not simply assuming an absence of grief. It necessitates an attention to other *additional* tasks that are a consequence of having to adapt to change. In this respect, our model is compatible with Worden's (1982/1991) task model. (5) Although the tasks of restoration are not directly linked with emotional adjustment to loss of the loved person, the two are, of course, closely related: even as they necessitate distraction from grief, they bring about reminders of it, which may then lead to what we call *oscillation.*

## The Process of Oscillation

Critical to the formulation is the notion of *oscillation*. Bereaved people typically move between loss- and restoration-oriented coping. At times, they will be confronted by their loss; at others, they will avoid memories, be distracted, or seek relief by concentrating on other things.

This is not, in contrast to Horowitz's or the traditional grief models, a phasal model. However, the model easily incorporates a *time perspective* with regard to oscillation. There is typically more loss-orientation in the early days of bereavement, with a move toward more restoration-orientation as time goes on.

Why should there be this oscillation, this need for approach-avoidance of the two orientations? Horowitz, as we saw, regarded intrusion-denial processes as *regulatory*: controlling confrontation with the stressor. He listed impediments versus facilitators to working through stress which acted as controls on the flow of ideas. Our analysis, in contrast, has concentrated on processes that regulate oscillation itself, or reasons why there is shifting from one orientation to the other, for example, habituation, forgetting, distraction, or exhaustion (see Stroebe & Schut, 1995). For example, it may be necessary to habituate to loss through repeated exposure and confrontation, but on the other hand, it may be necessary to allow for forgetting, since there is a tendency for reactions to become weakened over time, if left inactivated (cf. Kruglanski, 1993).

## Coping and Pathology/Health Consequences

This brings us to the issue of the impact on health of the way that one copes. For Horowitz, the impact on health is almost synonymous with one type of disturbance of coping, that is, of involuntary, highly intense, intrusion-avoidance. It is indicative that Horowitz (Horowitz et al., 1993) sees pathological grief as a potential diagnostic disorder that could be included within PTSD stressor criteria. Our model, on the other hand, accommodates different types of pathological grief, in relationship to different ways of coping.

The principle of oscillation postulates that there needs to be movement between the two orientations. This is critical to "normal grieving," and one could speculate that this pattern is associated with secure attachment styles (see Parkes & Weiss, 1983; Parkes, 1991 for application of attachment theory to bereavement). We would argue that complications or pathology would occur if either (1) oscillation does not occur (and maybe this is easier when there is no trauma—the demands of the situation may be critically different here), or (2) there is (involuntary) disturbance within this process (which may happen when a bereavement is also a trauma).

(1) Oscillation could be said to not occur if there is relentless, obsessive rumination. Chronic grief would be exemplary of this type of pathology. In terms of the model, chronic grievers would be entirely, or very predominantly, "loss-oriented" in their coping. It is a matter for empirical verification whether these will be related to insecure styles of attachment and associated with dependent relationships.

At the other extreme, there can be very marked avoidance. There may be persistent suppression (or even a less voluntary repression) of memories and denial of the painful impact of death. One can see parallels here with the syndromes of "inhibited" or "delayed" grief (cf. Lindemann, 1944; Parkes & Weiss, 1983). Again, one would propose that these patterns are related to avoidant attachment styles, associated with compulsive self-reliance.

(2) In identifying disturbance of oscillation as a form of pathology (turbulence), we are talking about the type of disturbed processes that Horowitz identified: disturbed intrusion-avoidance. Following this, such disturbance could be regarded as only one of three types of complication.

## CONCLUSIONS

Patterns of resemblance versus distinction between the phenomena of trauma and bereavement, their symptomatology, and their scientific interpretation have been discussed. There is clear overlap between the two phenomena, such that there are good reasons to analyze grief within the scientific study of traumatic stress reactions and to explore the relevance of theoretical approaches to bereavement for more general application to the trauma field. Nevertheless, we have identified limitations in adopting a general trauma framework for the study of grief. Examination of the symptomatologies of grief and traumatic reactions shows considerable differences in typologies. It became clear that reactions to bereavement covered a different, broader range of manifestations than those that have been described following traumatic losses. Furthermore, it was argued that most trauma research emphasizes pathological rather than normal reactions. The latter approach is important for, after all, a large majority of bereaved people, although suffering intensely, do not have complicated reactions, generally adjusting in time to their changed situation. It is noteworthy that this is also the case following traumatic experiences. Overall, the percentage of individuals who suffer PTSD following exposure to a traumatic life experience is estimated at only 25% (Kleber & Brom, 1989).

Furthermore, in viewing phenomena from a "pathological" stance, trauma research has concentrated on one type of complication, namely, extreme intensity and/or duration of avoidance and intrusion. In the case of bereavement, additional complications have been identified, for example, chronic or delayed grief. When a trauma has included a lost relationship, it would be useful to incorporate analyses such as we have described for the bereavement research field.

Finally, we noted that trauma research does not distinguish different components in the nature of the stressor itself. Yet we argued, in the case of bereavement, that adjustment not only requires coming to terms with the loss of the loved one, but also dealing with secondary stressors, such as the need to develop new roles and a new identity. This influences the coping process. This conceptualization also marks a departure from traditional models of adjustment to bereavement, which, in our view, have failed to provide explanations of such dual components. These two coping orientations were described in *The Dual Process Model of Coping with Loss* (Stroebe & Schut, 1995). Our conclusion is that, although the scientific analysis of grief and grieving can profit from incorporation of scientific understanding of traumatic events in general, such a stressor-specific model is necessary to understand the phenomena associated with bereavement. Just as traditional theories of bereavement lack explanatory power, so, in our view, does the most influential model of trauma. Only part of the complex psychological process of adjustment to bereavement can be understood through the framework provided by models of coping with traumatic experiences such as that of Horowitz (1986). Nevertheless, we are well aware that our own conceptualization needs further refinement and empirical confirmation.

## REFERENCES

American Psychiatric Association (1980/1994). *Diagnostic and statistical manual of mental disorders* (3rd & 4th eds.; DSM III/IV). Washington, D.C.: APA.

Bowlby, J. (1980). *Attachment and loss. Vol. 3. Loss: Sadness and depression.* London: Hogarth.

Breuer, J., & Freud, S. (1895/1937). *Studies in hysteria.* Boston: Beacon Press.

Doka, K. J. (Ed.). (1989). *Disenfranchised Grief: Recognizing Hidden Sorrow.* Lexington, MA: Lexington Books, D.C. Heath & Company.

Eitinger, L., & Strom, A. (1973). *Mortality and morbidity after excessive stress.* New York: Humanities Press.

Freud, S. (1917). Mourning and melancholia. In J. Strachey (Ed. & Trans.), *Standard edition of the complete psychological works of Sigmund Freud.* London: Hogarth.

Holmes, T. H., & Rahe, R. H. (1967). The social readjustment rating scale. *Journal of Psychosomatic Research, 11,* 213–218.

Horowitz, M. J. (1979). Psychological responses to serious life events. In V. Hamilton & D. M. Warburton (Eds.), *Human stress and cognition: An information processing approach* (pp. 235–263). Chichester, UK: Wiley.

Horowitz, M. J. (1983). Psychological response to serious life events. In S. Breznitz (Ed.), *The denial of stress.* New York: International Universities Press.

Horowitz, M. J. (1986). *Stress response syndromes.* Northvale, NJ: Aronson.

Horowitz, M. J., Bonanno, G. A., & Holen, A. (1993). Pathological grief: Diagnosis and explanation. *Psychosomatic Medicine, 55,* 260–273.

Horowitz, M., Wilner, N., Kaltreider, N., & Alvarez, W. (1980). Signs and symptoms of post traumatic stress disorders. *Archives of General Psychiatry, 37,* 85–92.

Kleber, R., & Brom, D. (1989). Incidentie van posttraumatische stress-stoornissen na frontervaring, geweldmisdrijven, ongevallen en rampen. *Tijdschrift voor Psychiatrie, 31,* 675–691.

Kleber, R., & Brom, D. (1992). *Coping with trauma: Theory, prevention and treatment.* Amsterdam: Swets & Zeitlinger.

Kruglanski, A. (1993). Discussant's comments. In A. Baum (Chair), *Cognitive processes in traumatic life events.* Meeting of the American Psychological Society, Chicago, IL.

Lazarus, R., & Folkman, S. (1984). *Stress, appraisal, and coping.* New York: Springer-Verlag.

Lindemann, E. (1944). Symptomatology and management of acute grief. *American Journal of Psychiatry, 101,* 141–148.

Parkes, C. M. (1972/1986). *Bereavement: Studies of grief in adult life.* Harmondsworth: Penguin.

Parkes, C. M. (1991). Attachment, bonding, and psychiatric problems after bereavement in adult life. In C. M. Parkes, J. Stevenson-Hinde, & P. Marris (Eds.), *Attachment across the life cycle* (pp. 268–292). London: Routledge.

Parkes, C. M., & Weiss, R. (1983). *Recovery from bereavement.* New York: Basic Books.

Prigerson, H., Frank, E., Kasl, S., Reynolds, C., Anderson, M., Zubenko, G., Houck, P., George, C., & Kupter, D. (1995). Complicated grief and bereavement related depression as distinct disorders: Preliminary empirical validation in elderly bereaved spouses. *American Journal of Psychiatry, 152,* 22–30.

Raphael, B., Middleton, W., Martinek, N., & Misso, V. (1993). Counseling and therapy of the bereaved. In M. Stroebe, W. Stroebe, & R. O. Hansson (Eds.),

*Handbook of bereavement: Theory, research and intervention* (pp. 427–453). New York: Cambridge University Press.

Raphael, B., & Nunn, K. (1988). Counselling the bereaved. *Journal of Social Issues, 44,* 191–206.

Schut, H., de Keijser, J., van den Bout, J., & Dijkhuis, J. (1991). Post-traumatic stress symptoms in the first years of conjugal bereavement. *Anxiety Research, 4,* 225–234.

Stroebe, M., & Schut, H. (1994). Grief. In A. Manstead & M. Hewstone (Eds.), *Blackwell dictionary of social psychology.* London: Blackwell.

Stroebe, M., & Schut, H. (1995). *The Dual Process Model of Coping with Loss.* Paper presented at the International Work Group on Death, Dying and Bereavement, St. Catherine's College, Oxford, UK, June 26–29.

Stroebe, M., Schut, H., & Stroebe, W. (1995). *Gender difference in patterns of grieving: Evidence and explanations considered.* Paper presented at the Annual Conference of the British Psychological Society, Warwick, UK, April 1–4.

Stroebe, M., & Stroebe, W. (1991). Does "grief work" work? *Journal of Consulting and Clinical Psychology, 59,* 479–482.

Stroebe, M., Stroebe, W., & Hansson, R. O. (Eds.). (1993). *Handbook of bereavement: Theory, research, and intervention.* New York: Cambridge University Press.

Stroebe, W., & Stroebe, M. (1987). *Bereavement and health.* New York: Cambridge University Press.

Stroebe, W., Stroebe, M., & Schut, H. (1993). *Working through loss: Does it help?* Santa Barbara, CA: Society of Experimental Social Psychology.

Stroebe, M., van Son, M., Stroebe, W., Kleber, R., Schut, H., & van den Bout, J. *On the classification and diagnosis of pathological grief.* Unpublished manuscript.

van den Bout, J., Kleber, R., & Brom, D. (1991). Traumaverwerking en rouw: eenheid in verscheidenheid? In J. Winnubst, P. Schnabel, J. van den Bout, & M. van Son (Eds.), *De metamorfose van de klinische psychologie* (pp. 73–85). Assen: Van Gorcum.

Wilson, J. P., & Raphael, B. (Eds.). (1993). *International handbook of traumatic stress syndromes.* New York: Plenum.

Worden, (1982/1991). *Grief counseling and grief therapy: A handbook for the mental health practitioner.* New York: Springer-Verlag.

World Health Organization (1992). *The ICD-10 classification of mental and behavioral disorders: Clinical description and diagnostic guidelines.* Geneva: World Health Organization.

# II

## *LOSSES WITHIN CLOSE RELATIONSHIPS*

# 7

# *The Dissolution of Close Relationships*

***Susan Sprecher***
*Illinois State University*

***Beverly Fehr***
*University of Winnipeg*

A large proportion of relationships that go through a growth and development trajectory will, at some point, reverse and deteriorate. This deterioration can be either abrupt or long and drawn out; furthermore, it can be either temporary and later repaired or irrevocable and result in a permanent breakdown of the relationship. Because the dissolution of close relationships is one of the most painful human experiences, and one that can also have costs for society, it has received the attention of scientists from a variety of disciplines. Research on relationship dissolution has focused on three major issues: (1) What causes relationships to break up? (That is, why does one relationship endure and another end?) (2) What is the process by which relationships end? and (3) How do people respond and cope after a breakup? This brief chapter can only touch the surface of the voluminous literature on the breakup (vs. the stability) of marriages and other close relationships. In the first section, we describe types of dissolution. The second section is a review of the causes of relationship (in)stability, both from the researcher's perspective and from the perspective of those who suffer through a breakup. In the final section, we discuss the process and aftermath of relationship dissolution.

## TYPES OF RELATIONSHIP DISSOLUTION

There are many types of relationships that can end. Furthermore, the dissolution phase of a close relationship can be experienced in a variety of ways. In this section, we describe the landscape of types of relationship dissolution and conclude by discussing how common the various types of breakups may be.

### Types of Relationships that End

There are many different types of close relationships, but one major distinction is between familial (nonvoluntary) and nonfamilial (voluntary) relationships. Although the emotional ties between family members may be severed, rarely does one become an ex-parent or ex-sibling. Just as one cannot choose one's relatives, one usually does not have the option of dissolving a relationship with a relative.

However, we can terminate our nonfamilial close relationships, which are the majority of close relationships most people develop over a lifetime. All voluntary close relationships have in common that the two members chose to enter the relationship and interdependence developed between them over time (e.g., Kelley et al., 1983). However, there are also distinctions among types of voluntary close relationships; the causes, the process, the aftermath, and how others react to a breakup are likely to differ as a function of the particular type of relationship. Voluntary close relationships can be distinguished in the following ways (Blumstein & Kollock, 1988; Marsiglio & Scanzoni, 1995): (1) sexual-romantic versus nonsexual-romantic; (2) shared legal status versus no legal status; (3) cohabiting versus noncohabiting; and (4) opposite-sex versus same-sex.

Most of the research on relationship dissolution has focused on the termination of marriage, which is usually a sexual/romantic, shared legal status, cohabiting, and opposite-sex relationship. However, other types of relationships end: dating heterosexual and homosexual couples, cohabiting heterosexual and homosexual couples, roommates, and friendships. Although it may take two partners to develop a relationship and create the interdependencies necessary to make it close, it takes only one member of the dyad to end the relationship. Thus, for one partner, the dissolution may be nonvoluntary, which can have a significant impact on the level of distress experienced, a topic we return to later.

## Types of Endings

Relationship dissolution is usually thought of as a dichotomous variable: a particular relationship either has terminated or has not. For example, in prospective studies of the determinants of relationship dissolution, researchers survey individuals or couples involved in a relationship and then contact them on at least one other occasion to assess the state of their relationship. Relationship state at the second or later wave of the study is usually operationalized as "broken-up" versus "still together." However, with the exception of legal divorce in the dissolution of marriage (one either has a legal divorce or does not), relationship dissolution is much more complex than an either-or distinction. The following factors or perspectives illustrate the complexity of relationship dissolution.

**Precursors to the final breakup**. Even before a relationship is defined by its members as officially over, the members engage in dissolution-type behaviors and cognitions. Some relationship theorists (Altman & Taylor, 1973; Baxter, 1983; Knapp, 1978) have speculated that the precursors to a breakup are the behaviors displayed in the growth stage in reverse. For example, because breadth and depth of self-disclosure and familiarity increase in the growth stage (Altman & Taylor, 1973), it has been argued that there is a reverse stage in which familiarity and self-disclosure decrease. However, only limited support has been found for this "reversal hypothesis" (Baxter, 1983, 1985; Baxter & Wilmot, 1986). Instead, the disengagement stage for most relationships seems to be characterized by particular behaviors that do not reflect the mirror image of what occurred in the growth stages (e.g., Bohannon, 1970; Edwards, Johnson, & Booth, 1987; Vaughan, 1986). These behaviors include complaining to the partner, seeking outside support, and beginning new relationships. They may occur over a period of time and are part of the breakup process even if some marking event (e.g., a legal divorce, the declaration that the relationship is officially over) has not yet occurred.

**Redefining relationships.** Some close relationships serve more than one role to its members. In many dating and marital relationships, for example, the two are each other's best friends (Hendrick & Hendrick, 1993; Schwartz, 1994). When the romantic/sexual aspect of such a relationship ends, the relationship may be redefined as a friendship rather than completely terminated (Ahrons & Wallisch, 1987; Juhasz, 1979; Metts, Cupach, & Bejlovec, 1989). In many cases, ex-partners continue to see each other as friends and support each other, although they have experienced the termination of the romantic/sexual aspect of their relationship (e.g., Masheter, 1991; Metts & Cupach, 1995).

**Active-to-passive ties.** Many friendships do not have a clear-cut dissolution point but rather simply "fade away," often without the friends' awareness (Fehr, 1996; Rose, 1984). The reduced interaction can be due to physical separation or other external factors (new friends or romantic involvements). The "fading away" can be conceptualized as a transition from active to passive ties, a distinction made by sociologists Marsiglio and Scanzoni (1995) in their conceptual model of primary relationships and network ties. We may not interact on a frequent basis with friends from an earlier period of our lives, but we view them as available to us if we need them, and often believe we can pick up where we left off, even if many years have passed since our last interaction. Furthermore, the endings of many dating relationships and marriages, particularly if they were amicable, might also be considered a shift from active to passive ties. Ex-romantic or ex-marital partners may continue to view each other as available for support and interaction.

## How Common are Various Types of Dissolution?

Fortunately, the breakup of a long-lasting and meaningful relationship does not occur very often in most people's lives. However, we speculate that almost everyone has experienced the dissolution of at least one very close relationship, and the majority of people have experienced multiple breakups. Furthermore, the redefinition of relationships (e.g., from best friend to a less important friend) and shifts from active to passive ties probably occur frequently for most people, particularly during young adulthood and middle age, when there is considerable mobility in geographic locations and job positions and movement in and out of organizations and clubs.

Of all types of relationship dissolutions, legal divorces are easiest to document. The divorce rate is calculated in various ways, but sociologists and demographers often report the *refined divorce rate*, which is the number of divorces in a year per 1,000 married women (or per marriages). Another common way of calculating a divorce rate is the number of divorces in a year per 1,000 people, which is called the *crude divorce rate*. There were 1.175 million divorces in 1990 in the U.S., which translates to a crude divorce rate of 4.70 and a refined divorce rate of 20.7. The divorce rate, regardless of how it is calculated, has been increasing dramatically in the past 50 years in most western nations as well as in preindustrial societies (Goode, 1993). The rate is higher in the U.S. than in most other industrial nations, including Canada, where the crude divorce rate was 3.05 in 1990. Demographers (e.g., Martin & Bumpass, 1989) have used current rates of divorce to estimate that one-half to two-thirds of new marriages in the U.S. will end in divorce.

The breakups of dating and cohabiting relationships are much more common, although nonmarital relationship dissolutions are not publically recorded. Evidence for the frequency of the dissolution of dating relationships comes from longitudinal studies of dating relationships. In their classic longitudinal study of 231 dating couples from the Boston area, Hill, Rubin, and Peplau (1976) found that 103 (45%) of the couples had ended their relationship over a two-year period. They also conducted a 15-year followup and found that 148 (64%) of the original couples were no longer together (Peplau, Hill, & Rubin, 1993). A similar rate was found in a more recent longitudinal study of dating couples conducted at Illinois State University (see Sprecher, 1994). Of the 101 dating couples who were surveyed annually over a four-year period, 60 couples (59%) broke up by the last contact. Most other longitudinal studies of dating relationships have followed couples for only a period of a few months, and have also provided evidence for the fragility of dating relationships (e.g., Felmlee, Sprecher, & Bassin, 1990; Simpson, 1987).

Cohabiting relationships are also not very stable. In an early review of the cohabitation literature, Macklin (1983) reported that 35% to 45% of U.S. cohabiting relationships break up within six months (see also, Bumpass, Sweet, & Cherlin, 1991). In a report based on the Boston Dating Couples study, Risman, Hill, Rubin, and Peplau (1981) found that the dissolution rate of the cohabiting couples in the sample was approximately the same as that for the dating (non-cohabiting) couples.

Of all types of sexual/romantic relationships, homosexual relationships may be least stable of all. In their *American Couples* study, Blumstein and Schwartz (1983) resurveyed some of the respondents from their national sample two years after the original study. Forty-eight percent of their lesbian sample, 36% of the gay respondents, 29% of the heterosexual cohabitors, and 14% of the married couples had broken up over the two-year period. However, breakups were rare across all couple types among those who had been together for more than 10 years. (Other studies conducted with lesbians and gays report that long-lasting relationships are common among the older respondents [as reported in Peplau, 1991].)

Friendships, too, are susceptible to termination, particularly when the partners experience changes in their lives such as moving away, romantic involvement, parenthood, retirement, and so on (e.g., Fehr, in press). In a study of college students' friendships, more than half of the participants (57.4%) reported losing at least one close friend in the previous five years (Rose, 1984). Among single and married undergraduate and graduate students, each respondent had experienced the dissolution of a close friendship, although only 27% reported that a best friendship had ended (Rose & Serafica, 1986).

## WHY RELATIONSHIPS END

Various theoretical and conceptual approaches identify factors that contribute to the likelihood of relationship dissolution. Most of these approaches are focused on explaining divorce and are rarely applied to the dissolution of other types of close relationships (Kurdek, 1993). However, one exception is the social exchange or interdependence approach in social psychology, which includes various models of commitment. In the first section below, we describe this theoretical approach to relationship dissolution. Then, we present a summary of findings from empirical investigations that have examined variables that predict or are associated with breakups.

## Social Psychological Models

A number of theories are relevant to the dissolution of relationships (e.g., Perlman & Fehr, 1986, 1987), although social exchange theories have generated the most research. The basic premise of these theories is that people calculate rewards and costs in relationships. Further, it is postulated that people will feel satisfied in relationships to the extent that outcomes are positive (rewards exceed costs). The variables that predict dissolution of relationships vary somewhat depending on the model that is being discussed.

According to interdependence theory (Kelley & Thibaut, 1978; Thibaut & Kelley, 1959), people develop a sense of the rewards and costs they feel they deserve in a relationship. This comparison level is the standard used to evaluate outcomes in a current relationship. If outcomes meet this standard, people will be satisfied with a relationship; if outcomes fall below this standard, they will be dissatisfied. Whether or not people remain in relationships is determined by another standard, the comparison level for alternatives. People will end a relationship if they perceive that more attractive alternatives are available to them. If not, they will remain in a relationship, even if they feel dissatisfied.

Rusbult's (1980a, 1980b) investment model is an extension of interdependence theory. She predicted that people will be committed to relationships to the extent that they are satisfied (rewards outweigh costs), attractive alternatives are not available, and they have invested in the relationship. Investments are defined as resources (e.g., time, money, emotional energy) that could not be recovered if the relationship ended. These variables in combination have been found to predict commitment to romantic relationships (e.g., Rusbult, 1980a), friendships (Rusbult, 1980b), gay and lesbian relationships (e.g., Duffy & Rusbult, 1986), and marital relationships (Rusbult, Johnson, & Morrow, 1986).

Finally, equity theorists (e.g., Hatfield, Traupmann, Sprecher, Utne, & Hay, 1985; Sprecher & Schwartz, 1994; Walster [Hatfield], Walster, & Berscheid, 1978) maintain that people do not calculate reward/cost ratios in isolation, but rather in reference to their partner's outcomes. An equitable relationship is one in which a person believes his or her outcomes are comparable to those of his or her partner. People who believe their partner's outcomes are more positive than their own are classified as underbenefitted, whereas those who believe their outcomes exceed those of their partner are categorized as overbenefitted. The theory predicts that people attempt to restore equity in inequitable (either over- or underbenefitted) relationships. If these efforts are unsuccessful, the relationship is likely to dissolve. Perceived equity has been found to influence commitment in dating relationships (Sprecher, 1988), marital relationships (e.g., Sabatelli & Cecil-Pigo, 1985), and friendships (Berg, 1984).

## Research on Causes of Relationship Dissolution

What causes relationships to end? Three major types of methodological designs have been used to address this question. Each design has focused on slightly different types of causal variables.

**Demographic studies of divorce**. In one type of design, national probability data sets are used to identify the demographic and background variables associated with having obtained a legal divorce. According to this research, the following demographic and background variables are associated with the greater likelihood of a marriage ending in legal divorce: lower socioeconomic status, unemployment of husband, younger age at marriage, premarital pregnancy, no or few children, cohabitation prior to marriage, parental divorce, being Afro-American, living in an urban area, and low level of religiosity (for a review, see White, 1990). This demographic research has identified which social groups are at greater risk for divorce, but has been largely atheoretical. Most of the demographic variables are hypothesized to be related to divorce due to an accumulation of stress or due to divorce-proneness that develops based on earlier experiences (e.g., having divorced parents).

**Prospective studies**. In a second type of design, researchers have conducted prospective (longitudinal) studies with one or both members of close dyads and examined how variables measured at the first wave, and occasionally at other early waves of a multiple-wave study, predict relationship stability over time or distinguish between the group that remains together and the group that breaks up. These studies are often designed for multiple purposes, and the identification of predictors of breakup may not become an articulated goal until the study has continued long enough to have a significant number of breakups. A majority of the prospective studies have been based on samples of dating individuals because of the higher rate of breakups among daters. However, analysis of longitudinal data on predictors of dissolution has also been conducted for marital relationships (e.g., Kurdek, 1993), homosexual couples (Kurdek, 1992), and friendship pairs (Griffin & Sparks, 1990). In prospective studies, the variables most commonly examined for their association with relationship dissolution are social psychological factors referring to aspects of the relationship (e.g., exchange) or feelings about the partner or the relationship (e.g., satisfaction). Some of these studies have been designed specifically to test the commitment models described above (e.g., Rusbult, 1983).

Most longitudinal studies that have included satisfaction and commitment as predictors of relationship stability have found that romantic or friendship pairs who are more satisfied and more committed at one time are less likely to break up later (Attridge, Berscheid, & Simpson, 1995; Kurdek, 1993; Rusbult, 1983; Sacher & Fine, 1996; Simpson, 1987). Feelings of love have also been found to be higher among pairs who stay together than among those who break up (Berg & McQuinn, 1986; Hill et al., 1976). Several studies have found that variables referring to interdependence, exchange, and other relationship dimensions have been found to be predictive of relationship longevity. The exchange variable that has been most consistently correlated with the dissolution of romantic relationships is quality of alternatives—those who perceive they have more and better alternatives are more likely to end their relationship (Berg & McQuinn, 1986; Felmlee et al., 1990;

Sacher & Fine, 1996). Other relationship variables that have been found to be predictive of relationship longevity in at least some studies include reward level (Lloyd, Cate, & Henton, 1984), amount of time spent together (Felmlee et al., 1990), self-disclosure (Berg & McQuinn, 1986; Sprecher, 1987), sexual involvement in the relationship (Simpson, 1987), interdependence and closeness (Attridge et al., 1995), dependency (Attridge, Berscheid, & Sprecher, 1998), and investments into the relationship (Attridge et al., 1995).

The external environment has also been found to affect the likelihood that a relationship will endure over time. In addition to the effect discussed earlier for alternatives available in one's social environment, positive reactions of family and friends to the relationship can decrease the likelihood that a relationship will terminate over time (e.g., Felmlee et al., 1990; Parks & Adelman, 1983; Sprecher & Felmlee, 1993).

**Retrospective studies**. Finally, in another type of study, individuals who have experienced a breakup are asked to provide their perspective on why the relationship ended, either by writing a detailed account (e.g., Cupach & Metts, 1986) or by responding to an investigator-provided list of reasons (e.g., Sprecher, 1994). In addition, in-depth interviews have been conducted with individuals who have experienced a relationship dissolution (e.g., Vaughan, 1986). Studies that focus on the insider perspective indicate that most people can construct an explanation for their breakup and that ex-partners have some agreement about the reasons for the breakdown of their relationship (Hill et al., 1976; Sprecher, 1994). The reasons people most frequently give for dissolution of a dating relationship have to do with interaction or communication processes (e.g., "communication problems"); incompatibility or dissimilarity is also a common reason (e.g., Sprecher, 1994). Studies done with divorced individuals have highlighted other reasons as well, including sexual infidelity, alcoholism, and financial problems (for a review, see White, 1990). When people are asked why a friendship ended, physical separation (one friend moving away) is a frequently mentioned reason, although it appears to be a more common explanation for the ending of casual friendships than of best friendships. Other reasons for the dissolution of friendships include involvement in a romantic relationship, the discovery of dissimilarities, and betrayal (e.g., Rose, 1984; Rose & Serafica, 1986). In this volume, Felmlee (Chapter 8) discusses how, in some relationship breakups, the qualities that are disliked in an ex-partner (and often presumed to contribute to the breakup) are related to the qualities that were initially attractive in the partner; Felmlee defines these as "fatal attractions." For example, a person may be initially attracted to someone because he or she is "successful" but later end the relationship because of his or her unavailability.

## THE PROCESS AND AFTERMATH OF RELATIONSHIP ENDINGS

### Process Models of Relationship Endings

The termination of a relationship is not a single, discrete event, but rather a multiphase process. According to Duck (1982), the first stage of relationship dissolution is the intrapsychic phase, in which the dissatisfied person privately mulls over his or her concerns with his or her partner, evaluates the relationship, and begins to consider the costs of withdrawing, availability of alternatives, and so on. In the next phase, the dyadic phase, the dissatisfied partner communicates that she or he is unhappy in the relationship and both partners engage in relationship talks. The outcome of these discussions may be a decision to make repair attempts or to dissolve the relationship. If the latter course is chosen, the social phase is entered. This phase involves informing members of the pair's social networks of the dissolution and working out details of the post-termination relationship between the partners and members of their respective social networks. The final phase, which is called the grave dressing phase, involves rehearsing and polishing accounts of the breakup for public distribution, forming final attributions about what went wrong, and so on.

Other theorists and researchers of relationship dissolution have also postulated that relationship dissolution occurs in stages (Bohannon, 1970; Knapp, 1984; Vaughan, 1986). Most stage or process models focus on the experience from the initiator's perspective.

## Strategies for Disengagement

How do people disengage from a relationship they no longer wish to continue? Baxter (1982) identified four major strategies for disengaging from romantic relationships and friendships: withdrawal/avoidance, positive tone (e.g., trying to prevent "hard feelings"), manipulatory strategies (e.g., asking a third party to bear the news), and open confrontation. For both types of relationships, participants reported that they would be most likely to use positive tone strategies, followed by withdrawal/avoidance. Generally, people are much more likely to use passive strategies such as withdrawal and avoidance to end relationships than active strategies such as directly communicating one's desire to terminate the relationship. Passive, indirect strategies are especially likely to be used when dissolving a friendship (see Fehr, 1996). For example, in one study, 72% of strategies participants reported using to disengage from a friendship were indirect (see Baxter, 1979). In contrast, dating and marital relationships tend not to simply fade away, particularly when only one partner desires the termination. Thus, the termination of these kinds of relationships may require the use of more direct strategies (see, e.g., Baxter, 1985).

## The Distress After a Breakup

The breakup of a close relationship can be one of life's most distressing events. Although no research, to our knowledge, has compared the level of distress experienced as a result of different types of breakups, it is assumed that the breakup of marriage is particularly distressing (Holmes & Rahe, 1967), in part because the two lives were so deeply intertwined. However, Orbuch (1992) has argued that the dissolution of dating and cohabiting relationships can be as painful or more painful than divorce because these nonmarital relationship endings are less socially recognized. Similarly, the ending of a friendship may be particularly distressful because others may not acknowledge it as a painful event. One new type of relationship ending that may be the least socially recognized is the termination of a "relationship" that was developed and sustained over electronic mail or another form of computer-mediated communication. Also not socially recognized but very painful is the ending that occurs when one realizes that a relationship exists only in one's own mind and that the other will never reciprocate one's feelings of love (Baumeister & Wotman, 1992).

In addition to the type of relationship, many other factors are likely to be related to the extent of distress individuals experience after a relationship breakup. Most breakups are nonmutual; thus, there are two roles, the "leaver" and the "left" (Hill et al., 1976; Sprecher, 1994; Vaughan, 1986; Weiss, 1975). Not surprising, research indicates that the person who is left experiences more distress than the person who leaves (Frazier & Cook, 1993; Gray & Silver, 1990; Sprecher, 1994).

The quality of the relationship while it was intact also affects how distressed the individuals become after the breakup. Berscheid (1983) has predicted that the extent to which individuals experience distress after a breakup is related to the degree to which the relationship facilitated one's goals (i.e., a more rewarding and more interdependent relationship is associated with greater post-dissolution distress). Furthermore, the investment model (e.g., Rusbult, 1983) has been used to predict not only relationship stability (as mentioned earlier) but also the distress following a relationship termination. In support of these predictions, greater interdependence and closeness, longer duration of the relationship, and lack of alternatives are associated with greater distress experienced after a breakup (Frazier & Cook; 1993; Orbuch, 1992; Simpson, 1987; Sprecher, Felmlee, Metts, Fehr, & Vanni, in press).

## Coping and Moving On

According to Brehm (1985), there is a continuum of reactions to the dissolution of a relationship. At one end, there are situations in which the dissolution of a relationship was unpredictable and uncontrollable. Situations where a person has a sense of understanding and feels in control of the breakup anchors the other end. Breakups where a person has some understanding of what went wrong, but feels powerless to change the situation (e.g., their partner had already made the decision to leave) fall in the middle. Brehm (1985) suggests that adjustment to the ending of a dissolution may parallel this continuum, with the poorest adjustment in situations where there is neither understanding nor control. A loss of control and the finality associated with death may be reasons the loss of a close other through death is usually more painful than the loss through relationship dissolution (e.g., Holmes & Rahe, 1967).

Research on account-making (see, e.g., Weber & Harvey, 1994) shows that after a relationship ends, obsession may become a primary activity as people try to make sense of what went wrong. For example, Weiss (1975) documented that people experiencing a marital separation frequently ruminated over the causes of the demise of their marriage. Once an account had been constructed, there was generally a reduction in the level of distress. The development of an account may be a significant element in the coping process because it brings some coherence or understanding to what may have been a chaotic, heart-wrenching, confusing event.

Understanding the event provides some reassurance that one is not destined to repeat the experience in the future (even though, of course, the account may lack veridicality). Thus, accounts may enable people to progress from the lack-of-understanding end of Brehm's continuum, and in so doing, improve their adjustment to the dissolution. Individuals cope with a distressing breakup in a number of other ways as well: by seeking advice and social support from friends, family, and professionals, and by beginning new activities (Orbuch, 1992).

Even though people may be devastated by the loss of a relationship, they generally move on and develop new ones. The high rate of remarriage (60%–80%, depending on gender, ethnic group, and age at divorce) attests to the basic optimism or resiliency of the human spirit. In a study of friendship loss, 35% of the participants reported the dissolution of a friendship since they had entered college. In many cases, the loss was accompanied by considerable sadness and regret. Importantly, 37% also reported that they had formed one or more new friendships (Rose, 1984; see also Duck & Miell, 1986). These new relationships can be a significant source of joy and satisfaction in people's lives.

## CONCLUSION

In this chapter, we have discussed the various meanings of relationship dissolution, the fragility of different types of relationships, the factors that contribute to (or predict) the breakdown versus the stability of close relationships, and the process and aftermath of breakups. Although relationship dissolution, similar to other losses discussed in this volume, is a painful experience, the human need for connectedness motivates people to seek out and develop new relationships. Furthermore, the dissolution of one relationship is buffered by the rewards that continue to come from other close relationships.

## REFERENCES

Ahrons, C. R., & Wallisch, L. S. (1987). The relationship between former spouses. In D. Perlman & S. W. Duck (Eds.), *Intimate relationships: Development, dynamics, and deterioration* (pp. 269–294). Beverly Hills, CA: Sage.

Altman, I., & Taylor, D. A. (1973). *Social penetration: The development of interpersonal relationships.* New York: Holt, Rinehart & Winston.

Attridge, M., Berscheid, E., & Simpson, J. A. (1995). Predicting relationship stability from both partners versus one. *Journal of Personality and Social Psychology, 69,* 254–268.

Attridge, M., Berscheid, E., & Sprecher, S. (1998). Measuring dependency and insecurity in romantic relationships: Development and validation of two self-report scales. *Personal Relationships, 5,* 31–58.

Baumeister, R. F., & Wotman, S. R. (1992). *Breaking hearts: The two sides of unrequited love.* New York: Guilford.

Baxter, L. A. (1979). Self-disclosure as a relationship disengagement strategy: An exploratory investigation. *Human Communication Research, 5,* 215–222.

Baxter, L. A. (1982). Strategies for ending relationships: Two studies. *Western Journal of Speech Communication, 46,* 223–241.

Baxter, L. A. (1983). Relationship disengagement: An examination of the reversal hypothesis. *The Western Journal of Speech Communication, 47,* 85–98.

Baxter, L. A. (1985). Accomplishing relationship disengagement. In S. Duck & D. Perlman (Eds.), *Understanding personal relationships* (pp. 243–265). London: Sage.

Baxter, L. A., & Wilmot, W. (1986). Interaction characteristics of disengaging, stable, and growing relationship. In R. Gilmour & S. W. Duck (Eds.), *The emerging field of personal relationships* (pp. 145–159). Hillsdale, NJ: Lawrence Erlbaum.

Berg, J. H. (1984). The development of friendship between roommates. *Journal of Personality and Social Psychology, 46,* 346–356.

Berg, J. H., & McQuinn, R. D. (1986). Attraction and exchange in continuing and noncontinuing dating relationships. *Journal of Personality and Social Psychology, 50,* 942–952.

Berscheid, E. (1983). Emotion. In H. H. Kelley, E. Berscheid, A. Christensen, J. H. Harvey, T. L. Huston, G. Levinger, E. McClintock, L A. Peplau, & D. R. Peterson (Eds.), *Close relationships* (pp. 110–168). New York: Freeman.

Blumstein, P., & Kollock, P. (1988). Personal relationships. *Annual Review in Sociology, 14,* 467–490.

Blumstein, P., & Schwartz, P. (1983). *American couples.* New York: Morrow.

Bohannon, P. (1970). The six stations of divorce. In P. Bohannon (Ed.), *Divorce and after* (pp. 33–62). Garden City, NY: Doubleday.

Brehm, S. S. (1985). *Intimate relationships.* New York: McGraw-Hill.

Bumpass, L., Sweet, J., & Cherlin, A. J. (1991). The role of cohabitation in declining rates of marriage. *Journal of Marriage and the Family, 53,* 913–927.

Cupach, W. R., & Metts, S. (1986). Accounts of relational dissolution: A comparison of marital and non-marital relationships. *Communication Monographs, 53,* 311–334.

Duck, S. (1982). A topography of relationship disengagement and dissolution. In S. W. Duck (Ed.), *Personal relationships. Vol. 4: Dissolving personal relationships*. New York: Academic Press.

Duck, S., & Miell, D. (1986). Charting the development of personal relationships. In R. Gilmour & S. Duck (Eds.), *The emerging field of personal relationships* (pp. 133–143). Hillsdale, NJ: Lawrence Erlbaum.

Duffy, S. M., & Rusbult, C. E. (1986). Satisfaction and commitment in homosexual and heterosexual relationships. *Journal of Homosexuality, 12,* 1–23.

Edwards, J. N., Johnson, D. R., & Booth, A. (1987). Coming apart: A prognostic instrument of marital breakup. *Family Relations, 36,* 168–170.

Fehr, B. (1996). *Friendship processes.* Thousand Oaks, CA: Sage.

Fehr, B. (in press). Commitment and stability in friendships. In W. H. Jones & J. M. Adams (Eds.), *Handbook of interpersonal commitment and relationship stability*. New York: Plenum.

Felmlee, D., Sprecher, S., & Bassin, E. (1990). The dissolution of intimate relationships: A hazard model. *Social Psychology Quarterly, 53,* 13–30.

Frazier, P. A., & Cook, S. W. (1993). Correlates of distress following heterosexual relationship dissolution. *Journal of Social and Personal Relationships, 10,* 55–67.

Goode, W. J. (1993). *World changes in divorce patterns.* New Haven, CT: Yale University Press.

Gray, J. D., & Silver, R. C. (1990). Opposite sides of the same coin: Former spouses' divergent perspectives in coping with their divorce. *Journal of Personality and Social Psychology, 59,* 1180–1191.

Griffin, E., & Sparks, G. G. (1990). Friends forever: A longitudinal exploration of intimacy in same-sex pairs and platonic pairs. *Journal of Social and Personal Relationships, 7,* 29–46.

Hatfield, E., Traupmann, J., Sprecher, S., Utne, M., & Hay, J. (1985). Equity and intimate relations: Recent research. In W. Ickes (Ed.), *Compatible and incompatible relationships* (pp. 91–117). New York: Springer-Verlag.

Hendrick, S. S., & Hendrick, C. (1993). Lovers as friends. *Journal of Social and Personal Relationships, 10,* 459–466.

Hill, C. T., Rubin, Z., & Peplau, L. A. (1976). Breakups before marriage: The end of 103 affairs. *Journal of Social Issues, 32,* 147–168.

Holmes, T. H., & Rahe, R. (1967). The social readjustment scale. *Journal of Psychosomatic Research, 11,* 213–218.

Juhasz, A. M. (1979). A concept of divorce: Not busted bond but severed strand, *Alternative Lifestyles, 2,* 471–482.

Kelley, H. H., Berscheid, E., Christensen, A., Harvey, J. H., Huston, T. L., Levinger, G., McClintock, E., Peplau, L. A., & Peterson, D. R. (1983). Analyzing close relationships. In H. H. Kelley et al. (Eds.), *Close relationships* (pp. 20–67). New York: Freeman.

Kelley, H. H., & Thibaut, J. E. (1978). *Interpersonal relations: A theory of interdependence.* New York: Wiley.

Knapp, M. L. (1978). *Social intercourse: From greeting to goodbye.* Boston: Allyn and Bacon.

Knapp, M. L. (1984). *Interpersonal communication and human relationships.* Boston: Allyn and Bacon.

Kurdek, L. A. (1992). Relationship stability and relationship satisfaction in cohabiting gay and lesbian couples: A prospective longitudinal test of the contextual and interdependence models. *Journal of Social and Personal Relationships, 9,* 125–142.

Kurdek, L. A. (1993). Predicting marital dissolution: A 5-year prospective longitudinal study of newlywed couples. *Journal of Personality and Social Psychology, 64,* 221–242.

Lloyd, S. A., Cate, R. M., & Henton, J. M. (1984). Predicting premarital relationship stability: A methodological refinement. *Journal of Marriage and the Family, 46,* 71–76.

Macklin, E. D. (1983). Nonmarital heterosexual cohabitation: An overview. In E. D. Macklin & R. H. Rubin (Eds.), *Contemporary Families and Alternative Lifestyles* (pp. 49–74). Beverly Hills, CA: Sage.

Marsiglio, W., & Scanzoni, J. H. (1995). *Families and friendships: Applying the sociological imagination.* New York: HarperCollins.

Martin, T. C., & Bumpass, L. L. (1989). Recent trends in marital disruption. *Demography, 26,* 37–51.

Masheter, C. (1991). Postdivorce relationships between ex-spouses: The roles of attachment and interpersonal conflict. *Journal of Marriage and the Family, 53,* 103–110.

Metts, S., & Cupach, W. R. (1995). Postdivorce relations. In M. A. Fitzpatrick & A. L. Vangelisti (Eds.), *Explaining family interaction* (pp. 232–251). Thousand Oaks, CA: Sage.

Metts, S., Cupach, W. R., & Bejlovec, R. A. (1989). "I love you too much to ever start liking you": Redefining romantic relationships. *Journal of Social and Personal Relationships, 6,* 259–274.

Orbuch, T. L. (1992). A symbolic interactionist approach to the study of relationship loss. In T. L. Orbuch (Ed.), *Close relationship loss: Theoretical approaches* (pp. 192–204). New York: Springer-Verlag.

Parks, M. R., & Adelman, M. B. (1983). Communication networks and the development of romantic relationships: An expansion of uncertainty reduction theory. *Human Communication Research, 10,* 55–79.

Peplau, L. A. (1991). Lesbian and gay relationships. In J. C. Gonsiorek & J. D. Weinrich (Eds.), *Homosexuality: Research implications for public policy* (pp. 177–196). Newbury Park, CA: Sage.

Peplau, L. A., Hill, C. T., & Rubin, Z. (1993). Sex role attitudes in dating and marriage: A 15-year follow-up of the Boston Couples study. *Journal of Social Issues, 49,* 31–52.

Perlman, D., & Fehr, B. (1986). Theories of friendship: The analysis of interpersonal attraction. In V. J. Derlega & B. A. Winstead (Eds.), *Friendship and social interaction* (pp. 9–40). New York: Springer-Verlag.

Perlman, D., & Fehr, B. (1987). The development of intimate relationships. In D. Perlman & S. Duck (Eds.), *Intimate relationships: Development, dynamics, and deterioration* (pp. 13–42). Newbury Park, CA: Sage.

Risman, B. J., Hill, C. T., Rubin, Z., & Peplau, L. A. (1981). Living together in college: Implications for courtship. *Journal of Marriage and the Family, 43,* 77–83.

Rose, S. M. (1984). How friendships end: Patterns among young adults. *Journal of Social and Personal Relationships, 1,* 267–277.

Rose, S. M., & Serafica, F. C. (1986). Keeping and ending casual, close and best friendships. *Journal of Social and Personal Relationships, 3,* 275–288.

Rusbult, C. E. (1980a). Commitment and satisfaction in romantic associations: A test of the investment model. *Journal of Experimental Social Psychology, 16,* 172–186.

Rusbult, C. E. (1980b). Satisfaction and commitment in friendships. *Representative Research in Social Psychology, 11,* 96–105.

Rusbult, C. E. (1983). A longitudinal test of the investment model: The development (and deterioration) of satisfaction and commitment in heterosexual involvement. *Journal of Personality and Social Psychology, 45,* 101–117.

Rusbult, C. E., Johnson, D. J., & Morrow, G. D. (1986). Predicting satisfaction and commitment in adult romantic involvements: An assessment of the generalizability of the investment model. *Social Psychology Quarterly, 49,* 81–89.

Sabatelli, R. M., & Cecil-Pigo, E. F. (1985). Relational interdependence and commitment in marriage. *Journal of Marriage and the Family, 47,* 931–937.

Sacher, J. A., & Fine, M. A. (1996). Predicting relationship status and satisfaction after six months among dating couples. *Journal of Marriage and the Family, 58,* 21–32.

Schwartz, P. (1994). *Peer marriage.* New York: The Free Press.

Simpson, J. A. (1987). The dissolution of romantic relationships: Factors involved in relationship stability and emotional distress. *Journal of Personality and Social Psychology, 53,* 683–692.

Sprecher, S. (1987). The effects of self-disclosure given and received on affection for an intimate partner and stability of the relationship. *Journal of Social and Personal Relationships, 4,* 115–127.

Sprecher, S. (1988). Investment model, equity, and social support determinants in close relationships. *Social Psychology Quarterly, 51,* 318–328.

Sprecher, S. (1994). Two sides to the breakup of dating relationships. *Personal Relationships, 1,* 199–222.

Sprecher, S., & Felmlee, D. (1993). The influence of parents and friends on the quality and stability of romantic relationships: A three-wave longitudinal investigation. *Journal of Marriage and the Family, 54,* 888–900.

Sprecher, S., Felmlee, D., Metts, S., Fehr, B., & Vanni, D. (in press). Factors associated with the distress experienced after a breakup of a close relationship. *Journal of Social and Personal Relationships.*

Sprecher, S., & Schwartz, P. (1994). Equity and balance in the exchange of contributions in close relationships. In M. J. Lerner & G. Mikula (Eds.), *Entitlement and the affectional bond* (pp. 11–41). New York: Plenum Press.

Thibaut, J. W., & Kelley, H. H. (1959). *The social psychology of groups.* New York: Wiley.

Vaughan, D. (1986). *Uncoupling: Turning points in intimate relationships.* New York: Oxford University Press.

Walster (Hatfield), E., Walster, G. W., & Berscheid, E. (1978). *Equity: Theory and research.* Boston: Allyn and Bacon.

Weber, A. L., & Harvey, J. (1994). Accounts in coping with relationship loss. In A. L. Weber & J. H. Harvey (Eds.). *Close relationships* (pp. 285–306). Boston: Allyn and Bacon.

Weiss, R. S. (1975). *Marital separation.* New York: Basic Books.

White, L. K. (1990). Determinants of divorce: A review of research in the eighties. *Journal of Marriage and the Family, 52,* 904–912.

# 8

# *Fatal Attractions: Contradictions in Intimate Relationships*

***Diane H. Felmlee***
*University of California, Davis*

The ending of an intimate relationship can be heartbreaking, both to the affected couple and to those close to them. A common assumption is that these painful endings are often unforeseen events unrelated to those events involved in the formation of a close relationship. Yet breakups may not always be as inexplicable or unpredictable as suspected. In fact, issues raised in relationship disengagement may be closely linked to choices made in relationship initiation.

The thesis presented in this chapter is that the qualities that are disliked in a romantic partner, and that are implicated in a breakup, are often very similar to those that were found to be initially attractive. This phenomenon is termed "fatal attraction," where the word "fatal" is used not in the sense of deadly, but in the sense of "foretelling a sequence." In this case the sequence begins with a romantic attraction and ends in disenchantment. Examples of fatal attractions include a woman who was attracted to a "light-hearted, easy to talk to, carefree" young man, but then later disliked that he was "not serious enough." Another example is a man who was drawn to his former girlfriend because, among other things, she was "confident" and "assertive"; yet he eventually judged her to be "arrogant" and "haughty."

The argument developed here is that such disenchanting attractions arise because of contradictory dilemmas faced by those in intimate relationships. As discussed in more detail below, members of a couple confront opposing tensions that are not easily resolved. Embracing one set of preferences in a relational partner may mean foregoing another contradictory set of preferences. This type of experiential loss is what crystallizes in a fatal attraction.

In this chapter, after a brief summary of relevant research on attraction and breakups, a number of important issues regarding fatal attractions are addressed. First, theoretical issues are discussed concerning reasons for fatal attractions and factors that influence their likelihood of occurrence. Next, existing empirical research on the prevalence and probability of fatal attractions in romantic attractions is summarized. Following that, a new empirical analysis is undertaken in which contradictory relationship themes that emerge in these types of disenchanting attractions are identified, and a discussion follows of the ways in which these contradictions entail a type of relationship loss. Finally, this chapter ends with a proposal for avenues of future research on this topic.

## RELATIONSHIP BEGINNINGS AND ENDINGS

People tend to be attracted to those who are in close geographical proximity (e.g., Priest & Sawyer, 1967), who are similar to themselves in attitudes (e.g., Byrne, 1971), physical attractiveness (Feingold, 1988), or sociodemographic background (Newcomb, 1961), and who like them (Backman & Secord, 1959). The process of interpersonal attraction also differs by gender. A recent national study finds youth and physical attractiveness to be more important for men than women when considering a potential marriage partner, whereas characteristics that influence earning potential are given more emphasis by women (Sprecher, Sullivan, & Hatfield, 1995). In addition, attraction is not a one-shot procedure, but a sequential, step-by-step process, according to stage theories of courtship (e.g., Kerchoff & Davis, 1962).

Regardless of their sources, nevertheless, romantic attractions can fizzle, come to a crashing halt, or fade away. Some of the common problems that are implicated in the dismantling of an intimate relationship include incompatibility or differences, desire for independence, external factors, and aspects of a partner's personality, according to respondent reports (e.g., Hill, Rubin, & Peplau, 1976; Sprecher, 1994). The argument proposed here, however, suggests that this process of relationship dissolution may be closely related to the initial phase of relationship attraction. In a fatal attraction, the incompatibilities and partner differences that become the eventual source of consternation in a relationship were at one time the very source of allure that propelled the attraction in the first place.

Note, however, that not all relationship endings involve fatal attractions. People may sever a connection to another because of troublesome aspects of that individual that are completely unrelated to those that were initially appealing. Or perhaps some fade away from closeness and involvement without developing new negative perspectives on their partners' qualities. Yet the particular phenomenon of fatal attraction is of interest here because of the paradox it presents and because of the symbolic loss that it entails.

## THEORETICAL ISSUES

### Explanations for Contradictions in Fatal Attractions

Why might individuals reject the very characteristics of a partner that originally appealed to them? Two different general explanations are possible, and each will be discussed in turn.

**Two sides of the same coin**. First, it is possible that the strengths and weaknesses of an individual's personality and character are linked. In their discussions of the "shadow side" of personality, psychologists and philosophers imply that an individual's virtues have a distinct negative dimension (e.g., Jung, 1973). Popular literature also reaches such a conclusion: "His strengths are his weaknesses," states one reporter describing a politician (Purdum, 1996), and "her imperfections turned out to be her virtues," writes a well-known author about a main character (Isaacs, 1991, p. 111).

If strengths and weaknesses are indeed two sides of the same coin, then being attracted to the virtues of another implies being confronted by their corresponding vices. It is not surprising, then, that people often identify pitfalls in the very qualities that initially appealed to them in a former companion. In such a case, a fatal attraction represents the loss of an illusion in the perfection of a partner's virtues. One's partner's virtues are not pure; they have distinct liabilities.

**Opposing relationship forces.** An explanation of fatal attractions that operates at the level of the dyad, rather than the individual, is also possible. According to Simmel (1955), members of groups are confronted by two competing alternatives, that of interdependence and that of independence, or freedom. By belonging to a group, individuals encounter social control and thereby lose some personal freedom. On the other hand, giving up group membership and embracing independence means depriving the individual of the benefits of group life, such as acceptance, security, and so on. Couples are also likely to face this dilemma, finding themselves torn between a need for connectivity and a need for personal freedom.

The work of dialectical relationship theorists echoes these notions (Altman, Vinsel, & Brown, 1981; Baxter & Montgomery, 1996). From a dialectical perspective, couples are thought to confront pairs of contradictory and ongoing tensions, such as those between (1) autonomy and connection, (2) novelty and predictability, and (3) openness and closedness. Couples are pulled in each direction of the two poles of a particular contradictory force. That is, individuals experience the need for both autonomy and connection in a relationship, for novelty and predictability, and so on. From a dialectical viewpoint, then, fatal attractions occur because one person chooses a partner on the basis of a quality that represents one pole of a contradictory force (e.g., connection), but then he or she inevitably finds the relationship lacking in the opposing pole (e.g., autonomy). Thus, the loss in a fatal attraction is the loss of one dimension of a contradictory dyadic group force.

## The Over-Time Process

These two explanations suggest why someone might dislike the characteristics that initially interested them in a partner. However, they do not speak to the over-time process of a fatal attraction. Why is it that individuals are drawn in the first place to qualities in an individual that they inevitably dislike—qualities that have a clear downside, or qualities that highlight only one valued relationship dimension at the expense of another? Why aren't these characteristics immediately rejected? There are at least three different possible social psychological mechanisms that could account for this developmental pattern, labeled as follows: (1) time will tell, (2) sour grapes, and (3) rose-colored glasses.

(1) *Time will tell.* One possibility is that fatal attractions occur over a period of time because partners are able to hide or suppress the negative aspects of their positive traits at the onset of a relationship, but are unable to maintain this facade indefinitely. Eventually a partner's liabilities surface, and it is these unanticipated liabilities that are rejected. Likewise, an imbalance in relationship dimensions may be obvious only after some significant amount of time has elapsed.

(2) *Sour grapes*. Another possibility, derived from cognitive dissonance theory (Festinger, 1957), is that fatal attractions simply represent a cognitive reframing of one's partner that occurs following a breakup. Relationship endings are likely to generate contradictory cognitions, and disparaging an ex-partner may be one way in which these stressful, dissonant cognitions can be dampened. For instance, little has been lost in a breakup if a former companion can be viewed as possessing prominent vices instead of virtues. Dissonance theory, therefore, can readily explain the critical nature of many breakup accounts; they are cases of "sour grapes." What is less clear on the basis of dissonance theory, however, is why individuals might deprecate qualities in a partner that are closely related, rather than completely unrelated, to those that once appealed to them.

(3) *Rose-colored glasses*. A final possibility is that individuals paint a loved one in a flattering light while in a state of infatuation, even though they are cognizant of that person's weaknesses and of potential relationship problems from the very beginning. Once the initial bloom has faded on the attraction, however, their evaluation of a partner becomes less idealized. In other words, similar to the cognitive dissonance argument in the second scenario, sour grapes, the rose-colored glasses scenario suggests that a fatal attraction involves a cognitive reinterpretation of a partner's positive qualities. In this third scenario, however, the partner's qualities are reconstrued in a more negative light because infatuation has subsided, not because of the dissonance generated by a breakup.

## The Role of Differences in Fatal Attractions

As has been seen thus far, there are several theoretical explanations possible for fatal attractions. However, not all attractions are equally liable to this pattern of partner disillusionment. In particular, attractions to partner qualities that are "different" are believed to be more likely than others to be susceptible to this type of disenchantment. Attractive partner characteristics can be seen as "different" in one of three ways: (1) dissimilar (different from the respondent's own characteristics), (2) extreme or unusual (different from average), or (3) culturally atypical (different from cultural expectations). Individuals may be drawn to one or more of these types of differences in a romantic companion because involvement with such a partner leads to an expanded sense of self (Aron & Aron, 1986) or because it makes them feel special or unique (Snyder & Fromkin, 1980).

On the other hand, a relationship with someone who is seen as "different" is also likely to have a downside. Similarity is rewarding because it reinforces our opinions and attitudes (Byrne & Clore, 1970), and thus, dissimilarity may be unrewarding. According to cognitive consistency theories (Newcomb, 1961), dissimilarities within a close dyad also may be stressful cognitively. In addition, interaction with partners who are different in the sense that they are dissimilar, unusual, or culturally atypical, may be challenging, because expectations for interaction in these situations are unclear. Finally, individuals involved with romantic companions who depart from social custom are likely to encounter resistance from social networks, and network approval is a powerful predictor of relationship stability (Felmlee, Sprecher, & Bassin, 1990).

## RESEARCH FINDINGS

Thus far, a number of theoretical issues concerning fatal attractions have been discussed. In the following section, two general questions are addressed: How common are fatal attractions in actual empirical data? What role, if any, do "differences" play in fatal attractions?

### Prevalence of Fatal Attractions

In previous research, the prevalence of fatal attractions was assessed using questionnaire data from 301 individuals (201 females and 101 males) reporting on a past, romantic relationship (Felmlee, 1995). Participants were college students from a relatively ethnically diverse population (43% White, 23% Asian, 20% Hispanic, 10% Black). Six reported on a homosexual relationship. Two of the questions asked of these participants were: "Describe the specific qualities that first attracted you to that individual" and "In retrospect, what were the qualities about that individual that you found least attractive?" Responses to those two questions were compared by coders in order to determine whether or not a fatal attraction occurred (with an intercoder reliability of .76). Fatal attractions were defined as occurring when a quality listed as "least attractive" was similar to (e.g., a synonym) or a negative interpretation of, a quality reported as being attractive initially. "Arrogance," for example, was defined as a negative interpretation of the positive quality of "confidence."

Fatal attractions surfaced for a substantial percentage of the respondents (29.2%). In other words, the characteristics reported as initially attractive in a former partner were quite similar to those reported as "least attractive" for close to one-third of the sample. Thus, these types of attractions arose frequently enough to suggest that this seemingly contradictory relationship phenomenon is worthy of further attention.

### Fatal Attractions to Differences in a Partner

Empirical findings show that two of the three types of partner differences are implicated in disenchantment (Felmlee, in press). First, findings from a multivariate logistic regression analysis reveal that when a respondent reports an attracting attribute in a partner that is dissimilar, then the probability of a fatal attraction increases fivefold. Attractions to a partner's similar qualities, on the other hand, are significantly less likely to be fatal; the odds of such an occurrence are lowered by approximately one-fourth in these cases. Second, results indicate that fatal attractions increase in likelihood when a partner's appealing quality is viewed as extreme, that is, different from average. In particular, describing the appealing qualities of a partner in extreme ways (e.g., "extremely successful," "very outgoing") on the part of a respondent doubles the odds that a trait is later disliked, i.e., a fatal attraction. The inclusion of a variety of control variables (e.g., gender, total duration of relationship, total number of attracting traits, sexual orientation) does not alter the general pattern of significance in the model.

Research to date does not provide support, however, for the argument that attracting characteristics of a romantic companion are highly susceptible to a pattern of disenchantment when they counter cultural normative expectations, at least in terms of cultural expectations regarding gender stereotypes (Felmlee, in press-a). Findings from a multivariate logistic regression analysis reveal that attractions to "gender atypical" partner qualities (e.g., nurturance in a man or assertiveness in a woman) are neither significantly more, nor less, likely to be "fatal" than attractions to more gender typical, or neutral, qualities. An in-depth investigation of open-ended responses finds that fatal attractions are common in either case: when individuals are attracted to qualities in a partner that are inconsistent, or consistent, with gender stereotypes.

In sum, attractions to dissimilar and unusual partners are particularly likely to be fatal. On the other hand, an examination of the questionnaire data reveals that there is a wide diversity in fatal attractions, and that they occur with respect to all general types of partner characteristics. For example, although uncommon, there are cases in which an individual reports similarity as the basis of an attraction, but then later appears to be repelled by that same quality (i.e., they find the relationship to be boring). It appears, thus, that there is no general type of appealing partner characteristic that is entirely immune to disillusionment.

### The Fatal Attraction Process

Research also provides information regarding the social psychological processes behind fatal attraction (Felmlee, in press-b). As discussed earlier, there are a number of different possible scenarios, including "time will tell" (partner's liabilities take time to uncover), "sour grapes" (evaluating a partner negatively after a breakup), and "rose-colored glasses" (assessing a partner in a more positive light while infatuated). Research finds that the likelihood of a fatal attraction does *not* increase linearly (nor nonlinearly) with the length of a relationship, and hence it fails to support the "time will tell" argument. Research also reveals that fatal attractions are significantly more likely when respondents report that it was their own idea, rather than their partner's idea, to end a relationship. Fatal attractions may not be simply a case of "sour grapes," therefore, because it is likely that cognitive dissonance (and the need for denigrating a partner) is lower, not higher, in cases in which the respondent initiated the breakup. On the other hand, this finding provides some support for the "rose-colored glasses" argument, because someone who terminates a romantic relationship is likely to be uninfatuated and capable of viewing the negative aspects of a partner's virtues with a clear lens. Thus, research suggests that the "rose-colored glasses" argument may be better at accounting for the fatal attraction process than the competing scenarios.

Thus far in this chapter, theoretical issues concerning fatal attractions have been discussed and existing research on the topic has been summarized. Nevertheless, important issues remain to be addressed. For example, one of the fundamental explanations for the paradox inherent in fatal attractions has to do with the existence of opposing relationship forces, as discussed by Simmel (1955) and dialectical theorists. It remains unknown, however, to what extent empirical data provide evidence of such contradictory themes. In the next section, this chapter presents the results of a new empirical analysis designed to address this issue.

## CONTRADICTORY THEMES

In the following analysis, 88 fatal attractions are examined for evidence of oppositional themes. Information is taken from the open-ended questionnaire responses of 301 individuals reporting on a breakup. The original data set was used to answer earlier research questions and did not address the issue raised here (see Felmlee, 1995). The research design is described in more detail earlier in this chapter.

There are a number of themes in the fatal attraction data that represent tensions between contradictory relationship forces. Five of the main themes are discussed below.

### Fun vs. Seriousness

Perhaps the most common contradictory theme found in fatal attractions concerns tensions between fun and seriousness. An example of this type of fatal attraction is one woman who was attracted to her partner because he "made me laugh" and was "a lot of fun." Nevertheless, what she least liked about this man was that he was "too carefree about life." In another case a woman disliked a man's "constant silliness" and the fact that he "never seemed to take the relationship seriously," but she was initially attracted to him because he was "funny" and "fun." The implication, then, is that while these women enjoyed the fun and humorous aspects of their relationships, these qualities had their limitations, and more serious qualities also were desired.

### Connection vs. Autonomy

Another theme that occurred in these data suggests that individuals experience conflict between the forces of connection and autonomy. Examples of this occur when respondents mention that a person's interest in them, or the amount of attention given to them, was appealing, which implies that they appreciated the connectivity between themselves and that person. Yet in several cases, these same individuals often report that what they least liked about their partner was his or her tendency toward jealousy and possessiveness. One woman, for instance, eventually found her "nurturing, loyal, warm, and gentle" boyfriend to be "smothering" and "codependent." Another was drawn to a man because he was "protective" and "cared for her," but was repelled by his tendency to be "clingy." These individuals were experiencing tensions between wanting a good deal of closeness with their partner, but at the same time wanting to preserve their autonomy.

In other cases, individuals were attracted to characteristics in another that were representative of autonomy, but at a later point in time they seemed to long for more connection with that partner. In one such instance a woman was attracted to a man because he was "independent" and "individualistic," but eventually she found him to be "too wrapped up in his own activities." Too much autonomy in a relationship, in other words, may generate a longing for more connection.

## Strength vs. Vulnerability

There are also a number of examples of fatal attractions that suggest tensions between strength and vulnerability. One man was drawn to his former girlfriend because of her "strong character and beliefs." He disliked, however, that she was "pushy, loud, domineering, and always took the initiative." In another example, a man was attracted to a woman's "confidence," but found her "ego" to be problematic. In such cases, individuals are drawn to strong aspects of another's character, but then appear to dislike that the person was "overly" strong, which may be indicative of a wish for more vulnerability, or flexibility, on the part of their partner.

In other situations demonstrating tensions between strength and vulnerability, individuals initially found the vulnerable, rather than the strong, aspects of a partner pleasing. For example, a man was initially attracted to his former girlfriend because of her qualities of "shyness," "timidity," and "modest[y]," but he later viewed her as being "insecure." In another instance, a woman eventually judged her "sweet," "sensitive," and "soft-spoken" boyfriend to be "boring," "fake," and "*too nice.*" Such individuals appear to have liked the vulnerable and "soft" aspects of their companions, but then desired that they display what they considered to be greater strength of character.

## Novelty vs. Predictability

Conflict between novelty and predictability also occurs in these disillusioning attractions. For example, a woman found a man's "offbeat personality" attractive initially, but then she later viewed him as "too hippie." In another case a man was drawn to a woman because, in addition to her physical attributes, she was "the opposite" of him. Later he disliked, however, that she was "too different."

In instances like these, individuals were initially intrigued by the novel or different aspects of a romantic partner. Eventually they were also repelled by this novelty, or differentness, which may mean that they wished for more predictability in their partner.

## Sexual vs. Chaste

An additional theme that emerges in fatal attractions is a tension between sexual experience and sexual innocence. In one such case, a man was drawn to a woman because of her "slutiness/experience," but then he later disliked the exact same qualities: "slutiness/experience." In another instance, a man described 10 different physical characteristics of a woman as being what initially interested him (e.g., face, legs). He was disturbed, however, that the relationship was "based too much on physical aspects. No true love just lust." In these cases (all male respondents), men appeared to appreciate the passionate, erotic, and physical aspects of their partners, but at the same time had misgivings about these same aspects.

## Additional Themes

Other oppositional themes represented in the data analyzed here include: relaxation and drive, closedness and openness, social and personal, maturity and youth, as well as flattery and honesty. Illustrations of the themes are listed in Table 1.

*Table 1.* Oppositional themes in fatal attractions, and illustrations of corresponding attracting and disliked partner qualities

| Theme | Attracting quality | Disliked quality |
|---|---|---|
| Fun vs. Seriousness | "funny and fun"<br>"sense of humor" | "constant silliness"<br>"jokes" |
| Connection vs. Autonomy | "nurturing"<br>"cared about me" | "smothering"<br>"clingy"; "held on too tightly" |
| Strength vs. Vulnerability | "strong-willed"<br>"spunk" | "domineering and macho"<br>"arguing ability" |
| Novelty vs. Predictability | "strange"<br>"spontaneity" | "too different"<br>"flighty" |
| Sexual vs. Chaste | "sexual experience"<br>"knew she would have sex" | "sexual experience"<br>"couldn't say no [to sex]" |
| Relaxation vs. Drive | "relaxed"<br>"successful and focused" | "constantly late"<br>"work commanded him" |
| Closedness vs. Openness | "shy"<br>"openness" | "too shy"<br>"too open to others" |
| Social vs. Personal | "very outgoing and social"<br>"friendly" | "too social"<br>"too concerned with pals" |
| Maturity vs. Youth | "older"; "looked up to him"<br>"older" | "age"<br>"treated me as younger" |
| Flattery vs. Honesty | "charming"<br>"flattering" | "deceptive and dishonest"<br>"superficial" |

## DISCUSSION

In sum, existing research demonstrates that fatal attractions seem to occur in a substantial number of breakup accounts. They are particularly likely when individuals are drawn to characteristics in a romantic companion that they view as extreme or different. Research also suggests that such attractions may occur because individuals inflate the image of a partner while in a preliminary relationship stage, but that once infatuation fades and the rose-colored glasses come off, the negative components of the partner become more salient.

New research presented here finds that there is abundant evidence of oppositional relationship themes in fatal attractions such as those suggested by Simmel (1955) and dialectics. The existence of these themes implies that one explanation for fatal attractions is that relational members face contradictory dilemmas that are not always easily resolved. Being drawn to a quality in a partner representative of one type of relationship dimension may be rewarding, but it also implies that the pairing is imbalanced and lacking in an opposing dimension.

These contradictory themes imply, also, that an attraction to another person often entails giving up something that is desirable. Relationships involve trade-offs, and such trade-offs mean that one experience is sacrificed at the expense of another. As indicated earlier, a common opposing theme occurred in cases in which respondents were attracted to a fun or funny partner. An abundance of fun in a relationship, however, may mean that there is less time for seriousness. On the other hand, an attraction to a serious, responsible partner may imply loss, too, since such a relationship may suffer from an excess of seriousness and an absence of light-heartedness or playfulness.

Note, however, that not all oppositional tensions are symmetrical. For example, tensions between novelty and predictability seemed to be much more evident when individuals were attracted to the novel, or different, qualities in a partner than when they were drawn to predictability, or similarity. Attractions to differences in a partner are significantly more likely to be fatal than those to other types of qualities, whereas attractions to similarities are significantly less likely to be fatal. These results imply, perhaps, that an excess of novelty in a relationship, and its accompanying loss in predictability, may be more problematic for a couple than an abundance of predictability and a subsequent loss in novelty. Thus, certain relational asymmetries are probably more tolerable than others.

There is also a subtle implication embedded in these fatal attraction themes that individuals in such romances "want it all." They want a partner who is extremely laid back and at the same time very motivated and successful. Or they want someone who is outgoing and social, but who spends plenty of exclusive time with them. Perhaps certain partners have the flexibility to fulfill such desires, allowing situations to determine the appropriateness of their behavior. Ideally, such individuals would be extremely easygoing and relaxed on weekends and vacations, for instance, but very driven and motivated in the workplace. They would be outgoing and friendly at parties, and yet focus exclusively on their partner on joint outings or within the home. Realistically, however, such desires for a loved one are probably inherently contradictory and are likely to remain unmet. To the extent that personality and behavioral tendencies are relatively stable and difficult to alter, the average person is unlikely to switch from one style of behavior to its opposite, situation by situation. Choosing a partner, thus, means embracing certain qualities in another at the expense of others. Furthermore, even if a companion was capable of shifting behavior to fit every occasion, that person no doubt would be at risk of being seen as "wishy-washy." Every virtue has its vice.

The lesson of fatal attraction, thus, is one of expectations. Individuals in such a romance may expect a flexibility in human behavior that is unrealistic. They want a partner to be both confident and humble, spontaneous and predictable, or sweet and assertive, all of which may be impossible. Or they fail to expect that the qualities of a loved one that are appealing in one context will be appalling in another. They also may have expectations that an intimate relationship can simultaneously provide experiences that are contradictory: interdependence and freedom, fun and seriousness, spontaneity and predictability. Ultimately, such expectations reflect a desire to protect themselves from loss—from the loss of valued dimensions of life.

In conclusion, this research has implications for the study of relationship loss. Loss in a close relationship can mean the departure of a loved one through relationship breakup or death, with an accompanying loss of companionship, intimacy, and/or material goods and services. What we see here, however, is that the ending of a close relationship can also entail the loss of hopes, dreams, and expectations, no matter how illusory these expectations may be.

## FUTURE RESEARCH

There are several unanswered questions that future work on this type of relationship disenchantment might address. One concerns the underlying process involved in a fatal attraction.

Research to date on this issue has been based on retrospective breakup accounts. One way to investigate further the developmental process of this type of partner disenchantment would be to follow couples over time, from the hint of an attraction, through the progressive stages of a relationship, and, in some cases, to the finality of a breakup. Diverse samples from representative groups of marital and nonmarital couples are also necessary to further examine these issues.

Another unanswered question involves individual differences in propensities towards fatal attractions. Perhaps certain individuals are more prone than others to experience these types of failed romances, in part because they have a tendency to be drawn to the extreme and different qualities in companions that are especially susceptible to disillusionment. Such individuals may be risk-takers, or they may be those who search for qualities in another that complement their own and that they desire to possess for themselves. Additionally, some may be more apt than others to "want it all" in a relationship and to find the absence of one dyadic dimension particularly taxing.

Finally, another question worth addressing is whether fatal attractions materialize only in unstable, terminal relationships. If vices and virtues are really one and the same, and if all couples face opposing tensions such as those discussed here, then partner disenchantment is likely to occur in continuing and stable relationships as well as in those that end. In other words, it is probable that members of an ongoing relationship learn to recognize each other's liabilities, and that these liabilities represent the "shadow side" of each person's assets. It is likely, too, that any given couple at any given time suffers from a surplus of particular relationship experiences at the cost of others. They may enjoy a good deal of connection, for example, but little autonomy, or they could have many serious pursuits, but little time for frivolity. The question, then, becomes one of how those in satisfactory and intact liaisons manage these dilemmas. Are the contradictions faced by satisfied couples less severe or less crucial than those confronting the disgruntled? Are happy couples able to manage relationship trade-offs more successfully than their unhappy counterparts by alternating between savoring one oppositional dimension and the other? Or are members of some satisfied pairs simply more accepting of each other's liabilities and of the inevitable compromises that must be made when confronting contradictory goals? The answers to such questions await further research on this intriguing relationship paradox.

## REFERENCES

Altman, I., Vinsel, A., & Brown, B. B. (1981). Dialectic conceptions in social psychology: An application to social penetration and privacy regulation. In L. Berkowitz (Ed.), *Advances in experimental social psychology. Vol. 14* (pp. 107–160). New York: Academic Press.

Aron, A., & Aron, E. (1986). *Love and the expansion of self: Understanding attraction and satisfaction.* New York: Hemisphere.

Backman, C. W., & Secord, P. F. (1959). The effect of perceived liking on interpersonal attraction. *Human Relations, 12,* 379–384.

Baxter, L. A., & Montgomery, B. M. (1996). *Relating: Dialogues and dialectics.* New York: Guilford.

Byrne, D. (1971). *The attraction paradigm.* New York: Academic Press.

Byrne, D., & Clore, G. L. (1970). A reinforcement model of evaluative processes. *Personality: An International Journal,* 1, 103–128.

Feingold, A. (1988). Matching for attractiveness in romantic partners and same-sex friends: A meta-analysis and theoretical critique. *Psychological Bulletin, 104,* 226–235.

Felmlee, D. H. (1995). Fatal attractions: Affection and disaffection in intimate relationships. *Journal of Social and Personal Relationships ,12,* 295–311.

Felmlee, D. H. (in press-a). "Be careful what you wish for . . .": Determinants of fatal attractions. *Personal Relationships.*

Felmlee, D. H. (in press-b). Fatal attraction. In B. H. Spitzberg and W. R. Cupach (Eds.), *The Dark Side of Relationships*, Hillsdale, NJ: Lawrence Erlbaum.

Felmlee, D., Sprecher, S., and Bassin, E. (1990). The dissolution of intimate relationships: A hazard model. *Social Psychology Quarterly, 53,* 13–30.

Festinger, L. (1957). *A theory of cognitive dissonance.* New York: Harper & Row.

Hill, C. T., Rubin, Z., & Peplau, L. A. (1976). Breakups before marriage: The end of 103 affairs. *Journal of Social Issues , 32,* 147–168.

Isaacs, S. (1991). *Magic Hour.* New York: Harper Collins.

Jung, C. B. (1973). *Memories, Dreams, Reflections.* Edited by A. Jaffe and translated by R. and C. Winston. New York: Pantheon Books.

Kerchoff, A. C., & Davis, K. E. (1962). Value consensus and need complementarity in mate selection. *American Sociological Review, 27,* 295–303.

Newcomb, T. M. (1961). *The acquaintance process.* New York: Holt, Rinehart & Winston.

Priest, R. T., & Sawyer, J. (1967). Proximity and peership: Bases of balance in interpersonal attraction. *American Journal of Sociology, 72,* 633–649.

Purdum, T. S. (1996, May 19). Facets of Clinton. *New York Times Magazine,* pp. 36–41.

Simmel, G. (1955). *Conflict and the web of group-affiliation.* Glencoe, IL: Free Press.

Snyder, C. R., & Fromkin, H. L. (1980). *Uniqueness: The human pursuit of difference.* New York: Plenum Press.

Sprecher, S. (1994). Two sides to the breakup of dating relationships. *Personal Relationships, 1,* 199–222.

Sprecher, S., Sullivan, Q., & Hatfield, E. (1994). Mate selection preferences: Gender differences examined in a national sample. *Journal of Personality and Social Psychology, 8,* 1074–1080.

# 9

# *Loss in the Experience of Multiracial Couples*

***Paul C. Rosenblatt and Carolyn Y. Tubbs***
*University of Minnesota*

Racism is complex and variable, different from situation to situation in how it is expressed, and different for different people in how it is experienced. Any definition of racism can be too simple. But as a beginning, to provide focus to this chapter, we offer the following definition: "Racism is hostile action with the intent to harm, based on the skin color of the intended victim" (Rosenblatt, Karis, & Powell, 1995, p. 2).

Racism can have many different consequences for its victims. In this chapter we explore one area of those possible consequences: loss and the feelings associated with loss. We talk about loss both as people in multiracial couples experience it and as we perceive it when attending to what they have to say. Racism can be said to create losses for every American. However, since racism is played out so much in the unspoken assumptions and taken-for-granted patterns of American life, it is often hard to grieve those losses or even to know that they are present. Some people do not know what they have lost. Some do not want to know what they have lost. Some do not want others to know how much they hurt.

Many white Americans who acknowledge the existence of racism think of it only as victimizing nonwhites, but it victimizes everyone. One way to recognize that is to look at the experience of black-white multiracial couples. Multiracial couples talk about losses experienced by the black partner as a target of racism and losses experienced by one or both of them because racism opposes interracial couples. There are also losses the white partner acknowledges that came from being white in a racist society. In this chapter we document all three kinds of loss resulting from racism: the losses of African-Americans resulting from racism, the losses of multiracial couples resulting from racism, and the losses the white partners in multiracial couples experience as they come to understand what white racism does to whites.

Although this chapter is about loss, it is important to note that many people who have considerable experience being targets of racism have learned how to live their lives so that racism does not burden them with grieving. They learn how to avoid racist attacks, to step away from them, to minimize their effects in their personal life, to live the life they want to live rather than the life (or death) that racism wants them to live. Thus, there is a paradox in that people can recurrently experience what seems to others and perhaps even to themselves as loss but not grieve constantly, often, or even at all.

## THE STUDY

The material for this chapter was drawn from a study of the relationships of black-white heterosexual couples (Rosenblatt et al., 1995). All interviews were carried out by Terri Karis and Richard Powell. The interviews involved open-ended questions focused on respondent experiences and perspectives.

Couples were recruited through announcements made at workshops for interracial families, notices placed in a YMCA newsletter for multiracial families, announcements posted on bulletin boards, and via word-of-mouth. Twenty-one interracial couples were interviewed, all residents of the Minneapolis-St. Paul metropolitan area. In 16 couples, the African-American partner was a man; in 5, a woman. At the time of interview, the couples had been together from 1 to 20 years.

The sample is not representative of black-white interracial couples in the Twin Cities metropolitan area, let alone of black-white couples in the United States. There were no elderly couples and no rural couples. There were no couples in public housing or on public assistance. The sample group was generally well educated and well off economically.

Interview tapes were transcribed verbatim. Transcriptions were checked, usually by a different person than the original transcriber, and corrected as appropriate. The corrected transcriptions were read closely for the topics that are at the focus of this chapter and were hypertext-searched for the following words or word parts: grief, grieving, mourn, sad, sorrow, loss, lost, identity, pain, hurt, privilege, depress, blue, bereav, ignorant, innocent, innocence, check, vacation, cry, cried, tears, sob, gave up, learn, heal, innocen, and weep.

With this sample and this qualitative methodology, the knowledge this chapter offers is the knowledge of possibility and perspective, not of generalization and quantification of effect.

## WHO ARE WE TO SAY PEOPLE HAVE EXPERIENCED LOSS?

Although this chapter includes extensive interview quotes, there is ambiguity about whose voice is speaking. In most of the couples interviewed, neither partner used the words "loss" or "grief." They talked about the illusions others have about multiracial couples and the ordinariness of their life together. But they also talked about the wounds experienced by the black partner and by the two of them because of racist attacks. One could say that there are losses in being the victim of racism, in having family members write one off or write one's partner off, in having one's child be the target of racism, and in losing credibility in one's own community. One could also say that there are losses that surprise some people, for example, continuing feelings of hurt after relationships with family of origin have in some sense been healed, or the loss of racial (as opposed to ethnic) identity and culture to pass on to one's children (something white partners did not know they had or that they would want to foster). But the people interviewed did not label these things as losses and did not claim to grieve them.

Perhaps for a person who has been the target of racism, treating losses as losses may be granting too much power to the racist words and actions that created the losses. That may make it hard to want to say one has experienced loss and is grieving. Then, too, one may have learned how to live in the environment in a way that sidesteps or distances many of the losses. Alternatively, the losses may not be experienced as much by the targets of racism, but rather by those who act in racist ways—losses from their own ignorance and malice. Is something grief when people do not call it grief and prefer to use emotion words other than those for grief (for example, words like, upset, frustrated, angry, or down)? And if people grieve a racist situation, would they say they are grieving losses, or would they say they are grieving betrayals, attacks, frustrations, deprivations? Although this chapter is written from a qualitative methodological and philosophical position that values and focuses on the realities of the people interviewed, it in some sense is disloyal to its own methods and philosophy in presuming to categorize experiences as losses and feelings as grief.

## THE LOSSES TO AFRICAN-AMERICANS RESULTING FROM RACISM

The list of losses experienced by African-Americans as a result of racism is extremely long, covering every area of life, and, unfortunately, it is still being written. African-American experiences and reactions are enormously diverse, so it is risky to generalize. Still, what one person says may apply to many. One area of loss that was poignantly described by an African-America man talking about struggles he and his white partner had in order to get along had to do with the defensive armor he had learned to wear.

> **John:** See the whole uncomfortable aspects of the relationship . . . I don't think it have anything to do with who she is. It has to do with me takin' off this armor that I've worn for so many years, and the thing about those armors is that see, a lot of things were thrusted at you when you had your armor on you. You thought that it didn't hurt you; but the armor hid the wounds. So when you take your armor off then you realize that you were stabbed . . . all through down the years. And there are all these wounds, and you're really like very vulnerable and then you have that kind of decision, sayin', well, should I keep it off and heal these wounds or should I just cover it back up and continue with the character?[1]

Another African-American talked about what he believed racism did to the health of its victims.

> **Robert:** I got to be ready to deal with any racial situation may comes up. A white person go into an all white area, he have no stress in mind like that whatsoever.

[1]Many of the quotations in this chapter are reprinted from Rosenblatt, Karis, and Powell (1995) with permission from Sage Publications, Thousand Oaks, CA. This quotation and the one on page 128 are not from that source.

What it does it causes more heart attack, gettin' sick often, gettin' headaches. It bring your health down because . . . you find yourself dealin' with racism. Then you wonder why we die early. That's why, some of the reasons why.

## THE LOSSES TO MULTIRACIAL COUPLES RESULTING FROM RACISM

Because of racism, multiracial couples may face discrimination, opposition, and hostility from family and community. And yet the people interviewed typically reported little of that and talked about learning to live in ways that minimized that. So, in balance, they could say they lived ordinary lives in which getting along with each other, buying groceries, paying bills, taking care of children, etc. were the focus—the everyday things that are the same for same-race couples. Still, many couples had experienced losses. What follows are illustrations of losses that were often mentioned.

### Loss of the Support of Family and Friends

**Dot:** [My] father . . . said, "For the first time in my life . . . I am glad that my own parents are dead so that they don't have to see the shame that you've brought on me." And we had no communication after that at all until he was dying, and then he asked for me, a few years later. My mother was a person who had never written a check, never paid a bill, had no idea what his salary was. What he said, she did. She snuck around. She would write me letters that he didn't know about, and I wasn't supposed to write back. . . . I made my choice. I've never had any regrets. I've kind of quit crying right now, because, it does (sounds tearful), I'll tell you what hurt the most. My dad, I guess you've gathered, was never a real warm come-home-and-play-in-front-of-the-fireplace kind of guy. I don't mean to say there was nothing good about him. He was a good provider. We always had a roof, a meal. He just was a person who will do his [worst] if you didn't please him. . . . My mother was the same way. So for them to withdraw their love . . . because I was going with a black man was not a real surprise. . . . I did make my choice, and I have never regretted it, and it hurt the most when [our daughter] was born. Because when she was born, . . . (crying) I knew immediately that there was nothing that we could do that would win their love. . . . I realized how little, how frail was their love to begin with. I think though that I have more love in my life than a lot of people ever will. . . . I feel lucky in the love department, although . . . I still feel the pain sometimes. . . . (Rosenblatt et al., 1995, p. 82)
**Wilson:** The pain is deep. I've seen the pain. Pain, I feel the pain. . . . She *loved* this man. He was her father! She had nothing to do with it. She loved the man; she had no choice whether to love or not. . . . This is her father. (Rosenblatt et al. (1995), p. 78)

**Joyce:** I think initially in the relationship it was like that choice [to be in this relationship] sort of cut us off from some people. . . . Like there were some of [my husband's] friends that were kind of disapproving. And it feels like those wounds have healed. . . . And with my family, my parents didn't come to our wedding, and my sisters did, but it's like it's, over time those kind of healed.

### Loss of Identity

**Gloria:** You always feel people will discount because you are with someone white. It's like, "Well we know where you stand!" I think in some ways that has been the most difficult piece of it, because I think people will assume a lot about your political beliefs, about how you grew up. A lot of people assume I didn't grew up in Harlem. I did grow up in an all-black community. I think when people start robbing my identity from me, and kind of making statements or discount me because I'm with someone white, that I have no concern about the black community, I'm not black-identified, that's been the hardest thing to deal with. . . . I started the black student union in my high school; I brought someone from the Black Panthers to my high. I don't feel like I should have to go through this itinerary of stuff that I've done in my life, where someone who just because they're with someone black that means they have their black-identity all intact. . . . It's hard not to take this stuff personal. (Rosenblatt et al., 1995, p. 180)

**Liz:** I don't think of John as being black and me as being white. There's difference, but I don't, I just see him as John. And I hadn't really even thought about the racial issue very much until he brought up he would like the kids to be in a day care situation with other black kids. . . . I started thinking about it, like do they, are they really black and do they really have to go to this black day care, or is it important that they be with other black kids? And so that's when it became more of an issue that there was a race difference. . . . I got the picture that the kids need to be prepared for society to see them or label them as black. Society at large maybe, . . . other people, they see the race more than I do. And that they seem to be prepared for that; I don't have to, in my house, like, tell them, "You're black." . . . Why do I have to call *them* black? . . . Then I don't get my ethn-, they don't carry my identity. . . . And then all of a sudden I realized I was labeling myself white, and it was like (laughs), well, I didn't know I really labeled myself white, and there I did it. (Rosenblatt et al., 1995, p. 191)

### Losses Resulting from Police Discrimination

Some couples told of shared discrimination. The story might deal with service in a restaurant or store, trying to find a motel room, trying to rent or buy a place to live, or trying to get a mortgage loan. Among the most common stories were those having to do with the police. Stories of trouble with the police were often told with strong feelings, perhaps because the police are armed and have the power to incarcerate and to entangle one in the courts. Here is one of a number of police stories that were told.

**Dot:** Police pulled us over. I was driving, got out, [my husband and son] had to put their hands up, and I had to show my license. [Then we were told we] could go. . . . We came home, and I called the . . . police station. And I said, "You have to understand that a certain amount of humiliation was suffered here. At least two neighbors drove by and looking at the (name) family with their hands on top of their head." And the man said, "Well, the thing is there has just been a . . . rash of stolen checks cashed and it is a black man and a white woman in a navy blue Cadillac or Lincoln or something." And I said, "We were a black man, a white woman, a black boy in a black Oldsmobile." And I understand the police have to do their job. I want them to do some soul-searching too, but we looked suspicious and the thing that identified us as suspicious was, once they heard that it was an interracial couple driving around with these checks it really didn't matter if it was Oldsmobile or Pinto. (Rosenblatt et al., 1995, pp. 145–146)

### Losses in Finding Places to Visit or Live

**Shirley:** We have to think really hard about where we're going to take our vacations, and it bothers me because we have to think that far ahead. And we can't live wherever we want, like some people can. (Rosenblatt et al., 1995, p. 174)

### Losses Because One's Children Have to Deal with Racism

**Tim:** I have concerns about my children. I already hurt in my heart for the pains that they may feel from somebody, some jerk's comment in the future. And I'm about ready to cry because I really feel very strongly that people are people and that their race should have nothing to do, whatsoever, with the way they are treated as a person, that they should be treated as people. (Rosenblatt et al., 1995, p. 76)

Central symbols of how children in multiracial families must deal with racism are the school and census forms that require that one be categorized as black or white. There are still, as of this writing, very few situations where one can write out one's own categorization of self or child or where there are multiracial options. So children have to fit into the category "white" or "black," and with that, lose an identity link and quite possibly get gated into one kind of school or other situation rather than another, whether it fits for them or not and is what their parents want for them or not.

**Ann:** It bothers me about our children. I mean what box do I check for [our younger daughter]? Our kids are a quarter black. Does that make them black? They're not white; they're not black. . . . I guess I say she's a biracial child or we're a multicultural family and . . . she's going to be a biracial child, and I'm not going to tell her she's black. How can you tell this kid she's black? She doesn't look black. . . . She can grow up and think she's white as long as she understands her dad is black. . . . She can identify whatever she feels is most comfortable as long as she accepts . . . her heritage. . . . (Rosenblatt et al., 1995, pp. 207–208)
**Bayard**: I think it's also real important that we . . . tell her that the people she deals with at school, society, whatever, when they see she has a black father they are going to consider her black, regardless of what she thinks she is.
**Ann**: Yeah, I worry a lot about our kids having completely different experiences and that there being some resentment [because one looks white and one looks much

darker]. . . . They're going to have a different life experience. (Rosenblatt et al., 1995, pp. 211–212)

### Loss of Status in the Community

**Gregory:** If I were married to an African-American woman, then I'd have a greater range of access outside. There are certain places that, as an interracial couple in either the black or the white communities, you don't go there. . . . I was teachin' a history class one day, and I don't know how we got on the subject, one of my students mentioned, well, Gregory, . . . how can you say that? Your wife is white? And I said, yes she is, . . . but that threw . . . the whole class into chaos at that time. It was like, "How can you teach this class if you're married to a white woman?" It was like everybody's feelings about it came out in that class, and that class just really wasn't able or capable of dealing with how you could have a relationship . . . separate from school. . . .
**Joyce:** Or how can you teach a black history class if you're married to someone white? And that was like beyond what they could understand.
**Gregory:** And these are students, and they're the ones that are growing up, so I think that probably the climate has not changed that much in terms of interracial relationships. I think the people are still pretty much opposed to 'em. And certainly if a kid were to ask me, "Should I marry somebody within my own race or outside of my race?" I'd probably say to them, "You have to do what you think is best for yourself." But then on another level I think, "If you want an easy way out (laughs), marry the person who's in your race," 'cause [a multiracial relationship] got its own set of struggles. . . . You don't see 'em on the surface when you look at the person. You fall in love; you think this will be a wonderful relationship, and there's a bigger realm outside of that relationship that you have to contend with. . . . I didn't give it that much thought! . . . If I was married to someone of my own race, . . . and this is just my projection and my imagining, I think I have more access in the black community. I mean there's a certain thing in the black community, it's called legitimacy, that you attain . . . with who you are and what type of outward appearance you have. So if you're an African-American man and you're in a relationship with an African-American woman, the African-American community sees you in high esteem. If you're an African-American man and you're married to a non-African-American woman, then there's segments of the community who say, this guy's gotta be viewed with suspicion (laughs). He (laughs) broke the code. The code is that you, if you are going to marry, marry in the race. And it's very strong! I think a lot of people think well the African-American community is very liberal about that, and I mean that's one of the few things that a person can do to really kinda chop yourself off at the knees! . . . They're gonna look and say, "You talk a good game, brother, but who'd you marry?" . . . If I were an ambitious person, I think I would feel a loss a lot greater. (Rosenblatt et al., 1995, pp. 180–181)

## THE LOSS TO WHITES FROM RACISM

One does not have to be in a multiracial relationship to learn how much one loses by being white in a racist society, but many whites talked about learning in a multiracial relationship how much racism costs whites. For those who had not in the past realized what racism had cost them, some losses were current and some were in the past but based on more recent insights.

### Losses from Having Been Ignorant of White Skin Privilege

White partners who discovered that their white skin had given them advantages unavailable to dark-skinned people could express gratitude that they had learned that unpleasant truth, feel sad over the costs their partner, their children, and others paid or may pay because they lack white skin privilege, and grieve their own past ignorance of skin privilege.

> **Eve:** I'm changed because I am more aware of the struggles that he as a black male faces. And I realize that my life if I were married to a white male would be very different. And I am thankful that I am married to him because I can see that. I am more aware of it because I see everyday the things that he has to go through. . . . I try to share with people that it's important, that issues that affect him really affect all of us. . . . The way that I've been treated differently . . . , for example, going to the grocery store and getting the third degree when I'm trying to write a check with him. You always wonder, is this racism, my skin, . . . am I feeling what it's like? . . . Because I don't know, and he always say, "It is, it is." But I really don't know what racism is, so I'm learning. . . . This past winter my husband was accused of doing something that he didn't do and we had to go through court with that . . . , and it was really hard on us. And the one thing that I noticed when we got into the court was that . . . the judge, everybody else was white; everyone on the other side of the system was a minority, Native American, black. . . . And I realized when I saw him in there charged with something that he didn't do that those other people just saw him as a black man, not as a person. He was just another black man who committed a crime, they sort of thought. . . . It didn't matter if he did it or not. He was just another black man. . . . Those are the type of things that I've seen with him, and other things . . . , like the police in this neighborhood they treat him differently. Like one night we had to call the police because our window had got broken in our house, and these two white policemen came, and he was in the alley with the three white kids that broke the window and the policemen pointed their guns at him. . . . You don't want to believe that things like that are true, but they are. And I think that situations I have seen like that have really changed [me]. (Rosenblatt et al., 1995, p. 220)

### Losses from Having a Part in Victimizing African-Americans

Some white partners had recognized long before they were in a multiracial relationship how they had been part of the racist system of victimizing African-Americans. But whether their stories were from years prior to their having an African-American partner or based on recent learning within a multiracial relationship, it was common to hear stories that included a sense of loss and horror in realizing how they had acted in support of a racist system.

**Dot:** I remember one time [I was little and at] a big store . . . , I got lost and I met up with a little black girl who also had lost her parents, and we decided to have a high good time. And I had on a bright red sweater and she had on a green sweater and we exchanged. And we were just very pleased with ourselves, . . . and here came my mother and aunt, . . . and my mother just (indrawn breath) and in fact my aunt was falling all over us . . . because we had changed clothes. And then I got a lecture on the way home, "Well, honey, you mustn't change clothes with a colored person." Now I'm here to tell you you shouldn't change clothes with anybody in the store. You should not pick up with strange people in the store. And I can remember thinking, I must have been maybe 6 at the time, and I can remember, I couldn't put it into words in my mind but I remember a sad feeling that I knew that wasn't right.

Once, another time . . . I hope I was really really young. . . . My sister said to me "I'll give you all of this" she had eleven cents, I'll never forget it, a dime and a penny, "if you'll say 'Hi, you dumb nigger' to that woman over there." There was a lady. . . . I remember looking at that money. I still remember my thought was that would buy a lot of candy. And I said, "okay," and so I hollered it, and I'll always be grateful to this woman. This must have been 1954 or 55, and this woman had every reason in the world to be afraid of a six or seven year old girl hollering at her. And the easiest thing for her to have done was to have kept right on walking. And this woman was so courageous! She stopped, she looked, well we're in the yard and she's across the street . . . on the public sidewalk. And she went like that, meaning "Are you talking to me?" She looked around. She was the only person there, and, now I realized my sister had run, not only was I not going to get this eleven cents but there was some problem here. And I stood like that, and she walked over . . . and she said, "Come here. What did you say to me?" And she repeated what I had said. And she said, "I know that you don't know what nigger means. I just know that. Do you?" And I went like that. And she said "Well you do know what dumb means?" She said, "I'm going to tell you what nigger means." And this lady gave me a little lesson in racism there, and I don't actually remember the exact words she used. I don't remember her definition. I'm real grateful to her. I didn't recognize courage until I was older, but that also added to my sense that something wasn't right. (Rosenblatt et al., 1995, pp. 55–58)

## The Loss to Whites of Being Ignorant about African-American Life

**Jill:** I learned a lot of things that I wasn't taught about black culture. It wasn't introduced in mine.

**Janet:** I'm still trying to get to know black people completely in this racist society, . . . but Charles has afforded me the ability to go into all black churches. . . . The opportunities are unique. . . . There is some kind of dissolve, slowly mental dissolving the color barriers.

**Dot:** I feel that as far as just the interraciality that there are *so* many people out there who never get to know anyone of a race other than themselves. And I guess

> ignorance is bliss. There are a lot of people out there who don't understand that. . . . The other day my boss was . . . trying to get some cultural diversity stuff going at work. . . . He's a white man who is not an evil person, but he's one of those who keeps the old institutionalized racism going. . . . He said, "Well, now, you bring these articles in, but then don't bring anything that's going to upset people. . . ." And I said, "You're a lucky fellow. You don't have to have any controversy in your life. . . ." Then I . . . started thinking I was dead wrong. I am more lucky. . . . I wouldn't trade what I have for *any*thing in the world. . . . The parts I consider controversial have helped me to learn. . . . I will never stop being amazed at racism. I hope I never get to the point where it no longer shocks me.

## THE VALUE OF TAKING MULTIPLE PERSPECTIVES IN GRIEF RESEARCH

If the people quoted in this chapter were speaking for themselves, they might say they were living ordinary lives, not grieving more than other married people do. They might see our focus on grief as feeding into racist views that couples differing in race have something wrong with them. They might say that what we called "loss" was something else, for example, betrayal or injustice, and that feelings we called "grief" were something else, for example, feelings of regret. It is vital in researching grief or providing services to people who may be grieving that their perspectives be understood and respected. But it seems equally important that the researcher or clinician not give up the perspectives that can be brought to bear from theory and research. We have tried in this chapter to combine perspectives, providing detailed quotes while also offering our interpretations of what people said. We think that by doing so we have pointed out something that is not obvious and that people who might have been victimized by racism might not say, that there are losses that stem from racism and that victims of racism can be understood to grieve. At the same time, we have tried to make clear how complex and various are the words people use in talking about experiences of racism and how much that complexity and variety represents perspectives alternative to those couched in the language of loss and grief.

## RACISM AND LOSS

One route to understanding racism and to making more sense of what is going on in America is to accept that racism creates losses and to go about documenting and understanding those losses. What is lost? The American Dream? Individual and familial safety? Justice? Fairness? Community? A million things. Working within a paradigm that sees losses from racism, we are then free to apply all that we know about loss and grief to the situations of people who have been victimized by racism. For example, we know that grief for some losses recurs for a lifetime, that grieving can be set off by reminders of past losses, that grieving over a new loss can be entangled in and complicated by grieving for past losses, that in families, a grieving member may be lost in various ways to other family members, and that grief can undermine or strengthen religious faith. Such implications should be explored systematically at the intersection of studies of racism and studies of loss.

This article is written from an anti-racism stance. However, we do not advocate that all societal distinctions and boundaries be eliminated. Distinctions and boundaries seem to be intrinsic to how humans think and how they organize their social relations. But the distinctions and boundaries created by racism are extremely destructive, and we think the world would be well served were racism to end. In this regard, it might be useful to consider a typology of racisms. With such a typology, it might be well to single out some of the most destructive forms of racism—to study their effects and to eliminate them. The most virulent forms include "institutional racism," in which harmful actions are supported overtly or covertly by a substantial societal institution like a university, a national government, or the real estate dealers of a community. The most destructive forms would also include those intended to cause bodily harm or financial loss to their victims and those that block victims from access to general societal goods, legal recourse, grievance protocols, or formal public acknowledgment of hurt and injustice.

## THE IMPORTANCE OF MACROSYSTEMIC PROCESSES

This chapter focuses on the relationship of a macrosystemic force (racism that comes from and is sustained by society-wide processes) to grieving at the individual and family level. Much of the grief literature is about individual coping. Not enough is about the larger context that creates the losses. In the case of macrosystemic forces like racism, the most important question for those interested in helping others to deal with grief might not be: "How can people best cope with the losses they experience as a result of racism?" The most important questions might be: "How can racism be eradicated? How can the effects of racism be decreased through acting on the larger society?"

## REFERENCE

Rosenblatt, P. C., Karis, T. A., & Powell, R. D. (1995). *Multiracial couples: Black and white voices.* Thousand Oaks, CA: Sage.

# 10

# *Curbing Loss in Illness and Disability: A Relationship Perspective*

***Renee F. Lyons and Michael J. L. Sullivan***
*Dalhouse University, Halifax, Nova Scotia, Canada*

Sarah operates a futon shop in a small city in Eastern Canada. She is considering selling her business because fatigue and mobility problems due to multiple sclerosis make it impossible for her to rise to greet customers as they enter her shop. They are usually "put off" by her perceived lack of hospitality, and she is tired of having to explain that she has MS. A friend loans her a cane, a cue to customers that she has a mobility problem.

Harold has been left with a weak right arm from cerebral palsy. For most of his adult life, he avoids social gatherings. In Britain, it is important, when greeting others, to look them straight in the eye while extending a firm handshake. However, Harold would inevitably avert his gaze to his weak arm as a cue that a "normal" handshake was not possible. Finally, in his late fifties, he contacts a relationships researcher for advice and is offered several strategies to deal with his problem.

Amy makes homemade pumpkin soup and decides to invite her friends, Claire and Edgar, to dinner. Edgar, however, is a quadriplegic and Amy's home is inaccessible. So Edgar suggests that Claire go on her own. But Amy insists that they both come . . . that there is a solution to this problem. She and her family roll out a carpet, borrow electric heaters, and hold a candlelight dinner with music for Claire and Edgar, in the garage.

The stories of Sarah, Harold, and Edgar represent three examples of how individuals make efforts to preserve social integration, valued social roles, and the pleasures of social life. Each story involves a different approach to modifying traditional ways of relating to others. Although chronic illness and disability are typically discussed within the context of "loss," it is our contention that the degree of loss associated with health problems and disabilities is directly related to the number and severity of unresolved relationship stresses in family, in friendships, and in the workplace. Surprisingly little effort has been given to addressing such issues, although relational concerns have been identified as a major stressor in coping with disability or illness (Cohen & Wills, 1985; Moos & Tsu, 1977).

Serious health problems such as stroke, cancer, and multiple sclerosis have a way of enveloping their victims in loss (Gordon & Benishek, 1996). Decrease in physical function as a result of pain, paralysis or treatment often leads to disruption or loss of roles in work, family, and community, and loss of financial resources. These changes contribute to increased dependency, loss of self-identity, and hopelessness (Brooks & Matson, 1982; Lyons, Sullivan, Ritvo, & Coyne, 1995). Of course, illness and disability do not happen in a social vacuum. They are embedded within the context of family and friendships. Studies of family caregiver distress, burden, and burnout suggest that losses due to illness or disability can impact as strongly on family members as on the individual with the illness or disability (e.g., Gatz, Bengston, & Blum, 1990; Williamson & Shaffer, 1996).

There have been three major approaches to the study of losses associated with health problems. The *individual perspective* has focused on assessment of illness-related stressors and on helping individuals and distressed family members cope more effectively with illness/disability in their lives (e.g., Thompson, 1996). The *social change perspective* attributes loss to the social construction of illness and disability, and focuses on the need to change societal values, policies, and services, which will lead to personal empowerment, social role valorization, and community access (e.g., Duval, 1984). The *relationship perspective* proposes that social support is a key factor in curbing and adapting to loss (e.g., Atkins, Kaplan, & Toshima, 1991). This perspective has focused largely on the provision of emotional and instrumental support to persons with the health problems. However, it has been argued that the piecemeal approach taken to study aspects of social support has side-stepped key questions concerning what it is people need and the conditions that will elicit necessary relationship provisions (Heller & Rook, 1997; Vaux, 1988). With respect to illness and disability, such an analysis must include the nature of relationship change and loss (Bolger, Foster, Vinokur, & Ng, 1996; Meyerowitz, Levin, & Harvey, 1997; Thompson, 1996), the contribution of relationship tensions to illness/disability loss, and the conditions which contribute to the maintenance of quality relationships (Coyne & Fiske, 1992), the *primary determinant* of social support provision.

This chapter expands upon the conceptualization of the relationship perspective on illness/disability loss and calls for increased attention to the relationship stressors of health problems. We clarify the key relationship issues which arise from illness and disability and discuss factors in the successful negotiation of relationship tensions. Although our perspectives have evolved from considerable clinical and research activity on relationships, illness, and disability, we specifically draw upon findings and personal accounts from a recent focus group study of relationship issues and illness/disability.

The study comprised 16 three-hour focus group sessions in six locations in Canada and the United States. Eight sessions involved 63 adults with a range of acquired chronic health problems and disabilities, e.g., multiple sclerosis, cancer, spinal injury, and stroke. Another eight sessions included 32 researchers and clinicians (primarily clinical and social psychologists, and social workers) who study relationships and/or work with persons with chronic health problems/disabilities (Lyons et al., 1996). Accounts from focus group participants with illness/disability are identified by "I/D," and accounts from the clinician/researcher focus groups are identified by "C/R."

## DEALING WITH RELATIONSHIP LOSS AND CHANGE

*In terms of my practice, I guess one of the basic observations that I make is that once a family is touched significantly by illness and disability, their trajectories are altered perhaps for the full course of their family life. There is not really this question of being affected and then overcoming it, or adapting to it, and getting back to "normal." There isn't such a thing.*
—(C/R, Toronto Group)

Illness and disability can substantively change relationships. Several impacts on network structure, function, and quality are surprisingly similar across a broad range of disabling health problems (e.g., cancer, multiple sclerosis, spinal injury). Changes in *social network structure* typically include decreased size of network, decreased frequency of interaction, loss of friendships, and increased divorce in younger populations (Burman & Margolin, 1992; Coyne & Fiske, 1992; Janssen, Philipsen, & Halfens, 1990; Lyons, 1991). Changes in relationship *functioning* include a reduction in the multidimensionality or range of companionate activity, a decrease in social space (Guay, 1982; Brent, 1982), and discomfort in communication and support processes (Dunkel-Schetter & Wortman, 1982; Meyerowitz et al., 1997). Inevitably, relationship *quality* is affected as a result of the absence of valued relationship provisions and difficulty negotiating relationship constraints produced by illness and disability (Lyons, 1991; Burman & Margolin, 1992). The impact appears more substantial with degenerative or unpredictable health problems and/or conditions involving severe chronic pain or cognitive functioning (Lyons, 1991). Nevertheless, both sets of focus groups discussed the substantial relational impact of illness and disability on relationships across a large range of acquired illnesses and disabilities.

*There is a lot of loss related to this condition (MS). A lot of people we talk to talk about the social isolation, the loss, I think, of relationships.* (C/R, Cleveland Group)

*I'm sure we've all had friends who just evaporated. Compatriots at work and partners in business and neighbors and what not who shared in the sort of trivialities of the community and they are all gone.* (I/D, Toronto, Prostate Cancer Group)

*It (the divorce) was brought on by the MS, I think. It was beginning to be bad. But the MS, I was totally rejected and neglected at that time. I basically wasn't fed. I ruined his life, shattered his dreams. . . .* (I/D, Cleveland, MS Group)

Not only are individuals often confronted with relationship loss, but with the prospect of losing valued relationships, or being rejected.

*[P]eople are scared of being dumped, either by the medical profession or . . . I think it's also very much with the couples. That they feel they are going to be dumped by the other person. . . . And there is a lot of talk about fear and anxiety about losing the*

*loved one.* (C/R, Ottawa Composite [persons with a variety of health problems/disabilities] Group)

Such fears lead to actions which may have been contraindicated by the health problem in order to preserve the relationship.

*I think that (fear of marriage breakup) is a lot of the reason why I try to do more. Because as long as I can do, I will do, so he won't get tired of me real fast, real early.* (I/D, Cleveland, MS Focus Group)

Illness and disability violate the implicit relationship "contract," the expectations and roles that were in place when both partners or friends were healthy and able-bodied. It is perhaps the understanding that I, as the person with the illness or disability, have changed the conditions of this contract, that makes me fear the loss of relationships. Denial of the illness/disability by significant others or resistance to the changes that are required to accommodate illness in the relationship supports this belief.

*It was with my family that I had the worst problem. It was so hard to get a ride even down here for treatment. Because if they brought me for treatment, they would have to acknowledge that I had a problem. That there was something wrong with me.* (I/D, Toronto, Breast Cancer)

Also supporting this fear of loss is the notion that illness and disability are inconveniences in our fast-paced, individualistic culture. I have now become burdensome.

*It's almost a matter of inconvenience. . . . People seem to be inconvenienced by you. And they take that, it seems to me in our conversation, quite personally.* (I/D, Halifax, Composite Group 1)

*It's easy. A lot of people will give you help and pat you on the back and give you a cigar and see you out the door. But somebody who will stick through the times when you're really scared shitless and you just need somebody there. . . .* (I/D, Toronto, Prostate Cancer)

Teenagers, in particular, often perceived health problems in a parent as a personal inconvenience.

*Teenagers are very selfish. So my cancer has been a total inconvenience to their lives.* (I/D, Toronto, Breast Cancer Group)

*I registered for school and I went back. And they all fought me every step of the way. And the teenagers . . . They weren't teenagers. Actually, young adults by then. My son was 16 when I was diagnosed. And I would come home to sinks full of dirty dishes. This was my punishment for not being there.* (I/D, Toronto, Breast Cancer Group)

Managing a net*work* of friends, family, work mates, and the health care system takes tremendous energy, a scarce resource for persons devoting considerable effort to their health problem, and the need for network shrinkage is exacerbated by relationship tension which is not addressed.

> *With chronic illness, one of the things that you have to do, with these types of disabilities, is that you have to pare down your friends. There is no sense spending time to save a relationship with someone who doesn't appreciate your strengths and weaknesses, what you can and cannot do. You'll put an enormous amount of effort into it and all they are going to do is lead you down the garden path into situations that are going to make your health worse.* (I/D, Halifax Composite Group 2)

Thus, for the individual with chronic illness and disability, the stress of illness is not restricted to the loss of physical abilities and function that will ensue for illness symptoms. The stresses go beyond physical symptoms to encompass changes in relationship systems. As indicated by the accounts, however, the person with the disability may feel responsible for changing the rules of the relationship and for demanding more resources of the relationship. Feeling burdensome increases the perception that relationships will be lost or will be maintained as a social obligation.

## THE INCREASED NEED FOR QUALITY RELATIONSHIPS

It is ironic that relationship loss and change occur precisely at the time of heightened need for smooth-functioning and supportive relationships. Well-functioning relationships are not a frill for persons with health problems. They can mean the difference between isolation and social integration. They will strongly influence whether the individual will be living at home or in an institution. With changes in health care and greater reliance on family, the need for family support has become even more critical.

> *I think family is so much more important to me today than it would have been if I hadn't had a stroke.* (I/D, Iowa, Stroke Group)

> *Just for spinal cord injury, the presence of good relationships for somebody who is a quad is a key issue between being in the community or being in an institution. And I was just talking to some folks I work with about somebody who has been in the community for 10 years as a quad. And because the social support system has broken down, he's going to an institution. He has no other choice. I think the way health care is going, and we already know that the presence of a good support system is needed in the community. And how do we identify relationship problems early on?. . . It is such an important issue.* (C/R, Cleveland Group)

Relationships are also central to self-identity. Although difficult to verify, personal identity and self esteem have social origins, stemming possibly from the reciprocal chaining of processes of personal performance and recognition (Heller & Rook, 1997). Typically, illness and disability result in the reassessment of personal identity (Brooks & Matson, 1977; Charmaz, 1991; Hutchinson, 1996; Mathieson

& Henderikus, 1995). The individual with the illness/disability as well as those sharing in their personal relationships engage in a process of individual and relationship schema reformatting. Who am I? Who are we? What can I contribute to this relationship? How can we have a satisfactory relationship, given this illness/disability? What are realistic expectations for my relationships?

> *I thought, well this is pretty scary, like who the hell am I and who is my wife and what is our relationship? Who are my children and what is our relationship?* (I/D, Toronto, Prostate Cancer Focus Group)

> *It colors people's perception. Like if they get MS when they are single, "Can I ever marry? Can I have children? Can I follow through on those plans that I thought I had? Should I go to college? Should I buy a house?" You know, all of that kind of thing. So I think in that way it affects relationships. Or even the expectation of having relationships.* (C/R, Cleveland)

Relationships with health professionals, doctors in particular, dramatically influence self-appraisal.

> *I think still there is a great deal of discomfort on the part of physicians and how they relate to persons with disabilities. . . . The only accessible examination table that I've ever seen in a doctor's office is the one in the Rehab. There's a message right there. If they can't examine you, it looks as if they don't want you. Or if there are stairs to the office, how do you get into their office?* (I/D, Ottawa, Composite Group)

The belief that relationships define the self and that being on one's own is a sign of personal failure (Peplau & Perlman, 1982) adds pressure to be in relationships.

> *Our culture puts so much emphasis on having a relationship that I feel that in order to be self-fulfilled, I must have one. I should have one. And my disability compounds that problem in a very significant way.* (I/D, Halifax, Composite Group 3)

The strong desire for a partner may lead one to rush close relationship development or to misperceive the willingness of others for an intimate relationship.

> *I feel that in order for me to feel complete, I want to be married. I want to date. I want to have an emotional and physical relationship. You strive for those. You strive for that. You work towards that. And that creates problems for you because you put so much emphasis on it, you tend to overcompensate. You tend to try too hard. Or, you tend to misread situations from time to time as well.* (I/D, Halifax, Composite Group)

The accounts above indicate that the threat of loss of relationships is highlighted by disability. So too, is the threat of loss of self. Relationships play a role in how we feel about ourselves and how we think about ourselves. Paradoxically, we not only lose ourselves in relationships, we also find ourselves in relationships.

## ADDRESSING SPECIFIC RELATIONSHIP CHALLENGES

The negotiation of stresses associated with illness and disability involves clarifying and addressing the relationship issues that were created by illness and disability. These issues are not pathologies or personal functional deficiencies, but products of changed health circumstances. We examine issues in communication, companionate activity, and social equity.

### Communication Challenges

Interactions with individuals with a disability are often stressful, and people typically avoid them. (Eisenberg, Griggens, & Duval, 1982). The scripts we learn in life to manage interpersonal situations may no longer be useful in interpersonal situations which are ambiguous and uncertain. We don't know how to approach people and feel less secure about interpreting their responses. From the perspective of the person with the illness or disability, relationship tensions stem from the need to disclose the health problem and its impact on functioning. Individuals with an illness or disability are faced with the task of educating others about their condition and their needs. This process is particularly important in circumstances such as Sarah's and Harold's, where there are few visual cues to the disability and everything needs explaining. Communication issues surround who to tell, how to tell, how much to tell about symptoms, prognoses, or changes in performance, and in particular, to explain how it feels.

> *For the last couple of years, I've been trying to think of a way to express to people what I feel. What it feels like. Because I guess that I feel that I want somebody who doesn't have MS to go through this for one day, or a couple of hours. . . . The actual sensation that your body has or does not have is hard to explain.* (I/D, Cleveland, MS group)

The task of informing and educating can become quite stressful and tiresome, particularly for individuals who did not have a fluent interactional style prior to the illness.

> *It's a big job sometimes to educate somebody every day, every day of your life. You get tired of it.* (I/D, Halifax, Composite Group 1).

> *I was never much of a talker. And my actions were louder than my words. I always rested on my laurels with that. It doesn't work any more. I have to explain so much and negotiate so much more.* (I/D, Halifax, Composite Group 1)

For some individuals social withdrawal may be the less stressful adaptational option.

> *We avoid communication (with family) because of the misinterpretation and misunderstanding.* (I/D, Ottawa, Composite Group)

Individuals in our society, particularly men, have difficulty tolerating distress or disability in others. Their propensity for wanting to "fix things" makes them feel helpless when confronted with another person's disability. So individuals with disabilities are frequently urged to "get on with it" or "snap out of it"—anything, except talk about it.

*My husband is having trouble dealing with the fact that I'm involved with the group, (cancer support group) and very much involved with the group. . . . [H]e thinks I should go into a severe depression. And this is really morbid stuff. You know, why do I have to talk to women with breast cancer? Like, "Just get over it." And this has been a long time for him to come to terms with.* (I/D, Toronto, Breast Cancer Group)

Social comparison stories were shared about insensitive comments relating to less fortunate circumstances.

*My pet peeve is that people are somehow compelled to tell you about their worst, worst, worst friend of a friend who was dying and suffering.* (I/D, Toronto, Breast Cancer Group)

*I don't like people to tell me how lucky I am. I know I'm lucky to be walking and everything but I just don't want people to tell me that.* (I/D, Iowa, Stroke Group)

Part of the process of adjustment typically involves a drop in self-esteem. So relationships become risky ventures, inviting considerable opportunity to say the wrong thing. Blows to a fragile identity are readily provided by people with, perhaps, kind hearts, but lack of skill in communicating with persons with health problems.

### Companionate Activity Adaptation

Reducing relationship tension and finding mutually enjoyable activities were perceived by focus group members as key factors in the maintenance of satisfying relationships with family, work mates, and friends. Toward these ends, patience and flexibility were required to change traditional ways of performing activity in every social context, including leisure, sexual intimacy, and work.

*In order to have a relationship with a disabled person, flexibility is absolutely essential. You must be flexible.* (I/D, Halifax, Composite Group 3)

Activities had to be organized to accommodate for accessibility, transportation, increased support needs, symptoms, and energy. A major constraint was fatigue.

*There just comes a time when you say "Okay, I've seen enough of you people, go home." Your fatigue has hit a point where you don't want to be sociable any more. I don't want to put a strain on a relationship, but it (fatigue) will always affect a relationship with your family and spouse.* (I/D, Cleveland, MS Group)

Loss of cherished companionate activity, which in some instances, was the focal point of valued relationships, was difficult. The choice was often between sacrificing companionate leisure or exacerbating a health problem.

> *At first it was really tough getting used to what I could do physically and what I couldn't do. And I think my active lifestyle had a lot to do with that because I was involved in sports. . . . Like friends have asked me, "Would you like to go snowmobiling?" Well, sure I would love to go snowmobiling. But I know if I hop on a snowmobile with friends of mine, that just the bumping is going to break my rearend. So I'm saying to myself, "Well, I'm not going to do that because I'm not going to jeopardize my job and end up in bed for 3 months just for an hour's enjoyment going snowmobiling with some friends." So these are some of the decisions that you make, that you have to make.* (I/D, Halifax, Composite Group 2)

There was also considerable tension regarding how much to expect family and friends to adapt their agenda (as in Edgar's case), or when to just "stay home."

> *We've all given up things. We know that we cannot do everything that we did pre-MS as far as entertainment and enjoying the family and all that. Those of us who are married, a lot of times our spouses will . . . We're almost holding them back. My wife loves to dance and I'm not real good at the polka any more. . . . People would invite me somewhere, and I got so depressed because other people could dance and I couldn't. So I decided to stop going to those functions.* (I/D, Cleveland, MS Group)

Many participants in the focus groups gave up or substantially reduced sexual activity as a function of their health problems.

> *My sex life is "What is sex?"* (I/D, Toronto, Prostate Cancer Group).

Spontaneity and casual sexual relationships were usually out of the question.

> *Speaking from personal experience, we're not likely to have too many one night stands.* (I/D, Halifax, Composite Group 1)

There were reduced feelings of sexual attractiveness, and this was exacerbated by perceived lack of interest from one's partner. Perceived rejection occurred at a time of increased need for love and social validation.

> *We all need to be loved and cared for. When I was discharged and went home, I couldn't believe that my wife didn't want to have anything physical to do with me. And that is a real shock . And you feel . . . You're dying to be loved, and to love, and it isn't there. So that is a very difficult part of a relationship for people who have disabilities, I think.* (I/D, Ottawa, Composite Group)

The impact of relationship tensions on illness/disability loss was very apparent in attributions for quitting work. Although some participants in the focus groups were employed, most had stopped working as a result of disability. There was a strong desire among many participants to continue to perform meaningful activity, but with reasonable performance expectations. Negotiation of adaptation to work performance issues was not resolved in most work situations.

> *I used to absolutely exhaust myself. I'll show them. I'll get beyond this.* (I/D, Ottawa, MS Group)

The message becomes very apparent that our work environment is not flexible enough to accommodate performance changes. We are now a burden to the system.

> *I worked in an extremely busy office where it's just go from the moment you step into the door until you walk out. And when you're not there, it puts stress on everyone else because everyone else has to fill your shoes. So you get guilt feelings as a result of not being there, and wanting to be there. And you get a bit of odd comments when you do return to work. In relation to, "Well, we were really busy while you were gone." Or, "I had to do this and this for you while you were gone," and that type of situation. So it did not help our relationships at work at all. I tended to withdraw from work more and more as time occurred, talking less to my peers, and interacting with them less.* (I/D, Halifax, Composite Group 1)

## Issues of Support and Equity

Social support is not merely the process of receiving help, but is tied intimately to issues of reciprocity, equity, and power (Antonucci & Jackson, 1990; Heller & Rook, 1997). Focus group participants expressed considerable awkwardness about the activities of giving and receiving. Numerous accounts were provided by focus group participants of how people had been helpful, but the process of support provision could also easily misfire. Issues that had to be negotiated in relationships included: fairness and reciprocity, obligation vs. desire, expectations regarding performance, overprotectiveness, and asking for help. There was an awareness that increased needs altered the balance of power markedly. Whereas prior to the illness, the relationship may have enjoyed a comfortable give-to-take ratio, this balance had now been upset. Individuals now may fear that expressions of distress must be censored so as to avoid stressing the relationship.

> *Maybe before you weren't an individual who needed to depend on others. And now, because of your disability, you have to. And so in order for you to survive, you have to swallow your pride, and you ask for the help and the support of people who have always been around you.* (C/R, Halifax Composite Group 1)

> *Having to ask makes you angry. And having to say "thank you." It's a funny role in life that I guess we're stuck with and can't do much about. But none of us like it.* (I/D, Cleveland, MS Group)

Long term needs for support require continuous negotiation around equity issues and shared roles of companionship and support within friendship and family networks. The closest family member is too often left with overwhelming responsibilities for the well-being of the person who is ill. This circumstance also overwhelms the relationship.

Respondents in the focus groups also expressed a desire to be useful to others, and not to be identified as a person who is continuously needy.

> *Usually you go to a minister with your problems . . . but I have a minister coming to me. And this minister has prostate cancer. And I was able to advise him. Like, "Tell me the fears that you have." He and his wife spent from 6:00 when they came until 10:00 when they left there talking about cancer, prostate cancer. And he was much more relieved when he left there. He had a living example of someone who had gone through it. So I did probably well advising him and listening. And I felt good after.* (I/D, Toronto, Prostate Cancer Group)

Many relationship stresses exist across a broad range of health problems and disabilities and are present in most relationship activities including communication, activities of work, leisure, intimacy, and social support. Addressing such issues takes time, flexibility, creativity, and a commitment to the quality maintenance of relationships. For persons with chronic health problems, these adjustments are not simply a new chapter in the book of life experience, but create a new story line which will extend throughout the rest of their book and contribute to the life chapters on enjoyment, meaningful activity, social validation, and social integration.

## DETERMINANTS OF RELATIONSHIP ADAPTATION

What are the messages the focus group participants gave about the efforts required to curb such losses? Persons with disabilities, researchers, and clinicians give fairly straightforward, consistent indications about what is needed to facilitate the relational well-being of persons with disabilities, such as the following.

(1) Teach people more about illness and disabilities and their impact on quality of life. This should occur in the general population and also in specific instances of chronic illness and disability and be facilitated by the health care system.
(2) Increase awareness about the linkages between relational well-being and the quality of life of persons with health problems.
(3) Increase dialogue about personal and shared roles regarding the presence of disability in the family, workplace, and community.
(4) Increase relational competence around illness and disability. Individuals need to know how to communicate more effectively with individuals with illness and disability. They need to know how to provide effective social support and to learn strategies regarding adapting activities. They need to be able to negotiate relationship adaptation for various relational contexts, including work, family, leisure, and community.
(5) Individuals with disabilities and family members need license to discuss relationship issues and share relationship stories and strategies, through informal dialogue, individual and family counseling, or support groups, and there needs to be models provided of successful relationship adaptation.

(6) Public policy and its linkage to relationship maintenance in disability must be examined, e.g., support services, transportation, work adjustment programs, accessibility, and transportation.

We examine two key factors in implementing the above-named actions: commitment and the place of relationship-focused issues in the health care system.

## Commitment

> *I think there is a denial of the complexity, usually, of family relationships and of couple relationships, as well as parental relationships. I think there is a denial of death and of illness altogether in our society. And there is a tremendous amount of confusion about commitment. And all of the issues which are present in every relationship, I would argue, become more cued when one or more members become ill or disabled.* (C/R, Toronto Group)

What is the meaning of commitment when a family member, friend, or employee has a disability? Commitment is a complex concept involving social obligation, relationship rules and roles, relationship history, degree of attachment, other roles and commitments, and relationship expectancies. Obviously, the commitment to establish, maintain, and adapt relationships in the context of illness/disability plays a central role in the quality of life of a person with a disability. With the relaxing of societal rules about commitment in relationships in general, people are left to sort their respective roles and methods for rewriting a relationship script on their own.

In fact, there may be considerable resistance to the relationship perspective on loss which calls for more attention to relationship tensions and more effort at negotiation. The relational agenda is in conflict with the personal agenda. In a poignant "letter to the editor" in response to an article on caregiving, Charlwood (1997) speaks of the time and effort required to understand his wife's abilities (early-onset Alzheimer's) and the obvious direct relationship between this knowledge and his attention and her physical and emotional well-being. One is struck by the guilt he expresses for the time he reduced his involvement with his wife due to increased work demands. His letter highlights the meaning of commitment and the efforts required to be supportive and to address relationship issues/adaptations when a partner has a disability such as Alzheimer's Disease.

The extent to which illness/disability is perceived as an individual or communal issue will contribute to the nature of the effort (i.e., commitment) given. Persons with a strong individual agenda will continuously resist accommodation and change for others. Where there is a weak sense of interdependence, the responsibility is placed on the individual for problem solving (Sampson, 1977). Heller and Rook (1997) state: "This country (the US) was built upon the spirit of individualism and non interference from others, with the typical response to group conflict being separation" (p. 651). Accordingly, people with a communal orientation will feel less burdened or distressed by the relationship negotiation, adaptation, and support provision required of illness and disability. Persons with a communal orientation should experience interpersonal loss more strongly (Williamson & Schultz, 1995) and invest more in efforts to address relationship issues. The problem with this perspective, however, is that those with a stronger communal orientation are typically left with the overriding responsibility for negotiating relationship issues. The need is for sharing the load and finding some means for establishing equitable responsibility within families, workplaces, etc. What is a fair commitment for a family member or friend is a difficult question to answer, but is certainly one that requires family and public debate.

## The Place of Relationships in Health Care Services

The quality of personal relationships is the key to social support and social integration, but this area has not received sufficient attention in the health care system. The prevalent acute care model of health does not accommodate the stresses of chronic health problems and disabilities, including relationship issues. Relationship problems often fall through the cracks. Health professionals need to be more aware of the fact that chronic illness and disabilities *are* relationship issues and examine how relationships feature in their treatment and services. There were numerous accounts of the lack of preparedness for the impact of illness and disability on the relationship.

> *I had more instructions when I bought a toaster, in English and in French, than I did when I left the doctor.* (I/D, Toronto, Breast Cancer Group)

Persons with illness/disabilities and family members are not given license to discuss relationship issues.

> *Most people tend to want to at least speak openly and honestly about these issues because they are more important than what people tend to realize.* (I/D, Halifax, Composite Group 2))

There is a need for individual and family counseling.

> *This is where I think the medical profession is really letting us down. And where I feel that a price is put on our heads. Because we are not offered the services of counseling for the family. . . .* (I/D, Toronto, Breast Cancer Group)

> *What I notice in my clinical experience, that the more people I brought in from the family or from the significant others that help the patient, made a tremendous difference.* (C/D, Toronto)

There is also a need for health professionals to facilitate discussion of relationship issues in support groups. Coping assistance is often more helpful when it comes from others who have faced similar stressors (Thoits, 1986), and so the benefit of sharing relationship experiences and strategies with others can be enormous.

> *When they came to their first self-help group and found that other people had problems like they did, it was like a reawakening. It was like finding that they weren't so different.* (I/D, Ottawa, MS Group)

*The very fact that we belong to the Stroke Club and I find out that other people have the same problems that I have, man that helps a lot. You get a lot of help just listening.* (I/D, Iowa, Stroke Group)

However, there appears to be a need for support groups to feature the examination of relationship issues more systematically. There is also the need for relationship-illness protocols with tools for identifying and addressing issues in disability.

*But I just think, for a lot of people, they say, "Life isn't very good. And I'm not very happy in my relationships. But I'm not really sure what is going on." It's like they can identify the symptoms but they can't identify the underlying layer.* (C/D, Toronto)

## A FINAL WORD ON LOSS

It is easy to be drawn into the compelling stories of loss in illness and disability, the near-death stories, the active treatment phase, etc. In a review of a recent book on coping with stroke, Drainie (1997) admits that "the crisis portion" of stroke survival was a compulsively readable story, but that the portion on acceptance and adaptation was "tougher slogging." She realizes, however, that this latter portion is the primary story of loss and adaptation in illness and disability.

*Even as the reader allows these negative reactions to surface, however, awareness dawns that this is what disabled people have to put up with everyday. As humans, we are all fascinated by the high drama, the great tragedy that strikes someone low, but long boring aftermath of a life of daily struggle is something we'd rather ignore.* (p. D16)

For persons with illness/disability, the everyday relationship experiences are central to understanding the meaning of loss, but the particularly compelling portions of this story are the commitments and successes in renegotiating relationships. With relief from the burden of unrelenting dependence and burden, one can experience the challenges and rewards of engaging in interdependence. It is not merely a sad story of personal loss, but an opportunity for intimacy and collaboration. In fact, an overemphasis on loss will not contribute to adjustment. The loss perspective must be contained in order to appreciate the opportunities.

## REFERENCES

Antonucci, T. C., & Jackson, J. S. (1990). The role of reciprocity in social support. In B. R. Sarason, I. G. Sarason, & G. R. Pierce (Eds.), *Social support: An interactional view* (pp. 173–198). New York: Wiley.

Atkins, C. J., Kaplan, R. M., & Toshima, M. T. (1991). Close relationships in the epidemiology of cardiovascular disease. In W. H. Jones & D. Perlman (Eds.), *Advances in personal relationships, 3* (pp. 207–231). London: J. Kingsley.

Bolger, N., Foster, M., Vinokur, A. D., & Ng, R. (1996). Close relationships and adjustment to a life crisis: The case of breast cancer. *Journal of Personality and Social Psychology, 70,* 283–294.

Brent, R. S. (1982). Community and institutional social spaces. *Therapeutic Recreation Journal, 16* (1), 41–48.

Brooks, N. A., & Matson, R. R. (1982). Social psychological adjustment to multiple sclerosis. *Social Science and Medicine, 16,* 2129–2135.

Burman, B., & Margolin, G. (1992). Analysis of the association between marital relationships and health problems: An interactional perspective. *Psychological Bulletin, 112,* 39–63.

Charmaz, K. (1991). *Good days, bad days: The self in chronic illness and disability.* New Brunswick, NJ: Rutgers University Press.

Charlwood, R. G. (1997). Caring for someone with Alzheimer's. In Letters to the Editor, *The Globe and Mail,* January 25, p. D.9, Toronto, ON, Canada.

Cohen, S., & Wills, T. A. (1985). Stress, social support and the buffering hypothesis. A theoretical analysis. In A. Baum, J. E. Singer, & S. E. Taylor (Eds.), *Handbook of psychology and health. Vol. 4* (pp. 253–267). Hillsdale, NJ: Lawrence Erlbaum.

Coyne, J. C., & Fiske, V. (1992). Couples coping with chronic illness. In T. J. Akamatsu, J. C. Crowther, S. C. Hobfoll, & M. A. P. Stevens (Eds.), *Family Health Psychology.* Washington, D.C.: Hemisphere.

Drainie, P. (1997). Slowdance: A story of stroke, love, and disability by B. Sherr Klein (book review). *The Globe and Mail,* February 8, p. D.16, Toronto, ON, Canada.

Duval, M. L. (1984). Psychosocial metaphors of physical distress among MS patients. *Social Science and Medicine, 19,* 635–638.

Dunkel-Schetter, C., & Wortman, C. B. (1982). The interpersonal dynamics of cancer: Problems in social relationships and their impact on the patient. In H. S. Friedman & M. Robin DiMatteo (Eds.), *Interpersonal issues in health care* (pp. 69–100). New York: Academic Press.

Eisenberg, M., Griggins, C., & Duval, R. (1982). Disabled people as second class citizens. New York: Springer-Verlag.

Gatz, M., Bengston, V. L., & Blum, M. J. (1990). Care-giving in families. In J. E. Birren & K. W. Schail (Eds.), *Handbook of the psychology of aging* (pp. 404–426). New York: Academy Press.

Gordon, P. A., & Benishek, L. A. (1996). The experience of chronic illness: Issues in loss and adjustment. *Journal of Personal and Interpersonal Loss, 1,* 299–307.

Guay, J. (1982). The social network of the ex-patient. *Canada's Mental Health, 30* (4), p. 22.

Heller, K., & Rook, K. S. (1997). Distinguishing the theoretive functions of social ties. In S. Duck (Ed.), *Handbook of personal relationships* (2nd ed., pp. 648–670). Chichester, UK: Wiley.

Hutchinson, S. L. (1996). *The altered self. An exploration of the process of self identity reconstruction by people who acquire a brain injury.* Master's thesis, Dalhousie University, Halifax, NS, Canada.

Janssen, M., Philipsen, H., & Halfens, R. (1990, July). Personal networks of chronically ill people. *Fifth International Conference on Personal Relationships,* Oxford University, Oxford, UK.

Lyons, R. (1991). The effects of acquired illness and disability on friendships. In D. Perlman & W. Jones (Eds.), *Advances in Personal Relationships. Vol. 3* (pp. 223–277). London: J. Kingsley.

Lyons, R. F., Sullivan, M. J. L., Ritvo, P. G., & Coyne, J. C. (1995). *Relationships in chronic illness and disability.* Thousand Oaks, CA: Sage.

Lyons, R. F., Coyne, J. C., Duck, S., Fitch, M., Gunter, A., Hood, C., Jackson, Z., Miller, D., Ritvo, P., Thompson, P., & Langille, L. (1996, July). *Social integration and disability: Clarification of relationship issues in work, family and community.* Research report to the Social Sciences and Humanities Research Council of Canada, Ottawa, ON, Canada.

Mathieson, C. M. & Henderikus, S. J. (1995). Renegotiating identity: Cancer narratives. *Sociology of Health & Illness, 17,* 283–306.

Matson, R. R., & Brooks, N. S. (1977). Adjusting to multiple sclerosis: An exploratory study. *Social Science and Medicine, 11,* 245–250.

Meyerowitz, B. E., Levin, K., & Harvey, J. H. (1997). On the nature of cancer patient's social interactions. *Journal of Personal and Interpersonal Loss, 2,* 49–69.

Moos, R. H., & Tsu, V. D. (1997). The crisis of physical illness. In R. H. Moos (Eds.), *Coping with physical illness* (pp. 3–21). New York: Plenum.

Peplau, L. A. & Perlman, D. (1982). Perspectives on Loneliness. In L. A. Peplau & D. Perlman (Eds.), *Loneliness: A source book of current theory, research, and therapy.* New York: Wiley.

Sampson, E. E. (1977). Psychology and the American ideal. *Journal of Personality and Social Psychology, 35,* 767–782.

Thompson, S. C. (1996). Barriers to maintaining a sense of meaning and control in the face of loss. *Journal of Personal and Interpersonal Loss, 1,* 333–357.

Thoits, P. A. (1986). Social support as coping assistance. *Journal of Consulting and Clinical Psychology, 54,* 416–423.

Vaux, A. (1988). *Social support: Theory, research and intervention.* New York: Praeger.

Williamson, G. M., & Schulz, R. (1995). Caring for a family member with concern: Past communal behavior and affective reactions. *Journal of Applied Social Psychology, 25,* 93–116.

Williamson, G. M., & Shaffer, D. R. (1996). Interpersonal loss in the context of family care-giving: Implications of communal relationship theory. *Journal of Personal and Interpersonal Loss, 1,* 249–274.

# 11

## *Passion Lost and Found*

***Michael R. Cunningham***
***Anita P. Barbee***
*University of Louisville*

***Perri B. Druen***
*York College*

A friend of ours, who we will call Angie, was head-over-heals in love. The object of her affection, Brad, worked in a different division of a medium size organization, and they had met at lunch through mutual friends. The members of the group were all young, well-educated, with careers on the rise, and they enjoyed one another's company. Soon, Angie, Brad, and their friends were having lunch together several times a week. Lunchtime contact evolved into plans for afterhours workout sessions at the company gym. But exercise is more demanding than eating. One person dropped out of the workout group because of family responsibilities, another because he could never seem to finish his work by 5:30, and a third because of an injured Achilles tendon. Just Angie and Brad were left, chatting and sweating together on adjacent stairclimbers, learning about each other's pains from the past and hopes for the future.

Perhaps because of personal compatibility, the physical attraction-enhancing qualities of spandex exercise togs, continued proximity causing familiarity and attachment, or misattribution of the heart-thumping arousal from the exercising, soon Angie and Brad felt irresistibly attracted to one another. She saw him as smart and funny, and felt intoxicated in his presence; she wanted to spend every minute of her spare time with him.

But this story does not end with Angie and Brad strolling off into the sunset together. They were both married to someone else at the time, and Brad had children to whom he was devoted. Angie recognized that it could never work out as a traditional storybook romance. But after one month of shared passion, she believed that what she felt was too good to give up. She wondered if she and Brad could not continue to enjoy their passionate feelings in a covert affair for the next 20 years.

### PASSION AND LOVE

Apart from the moral issues, and the possibility that their affair would be discovered and derail both of their marriages or careers, the story of Angie and Brad raises other questions. How important is passion in romantic relationships and in life satisfaction? How long can strong passionate feelings, like those of Angie and Brad's, last? Why were not Angie and Brad still passionately attracted to their spouses, and consequently inoculated from being attracted to each other? What causes such passionate feelings to ebb or die, if they do? Do people differ in the trajectories of their passionate feelings?

The importance of passion for love and life should not be overrated. In a survey of 130 undergraduates (Druen, 1997), relations based on passion alone were perceived to be of lower quality ($M$ = 4.14) than those based on intimacy alone ($M$ = 5.77) or commitment alone ($M$ = 5.17). Passion was also rated as lower than intimacy ($M$ = 6.17) and commitment ($M$ = 5.45) in importance for romantic relationships, and its importance for relationship success or happiness is unclear (Argyle, 1987; Sprecher, 1997). Nonetheless, Druen's (1997) respondents rated passion as very important ($M$ = 5.25 on a 7-point scale), so it should not be dismissed either.

Initial information on the duration of passion was offered by Elaine Hatfield and her associates. Hatfield and Rapson (1993) describe passionate love in the following way.

> *A state of intense longing for union with another. Passionate love is a complex functional whole including appraisals or appreciations, subjective feelings, expressions, patterned physiological processes, action tendencies, and instrumental behaviors. Reciprocated love (union with another) is associated with fulfillment and ecstasy; unrequited love (separation) with emptiness, anxiety, or despair. Other theorists have labelled this experience puppy love, a crush, fatal attraction, lovesickness, obsessive love, infatuation or being in love.* (p. 5)

The foregoing definition of passionate love involves the fusion of powerful sexual attraction (Hatfield & Rapson, 1987a) with intense idealization and intimacy, such as a strong desire to incorporate the wonderful other into the self (Aron, Dutton, Aron, & Iverson, 1989). Such feelings may induce new couples to stay up until 4 a.m., alternately discovering the pleasure of each others' bodies and minds, accelerating in excitement as each self-disclosure uncovers a new point of similarity (Adams & Shea, 1981).

Discriminating passion from feelings of idealization or intimacy can be challenging. Individuals with a Ludic love style may enjoy sexual passion without intimacy and commitment (Hendrick & Hendrick, 1991), and sexual passion that is manifested as arousal to pornography, or intimate behavior with a stranger, is different from passionate love. The passionate component of love (Sternberg, 1986) can be measured with items asking about seeing only the other's good qualities, gazing at the other, feeling euphoria, heart rate increase, sex appeal, energy, and touching, and such measures show good discriminant validity from measures of intimacy and commitment (Aron & Westbay, 1996). But separating passion from intimacy and commitment in the context of a romantic relationship remains problematic (Acker & Davis, 1992; Whitley, 1993). Increases in passion tend to be associated with increases in intimacy and commitment, and vice versa (Aron & Westbay, 1996).

Indeed, it has been suggested that the prospect of enhanced intimacy is usually necessary to create passion. Strong passion may entail the idealized expectation that the partner is going to meet all of one's needs, dependent as well as sexual

(Reik, 1972), and at a rate even faster than one expected (Berscheid, 1983; 1985). Extraneous sources of arousal may contribute to passion, when such stimuli are misattributed to the object (Dutton & Aron, 1974). But it is not clear that passion remains after the misattributed arousal has faded, or as life goes on.

Pillemer and Hatfield (1981) interviewed a variety of people, including those who had just begun dating each other steadily, couples who were newly married, and a group of older women, who had been married an average of 33 years. Whereas the dating couples and newlyweds expressed considerable passion for their partners, the married women stated that they (and their husbands) felt only "some" passion for one another. The duration of intense passionate feelings varied from a couple of months to a couple of years in retrospective accounts, but did not seem to extend to the 20 years that Angie hoped for. This pioneering work did not explore the causes of the shorter versus the longer enduring passions, but Hatfield and Rapson (1993) implicated biological adaptation mechanisms in passion's decline.

## BIOLOGY, EVOLUTION, AND PASSION

Richard Solomon's (1980) opponent-process theory of motivation proposed that many stimuli that produce euphoria, such as cocaine, heroin, gambling, or passionate love, not only produce addiction, or the intense desire to reexperience the stimulus, but also habituation, such that each encounter with the stimulus produces less positive affect. Either the strength of the arousing stimulus must be increased, or the highs will be increasingly weak and fleeting.

It might seem appropriate for the person to develop a tolerance for destructive stimuli, such as cocaine or gambling, but why should passionate love have to fade? Evolutionary theory offers one possible answer. Anthropologist Helen Fisher (1992) suggested that feelings of love evolved to induce men and women to consummate their passionate attraction through repeated acts of coitus until pregnancy was produced, and then stay attached to one another until the child was about two to four years old. After the mother had recovered from pregnancy, and the child had reached the age of mobility, the contribution of the father was no longer crucial for survival, at least in pre-industrial societies in Africa and Oceana. After a few years together, the partners could seek out other sexual opportunities, or again roll the genetic dice with each other.

This logic can be extended to suggest that the decline of passion may be nature's way of encouraging people to take off their rose-colored glasses, rationally examine their comparison level for alternatives, and decide if they should stay together with their current partner or try to do better elsewhere. Those whose sentiments are monogamous and who find this analysis distasteful may derive some cheer by downward phylogenetic comparison. Whereas human males may take two to four years to lose passion for their mate and develop a roving eye, roosters are far less faithful. As recounted in the well-known Coolidge effect, a rooster whose passion is sated with one hen may quickly recover his virility and mate passionately with a second hen (Carlson & Hatfield, 1992). And females in estrous may present themselves sexually to any number of males, and allow their sperm to compete for fertilization opportunities (Wilson, 1975). By contrast with the behavior of many other species, human passion seems quite stable (cf. Buss, 1994).

Evolutionary interpretations of human behavior, such as Fisher's, may offer useful heuristics for research (Cunningham, 1981), but they may also miss some of the complexity of human social dynamics. While passion may be increasingly important in mate choice (Simpson, Campbell, & Berscheid, 1986), romantic love may endure longer in societies with arranged marriages (Gupta & Singh, 1982), perhaps because of the greater attention of families than lovers to assortative mating variables that lead to intimacy and commitment.

The multiple fitness model's extension of parental investment theory (Cunningham, Barbee, Graves, Lundy, & Lister, 1996) noted that humans are uniquely slow to physically mature, and even slower to reach the point at which they can successfully compete for resources and invest in their offspring. In temperate and frigid climates, the resource contributions of the father may have been required to guarantee the survival of his offspring well past their third or fourth year. In post-industrial society, the contribution of the father may be necessary to secure the well-being and mating opportunities of his offspring for at least 22 years. Few single mothers can afford to subsidize the cost of their children attending first-rate universities, which provide access to higher-quality mates and more lush ecologies after graduation. Indeed, the support and resource contribution of grandparents may be helpful, if not crucial, to insure the continuity of their descendants. As a consequence, rather than operating exclusively in favor of serial polygamy and against the persistence of monogamous lust, evolutionary processes could have favored those who maintained long-term passion for their mates, especially in more challenging environments. Thus, there are good grounds for further consideration of the variables that instigate or reduce passion. Qualities of the perceiver, the target, and their relationship may all play a role in the relative persistence of passion.

## THE MORE OR LESS PASSIONATE RECEIVER

People may differ in how long their passionate feelings last. Extraverts, sensation seekers, and those who are high on sociosexuality reported having more sexual partners and romantic relationships compared to their counterparts (Simpson & Gangestad, 1991; Zuckerman, 1991). It is possible that the passion of such people burns both brighter and faster than that of others. Introverts, low sensation seekers, and those low in sociosexuality may never display quite the passionate intensity of their counterparts, but perhaps research may find that the flame of their passion lasts longer.

The alleviation of a temporary personal deficit may also cause passion to fade. For example, a person who starts a new job in an unfamiliar city may initially feel rather lonely and overwhelmed. If the new arrival begins a dating relationship with a local person, that partner may stir passion by offering an abundance of riches, including reduction of loneliness, introduction to new friends, and tours of a variety of exciting locations in the new city. But, as the new arrival becomes more comfortable with the city and the job, meets more people, develops a tighter social support network, and feels less lonely, the benefits that the local person offers may seem pale and superfluous; passion may fade (cf. Shaver & Hazan, 1987).

Erik Erikson (1950) suggested that the development of identity must precede the development of intimacy. Carl Rogers (1961) suggested that people must unconditionally love themselves before they can love someone else. Low self-esteem may entail dynamics that are similar to that of loneliness, in creating greater proneness to passion, but lower durability. Compared to people with high self-esteem, individuals whose self-esteem has been temporarily lowered are more attracted to friendly members of the opposite sex, especially those who give them unambiguous compliments (Walster, 1965). Individuals whose self-esteem is threatened may unconsciously long for a passionate experience with another person to replace self-doubt with excitement, validation, and tenderness. Individuals who have low self-esteem fall in love less often than others, but when they do it tends to be a very passionate experience (Dion & Dion, 1975), perhaps because the change in emotion is more extreme than in that of a person who was already happy. Prospective research on extramarital affairs was not located, but the combination of threats to self-esteem (cf. Walster, 1965; Jacobs, Berscheid, & Walster, 1971) and an available alternate paramour (cf. Simpson, 1987) seem like two possible predictors of affairs.

Yet, once people with temporarily lowered self-esteem return to their customary plateau of feeling satisfied with themselves, their passion for their partner may wane. Indeed, a supportive and solicitous partner may seem condescending and sex-role stereotyped if the ministrations are not needed. Water is desperately craved when one is thirsty, and tastes sweet and refreshing when the need is being slacked; but afterwards water tastes like nothing at all. Further research on how low-self-esteem people seek out and then undermine their relationships seems needed.

Some people may have personal needs that can never be completely filled. Those with an anxious-ambivalent (Hazan & Shaver, 1994) or dismissive (Bartholomew & Horowitz, 1991) attachment style may have exceptionally stringent standards for what they desire from their romantic partners. Such people may experience passionate excitement when they believe that they finally have found what they are looking for, perhaps because they project their ideals onto their dimly perceived new partner. Unfortunately, projections tend to evaporate; the anxious-ambivalent or dismissive person may become disenchanted when their partners are found to have feet of clay, and their passion may plummet.

Although familiarity can cause a pleasant sense of comfort (Zajonc, 1968), it can also cause boredom (Brickman & D'Amato, 1975). People may be passionately excited by novelty; individuals generally give potential romantic partners more positive appraisals initially than subsequently. Graziano, Jensen-Campbell, Shebilski, & Lundgren (1993) reported that people's second rating of another person's physical attractiveness was almost always less positive than their first rating had been, including one made just half an hour earlier. A more extreme pattern of overidealization and devaluation is characteristic of several personality disorders, including histrionic, narcissistic, and borderline (Apt & Hurlbert, 1994).

## THE OBJECT OF PASSION

Just as some people may be more prone to losing or sabotaging their own passionate feelings, some who are beloved may be highly prone to turning their partner's fire into rain. Felmlee's (1995) study of "fatal attractions" found that the same unique qualities that drew people to romantic partners often were later perceived to be the things that drove them apart. (See also Felmlee's contribution, in Chapter 8 of this volume, on the same topic.) Thus, a relaxed and playful style could later be recognized as immaturity and laziness; exceptional poise and beauty could be seen as obsession with appearances; intelligence and erudition could be reinterpreted as a know-it-all attitude; devotion could be viewed as possessiveness; a sense of humor could be reframed as the sarcastic inability to take anything seriously; and ambition could be seen as workaholism.

Part of the cause of a fatal attraction could be the bedazzling novelty of an available person with charismatic qualities. Extraordinary beauty, knowledge, humor, or ambition is rare, and may cause the perceiver to leap into passion without evaluating overall personal compatibility, thereby increasing the likelihood of a flame-out. But a portion of the responsibility for the loss of passion may lay with the target.

A person who is extremely invested in a single motive, whether it be athletic accomplishment, popularity with friends, monetary wealth, scientific productivity, political power, fame as a celebrity, or simply self-indulgence, may not have the time, energy, skill, or inclination to stay focused on a romantic relationship for the long term. Such a unidimensional person may invest enough in a romantic relationship to stimulate passion, but not enough to nurture and maintain it. In such cases, the target of a fatal attraction is not just seen more realistically; the behavior of the target has changed for the worse. The partner's romantic passion may wither because it is in the shadow of the real passions of the monomaniac, which lay elsewhere.

Other personal qualities of the target may create relationship time bombs that cause the loss of passion. High self-monitors (SMs), out of concern for situational appropriateness, are particularly sensitive and attentive to their self-presentation (Snyder, 1987). When the situation involves the possibility of a dating relationship, high SMs may cross the line from flexibility into deception.

We provided men who were high or low in self-monitoring with information on the date qualities that were sought by a pair of women, one of whom was high and the other low in attractiveness. The men then had the opportunity to describe themselves to the women. We found that high SMs engaged in more deceptive self-presentation than low SMs. For example, if the woman to whom they were attracted desired a great deal of masculinity in her date, the high SMs described themselves as masculine; if she wanted femininity, they described themselves as feminine. A second study replicated these findings, and further revealed that high SMs hold more favorable attitudes toward using deception in dating initiation and admitted altering their self-presentation in an attempt to initiate a date (Rowatt, Cunningham, & Druen, 1997).

Given such mate attraction behavior, it is not surprising that high SMs, on average, prefer establishing and maintaining less close and less exclusive romantic relationships, compared with low SMs (Snyder & Simpson, 1984). Such a relationship style may allow the SM's internal disposition to go unscrutinized and unchallenged for a longer period of time: when the woman discovers that the rugged and self-reliant, or tender and caring, man whom she thought she was choosing is a duplicitous chameleon, the feeling of betrayal may extinguish her passion.

Internal qualities, such as personality, exert a greater influence than do external qualities, such as appearance, on the mating choices of both males and females (Cunningham, Barbee, & Druen, 1997). Yet studies of physiological responses to pornography, as well as self-reported attraction to photos (Cunningham, Roberts, Barbee, & Druen, 1995) clearly demonstrate that a desirable physical appearance can enhance passion.

But life is not always kind to personal appearance. A stigmatizing injury, a disfiguring surgery, or the gradual effect of age, menopause, sun, and gravity can all reduce external attractiveness (Herman, Zanna, & Higgins, 1986). Neglect of hygiene, nutrition, exercise, or contraception can have comparable effects. The impact of loss of physical attractiveness on passion may depend upon the attributions of responsibility for the cause and controllability of the solution that a person makes about the partner's change in physical attractiveness. For example, if a person views a partner's weight gain as both negative and controllable, and the overweight partner consumes alarming quantities of food in front of the person, feelings of disgust (cf. Rozin & Fallon, 1987) could inhibit passion for the overweight partner.

On the other hand, if weight gain was seen as caused by a positive stimulus or as uncontrollable, as when a woman is pregnant, passion may remain intact. If the woman remains larger after the birth, her partner may continue to see her as physically attractive and continue to feel passion. But if a new mom continues to consume the calorie levels of pregnancy or feels unable to exercise often or to return to prior levels of grooming because of the added stress of the baby, then her partner's evaluation of her attractiveness may drop, her self-esteem may suffer, and her own passion, as well as that of her partner, may be lost. Disagreement with the partner over attributions of controllability and other dimensions may generate additional conflict and create reciprocal feelings of unjust treatment (Fincham & Bradbury, 1992).

Changes in the male may cause a loss of passion in the female. A woman may feel passionate, in part, because her man expresses a great deal of sexual interest in her. But male testosterone levels decline with age, such that men in middle age may produce half as much as men in their teens (Persky, Smith, & Basu, 1971). If the man displays less passion, then less passion may be reciprocated by the woman, for a net loss of passion in the relationship.

Other genetically based mechanisms in males may affect passion in females. We found that male pattern baldness decreased social perceptions of a male's attractiveness and aggressiveness, perhaps making him appear less suitable for passionate love. But baldness increased perceptions of the males' maturity and appeasement, perhaps making him seem more suitable for stable domesticity (Muscarella & Cunningham, 1996). Thus, male pattern baldness may serve to inform both the man who has it and the women who view him that he may be more suitable for a companionate than an exclusively passionate relationship. Many women might accept a small loss in passion for a potential increase in supportiveness and loyalty.

## STRUCTURAL INTERACTION EFFECTS

Passion may be fueled by a variety of extraneous sources of arousal, and some of these sources of arousal may not endure. Wegner, Lane, & Demetri (1994), for example, demonstrated that people felt more excited about romantic relationships that were secret compared to those that were public. Yet, while secrecy may fuel passion, keeping a relationship secret for 20 years, as Angie hoped to do, is unlikely. Bad luck or carelessness may cause the secret to be revealed, or lying and sneaking around may become repellant with repetition, and be replaced by the desire to make the relationship legitimate. Paradoxically, even if a once-secret relationship can withstand the glare of public scrutiny, it still may wilt. All of the plotting and worrying that it took to maintain the relationship may have kept the couple on their toes and at their best. As danger and effort justification is eliminated, arousal and passion may also decline. Ironically, consistent declarations of love can hinder the maintenance of passion (Hatfield & Rapson, 1993) because the arousal of insecurity is gone.

Passion may contain the seeds of its own destruction, if it is not rationed and controlled. Sexual passion leads to intercourse, which accelerates to orgasm, but ends in warm, but passionless, resolution. The passion to incorporate the other into the self can cause increasingly fascinated curiosity, until the other person is exhaustively known, leaving no surprises left to unwrap. Romantic passion leads to a quickening desire for closeness, and closeness leads to interdependent lifestyles (Berscheid, Snyder, & Omato, 1989), but a close and stable lifestyle may destroy the euphoric illusion of unlimited possibilities.

When pondering whether to book a flight on the Concorde and have breakfast in Paris or to save the money for a downpayment on a house, most couples choose the latter. After a few months of dating, the expense of going out to dinner and a film may be reduced in favor of drive-through fast food and a rented videotape. The joint savings account may grow, but passion may decline. Soon, rather than being associated exclusively with luxurious forms of entertainment, soulful self-disclosure, and delirious sexual expression, the partner becomes associated with the unglamorous monotony of daily hassles (Hatfield, Traupman, & Sprecher, 1984). Instead of serving as a distraction from the cares of living, the partner may contribute to them, with his requests for laundry and ironing service, her requests for car maintenance, or their child expressing constant needs (Argyle, 1987, Surra, Chandler, Asmussen, & Wareham, 1987). If it is not certain that being with the other person will be an occasion for unambivalent ecstasy, then passion at the prospect may decline.

The more frequently one sees the beloved, the more likely it is that one will witness actions and qualities that are usually kept backstage, away from public view. A partner's flatulent indigestion, sinus infection, intoxication, premenstrual syndrome, fatigue, and other weaknesses to which the flesh is heir, all may be tolerated in a close relationship. But they may also cause a social allergy (Cunningham et al., 1997), reduce the idealization of the partner, and undermine passion. Thus, while passion may have evolved to increase intimacy and commitment, distasteful intimacy and stifling commitment may destroy passion.

## PASSION GONE AWRY

Ironically for those who are nostalgic for more zest in their romantic lives, passionate feelings may sometimes be troublesome and difficult to dispel. In the case of unrequited love, for example, an individual may experience heartbreak or humiliation by being passionately attracted to someone who does not share those feelings (Baumeister, Wotman, & Stillwell, 1993). It has not been reported whether unrequited passion felt stronger or lasted longer than requited passion, nor was it clear whether unfulfilled sexual desire versus unfulfilled intimacy desire, including curiosity and the desire to incorporate the other into the self, were the driving motives.

Further research on the processes involved in resolving unrequited love, and thereby consciously killing passion, would be informative. Strong arousal associated with the initial perceptions (cf. Abbey, 1982) may retard, but clear rejection messages (Folkes, 1982) may hasten, the decline of unrequited love. As cases of obsessive passion toward and stalking of celebrities illustrate (Dietz et al., 1991), such feelings may be difficult to extinguish. Paradoxically, deliberately suppressing thoughts of the unrequited love object are likely to stimulate rather than reduce passion (cf. Wegner & Gold, 1995).

There are times when passionate feelings were initially reciprocated, but then lost through a unilateral breakup. Relationship disengagement may follow a variety of trajectories (Baxter, 1984) and may have multiple effects. Severing an attachment relationship causes a loss of feelings of intimacy and belongingness (Baumeister & Leary, 1995) and erodes self-esteem (cf. Mathes, Adams, & Davies, 1985), besides circumventing passion. Tracking the diminution of passion in such cases may be challenging, although cases of post-breakup sex have been observed.

Even the possibility of the loss of a partner may inspire jealousy (Fitness & Fletcher, 1993) and aggressive behavior to retain or restore the relationship (Barnett, Martinez-Tomas, & Bluestein, 1995). It may be that the more often that one partner unsuccessfully attempts to disengage, the more that the other person is aroused, which is transferred into more romantic, as well as aggressive, passion. The honeymoon period that has been observed to follow domestic abuse may be due to enhanced passionate love, rather than just guilt and remorse.

But when emotional needs are unmet, the heart may become a lonely hunter and contribute to some people, such as Angie and Brad, being passionately attracted to those who are not their legitimate partners. Those who feel low self-esteem (Sheppard, Nelson, & Andreoli-Mathie, 1995) and those who generally feel underbenefitted in the relationship (Walster, Traupmann, & Walster, 1978) seem most prone to infidelity. Women may be more willing than men, however, to believe that falling in love justifies sexual involvement (Glass & Wright, 1992). As long as passionate feelings last, the belief that the relationship represents romantic love may sustain the decision to continue an extramarital affair (cf. Hurlbert, 1992).

## SOLUTIONS TO PASSION'S DECLINE

A variety of cognitive mechanisms may delay passion's decline. The prospect of continued interaction with another person may cause people to repress their reservations and enhance their ratings of the desirability of the potential person (Berscheid, Graziano, Monson, & Dermer, 1976). Individuals in generally satisfying relationships may accentuate the positive and minimize the negative qualities of the relationship (Van Lange & Rusbult, 1995), including minimizing the attractiveness of alternate partners (Johnson & Rusbult, 1989; Simpson, Gangestad, & Lerma, 1990). While such mechanisms may be useful in maintaining a warm glow, they may not rekindle the flame passion.

Couples must understand what caused the passionate feelings in each of them to first burn brightly, and then what caused those fires to fade, before they develop strategies to bring them back. Developing procedures to address the loss of passion may require the use of a range of interactive coping procedures (Barbee et al., 1993; Barbee & Cunningham, 1995; Yankeelov, Barbee, Cunningham, & Druen, 1995). Indeed, a survey of 221 undergraduates (Druen, 1995) suggested that it may be more difficult to increase the passion ($M = 5.85$) through effort in a relationship than the intimacy ($M = 6.07$) or commitment ($M = 6.02$).

Druen's (1997) participants were asked the qualities necessary, and those to avoid, for a relationship high in passion. Many mentioned qualities that are stereotypically romantic. One respondent, for example, stated that she desired a partner who was physically attractive, romantic, and sponateous, and would avoid someone who is physically unattractive, boring, and who doesn't care about her feelings. Another respondent indicated desiring a romantic person, who is daring and energetic, while avoiding someone who is calm, uptight, or reserved.

To rekindle passion, it may be necessary to again be the kind of person with whom a partner would wish to fall in love. Even if it is impossible to recapture all of the physical attractiveness and spontaniety of decades past, it may be possible to return to courting behaviors (e.g., Tolhuizen, 1989). The effectiveness in restoring lost passion of apparel that enhances physical appearance, pretending great secrecy and intrigue (Wegner et al., 1994), novel settings or films that induce arousal (Stephan, Berscheid & Walster, 1971), or reaffirmations of intimacy and commitment, however, will depend on intuitive insight or effective communication concerning what the partner needs most, just as it did in the beginning of the relationship.

There is some evidence to suggest that the loss of any component of consummate love (Sternberg, 1986), including intimacy and commitment, can cause a loss of passion (Aron & Westbay, 1996). If passion was lost because the couple drifted apart and lost the intimacy component of passionate love (cf. Barbee, Cunningham, Druen, & Yankeelov, 1996), then efforts might be devoted to restoring closeness and warmth before reigniting the fires of passion. Passion lost due to the perception of reduced commitment or to betrayal (Jones & Burdette, 1994) must be addressed differently than passion that was lost through familiarity and boredom. For example, the case of a husband who is discovered by his wife in a torrid affair with his young secretary because he is unwilling to face his own aging or because of regret over missed opportunities must be handled differently from the situation of a husband and wife whose passion was undermined by the stress of having sex while the children were sleeping (Sanders & Cairns, 1987). Feelings of passion may precede those of intimacy and commitment in the development of a consummate relationship, but we suspect that the latter feelings must either be intact or be restored before passion can be regained.

Studies of maintenance behaviors (Baxter & Dindia, 1990; Bell, Daly, & Gonzalez, 1987; Shea & Pearson, 1986; Stafford & Canary, 1991), for example, concentrate on dimensions such as positive acts (giving gifts, building self-esteem), assurances (emphasizing commitment), sharing (helping with tasks, doing favors), and network activities (spending time with the partner's friends and family), which may build passion, intimacy, or commitment.

The actions that cause, and those that are taken to resolve, conflict in the relationship may have an impact on the maintenance or loss of passion (cf. Rusbult, Verette, Whitney, Slovik, & Lipkus, 1991). Individuals who have unstable self-esteem (Kernis, Grannermann, & Barclay, 1989) or who are prone to shame (Tangney, Wagner, Fletcher, & Gramzov, 1992) are both likely to manifest high levels of aggressiveness when problems arise. If the partner seems to be critical and fault-finding (Rosenblatt, Titus, & Cunningham, 1979), then the couple may lock into a vicious circle, with most passion focused on aggression and defense. But if the arousal from an argument is transferred into sexuality, passion may be strengthened (cf. Carlson & Hatfield, 1992; Dawes, 1979). Even relationships that seem doomed, such as an anxious-avoidant female paired with an avoidant male, may be resilient, perhaps because the thrill of the chase remains (Kirkpatrick & Davis, 1994).

The success of efforts to restore passion may also depend on the emotional intelligence (Mayer, Salovey, Gomberg-Kaufman, & Blainey, 1991) and motivation of the two members of the couple. If one member of the couple has an external locus of control, and believes that passion is a function of meeting the "right" person, that it is something that sweeps over one, and can be neither predicted nor controlled, then interventions may be dismissed. If a member of the couple is distrustful and does not want to open up to passion because it risks disappointment and hurt, then interventions may be resisted. It may be necessary to address meta-feelings about passion before passion itself can be restored.

It has become a truism that passionate love must mature into the "far less intense emotion" of companionate love, which "combines feelings of deep attachment, commitment and intimacy," and includes "the affection and tenderness we feel for those with whom our lives are deeply entwined" (Hatfield & Rapson, 1993, pp. 8–9). Yet it must be recognized that much of the research on the decline of passion has been cross-sectional; longitudinal studies are inconsistent on the trajectory of passion, perhaps because of the use of different samples and measures (cf. Acker & Davis, 1992; Ard, 1977; Hatfield & Sprecher, 1986; Sprecher, 1997; Huston & Vangelisti, 1991; Swensen, Eskew, & Kohlhepp, 1981, Tucker & Aron, 1993). Declines may be greater when passion is measured by the frequency of sexual intercourse, and less when measured by the surge of affection that people feel when their mate enters the room. There are reasons to be skeptical that passion must inevitably be exchanged for commitment, and that romantic love must be replaced by companionate love.

As people who fall in love in their 70s and 80s remind us, the capacity for complete, consuming passionate love may never entirely leave us. And what once was lost, sometimes, can be found. Those of us who are fortunate may continue to receive and to give passionate feelings as we look into the older but still glowing eyes of our beloved. We may feel overwhelming passion when we look into the eager and untroubled eyes of our children. With effort and with luck, we may sustain passion, as passion sustains us, as long as we have life and hope.

## REFERENCES

Abbey, T. (1982). Sex differences in attributions for friendly behavior: Do males misperceive females' friendliness? *Journal of Personality and Social Psychology, 42,* 830–888.

Acker, M., & Davis, M. H. (1992). Intimacy, passion and commitment in adult romantic relationships: A test of the triangular theory of love. *Journal of Social and Personal Relationships, 9,* 21–50

Adams, G. R., & Shea, J. A. (1981). Talking and loving: A cross-lagged panel investigation. *Basic and Applied Social Psychology, 2,* 81–88.

Apt, C., & Hurlbert, D. F. (1994). The sexual attitudes, behavior, and relationships of women with histrionic personality disorder. *Journal of Sex and Marital Therapy, 20,* 125–133.

Ard, B. N. (1977). Sex in lasting marriages: A longitudinal study. *Journal of Sex Research, 13,* 274–285.

Argyle, M. (1987). *The psychology of happiness*. London: Methuen.

Aron, A., Dutton, D. G., Aron, E. N., & Iverson, A. (1989). Experiences of falling in love. *Journal of Social and Personal Relationships, 6,* 243–257.

Aron, A., & Westbay, L. (1996). Dimensions of the prototype of love. *Journal of Personality and Social Psychology, 70,* 535–551.

Barbee, A. P., & Cunningham, M. R. (1995). An experimental approach to social support: Interactive coping in close relationships. In B. Burleson (Ed.), *Communication Yearbook. Vol. 18* (pp. 381–413). Thousand Oaks, CA: Sage.

Barbee, A. P., Cunningham, M. R., Druen, P. B., & Yankeelov, P. A. (1996) Loss of Passion, Intimacy and Commitment: A Conceptual Framework for Relationship Researchers. *Journal of Personal and Interpersonal Loss, 1,* 93–108.

Barbee, A. P., Cunningham, M. R., Winstead, B., Derlega, V., Gulley, M. R., Yankeelov, P. A., & Druen, P. B. (1993). Effects of gender role expectations on the social support process. *Journal of Social Issues, 49,* 175–190.

Barnett, O. W., Martinez-Tomas, E., & Bluestein, B. W. (1995). Jealousy and romantic attachment in maritally violent and nonviolent men. *Journal of Interpersonal Violence, 10,* 473–486.

Bartholomew, K., & Horowitz, L. M. (1991). Attachment styles among young adults: A test of a four-category model. *Journal of Personality and Social Psychology, 61,* 226–244.

Baumeister, R. F., & Leary, M. R. (1995). The need to belong: Desire for interpersonal attachments as a fundamental human motivation. *Psychological Bulletin, 117,* 497–529.

Baumeister, R. F., Wotman, S. R., Stillwell, A. M. (1993). Unrequited love: On heartbreak, anger, guilt, scriptlessness, and humiliation. *Journal of Personality and Social Psychology, 64,* 377–394.

Baxter, L.A. (1984). Trajectories of relationship disengagement. *Journal of Social and Personal Relationships, 1,* 29–48.

Baxter, L. A., & Dindia, K. (1990). Marital partners' perceptions of marital maintenance strategies. *Journal of Social and Personal Relationships, 7,* 187–209.

Bell, R. A., Daly, J. A., & Gonzalez, C. (1987). Affinity-maintenance in marriage and its relationship to women's marital satisfaction. *Journal of Marriage and the Family, 49,* 445–454.

Berscheid, E. (1983). Emotion. In H. H. Kelley et al. (Ed.), *Close relationships* (pp. 110–168). New York: W.H. Freeman.

Berscheid, E. (1985). Interpersonal attraction. In G. Lindzey, & E. Aronson (Eds.), *The Handbook of Social Psychology. Vol. 2* (pp. 413–484). New York: Random House.

Berscheid, E., Graziano, W., Monson, T., & Dermer, M. (1976). Outcome dependency: Attention, attribution, and attraction. *Journal of Personality and Social Psychology, 34,* 978–989.

Berscheid, E., Snyder, M., & Omato, A. M. (1989). The relationship closeness inventory: Assessing the closeness of interpersonal relationships. *Journal of Personality and Social Psychology, 57,* 792–807.

Brickman, P., & D'Amato, B. (1975), Exposure effects in a free-choice situation. *Journal of Personality and Social Psychology, 32,* 415–420.

Buss, D. M. (1994). *The evolution of desire.* New York: Basic Books.

Carlson, J. G., & Hatfield, E. (1992) *Psychology of Emotion.* Fort Worth: Hartcourt Brace.

Cunningham, M. R. (1981). Sociobiology as a supplementary paradigm for Social Psychological research. In L. Wheeler (Ed.), *Review of Personality and Social Psychology, Vol. 2* (pp. 69–106). Beverly Hills, CA: Sage.

Cunningham, M. R., Barbee, A. P., & Druen, P. B. (1997). Social Antigens and Allergies: The development of hypersensitivity in close relationships. In R. Kowalski (Ed.), *Aversive Interpersonal Behaviors.* Beverly Hills, CA: Sage.

Cunningham, M. R., Barbee, A. P., Graves, C. R., Lundy, D. E., & Lister, S. C. (1996, August). *Can't buy me love: The effects of male wealth and personal qualities on female attraction.* Paper presented at the Convention of the American Psychological Association, Toronto, ON, Canada.

Cunningham, M. R., Roberts, R., Barbee, A. P., & Druen, P. B. (1995). "Their ideas of beauty are, on the whole, the same as ours": Consistency and variability in the cross-cultural perception of female physical attractiveness. *Journal of Personality and Social Psychology, 68,* 261–279.

Dawes, R. M. (1979). The robust beauty of improper linear models in decision making. *American Psychologist, 34,* 571–577.

Dietz, P. E., Matthews, D. B., Daryl, B., Van Dyyne, C., Martell, D. A., Parry, C. D. H., Stewart, T., Warren, J., & Crowder J. D. (1991). Threatening and otherwise inappropriate letters to Hollywood celebrities. *Journal of Forensic Sciences, 36,* 185–209.

Dion, K. K., & Dion, K. L. (1975) Self-esteem and romantic love. *Journal of Personality, 43,* 39–57.

Druen, P. B. (1995). *Cumulative relationship experience and partner selection strategies: Associations and implications for relationship quality.* Unpublished doctoral dissertation, University of Louisville, Louisville, KY.

Druen, P. B. (1997). *Beliefs about a partner's personal qualities that facilitate passion, intimacy, commitment, and exclusivity.* Unpublished manuscript, York College, York, PA.

Dutton, D. G., & Aron, A. P. (1974). Some evidence for heightened sexual attraction under conditions of high anxiety. *Journal of Personality and Social Psychology, 30,* 510–517.

Erikson, E. (1950). *Childhood and Society.* New York: Norton.

Felmlee, D. (1995). Fatal attractions: Affection and disaffection in intimate relationships. *Journal of Social and Personal Relationships, 12,* 295–311.

Fincham, F. D., & Bradbury, T. N. (1992). Assessing attributions in marriage: The relationship attribution measure. *Journal of Personality and Social Psychology, 62*(3), 457–468.

Fisher, H. (1992). *Anatomy of love.* New York: W.W. Norton.

Fitness, J., & Fletcher, G. J. O. (1993). Love, hate, anger, and jealousy in close relationships: A prototype and cognitive appraisal analysis. *Journal of Personality and Social Psychology, 65,* 942–958

Folkes, V. S. (1982). Communicating the reasons for social rejection. *Journal of Experimental Social Psychology, 18,* 235–252.

Glass, S. P., & Wright, T. L. (1992). Justifications for extramarital relationships: The association between attitudes, behaviors, and gender. *Journal of Sex Research, 29,* 361–387.

Graziano, W. G., Jensen-Campbell, L., Shebilski, L., & Lundgren, S. (1993). Social influence, sex differences and judgments of beauty. Putting the "interpersonal" back in interpersonal attraction. *Journal of Personality and Social Psychology, 65,* 522–531.

Gupta, U., & Singh, P. (1982). Exploratory study of love and liking and types of marriages. *Indian Journal of Applied Psychology, 19,* 92–97.

Hatfield, E., & Rapson, R. L. (1987). Passionate love/sexual desire: Can the same paradigm explain both? *Archives of Sexual Behavior, 16,* 259–278.

Hatfield, E., & Rapson, R. (1993). *Love, sex, & intimacy: Their psychology, biology and history.* New York: Harper Collins.

Hatfield, E., & Sprecher, S. (1986). Measuring passionate love in intimate relationships. *Journal of Adolescence, 9,* 383–410.

Hatfield, E., Traupman, J., & Sprecher, S. (1984). Older women's perceptions of their intimate relationships. *Journal of Social and Clinical Psychology, 2,* 108–124.

Hazan, C., & Shaver, P. R. (1994). Attachment as an organizational framework for research on close relationships. *Psychological Inquiry, 5,* 1–22.

Hendrick, C., & Hendrick, S. S. (1991). Dimensions of love: A sociobiological interpretation. *Journal of Social and Clinical Psychology, 10,* 206–230.

Herman, C. P., Zanna, M. P., & Higgins, E. T. (1986). *Physical appearance, stigma, and social behavior: The Ontario Symposium. Vol. 3.* Hillsdale, NJ: Lawrence Erlbaum.

Hurlbert, D. F. (1992). Factors influencing a woman's decision to end an extramarital sexual relationship. *Journal of Sex and Marital Therapy, 18,* Sum.

Huston, T. L., & Vangelisti, A. L. (1991). Socioemotional behavior and satisfaction in marital relationships: A longitudinal study. *Journal of Personality and Social Psychology, 61,* 721–733.

Jacobs, L., Berscheid, E., & Walster, E. (1971) Self-esteem and attraction. *Journal of Personality and Social Psychology, 17,* 84–91.

Johnson, D. L., & Rusbult, C. E. (1989). Resisting temptation: Devaluation of alternate partners as a means of maintaining commitment in close relationships. *Journal of Personality and Social Psychology, 57,* 967–980.

Jones, W. H., & Burdette, M. P. (1994). Betrayal in relationships. In A. L. Weber & J. H. Harvey (Eds.), *Perspectives on close relationships.* Boston: Allyn and Bacon.

Kernis, M. H., Grannermann, B. D., & Barclay, L. C. (1989). Stability and level of self-esteem as predictors of anger arousal and hostility. *Journal of Personality and Social Psychology, 56,* 1013–1022.

Kirkpatrick, L., & Davis, K. (1994). Attachment style, gender and relationship stability. *Journal of Personality and Social Psychology, 66,* 502–512.

Mathes, E. W., Adams, H. E., & Davies, R. M. (1985). Jealousy: Loss of relationship rewards, loss of self-esteem, depression, anxiety, and anger. *Journal of Personality and Social Psychology, 48,* 1552–1561.

Mayer, J. D., Salovey, P., Gomberg-Kaufman, S., & Blainey, K. (1991). A broader conception of mood experience. *Journal of Personality and Social Psychology, 60,* 100–111.

Muscarella, F., & Cunningham, M. R. (1996). The evolutionary significance and social male pattern baldness and facial hair. *Ethology and Sociobiology, 17,* 99–117.

Persky, H., Smith, K. D., & Basu, G. K., (1971). Relation of psychologic measures of aggression and hostility to testosterone production in man. *Psychosomatic Medicine, 33,* 265–277.

Pillemer, J., & Hatfield, E. (1981). Love and its effects on mental an physical health. In R. Fogel, E. Hatfield, S. Kiesler, & S. Shanas (Eds.), *Aging: Stability and change in the family* (pp. 253–274). New York: Academic Press.

Reik, T. (1972). *A psychologist looks at love.* New York: Holt, Rinehart & Winston.

Rogers, C. R (1961). *On becoming a person.* Boston: Houghton Mifflin.

Rosenblatt, P. C., Titus, S. L., & Cunningham, M. R. (1979). Disrespect, tension, and togetherness-apartness in marriage. *Journal of Marital and Family Therapy, 5,* 47–51.

Rowatt, W. C., Cunningham, M. R., & Druen, P. B. (in press). Deception to get a date. *Personality and Social Psychology Bulletin.*

Rozin, P., & Fallon, A. E. (1987). A perspective on disgust. *Psychological Review, 94,* 23–41.

Rusbult, C. E., Verette, J., Whitney, G. A., Slovik, L. F., & Lipkus, I. (1991). Accommodation processes in close relationships: Theory and preliminary empirical evidence. *Journal of Personality and Social Psychology, 60*(1), 53–78.

Sanders, G. L., & Cairns, K. V. (1987). Loss of sexual spontaneity. *Medical Aspects of Human Sexuality, 21,* 88–96.

Shaver, P., & Hazan, C. (1987). Being lonely, falling in love: Perspectives from attachment theory. Special Issue: Loneliness: Theory, research, and applications. *Journal of Social Behavior and Personality, 2,* Pt 2., 105–124.

Shea, B. C., & Pearson, J. C. (1986) The effects of relationship type, partner intent, and gender on the selection of relationship maintenance strategies. *Communication Monographs, 3,* 354–364.

Sheppard, V. J., Nelson, E. S., & Andreoli-Mathie, V. (1995). Dating relationships and infidelity: Attitudes and behaviors. *Journal of Sex and Marital Therapy, 21,* 202–212.

Simpson, J. A. (1987). The dissolution of romantic relationships: Factors involved in relationship stability and emotional distress. *Journal of Personality and Social Psychology, 53,* 683–692.

Simpson, J. A., Campbell, B., & Berscheid, J. (1986). The association between romantic love and marriage. Kephart (1967) twice revisited. *Personality and Social Psychology Bulletin, 12,* 363–372.

Simpson, J. A., & Gangestad, S. W. (1991). Individual differences in sociosexuality: Evidence for convergent and discriminant validity. *Journal of Personality and Social Psychology, 60,* 870–883.

Simpson, J. A., Gangestad, S. W., & Lerma, M. (1990). Perception of physical attractiveness: Mechanisms involved in the maintenance of romantic relationships. *Journal of Personality and Social Psychology, 59,*1192–1201.

Snyder, M. (1987). *Public appearances/private realities: The psychology of self-monitoring.* New York: W. H. Freeman.

Snyder, M., & Simpson, J. A. (1984). Self-monitoring and dating relationships. *Journal of Personality and Social Psychology, 47,* 1281–1291.

Solomon, R. L. (1980). The opponent process theory of acquired motivation. The costs of pleasure and the benefits of pain. *American Psychologists, 35,* 691–712.

Sprecher, A. (1997). "I love you more today than yesterday": Romantic partners perceptions of changes over time in their relationship. Under review.

Stafford, L., & Canary, D. J. (1991). Maintenance strategies and romantic relationship type, gender and relational characteristics. *Journal of Social and Personal Relationships, 8,* 217–242.

Stephan, W., Berscheid, E., & Walster, E. (1971) Sexual arousal and heterosexual perception, *Journal of Personality and Social Psychology, 20,* 93–101.

Sternberg, R. J. (1986). A triangular theory of love. *Psychological Review, 93,* 119–135.

Swensen, C. H., Eskew, R. W., & Kohlhepp, K. A. (1981). Stages of family life cycle, ego development, and the marriage relationship. *Journal of Marriage and the Family, 43,* 841–853.

Surra, C. A., Chandler, M., Asmussen, L., & Wareham, J. (1987). Effects of premarital pregnancy on the development of interdependence in relationships. *Journal of Social and Clinical Psychology, 5,* 123–139.

Tangney, J. P., Wagner, P., Fletcher, C., & Gramzov, R. (1992) Shamed into anger? The relation of shame and guilt proneness to anger and self-reported aggression. *Journal of Personality and Social Psychology, 62,* 669–675.

Tolhuizen, J. H. (1989) Communication strategies for intensifying dating relationships: Identification, use and structure. *Journal of Social and Personal Relationships, 6,* 413–434.

Tucker, P., & Aron, A. (1993). Passionate love and marital satisfaction at key transition points in the family life cycle. *Journal of Social and Clinical Psychology, 12,* 135–147.

Van Lange, P. M., & Rusbult, C. E. (1995). My relationship is better than-and not as bad as-yours is: The perception of superiority in close relationships. *Personality and Social Psychology Bulletin, 21,* 32–44.

Walster, E. (1965). The effect of self-esteem on romantic liking. *Journal of Experimental Social Psychology, 1,* 184–197.

Walster, E., Traupmann, J., & Walster, G. W. (1978). Equity and extramarital sexuality. *Archives of Sexual Behavior, 7,* 127–142.

Wegner, D. M., & Gold, D. B. (1995). Fanning old flames: Emotional and cognitive effects of suppressing thoughts of a past relationship. *Journal of Personality and Social Psychology, 68,* 782–792.

Wegner, D. M., Lane, J. D., & Dimitri, S. (1994). The allure of secret relationships. *Journal of Personality and Social Psychology, 66,* 287–300.

Whitley, B. E. (1993). Reliability and aspects of the construct validity of Sternberg's Triangular Love Scale. *Journal of Social and Personal Relationships, 10,* 475–480.

Wilson, E. O. (1975). *Sociobiology: The new synthesis.* Cambridge, MA: Belknap.

Yankeelov, P. A., Barbee, A. P., Cunningham, M. R., & Druen, P. B. (1995). The influence of negative medical diagnoses and verbal and nonverbal support activation strategies on the interactive coping process. *Journal of Non-Verbal Behavior, 19,* 243–260.

Zajonc, R. B. (1968) Attitudinal effects of mere exposure. *Journal of Personality and Social Psychology Monograph, 9* (2, Part 2), 1–27.

Zuckerman, M. (1991). *The psychobiology of personality.* New York: Cambridge University Press.

# III

## *LOSSES FACED BY SURVIVORS AND CARETAKERS*

# 12

# *Implications of Communal Relationships Theory for Understanding Loss among Family Caregivers*

***Gail M. Williamson and David R. Shaffer***
*University of Georgia*

Over the last decade, research on the effects of providing care to a seriously ill or disabled family member has mushroomed into one of the largest and most conceptually sophisticated literatures in health psychology and gerontology. As a result, we can now say with confidence that although there is wide variability in reactions to the caregiving experience, substantial percentages of caregivers are emotionally distressed by the caregiving role (e.g., Gatz, Bengtson, & Blum, 1990; Pruchno, Kleban, Michaels, & Dempsey, 1990). Surprisingly, however, researchers have paid little attention to the extent to which caregiver emotional distress is due to the losses they experience in the context of providing care to a family member who no longer is able to occupy roles on which the relationship was formerly grounded. In this chapter, we consider a number of issues relevant to caregiver loss. We begin with a brief discussion of the current state of knowledge on the effects of caregiving on the emotional well-being of caregivers. We then turn to the current state of the literature on the role of loss in caregiver well-being. Next, we discuss a body of theoretical work that may inform the study of loss among caregivers and present some preliminary support for our theoretical position.

## THE CAREGIVING ROLE AND PSYCHOLOGICAL WELL-BEING

Most community-dwelling older people (i.e., those who are not institutionalized) depend on a family member for care when they become ill or disabled (e.g., Select Committee on Aging, 1987; Stull, Kosloski, & Kercher, 1994; Thompson, Medvene, & Freedman, 1995). These informal caregivers represent our society's primary line of defense against institutionalization and nursing home placement of frail elderly persons (e.g., Himes, 1992; Montgomery & Kosloski, 1994). Frequently, they are uniquely challenged by finding themselves in a role they are

Preparation of this chapter was facilitated by a fellowship from the Institute for Behavioral Research at the University of Georgia to the first author.

ill-prepared to assume (e.g., Allen, 1994; Hinrichsen & Niederehe, 1994) and which may be detrimental to their well-being.

At this point, what do we know about how detrimental caregiving is to the emotional health of caregivers? Despite the fact that many caregivers adapt quite well to providing care (see, for example, Williamson & Schulz, 1993), a substantial literature now documents that caregivers are at risk for poorer mental health outcomes compared to their non-caregiving peers (see, for example, reviews by Schulz, O'Brien, Bookwala, & Fleissner, 1995; Schulz, Visintainer, & Williamson, 1990; Wright, Clipp, & George, 1993). A common finding is that caregivers are subject to increased levels of depressive symptomatology (e.g., Schulz et al., 1995; Schulz & Williamson, 1991), and this is particularly likely among those who appraise caregiving as burdensome[1] (e.g., Pruchno et al., 1990; Williamson & Schulz, 1995).

Much less is known about other affective reactions to caregiving. However, some research indicates that caregivers may also experience more anger/hostility (e.g., Anthony-Bergstone, Zarit, & Gatz, 1988) and anxiety (Anthony-Bergstone et al., 1988; Bodnar & Kiecolt-Glaser, 1994; Vitaliano, Becker, Russo, Magana-Amato, & Maiuro, 1989; Vitaliano, Russo, Young, Teri, & Maiuro, 1991) than their non-caregiving peers.

## LOSS AS A COMPONENT OF CAREGIVER WELL-BEING

A comprehensive review of literature on the effects of providing care to an older adult family member yields little information about the loss caregivers may experience. For example, although it has often been speculated that caregivers whose relationship with the patient has been especially rewarding in terms of closeness and affection may be highly vulnerable to emotional distress because of the loss of that relationship (e.g., Biegel, Sales, & Schulz, 1991; Williamson & Schulz, 1990), empirical evidence for this proposition is scarce. In fact, available data strongly suggest the reverse. That is, caregivers whose relationship with the recipients of their care before illness onset was closer and more affectionate report less burden and depressed affect (e.g., Uchino, Kiecolt-Glaser, & Cacioppo, 1994; Williamson & Schulz, 1990).

We suspect that the dearth of evidence confirming an association between loss and caregiver distress is due to both methodological and conceptual issues. Methodologically, caregiving research has traditionally focused on the burdens and strains of providing care to the virtual exclusion of distress that might result from losing some (or all) aspects of a long-standing relationship. If aspects of loss

[1]The construct of caregiving burden can be operationalized as either a measure of *objective* burden (most frequently, the magnitude of assistance required of the caregiver due to severity of care recipient illness or disability) or an assessment of *subjective* burden (e.g., the extent to which caregivers perceive that providing care is burdensome). Because it is not uncommon for researchers to find that degree of patient impairment and amount of care provided by caregivers are related modestly, if at all, to caregiver distress (e.g., Schulz et al., 1990, 1995; Schulz & Williamson, 1991; Williamson & Schulz, 1990, 1993), in this chapter, caregiver burden refers to the caregiver's own self-reports of subjective (rather than objective) burden.

are assessed at all, they are most frequently imbedded in measures of burden that include a variety of caregiving costs (e.g., Walker, Martin, & Jones, 1992). Yet, indirect evidence for the idea that loss is associated with caregiver distress comes from studies showing that caregivers are less distressed when they have social support resources that may replace some valued aspects (e.g., recreation and pleasurable interactions) of their former relationship with the care recipient (e.g., Thompson, Futterman, Gallagher-Thompson, Rose, & Lovett, 1993).

Conceptually, we suspect that loss may have both direct and indirect effects on caregiver depressed affect and that the character of those influences may depend very critically on the nature of the pre-existing relationship between caregivers and their care recipients. Two theories are directly pertinent to this notion. The theory of communal relationships (e.g., Clark & Mills, 1979; Mills & Clark, 1982) proposes that in close relationships, benefits are given in response to *needs* as they arise rather than out of concern for maintaining balance. By contrast, equity theory predicts that judging the exchange of benefits in a relationship to be balanced leads to satisfaction with the relationship (e.g., Walster, Berscheid, & Walster, 1973). Being underbenefitted, as would be the case for caregivers, is then supposed to cause resentment of one's relationship partner. However, spouse caregivers of cardiac patients who perceive that they are underbenefitted appear to resent their caregiving responsibilities *only* when they have less communal feelings toward the care recipient, that is, do not feel their relationship with the patient justifies providing large amounts of aid to that person (Thompson et al., 1995). Similarly, segments of the population whose cultural norms characterize caregiving behavior as "unconditional, value-congruent, satisfying, and less taxing," in other words, a communal orientation specifying that family members should willingly help each other, have been shown to appraise providing care as less burdensome (Lawton, Rajagopal, Brody, & Kleban, 1992).

Therefore, in this paper, we rely on Clark and Mills' (e.g., 1979; Mills & Clark, 1982) theory of communal relationships to derive some predictions about how loss is likely to influence reactions to the caregiving role. Before turning to those predictions, in the next section, we describe communal relationships theory in some detail and illustrate its application to caregiving with the results of recent research.

## THE THEORY OF COMMUNAL RELATIONSHIPS AND ITS IMPLICATIONS FOR CAREGIVER BURDEN AND DEPRESSED AFFECT

It is often assumed that qualitative aspects of the interpersonal relationship between caregiver and care recipient influence caregiving outcomes and may, in fact, have an impact on the decision to assume or continue caregiving responsibilities (e.g., Brody, 1990; Cicirelli, 1993; Pruchno, Michaels, & Potashnik, 1990). Research tends to support this view. For example, caregivers who feel high levels of affection toward the care recipient have been shown to perceive caregiving as less stressful (Horowitz, 1979; Horowitz & Shindleman, 1983) and to be less likely to place care recipients in nursing homes (Montgomery & Kosloski, 1994). Similarly, stronger attachment and greater relationship closeness have been associated with lower levels of caregiver burden, frustration, and anxiety (Cicirelli, 1993; Walker et al., 1992; Williamson & Schulz, 1990).

Unlike these earlier studies of the effects of relationship quality on caregiving outcomes, recent research by Williamson and Schulz (1995) focused on a quantitative aspect of relationships between caregivers and the recipients of their care. Specifically, these researchers investigated the extent to which caregiver distress could be predicted by how frequently caregivers and care recipients engaged in mutual communal behaviors before onset of care recipient disability. Hypotheses tested in this study were derived from a theory of interpersonal relationships originated by Clark and Mills (e.g., 1979, 1993; Mills & Clark, 1982) and from a body of experimental research in the social psychology literature supporting the theory. Clark and Mills have proposed that *communal relationships* are exemplified by behaviors that are responsive to (or indicative of a desire to respond to) a partner's needs. Communal relationships are most likely to be found among close friends, romantic partners, and family members.[2] A primary assumption underlying the theory of communal relationships is that through the process of socialization, people come to have internalized norms about helping others with whom they have family or romantic relationships or with whom they have close friendships. These *communal norms* lead people to believe it is good to help family members, romantic partners, and close friends without expecting to be repaid (e.g., Williamson, Clark, Pegalis, & Behan, 1996).

It is important to note, however, that relationships that we think of as "close" (i.e., those between spouses, friends, and family members) may vary considerably in exactly how communal they are in practice. Highly communal relationships are those in which partners are routinely concerned about and attend to each other's needs as those needs arise. In contrast, less communal relationships are characterized by lower levels of mutual feelings of responsibility for the welfare of the relationship partner and less responsiveness to the partner's needs.[3]

The theory of communal relationships has fostered a variety of interesting predictions about how people allocate benefits and how they react to helping situations, and numerous empirical studies support these predictions. For example, individuals in communal relationships (as opposed to those in noncommunal, or exchange, relationships) pay more attention to their partners' needs (Clark,

[2]Communal relationships are often contrasted with those that Clark and Mills designate as *exchange relationships*, i.e., relationships exemplified by *quid pro quo* exchange of benefits and little concern for the other's needs and well-being. These types of relationships are most frequently found among strangers, business associates, and people who are merely acquaintances. This paper deals only with relationships that are most likely communal in nature, i.e., those between spouses and family members.

[3]Relationships can be classified along this dimension based on relationship partners' responses to the Mutual Communal Behaviors Scale (MCBS; Williamson & Schulz, 1995), which assesses frequency of behavioral expressions of communal feelings between caregiver and patient prior to illness onset. Caregivers are instructed to think about "the type of interactions you had with the patient *before* his/her illness." Five items evaluate caregiver communal behaviors toward the patient (e.g., "if the patient was feeling bad, I tried to cheer him/her up"). Five additional items evaluate patient communal behaviors toward the caregiver (e.g., "the patient did things just to please me"). Caregivers indicate frequency of these behaviors on a scale of 1 (never) to 4 (always).

Mills, & Powell, 1986; Clark, Mills, & Corcoran, 1989) and help each other more (Clark, Ouellette, Powell, & Milberg, 1987). They also do not keep track of individual contributions to joint tasks (e.g., Clark et al., 1989) and tend to react negatively to receiving specific repayment of help given (Clark & Mills, 1979). Several other findings from communal relationship studies are particularly relevant to reactions to caring for a seriously ill family member. For example, communal partners do not feel exploited when the other cannot reciprocate their aid (Clark & Waddell, 1985). Moreover, communal partners experience elevated affect after having helped their partners (Williamson & Clark, 1989a, 1992) and analogous declines in affect after failing to help (Williamson & Clark, 1992; Williamson, Clark, et al., 1996).

Communal relationships such as those between spouses and adult family members are most often mutual in nature (e.g., Clark & Mills, 1979, 1993; Williamson & Clark, 1989b). In other words, each partner helps the other when he or she needs help. Equity and exchange theories (e.g., Blau, 1964; Walster et al., 1973) would predict that when a chronic, debilitating, and potentially terminal illness (e.g., cancer, Alzheimer's disease) strikes one partner and a once mutual relationship becomes considerably more one-sided, the result could logically be distress in the partner whose needs must now take second place, i.e., the caregiver. Yet, we know from the substantial literature on the impact of providing care to a disabled elderly family member that many caregivers are not overly troubled by their role (e.g., Schulz et al., 1990; Schulz & Williamson, 1991; Williamson & Schulz, 1993).

Communal relationships theory suggests an explanation for why some caregivers become distressed while others do not. Williamson and Schulz (1995) speculated that although caring for a family member clearly qualifies as a communal behavior, differences in the factors that motivate people to provide care, and thus, to behave according to communal norms, may account for some of the variance in caregiving outcomes. Individuals may be motivated to follow communal norms for a variety of reasons. Among these is the fact that communal relationships are the relationships that are most valued by most people (e.g., Clark & Mills, 1993), and demonstrating concern for the other's welfare is good for the relationship (Williamson, Clark, et al., 1996).

A second factor that may motivate people to follow communal norms involves simply being concerned about the other person's well-being. Such concern could easily prompt a family member or spouse to give large amounts of help to someone with a debilitating illness. However, the motivation to provide care to a seriously ill family member might also stem from a desire to fulfill one's obligation, e.g., the societal sanction that one should behave in a communal manner toward the members of one's family. As Clark and Mills (1993) point out, both of these motivating factors, and doubtless, others as well, are consistent with the idea that in certain types of relationships (e.g., those between family members), most people believe behavior that follows communal norms represents the way that people should behave.

In their study of caregivers of family members with advanced cancer, Williamson and Schulz (1995) assumed that if a relationship has been mutually communal in the past, positive feelings about helping one's partner should continue even when one partner's needs far outweigh those of the other partner. In other words, in relationships historically characterized by mutual communal behavior, the caregiving partner should *not* become overly distressed by the burdens associated with providing care. It was also assumed that individuals in family relationships believe that following communal norms, e.g., responding to each other's needs when those needs arise, is the manner in which people *ought* to behave. In reality, however, even in relationships between spouses and family members, the extent to which people routinely behave in a communal manner toward each other can vary widely (Clark & Chrisman, 1994). For example, some marriages are characterized by lower levels of mutual feelings of responsibility for the other's well-being. Some spouses are less likely than others to do things simply to please their partners or to respond to their partners' needs. Williamson and Schulz (1995) reasoned that it is in these weaker communal relationships, i.e., those characterized by less frequent communal behaviors, that people are most likely to be motivated to follow communal norms because they believe it is their *duty* to do so rather than for purposes of maintaining the relationship or solely out of concern for the other's welfare. In addition, Williamson and Schulz (1995) speculated that a mechanism involved in the process through which infrequent communal behaviors might lead to more symptoms of depression would be the extent to which caregivers perceived providing care to be burdensome.

Consistent with hypotheses derived from the theory of communal relationships, Williamson and Schulz (1995) found that behaviors displayed in the relationship between caregiver and care recipient prior to illness onset played a role in how caregivers reacted to providing care. Specifically, in relationships historically characterized by frequent communal behaviors (e.g., mutual demonstrations of concern for and responsiveness to the other's needs), caregivers reported lower levels of burden and depressed affect than did those in relationships historically characterized by less frequent communal behaviors. These associations were found to operate beyond the effects of patient illness severity.

In addition, multivariate analyses suggested that past communal behavior was related to caregiver depressed affect in at least three different ways. First, communal behavior appeared to exert direct effects on symptoms of depression. Second, the effect of past communal behavior on caregiver symptoms of depression was partially mediated by caregiver burden. Finally, past communal behavior also appeared to interact with caregiver burden in influencing caregiver depressive symptomatology. These results were interpreted as suggesting that having a relationship with a family member or spouse in which the partners do not frequently behave in ways that are consistent with normative beliefs about how people should treat each other in these types of relationships is a situation that, in and of itself, can contribute to a propensity toward experiencing depressive symptomatology. When one partner is then stricken by an illness and requires care, the caregiving partner feels burdened in part because of the noncommunal nature of the past relationship, and these feelings of burden contribute to additional depressed affect.

Interestingly, high levels of past communal behavior between patient and caregiver seemed to have the greatest beneficial impact on caregiver depressed affect when perceived burden was relatively low. Caregivers reporting high levels of communal behavior and low levels of burden reported levels of depressive symptomatology much lower than the other caregivers—levels that, in fact, compared quite favorably to those typically found in the general population. In contrast, caregivers recalling low levels of communal behavior experienced levels of depressed affect substantially higher than typically found in the general population, and this was the case at both low and high levels of perceived burden.

## LOSS AS A CONTRIBUTOR TO CAREGIVER DEPRESSED AFFECT

As noted earlier, researchers have devoted little attention to the extent to which caregiver depressed affect may stem from the loss they experience when caring for a family member who is no longer capable of fulfilling the roles on which the relationship was previously grounded. When speaking of *loss*, we refer to changes resulting directly from the care recipient's inability to provide the affection and emotional support, instrumental/financial support, and/or advice and informational resources that characterized the relationship before illness onset. Stated another way, interpersonal loss reflects caregivers' personal reactions to changes in the typical, day-to-day interpersonal exchanges that had characterized their relationship with the care recipient.[4] We assume that loss will vary dramatically across caregivers (and relationships), ranging from highly negative for caregivers whose relationship with the care recipient was especially satisfying, to evaluatively neutral (and perhaps positive) for caregivers whose ties to the recipient were especially conflictual, unsatisfying, or even exploitative. Our assumptions are similar to those of Pincus and Gurtman (1995), who recently speculated that depressive reactions to loss depend, to a large extent, on what is lost in the context of a particular relationship.

Caregivers who have suffered substantial loss should be more susceptible to experiencing depressed affect. This may be especially true during the months immediately following changes in the character of the relationship, when it becomes quite apparent that such changes are permanent, and when caregivers have not yet adapted to them (Harris, 1993). In other words, loss may often be a direct contributor to depressed affect. Loss may also contribute indirectly to depressed affect by influencing whether caregivers are likely to appraise providing care as burdensome. Yet, it is not immediately obvious exactly how loss affects caregiver appraisals of the stresses and burdens associated with caregiving. As a working hypothesis, we propose that the loss that caregivers experience as well as the contributions of loss to depressed affect, will vary both directly and indirectly (through the impact of loss on perceived burden) according to the type of relationship that existed between caregiver and care recipient prior to onset of illness and disability. In our view, the theory of communal relationships (e.g., Clark & Mills, 1979, 1993; Mills & Clark, 1982) is an especially useful framework for conceptualizing how loss may differentially affect caregivers who had different types of relationships with their care recipients.

[4]Note that loss associated with caregiving is viewed as conceptually distinct from the loss (e.g., bereavement) caregivers may experience when the care recipient dies.

## Loss in the Context of Highly Communal Relationships

Williamson and Shaffer (1996) have speculated that caregivers who have previously enjoyed highly communal relationships with care recipients will feel a strong sense of *interpersonal* loss. That is, their relationship was previously characterized by affection and mutual desire to attend to the needs of the other. Now, that relationship is becoming one-sided, with caregivers continuing to respond to the other's needs while care recipients become less capable (perhaps even incapable) of providing the emotional, instrumental, and informational support to which caregivers have grown accustomed. In short, these caregivers have much to lose and are likely to long for the intimacy and mutual concern that is no longer apparent in their relationship. Moreover, the physical and/or mental deterioration of a care recipient to whom they are strongly attached may be particularly painful for these caregivers. Thus, we suspect that interpersonal loss in the context of losing a previously highly communal relationship will be keenly felt and will contribute directly to caregiver depressed affect.

However, interpersonal loss in the context of a highly communal relationship is unlikely to cause caregivers to appraise their care as particularly burdensome. Attending to the needs of a highly communal relationship partner often produces positive affect (Williamson & Clark, 1992) and few feelings of exploitation, even when one's relationship partner cannot reciprocate these kindnesses (Clark & Waddell, 1985). Thus, caregiving in the context of a previously highly communal relationship may often be perceived as a continuation of "in-role" behavior rather than a distasteful responsibility that one must endure. Although appraisals of caregiving burden may still predict the depressive symptomatology of highly communal caregivers if burden is severe (Williamson & Schulz, 1995), we believe that factors other than interpersonal loss (i.e., lack of social support) are primarily responsible for burden among caregivers in highly communal relationships.

## Loss in the Context of Less Communal Relationships

A cursory reading of communal relationships theory might tempt one to conclude that caregivers are likely to feel little, if any, loss when disengaging from the normal behavioral aspects of a less communal relationship—one characterized historically by low levels of mutual responsiveness to relationship partners' needs. Yet, this perspective may miss the mark. As Williamson and Shaffer (1996) have noted, caregivers in less communal relationships may have long since adjusted to their partner's lack of contingent responsiveness to their own needs and may nonetheless miss whatever levels of support that their care recipient had provided once such support is no longer forthcoming. Thus, while interpersonal loss may not be felt as keenly by those in historically less communal relationships, other types of loss (e.g., financial hardship resulting from care recipient illness) may color the experience of these caregivers and perhaps make a modest direct contribution to the depressed affect they experience.

However, in contrast to predictions for caregivers in highly communal relationships, Williamson and Shaffer (1996) speculated that some types of loss (e.g., financial) would make a substantial *indirect* contribution to caregiver depressed affect by virtue of its impact on appraisals of caregiving burden. Such feelings of burden may be due, in large part, to the fact that caring for an ill/disabled relationship partner qualifies as highly communal but "out-of-role" behavior for those who are not accustomed to placing their partner's needs ahead of their own (or to having their partners behave in kind to them). Consequently, although loss may make a small direct contribution to depressed affect among caregivers in previously less communal relationships, its primary impact may be to increase depressive symptomatology *indirectly* by leading these caregivers to appraise their roles as particularly burdensome.

## PRELIMINARY TESTS OF THE MODEL

Recently, we have explored the associations among aspects of caregiver loss, appraisals of caregiving burden, and caregiver depressive symptomatology in a study of 75 cancer patients (*M* age = 63.4 years) and their spousal caregivers.[5] Two loss measures were employed: (1) *financial loss* (i.e., extent to which the patient's illness had required the couple to make financial sacrifices in 10 domains such as borrowing money or using savings) and (2) *interpersonal loss* (i.e., severity of patient's cancer-related symptoms, which served as an estimate of change in the nature, or character, of the couple's interpersonal behaviors/interactions). Both loss measures utilized data provided by care recipients, thus eliminating negative reporting biases on the part of caregivers.

Perceived caregiving burden was reported by caregivers and indexed by a shortened version of the Caregiver Burden Scale (CBS; Zarit, Reever, & Bach-Peterson, 1980) previously used successfully in studying subjective burden among caregivers of stroke, cancer, and Alzheimer's disease patients (Schulz, Tompkins, & Rau, 1988; Williamson & Schulz, 1990, 1995). Caregivers also completed the Center for Epidemiologic Studies Depression Scale (CES-D; Radloff, 1977) and the Mutual Communal Behaviors Scale (MCBS; Williamson & Schulz, 1995) to assess the character of their relationship with the care recipient prior to illness onset. For purposes of data analysis, the sample was divided at the median for the MCBS such that caregivers with scores of 34 or lower were classified as having had a past relationship with the patient that was low in mutual communal behaviors (low-MCBS; *N* = 37); those with scores of 35 or higher were classified as having had a relationship that was high in mutual communal behaviors (high-MCBS; *N* = 38).

Figure 1 illustrates the simple associations among two types of loss (financial and interpersonal), perceived caregiving burden, and caregiver depressive symptomatology for caregivers in relationships classified as high or low in mutual communal behaviors. Focusing first on dyads classified as high-MCBS (Panels A & B), we see that both financial loss and interpersonal loss were significant direct predictors of caregiver depressive symptomatology, as were caregivers' percep-

[5]Data for these analyses were collected as part of research supported by Grant CA48635 from the National Cancer Institute (R. Schulz, principal investigator). These analyses were originally reported in Williamson, Shaffer, and Schulz (1996).

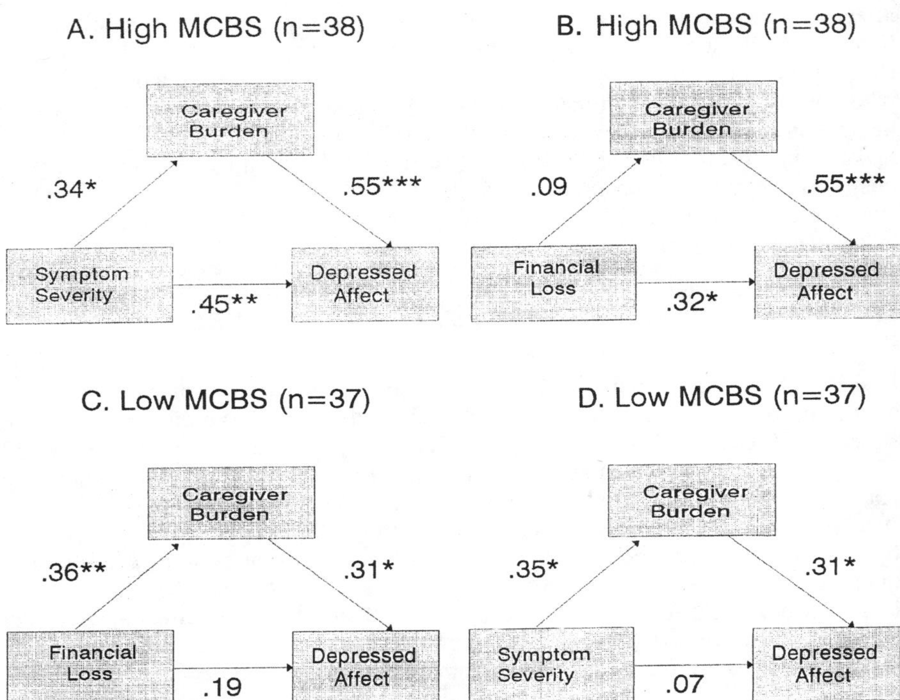


*Figure 1.* Associations among Loss, Perceived Burden, and Depressed Affect for Caregivers whose Past Relationships with Care Recipients were Low or High in Mutual Communal Behaviors Prior to Illness Onset. (Note: * $p < .05$; ** $p < .01$; *** $p < .001$.)

tions of caregiving burden. These findings are quite consistent with Williamson and Shaffer's (1996) model of interpersonal loss in the context of family caregiving. Also consistent with the model is the finding that financial loss did *not* predict perceived caregiving burden among high-MCBS caregivers. However, one finding was contrary to expectations: our measure of interpersonal loss *did* predict the amount of burden perceived by the high-MCBS caregivers. This unanticipated outcome may stem from our reliance on patient reports of symptom severity as a stand-in for caregiver interpersonal loss. Although illness severity does undoubtedly reflect declines in the quality of the couple's personal and interpersonal lives, it is likely that patients with the more severe symptoms require more extensive care from their spouses. Thus, the symptom severity measure may also tap objective burdens that high-MCBS caregivers experience in ways that purer or more direct measures of interpersonal loss (e.g., loss of affection, loss of valued shared activities) may not.

Findings for dyads classified as low-MCBS prior to patient illness onset (Panels C & D) were notably different from those for the high-MCBS couples. Perhaps the most noteworthy contrast to data from the high-MCBS dyads was that neither financial loss nor interpersonal loss directly forecasted levels of depressed affect among the low-MCBS caregivers. These findings are in accord with our premise that loss per se should have a stronger proximal impact on the depressive symptomatology of caregivers whose previous relationship with the care recipient had been close and mutually supportive. However, it is important to note that both loss measures did have the predicted *indirect* effect on low-MCBS caregivers by influencing their perceptions of caregiving burden, which, in turn, predicted their levels of depressive symptomatology.

## CONCLUDING COMMENTS AND IMPLICATIONS

These results are based on a relatively small number of caregiver/care recipient dyads and, consequently, are best viewed as preliminary support for our model of loss in the context of family caregiving. Nevertheless, they suggest that measuring the frequency of past mutual communal behaviors at the early stages of a caregiving situation can help specify how particular caregivers are likely to respond to the loss of normal behavioral aspects of their relationship with the care recipient. More importantly, our data provide some clues about the kind of support that might be provided to decrease caregiver vulnerability to depressed affect.

Specifically, the clear and consistent associations between loss measures and perceived caregiving burden for *low-MCBS* caregivers imply that these individuals may profit substantially from interventions emphasizing *caregiving support*, that is, actual assistance provided by others (e.g., friends, family members, formal services) with caregiving tasks to help relieve the strains low-MCBS caregivers experience (and presumably, promote the care recipient's welfare as well). In terms of affective reactions and emotional well-being, we suspect that support with the actual tasks of providing care will reduce the likelihood that loss will have an indirect effect on caregiver depressed affect by lowering caregiver perceptions of burden.

This is not to say that high-MCBS caregivers would not also profit from caregiving support. However, losses experienced by high-MCBS caregivers were directly linked to depressed affect and were not consistently associated with perceptions of burden. Our data suggest that high-MCBS caregivers were more upset than their low MCBS counterparts by the physical deterioration of their care recipients and by the corresponding decline of affectional, financial, and instrumental support to which these high-MCBS caregivers had become accustomed. Thus, we propose that *high-MCBS* caregivers may profit most from interventions emphasizing *compensatory support*, that is, contacts with friends and family members that focus less on caregiving assistance per se and more on other activities intended to replace some positive aspects of the caregiver/care recipient relationship that the recipient can no longer provide. Although such compensatory support can obviously neither eliminate the sadness that high-MCBS caregivers may experience over the decline of their loved ones nor replace all valued aspects of a previously close and mutually supportive relationship with these care recipients, it should nonetheless moderate the direct impact of such losses on caregiver depressive symptomatology. Conversely, high-MCBS caregivers who receive little compensatory support should be more likely to feel "alone" and to ruminate about the loss of their closest and most supportive relationship, thus becoming (or remaining) highly vulnerable to depressed affect.

In summary, we believe that considering past mutual communal behavior at or near the onset of caregiving can help identify those family members who are likely to adapt poorly to the caregiving role. These individuals may not only be those most vulnerable to psychological (and, perhaps, physical) distress, but also those who are least capable of providing high-quality care. Identifying family caregivers who are most likely to become distressed means that those individuals can be targeted early on for interventions aimed at lessening their burden and increasing the quality of care provided to the patient.

## REFERENCES

Allen, S. M. (1994). Gender differences in spousal caregiving and unmet need for care. *Journal of Gerontology, 49,* 187–195.

Anthony-Bergstone, C., Zarit, S., & Gatz, M. (1988). Symptoms of psychological distress among caregivers of dementia patients. *Psychology and Aging, 3,* 245–248.

Biegel, D. E., Sales, E., & Schulz, R. (1991). *Family caregiving in chronic illness.* Newbury Park, CA: Sage.

Blau, P. M. (1964). *Exchange and power in social life.* New York: Wiley.

Bodnar, J. C., & Kiecolt-Glaser, J. K. (1994). Caregiver depression after bereavement: Chronic stress isn't over when it's over. *Psychology and Aging, 9,* 372–380.

Brody, E. M. (1990). *Women in the middle: Their parent care years.* New York: Springer-Verlag.

Cicirelli, V. G. (1993). Attachment and obligation as daughters' motives for caregiving behavior and subsequent effect on subjective burden. *Psychology and Aging, 8,* 144–155.

Clark, M. S., & Chrisman, K. (1994). Resource allocation in intimate relationships: Trying to make sense of a confusing literature. In M. J. Lerner & G. Mikula (Eds.), *Entitlement and the affectional bond: Justice in close relationships* (pp. 65–88). New York: Plenum Press.

Clark, M. S., & Mills, J. (1979). Interpersonal attraction in exchange and communal relationships. *Journal of Personality and Social Psychology, 37,* 12–24.

Clark, M. S., & Mills, J. (1993). The difference between communal and exchange relationships: What it is and is not. *Personality and Social Psychology Bulletin, 19,* 684–691.

Clark, M. S., Mills, J., & Corcoran, D. (1989). Keeping track of needs and inputs of friends and strangers. *Personality and Social Psychology Bulletin, 15,* 533–542.

Clark, M. S., Mills, J., & Powell, M. C. (1986). Keeping track of needs in communal and exchange relationships. *Journal of Personality and Social Psychology, 51,* 333–338.

Clark, M. S., Ouellette, R., Powell, M. C., & Milberg, S. (1987). Recipient's mood, relationship type, and helping. *Journal of Personality and Social Psychology, 53,* 94–103.

Clark, M. S. & Waddell, B. (1985). Perception of exploitation in communal and exchange relationships. *Journal of Social and Personal Relationships, 2,* 403–413.

Gatz, M., Bengtson, V. L., & Blum, M. J. (1990). Caregiving families. In J. E. Birren & K.W. Schaie (Eds.), *Handbook of the psychology of aging* (pp. 404–426). New York: Academic Press.

Harris, P. B. (1993). The misunderstood caregiver? A qualitative study of the male caregiver of Alzheimer's disease victims. *The Gerontologist, 33,* 551–556.

Himes, C. L. (1992). Future caregivers: Projected family structures of older persons. *Journal of Gerontology, 47,* 17–26.

Hinrichsen, G. A., & Niederehe, G. (1994). Dementia management strategies and adjustment of family members of older patients. *The Gerontologist, 34,* 95–102.

Horowitz, A. (1979). Families who care: A study of natural support systems of the elderly. *Aging International, 6,* 19–20.

Horowitz, A., & Shindleman, L. (1983). Reciprocity and affection: Past influences on current caregiving. *Journal of Gerontological Social Work, 5,* 5–20.

Lawton, M. P., Rajagopal, D., Brody, E., & Kleban, M. H. (1992). The dynamics of caregiving for a demented elder among black and white families. *Journal of Gerontology, 47,* 156–164.

Mills, J., & Clark, M. S. (1982). Communal and exchange relationships. In L. Wheeler (Ed.), *Review of personality and social psychology* (pp. 121–144). Beverly Hills, CA: Sage.

Montgomery, R. J. V., & Kosloski, K. (1994). A longitudinal analysis of nursing home placement for dependent elders cared for by spouses vs adult children. *Journal of Gerontology, 49,* 62–74.

Pincus, A. L., & Gurtman, M. B. (1995). The three faces of interpersonal dependency: Structural analysis of self-report dependency measures. *Journal of Personality and Social Psychology, 69,* 744–758.

Pruchno, R. A., Kleban, M. H., Michaels, J. E., & Dempsey, N. P. (1990). Mental and physical health of caregiving spouses: Development of a causal model. *Journal of Gerontology, 45,* 192–199.

Pruchno, R. A., Michaels, J. E., & Potashnik, S. L. (1990). Predictors of institutionalization among Alzheimer's disease victims with caregiving spouses. *Journal of Gerontology, 45,* 259–266.

Radloff, L. (1977). The CES-D Scale: A self-report depression scale for research in the general population. *Applied Psychological Measurement, 1,* 385–401.

Schulz, R., O'Brien, A. T., Bookwala, J., & Fleissner, K. (1995). Psychiatric and physical morbidity effects of Alzheimer's disease caregiving: Prevalence, correlates, and causes. *The Gerontologist, 35,* 771–791.

Schulz, R., Tompkins, C. A., & Rau, M. T. (1988). A longitudinal study of the psychosocial impact of stroke on primary support persons. *Psychology and Aging, 3,* 131–141.

Schulz, R., Visintainer, P., & Williamson, G. M. (1990). Psychiatric and physical morbidity effects of caregiving. *Journal of Gerontology, 45,* 181–191.

Schulz, R., & Williamson, G. M. (1991). A two-year longitudinal study of depression among Alzheimer's caregivers. *Psychology and Aging, 6,* 569–578.

Select Committee on Aging, U.S. House of Representatives. (1987). *Exploding the myths: Caregiving in America.* Washington, DC: U.S. Government Printing Office.

Stull, D. E., Kosloski, K., & Kercher, K. (1994). Caregiver burden and generic well-being: Opposite sides of the same coin? *The Gerontologist, 34,* 88–94.

Thompson, E. H., Jr., Futterman, A. M., Gallagher-Thompson, D., Rose, J. M., & Lovett, S. B. (1993). Social support and caregiving burden in family caregivers of frail elders. *Journal of Gerontology, 48,* 245–254.

Thompson, S. C., Medvene, L. J., & Freedman, D. (1995). Caregiving in the close relationships of cardiac patients: Exchange, power, and attributional perspectives on caregiver resentment. *Personal Relationships, 2,* 125–142.

Uchino, B. N., Kiecolt-Glaser, J. K., & Cacioppo, J. T. (1994). Construals of preillness relationship quality predict cardiovascular response in family caregivers of Alzheimer's disease victims. *Psychology and Aging, 9,* 113–120.

Vitaliano, P. P., Becker, J., Russo, J., Magana-Amato, A., & Maiuro, R. D. (1989). Expressed emotion in spouse caregivers of patients with Alzheimer's disease. *Journal of Applied Social Sciences, 13,* 215–250.

Vitaliano, P. P., Russo, J., Young, H. M., Teri, L., & Maiuro, R. D. (1991). Predictors of burden in spouse caregivers of individuals with Alzheimer's disease. *Psychology and Aging, 6,* 392–402.

Walker, A. J., Martin, S. S. K., & Jones, L. L. (1992). The benefits and costs of caregiving and care receiving for daughters and mothers. *Journal of Gerontology, 47,* 130–139.

Walster, E., Berscheid, E., & Walster, G. W. (1973). New directions in equity research. *Journal of Personality and Social Psychology, 25,* 151–176.

Williamson, G. M., & Clark, M. S. (1989a). Providing help and desired relationship type as determinants of changes in moods and self-evaluations. *Journal of Personality and Social Psychology, 56,* 722–734.

Williamson, G. M., & Clark, M. S. (1989b). The communal/exchange distinction and some implications for understanding justice in families. *Social Justice Research, 3,* 77–103.

Williamson, G. M., & Clark, M. S. (1992). Impact of desired relationship type on affective reactions to choosing and being required to help. *Personality and Social Psychology Bulletin, 18,* 10–18.

Williamson, G. M., Clark, M. S., Pegalis, L., & Behan, A. (1996). Affective consequences of refusing to help in communal and exchange relationships. *Personality and Social Psychology Bulletin, 22,* 34–47.

Williamson, G. M., & Schulz, R. (1990). Relationship orientation, quality of prior relationship, and distress among caregivers of Alzheimer's patients. *Psychology and Aging, 5,* 502–509.

Williamson, G. M., & Schulz, R. (1993). Coping with specific stressors in Alzheimer's disease caregiving. *The Gerontologist, 33,* 747–755.

Williamson, G. M., & Schulz, R. (1995). Caring for a family member with cancer: Past communal behavior and affective reactions. *Journal of Applied Social Psychology, 25,* 93–116.

Williamson, G. M. & Shaffer, D. R. (1996). Interpersonal loss in the context of family caregiving: Implications of communal relationships theory. *Journal of Personal and Interpersonal Loss, 1,* 249–274.

Williamson, G. M., Shaffer, D. R., & Schulz, R. (1996, November). *Interpersonal loss in family caregiving and the theory of communal relationships.* Poster presentation at the 49th Annual Scientific Meeting of the Gerontological Society of America, Washington, DC.

Wright, L. K., Clipp, E. C., & George, L. K. (1993). Health consequences of caregiver stress. *Medicine, Exercise, Nutrition, and Health, 2,* 181–195.

Zarit, S. H., Reever, K. E., & Bach-Peterson, J. (1980). Relatives of the impaired aged: Correlates of feelings of burden. *The Gerontologist, 20,* 649–655.

# 13

## *Brain Injury: A Tapestry of Loss*

**Kathleen Chwalisz**
*Southern Illinois University*

*I feel that despite the fact that I was a nurse, I was ill prepared for my husband's emotional response to a spinal cord injury—I initially devoted myself to his care, then became overwhelmed by guilt since I was driving when the accident occurred. I also tried "too hard" to solve his problems.*

*Some of his qualities he retained, for example, despite the psychological testing showing clearly he had problems, he could still do some mechanical work.*

*I believe he has lost ground intellectually and has changed personality otherwise. For several years I could never turn to him for any type of support. To adjust to his new personality took a lot of work. He has some sexual dysfunction and despite our attempt to communicate about this when we do have sex, I think he is focusing on his personal pleasure, not me. Sex is still very important to him but it is extremely unpleasant to me. I do my best to participate and I would never let him know how bad it is but is evident that I don't like it.*

*It is like being married to a man who looks like him and has some of his characteristics but it is no longer him and often he is doing exactly what I don't want in a man.*

*His family denied that he is different so I never brought it up again, I did it only once. I made the decision to stay married as long as he is not abusive (he was only once). Sometimes I wonder, is this really happening? I have at times doubted that it did, yet the evidence is all over the medical records.*

*We have grown together since the accident and I am in general reasonably happy. I have two friends I can talk to anytime I need to. I am still confused, however, as to who is this man I live with, and where is the other one, I unconsciously wait for him to return. I know that compared to other people we are lucky.*

This essay was written by a 50-year-old woman whose husband suffered a mild head injury and spinal cord injury in an automobile accident four years earlier. Her husband had regained his mobility, and he had been able to work after the injury, but there are still many losses being faced by this couple. This information was provided on the back of a traditional quantitative study of caregiver burden among spouses of persons with brain injuries (Chwalisz, 1996), in response to an invitation to share any additional information they thought researchers should have. Twenty-seven of the 135 participants in the study felt the need to tell their stories in addition to the information they provided on a rather extensive collection of standardized instruments. These stories were replete with accounts of the many losses sustained as a result of a brain injury.

Brain injury affects many families. The incidence of closed head injury alone has been estimated between 120 and 284 per 100,000 population (e.g., Kraus & Nourjah, 1989). Further, the majority of closed head injuries occur to men between the ages of 15 and 24 (Kalsbeek, McLaurin, Harris, & Miller, 1980), so many families cope with brain injury for a lifetime. Much research has been directed toward understanding the effects of brain injury on the survivor and his or her family, yet there are still many aspects of the psychological impact of brain injury that have not been identified and explored.

Virtually no literature has conceptualized the impact of brain injury in terms of loss, whereas loss may be quite salient to survivors and their families. Furthermore, the changes associated with brain injury that appear to be most stressful (e.g., personality changes, emotional changes) occur even among persons with mild brain injuries, suggesting that significant losses are experienced across the range of brain injuries from mild to severe. The account at the beginning of this chapter illustrates the many losses experienced by a family coping with a mild brain injury. One might expect more severe injuries to be associated with even more losses or different types of losses, although no research has been directed toward examining the relationship between loss and the severity of the injury.

## LOSSES SUSTAINED BY PERSONS WITH BRAIN INJURIES

A large body of literature has been devoted to describing the sequelae of brain injury. Various cognitive deficits, motor skills deficits, behavior changes, psychosocial difficulties, and emotional or characterological changes have been identified (e.g., Brooks, Campsie, Symington, Beatty, & McKinlay, 1986; Fahy, Irving, &

Millac, 1967; Levin, Benton, & Grossman, 1982; Lezak, 1978; Lezak & O'Brien, 1988). When an individual with a brain injury is aware of his or her impairments, negative psychological consequences such as anxiety, paranoia, and depression have also been reported (Lezak, 1978; Lezak, 1988). Gross neurological motor deficits and cognitive sequelae have been found to improve over time (e.g., Mandelberg & Brooks, 1975; Najenson et al., 1974), but personality and emotional changes have been found to remain stable or even deteriorate over time (Fordyce, Roueche, & Prigatano, 1983; Thomsen, 1984).

The various sequelae of brain injury clearly represent losses, yet virtually no attention has been directed toward addressing these changes from the theoretical perspective of loss. A brain injury often exerts multiple losses simultaneously, such as loss of physical integrity, loss of memories, loss of the ability to control one's emotions, loss of characteristics which used to comprise one's personality, loss of friendships, loss of employment, loss of financial security, and loss of freedom. Sustaining a brain injury can undercut all aspects of a person's life. Furthermore, brain injury can be a stigmatizing loss, depending on the extent of observable disability. Losses such as this may result in discrimination or even ostracism (Harvey, 1996). People with brain injuries and their families often describe how friends seem to disappear over time, because they are uncomfortable around the person with the injury.

Much work needs to be done to identify losses experienced by persons with brain injuries, the psychological meaning of those losses, and coping processes among persons with brain injuries. My research team reexamined some of our data as a first step in exploring loss among persons with brain injuries. A reanalysis of qualitative data provided by spouse caregivers of persons with brain injuries (Chwalisz & Stark-Wroblewski, 1996), with a specific focus on themes of loss contained in these general essays about their experiences, revealed a number of areas of loss experienced by the person with the injury. The most frequently reported care-receiver losses were *loss of purpose* (e.g., "He's very lonely and has no purpose"), *loss of personality* (e.g., "Sometimes, very rarely, there are fleeting glimpses of the person he was . . ."), and *loss of intellectual capacity* (e.g., "R___'s I.Q. dropped by 45 points after the accident," "My five year old son has more common sense than his father"). Other areas of loss directly related to brain injury included losses of *income/earning potential*, *quality of life*, *sexual function*, *capacity to love*, and *family relationships*. It should also be noted that in most cases, several losses were identified for a single individual. Of course, these areas of loss should be judged with caution, because they are based solely on spouse report, but they represent a starting place for examining loss among persons with brain injuries.

There are several factors that may affect loss experienced by persons with brain injuries that do not affect people experiencing other types of loss. Probably the most critical is the fact that the very nature of the loss event suggests diminished capacity to cope with the loss. For example, a person with diminished cognitive capacity (e.g., reasoning, social learning) may not be capable of engaging in the cognitive coping processes necessary to effectively recover from such a severe loss. On the other hand, people with brain injuries may not experience their losses as fully or in the same way due to diminished cognitive capacity. In addition, the stigmatizing nature of the loss may limit support available to the individual. The compound losses experienced across many life domains make coping much more complex. Of course, these multifaceted losses are not unique to people with brain injuries, but these individuals appear to be a part of a group of people who experience loss that cuts across most or all aspects of life. There doesn't appear to be much literature devoted to such complex loss situations.

## CAREGIVER LOSS

The remainder of this chapter will focus on loss as it is experienced by caregivers of persons with brain injuries, because the prognosis for the caregiver is not determined by the nature of the injury to the extent that it is for the person with the injury. That is, many psychological phenomena appear to mediate the relationship between a brain injury and the well-being of the caregiver. This chapter will also focus on spouse rather than parent caregivers, because many spouses experience perhaps the most significant loss of all: the loss of consortium (i.e., company, affection, assistance, sexual relations) with the injured person.

The concept of loss has received little attention in the caregiver literature in general (Williamson & Shaffer, 1996), and I was similarly unable to find any literature applying loss conceptualizations to issues among caregivers of persons with brain injuries. Clearly, caregivers of persons with brain injuries experience significant losses, but these caregivers' difficulties have not been examined within the frameworks of personal and interpersonal loss. The majority of literature on caregivers of persons with brain injuries has been focused on the relationship between caregiver burden and negative physical and mental health outcomes and on identifying variables predicting burden and negative outcomes for caregivers. A model of the caregiver burden process among spouses of persons with brain injuries containing stress, coping, and social support accounted for just 56 percent of the variance in caregiver mental health status (Chwalisz, 1992b). Clearly, other psychological phenomena are involved.

### Previous Research

Objective burden (e.g., severity and nature of the injury, physical and cognitive changes, caregiving responsibilities, financial strain) has not been a consistent predictor of caregiver burden or physical or mental health consequences for caregivers (see Livingston & Brooks, 1988, for a review). Emotional and characterological changes associated with brain injury, however, have been consistently associated with caregiver burden and negative physical and mental health outcomes (e.g., Brooks et al., 1986). Furthermore, measures of the spouses' subjective experience of the injury have consistently predicted a variety of physical and mental health consequences. Particularly, perceived stress (i.e., the perception that the caregiving situation exceeds one's available resources) has consistently predicted a variety of negative caregiver outcomes such as depression, anxiety, and stress-related illnesses such as ulcers and migraine headaches (Chwalisz, 1992a, 1996).

The emotional and characterological sequelae associated with brain injury are clearly the "culprits" in caregiver burden and negative caregiver outcomes. The characterological alterations associated with brain injury can be conceptualized in five categories: (a) impaired capacity for social perceptiveness (e.g., self-centered behavior, lack of empathy); (b) impaired capacity for control and self-regulation (e.g., impulsivity, random restlessness, impatience); (c) stimulus-bound behavior (e.g., social dependency, rigidity); (d) emotional alterations (e.g., apathy, silliness, lability, irritability, greatly increased or complete loss of sexual interest); and (e) inability to profit from experience which compromises the capacity for social learning (Lezak, 1978). Furthermore, these higher-order functions appear to be independent of other cognitive functions which might be affected by brain injury. They may be disrupted even when other cognitive functions remain intact (Lezak & O'Brien, 1988).

Spouses of persons with brain injuries often describe these characterological changes as being married to a different person. One caregiver reported, "it is like being married to a man who looks like him and has some of his characteristics but is no longer him" (Chwalisz & Stark-Wroblewski, 1996). Another spouse noted that "I have lost a friend and gained an enemy." This personality change is an unusual kind of interpersonal loss, somewhere between a death and the interpersonal loss associated with other caregiving situations in which previous roles or behaviors may be lost but the emotional quality of the relationship remains. One caregiver mused, "It is almost like a death that doesn't actually end" (Chwalisz & Stark-Wroblewski, p. 32).

Caregivers of persons with brain injuries can neither divorce with dignity nor grieve the loss of their spouse, because the familiar body remains (Lezak, 1978). Muir and Haffey (1984) described this grieving process as "mobile mourning," in which the tentative nature of the patient's prognosis leaves family members uncertain with regard to the extent to which they have permission to grieve the loss of the patient's former level of functioning. The grief process among spouses of persons with brain injuries, however, may represent more than tentativeness. Disenfranchised grief, or grief associated with a loss that cannot be openly acknowledged, publicly mourned, or given much social support (Doka, 1989), may be a more useful way of conceptualizing these caregivers' grief. Outsiders often deny or fail to recognize changes in the person with the injury and are unsupportive to the spouse (e.g., "It is a terrible feeling to know that there is something different about your spouse and have doctors, friends, and family not believe you. I lived in hell thinking I was losing my mind") (Chwalisz & Stark-Wroblewski, 1996). In fact, many persons with brain injuries are able to exercise some control over their aberrant behavior for short periods of time, making them appear normal to outside observers (Lezak, 1988). Interactions like these may contribute to the caregivers' experience of stigma associated with brain injury.

## Themes of Loss in Caregivers' Accounts

When essay data from our previous qualitative study (Chwalisz & Stark-Wroblewski, 1996) were reanalyzed specifically in search of loss issues, a number of themes of loss emerged. A major theme, which appears to reflect a *loss of consortium*, contains two categories of losses: (a) *personal and emotional losses*, which reflects emotional and sexual aspects of the relationship and loss of the care-receiver's premorbid personality (e.g., "I do miss the love he had for me," "I am still confused, however, as to who is this man I live with, and where is the other one, I unconsciously wait for him to return"), and (b) *supportive and tangible losses*, which reflects the supportive contributions previously made by the care-receiver (e.g., "For several years I could never turn to him for any type of support," "[I] feel like I have to do it all—can't depend on husband").

Another theme reflects a sense of *foundational or core loss*, a loss of something central to the caregiver (e.g., "I have no purpose in life," "Over the past six years, I am aware that I have walled off myself from myself," "[I] feel like I'm not me, yet feel I have great capabilities . . ."). A *loss of projected security* was also reported by these caregivers (e.g., "[I] find it hard to relax and let go," "Because of these costs we (I) have had to use all savings, put a large mortgage on the house, etc. with no actual plan of getting things under control"). Some caregivers described a *loss of their own physical integrity* as they struggled to manage the stress of their caregiving responsibilities (e.g., "I find I am exhausted physically and mentally by evening . . . ," "In the past 6 months my physical health has been worse than I can every remember—migraines, colds (3 times), and the flu—all of which seem harder to recuperate from"). A *loss of family support* was also described (e.g., "Another problem is family—trying to help them discover their son or brother is still a person with normal needs," "His family denied that he is different so I never brought the subject up again . . ."). This loss of family support suggests that brain injury may actually create compound interpersonal losses over time.

*Loss of dreams* because of the brain injury in the family also seems to be an important theme (e.g., "The head injury R__ suffered has totally dashed every dream of our lives," "[I] have not gotten to do things I want to do—no time, no money, no energy left," "life seems an existence"). Goals serve a central role in the perception that one has control over life (Thompson, 1996), and these caregivers who perceive themselves as no longer having goals may be particularly at risk for the negative consequences of loss. These caregivers also experienced a *loss of freedom* (e.g., "I am not living the way I want to live—yet I really do not have control of my life," "I have not enjoyed life as my friends have"). Some caregivers also reported *lost aspects of oneself* (e.g., "I am no longer fun," "I used to feel things intensely, either positive or negative. I liked that in myself").

Loss appears to be a significant, yet untapped, psychological process for spouses of persons with brain injuries. A number of substantial losses can be readily identified. Furthermore, the most common mental health outcome among spouses of persons with brain injuries is depression (e.g., Chwalisz, 1992b; Lezak, 1978; Oddy, Humphrey, & Uttley, 1978), and loss has been theoretically implicated in depression. I concur with Williamson and Shaffer's (1996) speculation that loss may have both direct and indirect effects on caregiver depression. For example, unsuccessful coping with the variety of losses, particularly the loss of consortium, would be directly implicated in depression. The loss of resources and support will also likely impact perceived stress (caregiver burden), and impact depression via increased stress. The description of burden which emerged from caregiver accounts

(Chwalisz & Stark-Wroblewski, 1996) contains suggestions of both direct and indirect effects of loss. These caregivers expressed traditional grief reactions which might be directly related to poor outcomes (e.g., "Sometimes I wonder if this is really happening," "It is like a death that doesn't actually end"). They also expressed how overwhelmed they felt by their situation (e.g., "I am exhausted physically and mentally by evening—sometimes by late afternoon . . . ," "[I] feel like I have to do I all . . .").

These caregivers' accounts also contained evidence of cognitive processes involved in working through their losses. Several caregivers engaged in social comparisons (e.g., "I didn't know what he was like before his injury and so I only have one side to deal with as opposed to someone who is dealing with the changes that have taken place in their spouse since the injury," "Most of this questionnaire doesn't apply to us at this time. I'm sure it will be most helpful to others whose circumstances are more difficult"). There were also examples of healthy positive-thinking (e.g., "Fortunately R__'s spirit didn't change—and that is what I was in love with").

### Factors Impacting Caregiver Losses

Thompson (1996) described a number of factors which impact the extent to which individuals finding meaning and control in the face of loss. The *extent and seriousness* of the loss impact one's ability to find meaning in it. Spouses of persons with brain injuries experience serious, life-altering losses. The *type of loss* (e.g., unexpected, misfortune created by trusted others, loss of control in a previously controllable situation) also appears to predict coping. Most brain injuries occur unexpectedly via accidents. Individuals who engage in the *cognitive work* necessary for effective coping also appear to recover more effectively from loss. A fairly common reaction identified among family members of persons with brain injuries is denial (e.g., Ridley, 1989; Roueche & Fordyce, 1983), which can be considered a hindrance to that cognitive work. *Opportunities to talk with others* are also critical to effective coping with loss (Harvey, 1996; Thompson). Caregivers often lose contact with previously supportive others because of the discomfort, stigma, and lack of understanding associated with brain injury (e.g., "People I know can't understand the problems I have. They brush it off and act like it is unimportant—or theirs is worse"). Therefore, not only do caregivers of persons with brain injuries experience a number of significant losses, they have a number of strikes against them in terms of finding meaning or reestablishing control in their lives.

## INTERVENTIONS WITH CAREGIVERS: CONFRONTING LOSS

Finding meaning and reestablishing a sense of control following a major loss are important contributors to successful coping (Thompson, 1996). However, many individuals do not find meaning in loss. Account-making and confiding with others appear to be important mechanisms through which individuals engage in the cognitive work involved in deriving meaning from loss (Harvey, 1996). These mechanisms might also underlie the success of support group interventions with caregivers. Support groups have been found to be effective interventions with caregivers of persons with brain injuries, although most of the findings have been based on facilitator impressions (Chwalisz, Wiersma, Stark-Wroblewski, & Cook, 1996). It has been suggested that support groups play a very significant role in combating the isolation experienced by caregivers (Colman, 1984).

## Critical Events in a Caregiver Support Group

In a study of member-reported critical events occurring in a support group for caregivers of persons with brain injuries (Chwalisz et al., 1996), a number of categories of events appear relevant to coping with loss, particularly account-making and confiding. One critical event which was articulated following discussion of caregiving situations was the *acknowledgment of loss*. Awareness of losses appears to be an important naturally occurring function of caregiver support groups. Specifically, these caregivers were referring to losses experienced by the care-receiver (e.g., "Dad [sic] has lost so many of the things that made his life good each day") and outcomes associated with these loss acknowledgment events included negative affect, positive affect, and coping thoughts.

Several events appear particularly relevant to the account-making and confiding processes. Interestingly, simply sharing their stories was not reported as a critical event by group members, suggesting that the process of confiding an account may operate at a less than conscious level or may be assumed in the context of a support group. However, sharing stories of their successes seemed particularly important to these group members (e.g., "[we] talked about . . . skill and success as a caretaker, especially . . . comfort and ease in handling [the care-receiver]"). Sharing successes allowed them to receive some validation and helped them to balance positive and negative material discussed in the group (e.g., "This is important. I'm glad this is happening. This helps balance the long list of troubles and complaints"). *Displaying or discussing negative emotions* was also a recurrent critical event for the majority of members on several occasions. This kind of self-disclosure was associated with feeling understood and accepted, coping thoughts, and some negative affect. This may reflect some working through of the losses these caregivers experience. Another critical event involved experiencing *companionship* in the group (e.g., "having someone to talk to and to listen to"). Again, the presence of confidants in a support group appears to be critical for this otherwise isolated group.

Two other categories of events suggest that there may be some benefit to simply hearing the accounts of people whose experiences are similar to one's own. Several group members identified a *vicarious emotional experience* (e.g., observing another member cry) as a critical event for them, resulting in universality (e.g., "I found out that all of us had guilty feelings at times . . ."), altruism (e.g., "I try to help out by being a listener"), and coping thoughts (e.g., "I am a very happy person and will conquer whatever I have to"). Group members also reported that events involving *receiving information* were also very important to them. It appears that these caregivers gained from the accounts of others, and perhaps these gains shaped future account-making of their own.

Another type of critical event involved *reflecting on the group* (i.e., at termination), in which group members created a joint account of what they had gained by participating in the group. A number of members reported coping thoughts coming out of their reflections. Other outcomes included planning the next step (e.g., "I am going to go back to church . . ."), a sense of benefit (e.g., "getting some help . . ."), relaxation (e.g., "the stress level has gone down and I'm more relaxed"), increased cohesion (e.g., "being with other people with the same problems"), and altruism toward group members (e.g., "I thought about who could help her"). Such group accounts have yet to be explored. It would seem that the process of reflecting on one's accomplishments with the support and assistance of others represents a unique and potentially powerful account-making process inherent in groups.

The *opportunity to help others* was also a critical event for the majority of support group members. Providing assistance in the context of other members' distress was one context in which altruism occurred among group members. The urge to assist a fellow group member was also prompted by learning more about her situation. Caregivers' essay accounts of their experiences (Chwalisz & Stark-Wroblewski, 1996) also contained expressions of a desire to help others (e.g., "I hope this research really helps the spouses," "I would be happy to talk to you and answer any direct questions you have"). It appears that helping others in the same situation plays an important role for many caregivers. If we think of such efforts as a means of coping with loss, helping others may be a way to find meaning in their adversity. Or, for some, taking a helping role may be associated with positive social comparison (e.g., offering help to less fortunate caregivers).

## Themes of Loss Discussed in a Support Group

A support group does, indeed, appear to be a place for caregivers to talk about issues of loss. When I analyzed transcripts of sessions from the previous study of a caregiver support group (Chwalisz et al., 1996), looking specifically for loss, I identified a number of categories of loss experience by the care-receiver, caregiver, and the couple jointly. These issues of loss were identified throughout the content of the support group sessions.

**Care-receiver losses**. Caregivers discussed a number of losses they perceived the care-receiver to have experienced. The *loss of abilities* was a major area of loss, which encompassed loss of stamina, motor skills, and previously automatic behavior such as writing or other skills (e.g., "He plays piano by ear. I mean he can play like Liberace by ear. And now with only one hand, that's one less thing that he did for enjoyment that he's not able to do now").

Along with these lost abilities, there appears to be a much more impactful *loss of basic freedom*, which involved not being able to take care of oneself, protect oneself from harm, or engage in the things one used to enjoy (e.g., "The problem is he was so active. He was an outdoor person . . . just real physical person all his life . . . he just can't do anything he used to do"). A particularly poignant example of this fundamental type of loss is the experience of a care-receiver who was attacked by a stray dog while on his porch, and he could neither "beat the dog off" nor call for help.

Caregivers also reported *losses of memory* experienced by their family members. In some cases, memory loss was severe enough to represent loss of particular periods of time in their past or awareness of people they used to know. One caregiver reported, "He was unconscious for a few days, and for several weeks he didn't know anybody or anything. He doesn't remember anything that happened for about six months."

**Caregiver losses.** Two losses reported by caregivers were related to changes in the care-receiver as a result of the injury. Several caregivers reported that *the care-receiver is another person,* which encompassed differences in personality and appearance (e.g., "And when I first walked in, I couldn't hardly stand it . . . It was horrible, you know, that she came home in that kind of condition," "You know, why can't you take him back to the hospital and have them do something, then he'll be normal. There's nothing left up there"). These caregivers also expressed a *loss of consortium,* or lack of support or interaction with the care-receiver resulting in having to handle everything alone (e.g., "you are the one that's holding it together"). In one case, the caregiver was single-handedly caring for her paralyzed adult daughter and her daughter's four children (ages 4, 5, 14, and 15).

These caregivers' experiences of having to do it all alone was in some cases compounded by a *loss of family/friends* as a result of the injury (e.g., "As time went on, you never see anybody. They never even called. And I realize that a lot of people when this happened to B___ they didn't know what to say"). Consequently, several caregivers reported a *loss of autonomy,* which encompassed the heavy pull of their myriad responsibilities, a loss of personal space or time, and having to put one's own plans and goals on hold (e.g., "But I was planning on going back that fall and then she got hurt in early spring, so I didn't go back to school," "I can't even come in the house and sit down. . . . And she hears me at the back door and she starts hollering Mom, Mom, Mom"). A *loss of financial security* was also reported, associated with loss of employment and the costs associated with brain injury (e.g., "I had to take off work on average three days a week. I do not have an understanding boss," "She had no insurance. She had nothing. Chicago . . . back and forth . . . there's no help for that, no money to do anything with").

**Losses experienced jointly.** Two types of losses reported in the support group appeared to impact both the caregiver and the care-receiver in a similar way. A *loss of family interaction* appeared particularly significant. Having someone in a family sustain a brain injury changes the nature of the family system, and some authors have suggested looking at brain injury from a systems perspective (e.g., Graffi & Minnes, 1989). Caregivers in this group described strained interactions in the family, loss of communication, and fewer activities together (e.g., "He's short with me, I'm short with him. And if he's short with my daughter, then I'm short with him, and then she's developed an attitude out of this whole thing"). There was also a *joint loss of family/friends* (e.g., "They don't come around too much. . . ."). That is, sometimes it appears that the loss of family and friends is experienced by both caregiver and care-receiver (or the entire immediate family), whereas other times it appears that the caregiver experiences the loss of family or friends as a loss of support related to his or her caregiving efforts.

## IMPLICATIONS OF LOSS FOR SURVIVORS OF BRAIN INJURY

These initial findings suggest that loss is an important psychological phenomenon for survivors of brain injury and their families. Conceptualizing the experience of persons coping with brain injury in terms of loss opens up a variety of new avenues for research and practice. Psychological interventions could be directed toward assisting survivors and their families in the work required to grieve the losses and find meaning in their situations. Research could be directed toward investigating mechanisms surrounding loss and how they operate in or interact with existing models of the response to brain injury.

## REFERENCES

Brooks, N., Campsie, L., Symington, C., Beattie, A., & McKinlay, W. (1986). The five year outcome of severe blunt head injury: A relative's view. *Journal of Neurology, Neurosurgery, and Psychiatry, 49,* 764–770.

Chwalisz, K. (1992a). Perceived stress and caregiver burden after brain injury: A theoretical integration. *Rehabilitation Psychology, 37*(3), 189–203.

Chwalisz, K. (1992b). *The perceived stress model of caregiver burden: Evidence from the spouses of head injured persons.* Unpublished doctoral dissertation, The University of Iowa.

Chwalisz, K. (1996). The perceived stress model of caregiver burden: Evidence from the spouses of persons with brain injuries. *Rehabilitation Psychology, 41*(2), 91–114.

Chwalisz, K., & Stark-Wroblewski, K. (1996). The subjective experience of spouse caregivers of persons with brain injuries: A qualitative analysis. *Applied Neuropsychology, 3,* 28–40.

Chwalisz, K., Wiersma, N. S., Stark-Wroblewski, K. S., & Cook, C. A. (1996, August). *Critical events in a support group for caregivers of persons with brain injuries.* Paper presented at the annual convention of the American Psychological Association, Toronto, ON, Canada.

Colman, (1984). Till death do us part: Caregiving wives of severely disabled husbands. *The Coordinator, 3*(1), 15–19.

Doka, K. J. (1989). *Disenfranchized grief: Recognizing hidden sorrow.* Lexington, MA: Lexington Books/D.C. Heath and Company.

Fahy, T. J., Irving, M. H., & Millac, P. (1967). Severe head injuries: A six-year follow-up. *Lancet, ii,* 475–479.

Fordyce, D. J., Roueche, J. R., & Prigatano, G. P. (1983). Enhanced emotional reactions in chronic head trauma patients. *Journal of Neurology, Neurosurgery, & Psychiatry, 46,* 620–624.

Graffi, S., & Minnes, P. (1989). Stress and coping in caregivers of persons with traumatic head injuries. *The Journal of Applied Sciences, 13*(2), 293–316.

Harvey, J. H. (1996). *Embracing their memory: Loss and the Social Psychology of Storytelling.* Needham Heights, MA: Allyn & Bacon.

Kalsbeek, W. D., McLaurin, R. L., Harris III, B. S. H., & Miller, J. D. (1980). The national head injury and spinal cord injury survey: Major findings. *Journal of Neurosurgery, 53,* S19–S31.

Kraus, J. F., & Nourjah, P. (1989). The epidemiology of mild head injury. In H. S. Levin, H. M. Eisenberg, & A. L. Benton (Eds.), *Mild head injury* (pp. 8–22). New York: Oxford University Press.

Levin, H. S., Benton, A. L., & Grossman, R. G. (1982). Neurobehavioral consequences of closed head injury. In H. S. Levin, A. L. Benton, & R. G. Grossman (Eds.), *Mild head injury* (pp. 49–62). New York: Oxford University Press.

Lezak, M. D. (1978). Living with the characterologically altered brain injured patient. *Journal of Clinical Psychiatry, 39*(7), 592–598.

Lezak, M. D. (1988). Brain damage is a family affair. *Journal of Clinical and Experimental Neuropsychology, 10*(1), 111–123.

Lezak, M. D., & O'Brien, K. P. (1988). Longitudinal study of emotional, social, and physical changes after traumatic brain injury. *Journal of Learning Disabilities, 21*(8), 456–463.

Livingston, M. G., & Brooks, D. N. (1988). The burden on families of the brain injured: A review. *Journal of Head Trauma Rehabilitation, 3*(4), 6–15.

Mandelberg, I. A., & Brooks, D. N. (1975). Cognitive recovery after severe head injury 1. Serial testing on the Wechsler Adult Intelligence Scale. *Journal of Neurology, Neurosurgery, and Psychiatry, 38,* 1121–1126.

Muir, C. A., & Haffey, W. J. (1984). Psychological and neuropsychological interventions with the mobile mourning process. In B. A. Edelstein & E. T. Courture (Eds.), *Behavioral assessment and rehabilitation of the traumatically brain damaged.* New York: Plenum Press.

Najenson, T., Mendelson, L., Schecter, I., David, C., Mintz, N., & Groswasser, Z. (1974). Rehabilitation after severe head injury. *Scandinavian Journal of Rehabilitation Medicine, 6,* 5–14.

Oddy, M., Humphrey, M., & Uttley, D. (1978). Stresses upon the relatives of head-injured patients. *British Journal of Psychiatry, 133,* 507–513.

Ridley, B. (1989). Family response to head injury: Denial . . . or hope for the future? *Social Science and Medicine, 29*(4), 555–561.

Roueche, J. R., & Fordyce, D. J. (1983). Perceptions of deficits following brain injury and their impact on psychosocial adjustment. *Cognitive Rehabilitation, 1,* 4–7.

Thompson, S. C. (1996). Barriers to maintaining a sense of meaning and control in the face of loss. *Journal of Personal and Interpersonal Loss, 1,* 333–357.

Thomsen, I. V. (1984). Late outcome of very severe blunt head trauma: A 10-15 year second follow-up. *Journal of Neurology, Neurosurgery, & Psychiatry, 47,* 260–268.

Williamson, G. M., & Shaffer, D. R. (1996). Interpersonal loss in the context of family caregiving: Implications of communal relationships theory. *Journal of Personal and Interpersonal Loss, 1,* 247–272.

# 14

# *Loss Experienced in Chronic Pain and Illness*

***Patricia Kelley***
*University of Iowa*

Persons suffering from chronic pain or illness experience a sense of loss at the personal and interpersonal level. The losses incurred are existential and personal, as a sense of self and a sense of control over one's destiny is undermined. There is a sense of "not being who I was," and a loss of the way of living for both the sufferer and the caregivers and other family members. In addition, there are interpersonal losses such as a change in relationships with family members and other significant others, loss of employment, and loss of an active social life.

In this chapter, these personal and interpersonal losses are explored through a review of existing literature, and through reanalysis of materials gathered for a research project which assessed the use of narrative group approaches with fibromyalgia (Fm) sufferers. In that study, transcripts of group sessions as well as journals kept by the individuals were analyzed, and loss was found to be a major theme (Kelley & Clifford, 1997). Here, the stories of loss reported by those individuals are reexamined in light of the literature on the subject.

Chronic pain is of national concern, as it affects about 10% of the population in the United States in a given year (Osterweis, Kleinman, & Mechanic, 1987). It is also of concern to health and mental health professionals because of its negative effects on the social and psychological functioning of the afflicted, and because it goes beyond the patient to affect the family and other social systems (Miller, 1993). Chronic pain is differentiated from acute pain, with the approximate dividing line drawn at three months (Roy, 1989). As a group, persons suffering from chronic pain or chronic illness experience a sense of loss (Roy, 1989; Shapiro, 1993), more depression than non-pain sufferers (Hanson & Gerber, 1990; Miller, 1993; Roy, 1989), and, almost universally, a sense of having their pain discounted and their authenticity questioned by health professionals and by family members at some point (Kleinman, 1988).

Fm is an invisible and chronic pain condition affecting at least 3% to 6% of the population in North America (Smythe, Bennett, & Wolfe, 1993). The symptoms include muscle aches and pain with tender points on examination, sleep disturbance and fatigue, headaches, vascular reactivity, and urinary and bowel irritability

The author acknowledges Patricia Clifford, MSW, CSW, Social Worker in the Arthritis Unit of York County Hospital, Newmarket, Ontario, and Mary Cerda, Student of Social Work, University of Iowa, for their invaluable help in the preparation of this chapter.

(Smythe et al., 1993). It is a poorly understood condition which has been recognized only recently; the American College of Rheumatology developed a classification system in 1990 (Goldenberg, 1994). Fm sufferers are an important group to study in relationship to chronic pain because as a group they experience more pain and with less relief than do persons with other chronic pain conditions, and they report more symptoms of depression and fatigue than other pain patients (Gaston-Johansson, Gustafsson, Felldin, & Sanne, 1990; Soderberg & Norberg, 1995). In addition, the lower self-esteem, reduced self-confidence and alienation found in persons living with chronic pain (Gaston-Johansson et al., 1990; Miller, 1993) are often exacerbated for Fm patients because it is an invisible condition which often has not been taken seriously by health care providers and family members. This lack of social support increases the stress of living with pain (Gaston-Johansson et al.).

Shapiro (1993, p. 4) defines loss as "the disruption of an attachment—an attachment to other people, to body parts, to inanimate objects, to fantasies, to habits, and to life styles." She notes that the early literature on loss focused almost exclusively on the death of a loved one, but that it has been broadened more recently to include symbolic losses, life transitions, and the loss of physical functioning. Shapiro further notes that the literature on crisis intervention, based on Erich Lindemann's pioneering work in the field in 1944, tends to ignore the individual's need to confront grief and loss and favors instead the goal of returning the person to normal functioning. She agrees with Rando (1988) that coping with loss involves three stages of processing: acknowledging and understanding, experiencing the pain and reacting to the loss, and finally, moving into the new life without forgetting the old. These are important points in understanding the loss associated with chronic pain and illness, for one cannot return to normal functioning or "get beyond" the loss; the sufferers live with it daily. Yet, to cope with the condition effectivley, they must move beyond the "illness narrative" (Kleinman, 1988) to view the condition as "afflicting but not constituting" (Wynne, Shields, & Sirkin, 1992) themselves. Under this definition, coping involves keeping a sense of self while adapting to a new way of life.

## PERSONAL LOSS

The personal loss experience of persons suffering from long-lasting illness or pain has been well documented in the literature (Brooks & Matson, 1982; Flor, Turk, & Scholz, 1987; Holland & Beeson, 1993; Lebovitz, 1979; Lewis, 1994; Mann, 1985; Roy, 1989; Shapiro, 1993). As Lebovitz (1979) has noted, persons faced with a loss of health lose their sense of self and need to mourn the loss of their old selves and reorganize their identity. Lewis (1994) notes that with chronic illness there is a "loss of privacy, body image, and human relationships" (p. 9). When people go from being independent to being dependent, from being healthy to having a chronic condition, from feeling in control of their lives and their bodies to feeling powerless, and from feeling sexual desires and energy to feeling chronic fatigue and loss of desire, there is a sense of having lost who they were.

In the first group session of the Fm study, members explained their experiences with the syndrome, and one woman in the group noted that the Fm experience has been like "taking some of your life away by taking pieces out of it. There are lots of things you used to be able to do that you can't do now." Another said, "you've got nothing that you had before; I can relate with that. I have nothing that I had before. Absolutely nothing." Another said, "It's just like when somebody dies you have grieving, and go through a cycle of anger, disbelief, etc.—but with Fm you just get caught on a thing like a hamster where you just go round and round." In discussing the uncertainty and lack of control, one noted: "there's no point in having expectations." Another added, "It is so different all the time you don't know—today you'll be fine and tomorrow you're knocked out. You just don't know what's going to happen."

Lindgren, Burke, Hainsworth, and Georgene (1992) note that chronic illness is a constant source of loss, and they apply the term chronic sorrow to describe the experience. They differentiate chronic sorrow from grief and from depression. The experience of these pain sufferers seems to bear out that distinction. One woman said, "it is not a textbook depression; I am not irritable, angry, or even feeling sorry for myself. I am just so utterly dragged down by pain and fatigue. I don't cry for myself and I am relieved that I can still cry for others." Another added, "this is not the life I planned. The pain wears down my defenses; the tears flow endlessly in private."

Armentrout (1979) has noted that chronic pain negatively affects self-concept, as it is associated with the loss of many normal functions. Several members of the Fm group discussed how they used to like to have big family dinners for the holidays and how they could no longer do that. One said, "I just can't make the meals I used to." Another said, "I am limited to maybe four people; I cannot cook for more than that because I can't lift a bigger pan of potatoes." Another said, "my husband has to peel the potatoes now because I can not hold them in my hand."

Other areas of life were also discussed. One person said, "by the beginning of 1991 I simply could not work any longer and I stopped. Nothing has changed since then. I have pain all the time, and I never sleep properly." Another added, "I can not play tennis any longer, or go for walks, or garden as I loved. I can't even clean my house, not that I loved that. I can't easily manage a shopping mall, supermarket or post office anymore."

A related theme was one of independence. Several group members said that the loss of independence was the biggest loss of all. One member said, "I miss doing things for myself—it is hard to know you have to wait for someone to help you to do something." Charmaz (1994), in her study of chronically ill men, found that a major problem for them was an identity dilemma. In the Fm project, all of the participants were women, and they also had the problem with identity. One woman said, "I have had to learn to ask for help." Another said, "I use [sic] to consider myself a giver and a nurturer." Becoming more dependent does affect one's sense of identity. Mann (1985) said that this changing sense of self comes from the loss of the sense of mastery or control. As one participant expressed, "my home is my career and I feel like a failure at that. I feel like a burden to my husband and family, and I feel useless." The findings of this study of women with Fm are similar to the experiences reported in a study conducted by Soderberg and Norberg (1995), where the pain experiences of 14 Fm women patients were described.

Other personal losses discussed by these group members included loss of vision of what life was going to be, that is, the loss of an ideal life; loss of physical activity; loss of memory and ability to think as clearly; loss of interest in and enjoyment of sexuality (for some it was fatigue; others said it hurt to be touched); loss of self and loss of life as it used to be. Throughout the discussion they kept coming back to the dependency issue. Gannon and Gold (1988) refer to this phenomenon as the psychological death of the old self as people are thrust back into a state of dependency. They believe that this loss requires a mourning process and the rebirth of an adapted self.

## INTERPERSONAL LOSS

The interpersonal and social losses of chronic pain and chronic illness sufferers are also well documented in the literature (Brooks & Matson, 1982; Flor et al., 1987; Lebovitz, 1979; Manne & Zaurtra, 1989; Payne & Norfleet, 1986; Raymond & Bergland, 1994; Roy, 1989). Henriksson (1995) studied the consequences of Fm on 40 women in the U.S. and Sweden and found the psychosocial consequences to be severe and often minimized. These interpersonal losses are closely connected to the personal losses, for as noted by Shapiro (1993, p. 5), "our sense of identity, which encompasses our beliefs about our physical attributes and our worth as human beings, is shaped over a lifetime of interactions and personal growth." The feelings of dependence and the decrease in sexual activity are especially related to the interpersonal losses, as marital adjustment and family satisfaction are often reduced in families with a chronic pain sufferer (Flor et al.; Henriksson, 1995; Lewis, 1994; Payne & Norfleet, 1986; Roy, 1989). Further, as noted by Hanson and Gerber (1990), chronic pain may lead to negative emotional states, such as depression, anxiety, and anger, which can lead to negative thinking and produce a destructive cycle. In addition, caretakers of persons with chronic illness are at risk for more stress and depression themselves (Given et al., 1993), thus exacerbating the negative interactive cycle.

As noted, marital and family interactions suffer when one member has chronic illness or pain, and this loss is the most difficult of the interpersonal losses. Henriksson (1995), in his study of Fm sufferers, found the disruption of family life was one of the biggest losses experienced by these persons. The changes in everyday life, the inability to do tasks, and the changes in the ways they were perceived by family members were cited as some reasons for this disruption. The loss of the family role was cited by the women in both Henriksson's study and this author's study. In addition to not being able to care for family members as they used to do, there was the general feeling that intimacy was decreased with children and spouses. The lack of understanding on the part of family members regarding the condition and the afflicted member's lack of energy to get involved in others' lives were cited as two main reasons for the decreased sense of closeness. Lack of sexual desire was a major theme in the lives of these women. Flor et al. (1987), in their study of the impact of chronic pain on the spouse of the patient, found that both the patients and their spouses experienced considerable change in marital and sexual satisfaction. They found heightened stress and physical symptoms in the spouses as well.

Studies by Manne and Zaurtra (1989) of women with rheumatoid arthritis and by Given et al. (1993) of cancer patients and their families supported the findings of Flor et al. (1987) that the attitude, behavior, and mood of the caretaker affected the pain experience of the patient, and the pain experience of the patient affected the mood of the caretaker. Negative interactions have significant implications for mental health, stress level, and physical well-being of both the pain sufferer and the caretaker. Conversely, spousal support is associated with more adaptive coping (Manne & Zaurtra, 1989).

Discussing the changes in sexuality, the women in the Fm group had many comments. One noted, "I'm like everyone else (meaning in the group). I'm so tired—you know the old joke about being too tired again tonight dear." Another added, "it's painful, too. I've got pain all in my pelvis and in all the tendons and in all the bones. You have certain parts of the body you don't want touched—like it's ok to have sex; just don't touch me." Another added, "How do you convey this nebulous illness that produces this general pain and this fatigue and this poor sleep. That's hard to explain. Then, how do you deal with that in terms of sexuality and being able to tell your partner that my energy level is zero—I am exhausted?"

These comments relate to another loss faced by pain sufferers: the loss of feeling understood. Manne & Zaurtra (1989) noted that while the need for social support is greater for pain patients, it is more difficult for them to receive. Brooks and Matson (1982) note that pain management requires major efforts with minimal reinforcements. The women in Henriksson's study reported feeling rejected and misunderstood by family and friends as well as by health professionals. They reported anxiety over feeling misunderstood or minimized, and felt that receiving a diagnosis provided relief and validation.

In a discussion in the author's Fm group (Kelley & Clifford, in press), similar experiences were reported. In one session there was agreement that loss of validation by family members, friends, health professionals, and employers had been most difficult, and that receiving a diagnosis was validating. They expressed gratitude for the care and understanding that they finally received at the hospital where they were currently being treated, and felt more understanding from the health care providers and the other patients here than from their families and friends. Raymond and Berglund (1994) have noted that finding health professionals who understand the syndrome (Fm) is crucial in helping patients create a workable balance between the demands of the syndrome and their individual lifestyles. They also stressed the importance for professionals of educating the families, employers, and others regarding the physical and psychological aspects of Fm.

Loss of social life was reported by the women in the Fm group. This loss was associated with many other factors: their low energy level, which prevented them from seeking out their friends, their inability to plan ahead and to host activities, the loss of abilities to do certain activities which they used to do with friends, such as sports, and their friends not understanding their pain or limitations. As one group member said, "That's when your world gets small. It's not that you've chosen it, but it was chosen for you because you are not capable of doing things others do." The women in Henriksson's (1995) Fm study noted similar experiences, and some added that their friends distanced themselves from them, seeming to be fearful of their condition or to find it distasteful. The loss of social life experienced by these Fm patients is similar to the experiences found with other chronic illness patients (Brooks & Matson, 1982; Lebovitz, 1979).

A related interpersonal loss is that of occupation. Missed time from work, changes in type of employment, and job termination have been reported in the literature regarding chronic illness in general and Fm in particular, but other studies have suggested that work is usually maintained by Fm sufferers despite chronic pain and fatigue (Raymond & Berglund, 1994). In fact, Waylonis (1992), reporting from clinical experience, found that Fm sufferers are ideal employees because as a group they are often compulsive in personal appearance, quality of work, punctuality, and overall job performance. In the group discussed in this paper, however, most of the participants had been employed, but few still were, and they reported that the effects of Fm were the reason for current unemployment (Kelley & Clifford, 1997). As one woman noted, "I simply could work no longer."

The Fm sufferers in the Henriksson (1995) study also reported that their work was either stopped or decreased in time. Loss of sustainable income was reported as a problem for women with Fm in a literature review by Raymond and Berglund (1994), but they also cited reports that found 60% of Fm patients still employed with only 6% receiving disability. Wolfe and Potter (1996), on the other hand, found that 25.3% of the Fm patients in their study received some type of disability payments. Clearly, there are discrepancies in the data, with widely varying reports. Regardless of the exact number who can no longer work, Raymond and Berglund (1994) in their literature review on this subject note that Fm sufferers do face legitimate challenges, with diminished work capacity and decreased ability to perform standard tasks, and they reported more pessimism about the future of their work. One group member noted that before she quit her job she found herself "getting slower and slower" and the job getting "harder and harder." Other chronic illness and pain sufferers sustain as much or more difficulty in employment as Fm patients (Flor, Turk, & Scholtz, 1987; Lebovitz, 1979). Since occupation is a source of role identity, social satisfaction, and income, inability to work is a major loss.

## CONCRETE LOSSES

In addition to the personal and interpersonal losses, members of the Fm group reported several very concrete losses resulting from their condition. The loss of job and income are very good examples. Other specific concrete losses were noted by the participants in the Fm group, such as loss of mobility, loss of energy, loss of comfort, loss of physical activity, and even the loss of wearing pretty dress shoes that they used to enjoy. They discussed the loss of sleep and the loss of concentration and memory as very troubling and ongoing problems. Inability to drive a car and to get around on their own or to carry out specific tasks were also named by several members. Loss of comfort in social situations was named by several persons, and the memory loss and confusion were cited as contributing to the problem. The list of concrete losses varies by the individual and by the nature of the chronic condition, but together they mean a loss of the lifestyle which they knew and associated with themselves.

## RE-STORYING ONE'S LIFE

Up to this point, this chapter has been about the losses sustained by persons facing chronic pain or illness. It has been pretty grim reporting, but luckily it has been only one side of the story. In addition to being persons who have sustained losses and suffered pain, these are also people who have coped with adversity with varying degrees of success, and who have other aspects of their life stories besides the illness narrative. It is important for the persons who have the chronic conditions, their families, and the professionals who work with them to recognize both sides of the picture. Facing their own losses and feeling understood by the people around them is important, but it is also important for these people to not lose sight of the other aspects of themselves and their lives, so that they view themselves and are viewed by others as persons who live with and cope with a chronic condition rather than as people whose identity is the chronic condition.

What helps people cope with adversity and loss and move on in life? Several studies have addressed the problem of coping. Gannon and Gold (1988) discuss the rehabilitation process as "rebirth" of an adapted self, noting that after trauma people return to earlier functioning and dependency, and then go through developmental stages as they gradually differentiate and "hatch" out again. They relearn old skills and practice developing new skills. An intact sense of self is recognized as central to the process. Holland and Beeson (1993), on the other hand, note that the sense of self is often shaken by the loss and that the rehabilitation process needs to nurture a new self-image. The new self must include and be built upon the former self, however, or further fragmentation may occur.

Taylor (1983), in a discussion of adaptation to threatening events, isolated three themes in the adjustment process: a search for meaning in the experience, an attempt to regain mastery over the event, and an effort to restore self-esteem through self-enhancing evaluations. She maintained that the individual's efforts to resolve these three themes rest upon the ability to form and maintain a set of illusions. She cites Greenwald's (1980) view that maintenance of one's self-concept depends on the revision of one's personal history, perhaps remembering oneself as more successful than one really is. She notes that denial may be a useful defense for persons facing adversity. The helpfulness of downward comparison is also noted: that people can maintain their sense of self best when they see that others are worse off or not faring as well. Comparisons with people who were coping well with worse situations are especially helpful, for they can enhance a sense of self at the same time as they offer role models for coping.

Murphy (1985) and Thompson (1985) view adversity as a part of life which can enhance growth and potentially be a positive factor. Murphy notes that we suffer many losses in our lives, including loss of health, and she believes that the grieving process resulting from the loss can lead to growth and fulfillment. She argues that the grieving process should not end in acceptance, but should restore us to life as we become more conscious of our own strengths, abilities, and talents. Thompson, in a study of how people coped with traumatic events, found that those people who could find some positive meaning or could concentrate on the benefits brought by an undesirable event, rather than the costs incurred, coped better. In addition, those who took some responsibility for the undesirable events coped better than those who blamed others, perhaps because it heightened their feelings of control. She outlined five ways of focusing on the positive which were associated with better coping in her study: finding side benefits, social comparison, imagining worse situations, forgetting the negative, and redefining. It should be noted, however, that her subjects were survivors of fires which destroyed their homes, and the negative event was "over" for them, which is different from persons living with chronic and worsening pain or illness. With some modification, however, these coping mechanisms were similar to the coping devices which were useful for the participants in the Fm study.

In the study reported here (Kelley & Clifford, 1997), narrative group approaches were found useful for helping Fm sufferers develop their coping mechanisms. In the narrative groups, the participants could first tell and hear each others' stories of pain, which they believed was necessary before they could move on. Then they were able to assess their broader life stories, and to see how their adversity fit into their ongoing life story and could be incorporated into their existing sense of self. Then they were able to discover the strengths and coping mechanisms they were already using, which allowed them to take pride in their coping. They also shared coping ideas with each other and learned from each other, which enhanced their sense of self as helpers. For example, they discussed how they had found alternatives for certain activities: one woman took up swimming when she could no longer play tennis. Others talked about having to learn to be flexible, for example, to do their chores when they felt good and to let themselves wait on those activities when they did not feel good.

They did look for meaning in their circumstances, as discussed by Taylor (1983) and Murphy (1985). One member even said that she thought those who developed Fm were those who were strong in the first place, and that is why they were "chosen." Others found positive side-effects of it, saying Fm made them strong. As a group, they came to the conclusion that people with Fm were by nature stronger and more giving than others. They also believed that Fm sufferers were, by nature, more perfectionistic and independent, and that is why it is so difficult for them to learn to let go of chores and to ask others for help. These discussions bore out Taylor's (1983) contentions regarding the usefulness of denial and of maintaining illusions. Several positive side-effects were identified. One woman said, "Fm has made me more balanced;—I used to consider myself a nurturer and a giver, but now I can allow others to nurture me as well, sometimes." She added that perhaps she had helped others learn to nurture. Another said, "I have learned to ask for help."

As these women told their stories of pain, they were also able to find strengths and happiness as well. They challenged the meanings that they had created regarding their condition, and created new realities. For example, they found out that all days were not equally bad, as they had originally contended. They found that knowing there would be good days helped them get through the bad days. They also discovered that they were still the same persons they were before, but they had to live with some restrictions now. As one woman noted, she could still enjoy her classical music and her love of nature. They were also able to modify their expectations of others. There was so much anger at first about not being understood by family and friends. Later, they were able to see that they did not require

100% understanding from everybody, that if some people understood them somewhat they could live with that. They realized that different ones among their family and friends could be counted on for different types of help and different understanding, rather than having all of them good for everything. These findings bear out Seaburn, Lorenz, and Kaplan's (1992) contention regarding the importance of the meanings attributed to an illness and the importance of storying the experience. Taylor's (1983) theory of cognitive adaptation to threatening events is also supported by these findings. It is important to note, however, that some understanding by the family member seemed very important for these pain sufferers before they could move on into these other coping strategies.

## CONCLUSIONS

In this chapter, loss was examined from the viewpoint of persons experiencing chronic pain or illness. Relevant literature was reviewed and discussed in terms of experiences reported by participants in a research project of the author, which assessed the usefulness of narrative approaches on coping experiences of persons diagnosed with Fibromyalgia. The experience of these participants was congruent with the literature on the subject. Persons with chronic pain and chronic illness conditions do suffer from personal and interpersonal losses. As their sense of self and their way of life is lost, they go through a grieving process where they first mourn the loss of their old self and then go on to rediscover a newly developed sense of self. The importance of discovering strengths, of recognizing that the condition is one part of their life but not their whole life, and of adapting to the new life is underscored. For professionals who work with persons experiencing chronic pain, it is important to recognize the usefulness of educational groups for them and their families which highlight the stages of adaptation and which impart information on the condition. Narrative approaches which help people reauthor their lives and cognitive approaches appear especially useful.

## REFERENCES

Armentrout, D. P. (1979). The impact of chronic pain on self-concept. *Journal of Clinical Psychology, 35*, 517–521.

Brooks, N. A., & Matson, R. R. (1982). Social-psychological adjustment to multiple sclerosis. *Social Science Medicine, 16*, 2129–2135.

Charmaz, K. (1994). Identity dilemmas of chronically ill men. *The Sociological Quarterly, 35*, 269–288.

Flor, H., Turk, D. C., & Scholz, O. B. (1987). Impact of chronic pain on the spouse: Marital, emotional and physical consequences. *Journal of Psychosomatic Research, 31*, 63–71.

Gannon, S., & Gold, J. R. (1988). Rebirth: The rehabilitation process. *Professional Psychology: Research and Practice, 19*, 632–636.

Gaston-Johansson, F., Gustafsson, M., Felldin, R., & Sanne, H. (1990). A comparative study of feelings, attitudes and behaviors of patients with fibromyalgia and rheumatoid arthritis. *Journal of Social Science and Medicine, 31*, 941–947.

Given, C. W., Stommel, M., Given, B., Osuch, J., Kurtz, M. E., & Kurtz, J. C. (1993). The influence of cancer patients' symptoms and functional states on patients' depression and family caregivers' reaction and depression. *Health Psychology, 12*, 277–285.

Goldenberg, D. L. (1994). Fibromyalgia. In J. Klippel & P. Dieppe (Eds.), *Rheumatology* (Sec. 5, pp. 16.1–16.12). London: Mosby.

Greenwald, A. G. (1980). The totalitarian ego: Fabrication and revision of personal history. *American Psychologist, 35*, 603–618.

Hanson, R. W., & Gerber, K. E. (1990). *Coping with chronic pain.* New York: The Guilford Press.

Henriksson, C. M. (1995). Living with continuous muscular pain: Patient perspectives. *Scandinavian Journal of Caring Sciences, 9*, 67–76.

Holland, A. L., & Beeson, P. M. (1993). Finding a new sense of self: What the clinician can do to help. *Aphasiology, 7*, 581–584.

Kelley, P., & Clifford, P. (1997). Coping with chronic pain: Assessing narrative group approaches. *Social Work, 42,* 266–276..

Kleinman, A. (1988). *The illness narratives: Suffering, healing, and the human condition.* New York: Basic Books.

Lebovitz, R. (1979). Loss, role change, and values. *Clinical Social Work Journal, 7*, 284–295.

Lewis, K. S. (1994). *Successful living with chronic illness.* Dubuque, IA: Kendall/Hunt.

Lindgren, C. L., Burke, M. L., Hainsworth, M. A., & Georgene, G. E. (1992). Chronic sorrow: A lifespan concept. *Scholarly Inquiry for Nursing Practice: An International Journal, 6*, 27–42.

Mann, C. H. (1985). Aging—A developmental reality ignored by psychoanalytic theory. *Journal of The American Academy of Psychoanalysis, 13*, 481–487.

Manne, S. L., & Zaurtra, A. J. (1989). Spouse criticism and support: Their association with coping and psychological adjustment among women with rheumatoid arthritis. *Journal of Personality and Social Psychology, 56*, 608–617.

Miller, L. (1993). Psychotherapeutic approaches to chronic pain. *Psychotherapy, 30*, 115–124.

Murphy, M. (1985). Grief process and becoming one's own person. *Journal of Ongoing Formation, 4*, 379–385.

Osterweis, M., Kleinman, A., & Mechanic, D. (Eds.). (1987). *Pain and disability: Clinical, behavioral, and public policy perspectives.* Washington, DC: National Academy Press.

Payne, B., & Norfleet, M. A. (1986). Chronic pain and the family: A review. *Pain, 26*, 1–22.

Rando, T. A. (1988). *Loss and anticipatory grief.* Lexington, MA: Lexington Books.

Raymond, B., & Bergland, M. M. (1994). Psychosocial aspects of fibromyalgia syndrome. *Journal of Applied Rehabilitation Counseling, 25*, 43–46.

Roy, R. (1989). *Chronic pain and the family: A problem-centered perspective.* New York: Human Sciences Press.

Seaburn, D. B., Lorenz, A., & Kaplan, D. (1992). The transgenerational development of chronic illness meanings. *Family Systems Medicine, 10*, 385–394.

Shapiro, C. H. (1993). *When part of the self is lost.* San Francisco, CA: Jossey-Bass.

Smythe, H. A., Bennett, R. M., & Wolfe, F. (1993). Recognizing fibromyalgia. *Patient Care, 27,* 53–72.

Soderberg, S., & Norberg, A. (1995). Metaphorical pain language among Fibromyalgia patients. *Scandinavian Journal of Caring Sciences, 9*, 55–59.

Taylor, S. (1983). Adjustment to threatening events: A theory of cognitive adaptation. *American Psychologist, 38*, 1161–1171.

Thompson, S. C. (1985). Finding positive meaning in a stressful event and coping. *Basic and Applied Social Psychology, 6*, 279–295.

Waylonis, G. W. (1992). Fibromyalgia and the workplace. *Physical medicine and rehabilitation: State of the art reviews 6,* 245–256.

Wolfe, F., & Potter, J. (1996). Fibromyalgia and work disability: Is fibromyalgia a disabling disorder? In D. Goldenberg (Ed.), *Rheumatic diseases clinics of North American. Vol. 22(2) Controversies in fibromyalgia and related conditions* (pp. 369–391). Philadelphia: W. B. Saunders.

Wynne, L. C., Shields, C. G., & Sirkin, M. I. (1992). Illness, family theory, and family therapy: Conceptual issues. *Family Process, 31*(1), 3–18.

# 15

# *When a Loss is Due to Suicide: Unique Aspects of Bereavement*

***Lillian M. Range***
*University of Southern Mississippi*

Those persons who are bereaved from suicide share a common core of experiences with those who are bereaved from other causes (Range & Calhoun, 1990), as well as experiences that are more intense or unique to suicide (Silverman, Range, & Overholser, in press). This review will discuss research findings on these unique aspects of suicidal bereavement and make research and clinical suggestions.

For the bereaved person, some unique features of losing a loved one by suicide are *stigma*, feelings of *blame* and personal responsibility, *unusually strong emotional reactions*, an exacerbated *search for meaning*, and *deception* about the cause of death. Those bereaved from suicide are often *misunderstood,* and face others who *lack knowledge about what to say*, which may result in intrusive questions, sympathy from someone who is especially uncomfortable, and diminished social support. Although these reactions overlap, and although they may also be true of other bereavement experiences, they are singularly characteristic of suicidal bereavement.

## STIGMA

One unique initial aspect of suicidal bereavement is *stigma*, which is particularly acute when the death is by suicide. This negative view of the suicide extends beyond the victim to include the home environment and is exacerbated if the suicidal death is by violent (e.g., hanging, guns) as opposed to nonviolent means (e.g., drug overdose; Range, Bright, & Ginn, 1985; Rudestam & Imbroll, 1983). Further, the stigma is present regardless of whether the suicide attempt was successful (Range & Kastner, 1988). This stigma may be more pronounced when people are asked hypothetical questions than when they actually know someone, perhaps because knowing a specific person or actual circumstances can override initial preconceptions. Thus, stigma appears to be an initial global reaction when someone learns of a suicide or suicide attempt. An important implication for bereaved individuals is that they should get to know people before telling them about the suicide of their loved one. Research that focuses on ways to ameliorate the stigma of suicide, such as empathy training for nonbereaved individuals, is recommended.

## BLAME

Another unique feature of suicidal bereavement is *blame toward the bereaved person*, which is uniquely associated with suicidal and accidental deaths. For example, when asked about a hypothetical death, respondents blame the parents "a little" for a child's suicide but "very little" for a child's viral illness death (Calhoun, Selby, & Faulstich, 1980). Blaming the bereaved survivor for the suicide is more likely to be perceived by bereaved individuals (McNiel, Hatcher, & Reubin, 1988; Thompson & Range, 1992–1993) or funeral directors (Steelman, Calhoun, & Selby, 1984) than by potential comforters/blamers (Range & Thompson, 1987). Blame is also pronounced in hypothetical situations (Calhoun, Selby, & Walton, 1985–1986; Rudestam & Imbroll, 1983); but blame may (Silverman et al., 1994–1995) or may not (Range & Calhoun, 1990) be present when respondents are asked about the suicide of someone they actually know. When the deceased is a child, the parents are blamed even more in an accident than in a suicide (Ginn, Range, & Hailey, 1988; Range & Kastner, 1988), and even more for younger than older children (Range et al., 1985). However, despite extra doses of blame, suicidally bereaved persons recover more than others imagine (Thompson & Range, 1992–1993). Thus, blame is unique to suicidal and accidental bereavement, and depends somewhat on the specific circumstances involved, such as the age of the victim.

Regardless of the type of death, attributions of blame to the victim or family are unhelpful (Range & Calhoun, 1990) perhaps because they weaken the social support that is provided (Thompson & Range, 1992–1993). Research is recommended which delineates the parameters of this blame and establishes whether people can be taught to be less blaming of the family of a suicide victim or less blaming of themselves when a loved one commits suicide. For example, in a related study, people were given a vignette about a 13-year-old girl who had numerous problems. In half the vignettes she eventually committed suicide. Those who read about the suicide thought it was more foreseeable than those who only knew of the problems. The conclusion was that hindsight had disadvantages (Goggin & Range, 1985), one of which may be blaming oneself when there was actually no way to predict that the suicide would happen.

## A SEARCH FOR MEANING

Another feature of suicidal bereavement is *searching for meaning*, a common response to all deaths, which appears to be particularly acute when the death is due to suicide. This need for an explanation is felt by bereaved persons themselves (Silverman et al., 1994–1995); Smith, Range, & Ulmer, 1991–1992), but may be exacerbated by the questions of others, who ask for an explanation of suicide more often than in other causes of death (Range & Calhoun, 1990; Rudestam & Imbroll, 1983). Indeed, about 90% of suicidally and accidentally bereaved individuals report being asked to explain the nature of the death, whereas only about 33% of other bereaved individuals report being asked this question (Range & Calhoun). This search may be emotionally draining to bereaved individuals because they are struggling with existential questions for which there are no ultimate answers.

Still another unique feature of suicidal bereavement is *deception* on the part of the bereaved person. Such deception includes actively lying about the cause of death (Range & Calhoun, 1990) or concealing its nature (McNiel et al., 1988) and passively avoiding thinking about it (Thompson & Range, 1991). Lying about the nature of the death is reported by 30% (Rudestam, 1977) to 44% (Range & Calhoun, 1990) of suicidally bereaved individuals, but by no individuals bereaved in other ways. Deceiving others during this crisis leads to difficulty in sharing feelings (Ness & Pfeffer, 1990) and social isolation (McNiel et al., 1988). Thus, suicidally bereaved individuals may feel the need to deceive others about the nature of the death, and in so doing, decrease the social support they might otherwise receive.

In addition, *unique emotional repercussions* of suicidal loss include suicidality in the bereaved individual (Roy, 1983; Shafii, Carrigan, Whittinghill, & Derrick, 1985; Silverman et al., 1994–1995), feelings of rejection (Silverman et al., 1994–1995), anxiety (Farberow, Gallagher, Gilewski, & Thompson, 1987), shock (Ness & Pfeffer, 1990), and psychological intrusion, and avoidance (Thompson & Range, 1991). Recovery outcomes are mixed, with some research reporting better outcomes from suicidal bereavement (Shepherd & Barraclough, 1974), others reporting about the same outcomes (Demi, 1984), and still others reporting worse outcomes (Thompson & Range, 1991). Even though outcome is a complex concept, and may vary depending on how it is defined, the emotional repercussions of suicidal bereavement appear especially severe.

## BEING MISUNDERSTOOD

Another aspect of suicidal bereavement is *being misunderstood*. Potential comforters are unable to accurately imagine all aspects of a suicidal bereavement: they are correct about the psychological impact, but are incorrect about social support, recovery, and acceptance of the death (Thompson & Range, 1992–1993). In terms of social support, bereaved persons vary greatly in their memories of how much contact they had with others before the death, depending on type of death, but nonbereaved persons imagine similar levels of contact regardless of type of death (Thompson & Range, 1991). Despite what others expect, psychological recovery appears about the same (regardless of the cause of death) for the individual (Range & Niss, 1990) and the family (McNiel et al., 1988). Thus, potential comforters seem to understand the situation hypothetically, but cannot accurately picture all aspects of an actual, specific bereavement.

When people misunderstand the bereavement experience, their *support attempts may be inappropriate* or harmful (Wortman & Lehman, 1989). Not surprisingly, people are less helpful after a suicide than after other deaths (Silverman et al., 1994–1995; Thompson & Range, 1991; Thompson & Range, 1992–1993), though all bereaved persons perceive others as only somewhat helpful after the death (Thompson & Range, 1990–1991). For example, even in accidental deaths, a majority of bereaved respondents could clearly remember ways that others had been helpful, but most could also easily remember instances of failed support efforts

(Lehman, Ellard, & Wortman, 1986). After a suicide, potential comforters may need to take into account the cause of death in order to say something that is perceived as helpful (Range, Walston, & Pollard, 1992). One reason that comforting suicidally bereaved persons is so difficult is that there are more social constraints in suicide than in other deaths (Calhoun, Abernathy, & Selby, 1986). So, comforters know more what *not* to say than what to say to suicidally bereaved individuals. After a suicide, others often say the wrong thing.

## LIMITATIONS IN SUICIDAL BEREAVEMENT

Research on suicidal bereavement is in its infancy. It is healthy, but nevertheless has several limitations. One, it is typically retrospective (McNiel et al., 1988), leading to potential memory and self-serving bias errors. Rapid initial contact (Ness & Pfeffer, 1990) and consistent follow-up at various times after the death (Ness & Pfeffer, 1990) would begin to address this limitation.

Two, there is potential bias in those who participate in bereavement research versus those who do not. Participation rates of 30% to 35% are common in this area (Farberow et al., 1987; Smith et al., 1991–1992; Ulmer, Range, & Smith, 1991), although rates as high as 83% have been reported (Shafii et al., 1985). When participation rates are low, it is quite possible that those who respond are different in many ways from those who do not respond. This limitation is difficult to address because most researchers prefer not to intrude on those who refuse to participate. To begin to address this problem, researchers should make extra efforts to enhance responding, including assuring confidentiality, responding to the feelings generated by participating in the research, and offering follow-up services as needed.

Three, noncomparable controls are often a limitation of research comparing suicide and other deaths (McNiel et al., 1988). Recovery after someone's sudden death is much more difficult than from anticipated death (Parkes & Weiss, 1983), so matching for suddenness is critical. The age of the deceased is another frequent experimental confound of bereavement studies, with the suicide victim typically younger than the other victims (i.e., Range & Calhoun, 1990). All other things being equal, it may be that the death of an older person is an easier event from which to recover than the death of a younger person. Therefore, matching for age of the victim is also critical. Control groups should also be matched for time since the death, closeness to the victim, and for other important variables as well.

Four, research on suicidal bereavement is often characterized by idiosyncratic decisions about predictor and outcome variables (Osterweis, Soloman, & Green, 1984). Although interview data are often rich and revealing, there are possible experimenter biases and inconsistencies across respondents, so that it is difficult to generalize findings. In the future, standard research instruments should be used (McNiel et al., 1988). Particularly relevant to suicidal bereavement are the Grief Inventory (Barrett & Scott, 1989), Calhoun's Youth Suicide Scale (Calhoun et al., 1990; Range, McDonald, & Anderson, 1987), and the Impact of Event Scale (Horowitz, Wilner, & Alvarez, 1979). Psychometrically sound research assessment instruments would help to compare research results and build a more consistent knowledge base.

Five, research on suicidal bereavement often fails to examine family factors that could mediate reactions to bereavement (McNiel et al., 1988). People who commit suicide come from networks of families and friends, and social support makes a big difference in how someone reacts to any situation, especially a difficult one. Thus, the responses of the social support network may make a big difference in how suicidally bereaved individuals handle their loss.

A final limitation of suicidal bereavement research is that it typically focuses on the negatives rather than the positives. Although these concerns are appropriate, it is also appropriate to examine how people can adapt and grow in response to this tragic loss. Indeed, after traumatic events such as suicide some people report new-found maturity, increased emotional strength and independence, greater confidence in their ability to face crisis, and a better understanding of others (Tedeschi, Calhoun, Morrell, & Johnson, 1984). Research which delineates how these benefits occur might help many people.

## RESEARCH RECOMMENDATIONS

In addition to building a knowledge base, a goal of research is to help clinicians and potential comforters learn how to comfort suicidally bereaved individuals. Even though research is incomplete, some recommendations can already be made. One, group experiences with veterans and novices who have experienced similar traumas are helpful for some bereaved individuals. The specialized nature of such groups is one way of addressing the bereaved person's perspective that his or her suffering is unique, and that only someone who has been through the same experience can offer helpful support (Tedeschi & Calhoun, 1993). Therefore, suicidally bereaved people often see self-help groups as very helpful, especially if they include individuals who have undergone similar losses.

Two, clinicians should refrain from overly ambitious therapy goals, because resolution of feelings from suicidal losses are never complete (Ness & Pfeffer, 1990). Clinicians should recognize that there are an enormous variety of responses to grief (Lehman, Wortman, & Williams, 1987), and should communicate empathy, reassurance of normality, and support of creative attempts to deal with the client's loss (Tedeschi & Calhoun, 1993). Late in the counseling process, the professional may also recognize ways in which the bereaved person has personally grown because of his/her struggle with grief (Tedeschi & Calhoun, 1993).

Three, inasmuch as suicidality is one of the repercussions of suicidal bereavement, clinicians should ask all clients about a family history of suicide. Some of them may be reluctant to share this information (Ness & Pfeffer, 1990), so these questions should be sensitively framed and posed.

Four, most bereaved people appreciate expressions of concern, whether they are tangible, such as bringing food or sending cards, or intangible, such as allowing expression of grief (Range & Calhoun, 1990). Particularly helpful comments are, "If there is anything I can do, please let me know," and "I'm here if you need someone to talk to" (Range et al., 1992). When comforters are expressing concern toward a suicidally bereaved person, blaming comments may be especially tempting. They should be avoided, regardless of the cause of death.

Also, most suicidally bereaved people are searching for meaning themselves and cannot answer questions about why the person committed suicide. They do *not* appreciate detailed questions about the circumstances surrounding the death, the condition of the remains, or why it happened (Range & Calhoun, 1990). Rather, they appreciate someone encouraging or allowing their personal expressions of grief. So, expressions of concern and emotion-facilitating remarks are helpful, but questions about gruesome details or why the person did it are unhelpful.

Five, religion can help. Belief in both afterlife and a purpose in life buffer the difficulties of bereavement, but in different ways. Belief in afterlife is associated with greater recovery, less avoidance, and greater ability to find meaning in the death (Smith et al., 1991–1992). Purpose is associated with a relatively greater social support network, which may lessen the impact of the death and enhance life satisfaction (Ulmer et al., 1991). Comforters who bolster belief in afterlife may help the bereaved person struggle with personal existential questions, and those who bolster purpose in life may help enhance the bereaved person's social support network.

## CONCLUSION

Losing a loved one is a very difficult experience, which is made even worse when the death is by suicide. After a suicide, bereaved persons feel a stigma from society, blame themselves, and struggle hard to find meaning in the death. They sometimes feel that they must deceive others about the nature of the death. Not surprisingly, comforters sometimes fail to empathize, offer inappropriate social support, and ask intrusive, unhelpful questions. This psychological legacy of suicidal bereavement makes recovery especially difficult. People respond to grief in a vast diversity of ways, however (Wortman & Silver, 1989), and the interventions described here may be useful for clinicians, especially the admonition to focus on the bereaved person, not on the event. Fortunately, some suicidally bereaved individuals are remarkably able to bounce back over time. Though the pain never completely recedes, they do learn to deal with it, and go on with even more fulfilling lives.

## REFERENCES

Barrett, T. W., & Scott, T. B. (1989). Development of the Grief Experience Questionnaire. *Suicide and Life-Threatening Behavior, 19,* 201–215.

Calhoun, L. G., Abernathy, C. B., & Selby, J. W. (1986). The rules of bereavement: Are suicidal deaths different? *Journal of Community Psychology, 14,* 213–218.

Calhoun, L. G., Selby, J. W., & Walton, P. B. (1985–1986). Suicidal death of a spouse: The social perception of the survivor. *Omega: Journal of Death & Dying, 16,* 283–288.

Calhoun, L. G., Selby, J. W., & Faulstich, M. E. (1980). Reactions to the parents of childhood suicide: A study of social impressions. *Journal of Consulting and Clinical Psychology, 48,* 535–536.

Demi, A. S. (1984). Social adjustment of widows after a sudden death: Suicide and nonsuicide survivors compared. *Death Education, 8* (Supl.), 91–111.

Farberow, N. L., Gallagher, D. E., Gilewski, M. J., & Thompson, L. W. (1987). An examination of the early impact of bereavement on psychological distress in survivors of suicide. *Gerontologist, 27,* 592–598.

Ginn, P. D., Range, L. M., & Hailey, B. J. (1988). Community attitudes toward childhood suicide and attempted suicide. *Journal of Community Psychology, 16,* 144–151.

Goggin, W., & Range, L. (1985). The disadvantages of hindsight in the perception of suicide. *Journal of Social and Clinical Psychology, 3,* 232–237.

Horowitz, M., Wilner, N., & Alvarez, W. (1979). Impact of Event Scale: A measure of subjective stress. *Psychosomatic Medicine, 41,* 209–218.

Lehman, D. R., Ellard, J. H., & Wortman, C. B. (1986). Social support for the bereaved: Recipients' and providers' perspectives on what is helpful. *Journal of Consulting and Clinical Psychology, 54,* 438–446.

Lehman, D. R., Wortman, C. B., & Williams, A. F. (1987). Long-term effects of losing a spouse or child in a motor vehicle crash. *Journal of Personality and Social Psychology, 52,* 218–231.

McNiel, D. E., Hatcher, C., & Reubin, R. (1988). Family survivors of suicide and accidental death: Consequences for widows. *Suicide and Life-Threatening Behavior, 18,* 137–148.

Ness, D. E., & Pfeffer, C. R. (1990). Sequelae of bereavement resulting from suicide. *American Journal of Psychiatry, 147,* 279–285.

Osterweis, M., Solomon, F., & Green, M. (1984). *Bereavement: Consequences, reactions, & care.* Washington, D.C.: National Academy Press.

Parkes, C. M., & Weiss, R. S. (1983). *Recovery from bereavement.* New York: Basic Books.

Range, L. M., Bright, P. S., & Ginn, P. D. (1985). Public reactions to child suicide: Effects of age and method used. *Journal of Community Psychology, 13,* 288–294.

Range, L. M., & Calhoun, L. G. (1990). Responses following suicide and other types of death: The perspective of the bereaved. *Omega: Journal of Death and Dying, 21,* 311–320.

Range, L. M., & Kastner, J. (1988). Community reactions to attempted and completed child suicide. *Journal of Applied Social Psychology, 18,* 1085–1093.

Range, L., McDonald, D., & Anderson, H. (1987). Factor structure of Calhoun's Youth Suicide Scale. *Journal of Personality Assessment, 51,* 262–266.

Range, L. M., & Niss, N. M. (1990). Long term bereavement from suicide, homicide, accidents, and natural deaths. *Death Studies, 14,* 423–433.

Range, L. M., & Thompson, K. E. (1987). Community responses following suicide, homicide, and other deaths: The perspective of potential comforters. *Journal of Psychology, 121,* 193–198.

Range, L. M., Walston, A. S., & Pollard, P. M. (1992). Helpful and unhelpful comments after suicide, homicide, accident, or natural death. *Omega: Journal of Death and Dying, 25,* 25–31.

Roy, A. (1983). Family history of suicide. *Archives of General Psychiatry, 40,* 971–974.

Rudestam, K. E. (1977). Physical and psychological responses to suicide in the family. *Journal of Consulting and Clinical Psychology, 45,* 162–170.

Rudestam, K. E., & Imbroll, D. (1983). Societal reactions to a child's death by suicide. *Journal of Consulting and Clinical Psychology, 51,* 461–462.

Shafii, M., Carrigan, S., Whittinghill, J. R., & Derrick, A. (1985). Psychological autopsy of completed suicide in children and adolescents. *American Journal of Psychiatry, 142,* 1061–1064.

Shepherd, D., & Barraclough, B. M. (1974). The aftermath of suicide. *British Medical Journal, 2,* 600–603.

Silverman, E., Range, L., & Overholser, J. C. (1994–1995). Bereavement from suicide as compared to other forms of bereavement. *Omega: Journal of Death & Dying, 31,* 41–51.

Smith, P. C., Range, L. M., & Ulmer, A. (1991–1992). Belief in afterlife as a buffer in suicidal and other bereavement. *Omega: Journal of Death and Dying, 24,* 219–227.

Steelman, J. K., Calhoun, L. G., & Selby, J. W. (1984, March). Funeral directors' impressions of suicidal deaths: Individual and social elements. In L. Range (chair), *Exploring the impact of suicide.* Symposium at Southeastern Psychological Association, New Orleans, LA.

Tedeschi, R. G., & Calhoun, L. G. (1993). Using the support group to respond to the isolation of bereavement. *Journal of Mental Health Counseling, 15,* 47–54.

Tedeschi, R. G., Calhoun, L. G., Morrell, R. W., & Johnson, K. A. (1984, August). *Bereavement: From grief to psychological development.* Paper presented at the American Psychological Association, Toronto, ON, Canada.

Thompson, K. E., & Range, L. M. (1991). Recent bereavement from suicide and other deaths: Can people imagine it as it really is? *Omega: Journal of Death and Dying, 22,* 249–259.

Thompson, K. E., & Range, L. M. (1992–1993). Bereavement following suicide and other deaths: Why support attempts fail. *Omega: Journal of Death & Dying, 26,* 61–70.

Ulmer, A., Range, L. M., & Smith, P. (1991). Purpose in life: A moderator of recovery from bereavement. *Omega: Journal of Death and Dying, 23,* 279–289.

Wortman, C. B., & Silver, R. C. (1989). The myths of coping with loss. *Journal of Consulting and Clinical Psychology, 57,* 349–357.

# 16

## *Mental Health Professionals' Responses to Loss and Trauma of Holocaust Survivors*

**Zahava Solomon and Yuval Neria**
*Tel-Aviv University*

**Anca Ram**
*Sheba Medical Center, Tel-Hashomer, Israel*

The Nazi Holocaust is undoubtedly one of the most brutal and horrifying traumatic events of this century. Millions were tortured and murdered; millions were exposed for many years to uncertainty, humiliation, terror, and starvation. All the survivors lost loved ones. The better part of them lost most of their family, and some lost all of it. They lived to see the Jewish communities where they had lived exterminated, their homes and property confiscated, their friends killed, and their way of life forever gone. Exposed to inconceivable evil, the survivors also lost much of themselves: their innocence; their faith in order, justice, and human morality; their ability to trust and confide in others and to form and maintain intimate relationships; and sometimes, too, the ability to feel and to love.

At the same time, the vast majority sought not only to restore their physical losses and to build new, more secure lives, but also to regain or to reconstruct something of their shattered selves and social worlds. They longed for meaningful human ties which would provide them with a sense of belonging and help them to work through and eventually recover from their trauma and grief. There was an instinctive awareness of the healing effect of human connections. Most survivors went on to marry, raise children, and make friends among other survivors (Danieli, 1988).

The survivors who succeeded in healing themselves did so against tremendous odds, with little if any of the social support that has been found to mitigate the deleterious effects of a wide range of traumatic events (Quarantilli, 1985; Herman 1992), especially those, like the Holocaust, which were deliberately and maliciously created (Danieli, 1988). In some ways, the postwar period continued to be traumatic for the survivors. Most of them immigrated to new countries, where the opportunity to start afresh was accompanied by social and cultural uprooting and formidable economic difficulties. To make matters worse, in virtually all the countries to which they immigrated after World War II, they encountered an apathetic, baffled, or critical society. And those who needed professional help were met by a mental health community which totally ignored the pathogenic effects of the Holocaust.

This chapter discusses the responses of the Israeli mental health community to the Holocaust survivors who asked for professional help.

## TURNING A DEAF EAR

The reluctance of the mental health profession in the Western world to acknowledge the deleterious psychological effects of the twentieth century's man-made catastrophes is well documented (Herman, 1992; Black, 1985). The Holocaust is one example, the Vietnam War another. On first thought it might seem that Israeli mental health professionals would have been more sensitive than their peers abroad to their Holocaust survivor patients—mostly central and eastern European Jews like themselves. Sadly, this is not at all what happened.

Like their fellow professionals in Europe and the United States, they mostly turned a deaf ear. Information about the psychological suffering of the Holocaust survivors was already available at the end of World War II (Friedman, 1948). When the war ended, a variety of both international and Jewish organizations sent delegations to Europe to assess the survivors' needs and to help them resettle. Mental health professionals in these delegations reported high levels of emotional distress among the survivors and their need for both general emotional support and psychiatric help. Yet this abundant psychiatric evidence was largely unheeded by the mental health professionals in Israel, and calls by Jewish aid organizations outside of Israel for organized supportive psychiatric intervention for survivors were largely ignored (Segev, 1991).

The professionals who encountered survivors hospitalized in psychiatric facilities often ignored the possible connection between their suffering and their recent experiences of terror and loss (Dasberg, 1987). Nathan, Eitinger, and Winnik (1964), who examined the medical records of Holocaust survivor patients at the Talbieh psychiatric hospital in Jerusalem, found, to their surprise, that only 54% of the files contained any mention of the patients' Holocaust experience. This is a lower rate than that found in a similar study conducted by Axelrod, Schnipper, and Rau (1980) on Holocaust survivors in a mental hospital in the United States, where a third of the files made no mention of the patient's Holocaust experience.

It was only in the early 1960s that clinicians—notably, not Israeli clinicians—began to realize that their Holocaust survivor patients shared clusters of symptoms that stemmed from their traumatic experience. Eitinger (1962) grouped the symptoms under the term "concentration camp syndrome," and Niederland (1968), under "survivor syndrome." Both syndromes identified a specific clinical picture with symptoms ranging from memory disturbances, chronic depressive states, a tendency to isolation, pseudopsychosis, and changes in self-identity, to corpse-like behavior. Subsequently other clinicians confirmed and elaborated on this picture (Krystal, 1968). Even with the knowledge, however, clinicians found it very difficult to relate to their Holocaust survivor patients in a professionally appropriate manner. The well-known Israeli psychiatrist Raphael Moses (1984) confesses that he initially distanced himself emotionally from his survivor patients. Along with others in the profession (Davidson, 1980; Dasberg, 1987), he tells that most contemporary Israeli therapists wanted to "normalize" their survivor patients. Klein (1987) maintains that they refused to accept either the defenses, detachment or denial, that the survivors used to get through their ordeal and to cope with their losses, or the survivor guilt that emerged afterwards, and misinterpreted both as pathological. Danieli (1988) reports that many therapists resented their survivor patients' demands for attention, clung to their professional role, and retreated into method and theory.

This poor professional response can be attributed to three sources: (1) lack of knowledge in the early years after the Holocaust; (2) prevailing social attitudes towards the survivors; and (3) the professionals' own feelings of discomfort in dealing with the trauma victims.

## LACK OF KNOWLEDGE

Eitinger (1980) suggests that the failure to question mentally ill survivors about their Holocaust experience may have derived from a lack of professional knowledge in the early years after the Holocaust. The traumatogenic nature of catastrophic events was little understood in those years. Indeed, it was not until the 1980s, with the publication of the DSM III, that the American Psychiatric Association (APA, 1980) officially acknowledged Post Traumatic Stress Disorder (PTSD) as a diagnostic entity, and even today its validity is still in dispute. Moreover, the full reality of the conditions of the Holocaust, the odds facing the survivors, and their struggle to remain alive was little known and even less well grasped.

The psychoanalytic approach, which was highly influential and widespread both in Israel and abroad up until the 1980s, also probably contributed to the clinicians' failure to link their Holocaust patients' symptoms to their traumatic experience. Psychoanalytic theory locates all mental disorders in the events of childhood and undervalues the importance of traumas experienced in adulthood (Boulanger, 1990). The assumption is that any serious disorder that develops after exposure to traumatic stress must have stemmed from some predisposing psychopathology. Moreover, this theory tends to see external realities as less significant than fantasy in the formation and treatment of psychological disorder (Herman, 1992). As Boulanger observes (1990, p. 20): "In psychoanalysis and so many of the individual therapies that were influenced by this theory, reality is frequently ignored in favor of the fantasized traumas—battles being waged internally that found their expression in dreams, day dreams and associations. . . ." For many years it was almost professional heresy to publicly consider the possibility that long-term psychological disorder could result solely from exposure to an extreme stressor.

The blinding effect of the psychoanalytic lens is confirmed by the observations of the historian Tom Segev (1991), who surveyed the files of several hundred adolescents who had been sent for psychiatric evaluation within the framework of Aliat-HaNoar, a program to absorb youths who arrived in Israel without their parents. Segev reports that at the special clinic that was set up for this purpose, some of the staff came from the United States and knew only English, some knew only German, and all of them tended to diagnose the presenting problems with Freudian orthodoxy. In his opinion, the failure to connect the survivors' traumatic experiences with their subsequent mental distress opened the way for flagrant misdiagnoses. The staff diagnosed "oedipal complexes," "inferiority complexes[!]," "ego weaknesses," etc.

## PREVAILING SOCIAL ATTITUDES

In some ways, the new state of Israel, officially established in May 1948, provided the survivors with an ideal healing environment. Along with old-timers and other immigrants, the survivors were caught up in the common struggle of defending and building the new nation. According to the late Israeli psychiatrist and Holocaust survivor, Klein (1973), they found in the reestablishment of the Jewish homeland a theme that closely coincided with "the theme of personal, family and community rebirth" so central to their own lives; "a rationale for their escape from extinction"; and "a positive self-image as pioneers and builders of a new society" (p. 395). Eitinger (1980) suggests that they were "exposed to a sort of milieu therapy" (p. 1157), and Winnik (1979), that Israel provided "an essential prerequisite of a favorable social frame" (p. 22). Klein (1973) also emphasized the value of the annual rituals of commemoration and mourning held throughout Israel in allowing the survivors to work through their feelings of grief, anger, and fear.

On the other hand, the young state was hard on the survivors, as it was on other immigrants who did not fit into the prescribed mold. Abraham Maslow (1971) has pointed to the hierarchy of needs as the basis of which human beings develop. The first needs are for physical survival—for such basics as food, shelter, and safety—and emotional needs can enter awareness and be attended to only when these needs have been met. This order of priorities seems to have governed the treatment of the Holocaust survivors in Israel.

When the Holocaust survivors began to arrive in the mid-1940s, Israel was not yet a sovereign state. Its tiny population was engaged both in trying to throw off British Mandate rule and in fending off Arab hostility. With the acquisition of statehood, the country was plunged into a war for survival against five Arab armies. In the 1950s, it continued to fight for survival against persistent infiltration from neighboring Arab states, at the same time as it was occupied with the monumental, all-consuming task of building from scratch the infrastructure of a modern country and with absorbing a huge influx of immigrants, whose number by the end of the 1950s would swell the Jewish population to about five times its mid-1940s number.

In these conditions, the society lacked the resources to deal compassionately with the emotional suffering of the Holocaust survivors, or of anyone else for that matter. In fact, it could not allow itself to be too aware of their plight. It required people who could cope effectively with hardship and who had the emotional and physical stamina to take part in the survival effort. The value system that developed to support the survival effort eschewed weakness and extolled strength and demanded the subordination of personal needs to the needs of the community. The society thus sealed off the survivors' losses and traumas. For the first 20 years after the Holocaust, the survivors' distress went almost totally unacknowledged by the political establishment and veteran Israelis. Their plight was either not recognized at all or, where it was dimly glimpsed, denied legitimacy.

One manifestation of the society's unwillingness to cope with the survivors' experience was what numerous Israeli psychologists and psychiatrists (e.g., Danieli, 1981; Dasberg, 1987, Klein & Kogan, 1987; Moses, 1983) have termed an all-encompassing conspiracy of silence. According to Danieli (1981), people were not only unwilling to listen to what survivors had seen and experienced during the Holocaust, but also refused to believe that such horrors had taken place.

Another manifestation of this unwillingness to cope was a tendency to blame the victim. Holocaust victims were blamed both for surviving and for not surviving. They were accused of passivity, of going like sheep to the slaughter, and, on the other hand, of staying alive by shameful compliance with Nazi decrees, betrayal of their friends, and other ignominious means. There was a widespread feeling that the Holocaust victims who survived were selfish, immoral, and otherwise contemptible. Emissaries who were sent to help bring the survivors to Israel after the war described them as "a faceless crowd of subhuman[s] . . . a large band of depleted, run down, decrepit beggars . . . not only physically and mentally, but also morally base." One of the emissaries later recounted that "at first I thought they were animals" (cited in Segev, 1991, p. 106). Similar descriptions of the survivors as wretched and immoral made their way into the newspapers of the time (e.g., Gelblum, 1945). Looking back at those days, the famous Israeli paratrooper Yoel Palgi (1978) observes: "[W]e are ashamed of those who were tortured, shot, burned. Without realizing it, we had adopted the Nazi view that Jews were subhuman. . . . History mocks us bitterly: we ourselves had put them [the Holocaust victims] in the dock" (Palgi, 1978, p. 243).

In addition to the survival needs of the new state, other factors also contributed to the repudiation of the survivors by veteran Israelis. One was the prevailing ideology. In the first decades of statehood, veteran Israelis were engaged in the process of redefining Jewish identity. En masse, the more established Israelis, most of them themselves relatively recent arrivals from Eastern Europe, rejected the identity of the Diaspora Jew, depicting him/her as a sniveling, cowardly character whose personality had been distorted by centuries of persecution (Friedlander 1980), and sought to replace it with the image of the proud, brave, and unbowed Israeli. The survivors, who did not "fight" the Nazis in the fantasized heroic style, were a psychological threat to these Israelis as they sought to cut themselves off from their all-too-recent history in the Diaspora. In the general view, the survivors, like other immigrants, were not to be understood and accepted for who they were, but to be reeducated and made over in the image of the "New Jew" (Segev, 1991).

Another important factor in the social repudiation of the survivors was guilt, as it is in the rejection of other victims. Most of the old-timers had left family and friends in Europe when they emigrated to Israel as young men and women, and most of those they left behind perished in the Holocaust. A good proportion of the veteran population probably experienced the "survivor guilt" that we now know accompanies such losses. Adding to this guilt, and to the anger at the survivors that accompanied it, was the guilt that arose from the fact that the local settlers could do very little to help the Jews in Europe. The leadership made certain rescue efforts, which included sending paratroopers into Nazi-occupied Europe, pressuring foreign governments to intervene, and attempting to barter Jewish lives for money and goods. But the attempts were very few and mostly unsuccessful. Given Israel's distance from Europe, the paucity of money and manpower, and the obstructiveness of the British Mandate authorities, there was very little that the Jews in Palestine could do to save their European brethren (Porat, 1986). For the most part, like people everywhere, they carried on with their own lives. While objectively, there was nothing reprehensible in their conduct, once the dimensions of the Holocaust became known, many of them felt guilty for not having done more to avert it.

This guilt fed into yet another sort of blame, which was also associated with the prevailing ideology. Zionist political orthodoxy was that the Jew's place is in Israel. The unspoken accusation was that having chosen to remain in Europe, the Holocaust victims brought their sufferings on themselves. If they had been where they should have been—in their homeland with the veteran settlers—none of it would have happened. This is similar to the accusation flung at the rape victim: if she had been at home where she belonged, she wouldn't have been raped (Koss & Harvey, 1991).

Therapists, no less than other persons, inevitably imbibe the attitudes of their society (Levi, 1981). They shared the society's fear of weakness and veneration of strength, were similarly threatened by the image of the despised Diaspora Jew that the survivors represented, and possessed their own feelings of survival guilt and guilt for not having done anything to avert the disaster. Like other Israelis, they countered these threats by the avoidance, repression, and denial of the trauma of the Holocaust and by a judgmental and accusatory attitude towards the survivors. When they met survivors in their work, they engaged in the same conspiracy of silence as the rest of the society, the same blaming of the victims, and the same efforts to reform the survivors and mold them to the desired image (Danieli, 1988; Solomon, 1995).

## COUNTERTRANSFERENCE

Professionals who have treated Holocaust survivors have testified to the enormous emotional difficulty of the undertaking. They report feeling overwhelmed by the horror of the survivors' stories and the enormous intensity of their experiences, even at second hand, and feeling powerful and disturbing countertransference emotions that interfere with their treatment (Danieli, 1981). McCann and Pearlman (1990) suggest that the strong emotional responses that intimate encounters with survivors arouse often activate major unresolved unconscious conflicts in therapists. Krystal (1968) and Meerloo (1969), among others, write that therapists' old scars and injuries are constantly rubbed anew in their work with survivors.

Danieli (1981), whose studies were carried out in the United States, names guilt and rage as the dominant countertransference themes. Bystander guilt, she contends, was a common outcome of the therapists' sense of helplessness to undo the long-term destructive effects of the Holocaust on their patients. According to Danieli, therapists who felt guilt were fearful of hurting their patients, which led them to avoid raising painful issues in therapy. Some such therapists, not appreciating their patients' strengths, were afraid that their patients were so fragile that they would fall apart if pressed. Guilt feelings also made therapists unable to set reasonable limits for their patients, and in some cases, led them to adopt a masochistic position towards them.

Intense rage towards their survivor patients was often linked to the guilt in a vicious circle. The therapists' inability to set limits led to anger and resentment, as their patients became increasingly demanding; their anger then made them feel even more guilty for getting angry at a person who had already suffered so much. Intense anger was also produced by therapists' unrealistic expectations of the survivor patients and by intolerance of their no-end-in-sight mourning. Consciously or unconsciously, some therapists felt that having suffered so much from hate and discrimination, survivors should rise above such feelings and attitudes in themselves. When survivors came into their offices with declarations like "I hate all Germans/Poles," these therapists were filled with high-minded anger. Another source of anger was the great frustration therapists felt with the unending mourning of many survivor patients, which they were unable either to mitigate in their patients or to contain in themselves. Some therapists viewed their survivor patients as still living, passive and helpless, in the world of the camp, and responded with impatience, irritation, and the urge to "liberate" them. Yet another source of rage was the survivors' stories of Nazi brutalities, which forced them to confront their own sadistic and destructive urges (Freedman, 1978).

Other countertransference emotions that made it difficult for therapists to relate appropriately to their Holocaust survivor patients were shame and contempt and, alternatively, awe (Danieli, 1981). Some of the shame derived from therapists' acceptance of the sheep-to-the-slaughter myth that hounded the survivors for decades after the Holocaust. As part of the same people, Israeli therapists felt shamed by this image and were contemptuous of their survivor patients, whom they considered cowardly for not fighting the Nazi aggressor. A related source of shame was the therapists' fantasies of what the patients must have done or allowed themselves to suffer in order to survive. In the ghettos and camps, the Nazis strove to systematically deprive their victims of their humanity and to reduce them to the level of animals. Survivors' stories include such horrendous acts and, more commonly, accounts of deep humiliation and abuse. Disgust and loathing impelled some therapists to prohibit their survivor patients from telling these stories. The therapists who could neither abate nor tolerate the shame and contempt they felt became enraged at their patients.

In contrast to guilt, rage, and shame, the feeling of awe that some therapists felt towards their Holocaust survivor patients involved an idealization of their characters. Therapists who felt this emotion tended to glorify their survivor patients as superhuman figures (e.g., Gay & Shulman, 1979) and, conversely, to denigrate themselves as unlikely to have survived the hardships their patients recounted. The sense that their patients knew more than they did about human survival made such therapists hesitant and deferential in their treatment and blinded them to the pain, suffering, and problems in daily living that brought these patients to seek help. It could also lead to feelings of envy and competitiveness with the survivor patients. In one way or another, all these countertransference emotions sabotaged the ability of Israeli (and other) therapists to provide a supportive holding environment in which their survivor patients could grieve, mourn, and work through their traumatic experiences. It often made them intolerant or immobilized and led to their blaming their survivor patients for bringing their troubles on themselves and, sometimes, to premature termination of the treatment on the grounds of "the patient's resistance."

As shown above, the unhelpful response of Israeli mental health professionals to their troubled survivor patients in the early years after the Holocaust was fed by Israel's particular social setting at the time and the therapists' uncomfortable closeness in background to their European Jewish patients. At the same time, most of the countertransference emotions that they reported are universal responses to any man-made catastrophe, reported throughout the world, at different times, and in a range of social and cultural situations (Herman, 1992; Solomon, 1995). It is apparently very difficult for people to face the terrible vulnerability and aggressiveness of human beings. Despite our training and experience, we mental health professionals are no different from others in this respect. As professionals, however, we have accepted a special moral obligation to our suffering patients. It is thus incumbent upon us to recognize our failings and strive to overcome them.

## REFERENCES

American Psychiatric Association (1987). *Diagnostic and statistical manual of mental disorders* (3rd ed., revised). Washington, D.C.: APA.

Axelrod, S., Schnipper, O. L., & Rau, J. H. (1980). Hospitalized offspring of Holocaust survivors: Problems and dynamics. *Bulletin of the Menninger Clinic, 44,* 1–14.

Blank, A. S. (1985). Irrational reactions to posttraumatic stress disorder and Vietnam veterans. In S. M. Sonnenberg, A. S. Blank, & T. A. Talbott (Eds.), *The trauma of war: Stress and recovery in Vietnam veterans.* Washington, D.C.: American Psychiatric Press.

Boulanger, G. (1990). A state of anarchy and a call to arms: The research and treatment of post-traumatic stress disorder. *Journal of Contemporary Psychotherapy, 20,* 5–15.

Danieli, Y. (1981). *Therapists' difficulties in treating survivors of the Nazi Holocaust and their children.* Ph.D. dissertation. New York University, New York.

Danieli, Y. (1988). Confronting the unimaginable. In J. P. Wilson, Z. Harel, & B. Kahana (Eds.), *Human adaptation to extreme stress: From the Holocaust to Vietnam* (pp. 219–237). New York: Plenum Press.

Dasberg, H. (1987). Society facing trauma or psychotherapist facing survivors. *Sihot - Israel Journal of Psychotherapy, 1,* 98–103.

Davidson, S. (1980). On relating to traumatized/persecuted people. In *Israel-Netherlands symposium on the impact of persecution,* No. 2, Daffsen/Amsterdam: Ministry of Social Welfare.

Eitinger, L. (1962). Concentration camp survivors in the postwar world. *American Journal of Orthopsychiatry, 32,* 367–375.

Eitinger, L. (1980). The concentration camp syndrome and its late sequelae. In J. E. Dimsdale (Ed.), *Survivors, victims and perpetrators: Essays on the Nazi Holocaust.* New York: Hemisphere.

Friedlander, S. (1980). *When memory comes.* New York: Evon.

Friedman, P. (1948). The road back for the DP's: Healing the psychological scars of Nazism. *Commentary, 6,* 502–510.

Freedman, A. (1978). Psychoanalytic study of an unusual perversion. *Journal of the American Psvchoanalytic Association, 26,* 749–777.
Gay, M., & Shulman, S. (1979). Comparison of children of Holocaust survivors with children of the general population in Israel: Are children of Holocaust survivor parents more disturbed than others? In *Israel-Netherland symposium of the impact of persecution* (pp. 88–93). Rijisuijik, the Netherlands: Ministry of Cultural Affairs, Recreation and Social Welfare.
Gelblum, A. (1945). Fundamental problems in immigrant absorption. *Ha'aretz* (daily newspaper), September 28th (in Hebrew).
Herman, J. L. (1992). *Trauma and recovery,* New York: Basic Books.
Klein, H. (1973). Children of the Holocaust: Mourning and bereavement. In E. J. Anthony & C. Koupernik (Eds.), *The Child in His Family: The Impact of Disease and Death.* New York: John Wiley.
Klein, H. (1987). Life under existential threat—40 years after the Holocaust—Therapeutic aspects. *Sihot - Israel Journal of Psychotherapy, 1*, 94–97 (in Hebrew).
Klein, H., & Kogan, A. (1987). Denial and identification processes in survivors of the Holocaust. *Sihot - Israel Journal of Psychotherapy, 1,* 108–111 (in Hebrew).
Koss, M. P., & Harvey, M. R. (1991). *The rape victim.* Beverly Hills, CA: Sage.
Krystal, H. (1968). *Massive psychic trauma.* New York: International University Press.
Levi, A. (1981). The professional historical mistake: Psychiatric aspects. *Harefua: Journal of the Israel Medical Association, 121,* 10–12 (in Hebrew).
Maslow, A. (1971). *The Further Reaches of Human Nature.* New York: Viking Press.
Meerloo, J. A. M. (1969). Persecution trauma and the reconditioning of emotional life: A brief survey. *American Journal of Psychiatry, 125,* 1187–1191.
Moses, R. (1983). Emotional response to stress in Israel: A psychoanalytic perspective. In S. Breznitz (Ed.), *Stress in Israel.* New York: Van Nostrand Reinhold Company.
Moses, R. (1984). An Israeli Psychoanalyst look back in 1983. In S. A. Luel and P. Marcus (Eds.), *Psychological reflection on the Holocaust* (pp. 53–69). Denver: Holocaust Awareness Institute, Center for Judaism Studies, University of Denver.
McCann, I. L., & Pearlman, L. A. (1990). Vicarious traumatization: A framework for understanding the psychological effects of working with victims. *Journal of Traumatic Stress, 3,* 131–149.
Nathan, T. S., Eitinger, L., & Winnik, H. Z. (1964). A psychiatric study of the Nazi Holocaust: A study in hospitalized patients. *Israel Annals of Psychiatry and Related Disciplines, 2,* 47–80.
Niederland, W. G. (1968). Clinical observations in the survivor syndrome. *International Journal of Psychoanalysis, 49*(2–3), 313–315.
Palgi, J. (1978). *A great spirit is coming.* Tel Aviv: Am Oved Publishers (in Hebrew).
Porat, D. (1986). *An entangled leadership: The yishuv and the Holocaust, 1942-1945.* Tel Aviv: Am Oved (in Hebrew).
Segev, T. (1991). *The seventh million: The Israelis and the Holocaust.* Jerusalem: Keter Publishing House and Domino Press (in Hebrew).

Solomon, Z. (1995). From denial to recognition: Attitudes to Holocaust survivors from World War 2 to the present. *Journal of Traumatic Stress, 8*(2), 215–229.

Quarantelli, E. L. (1985). An assessment of conflicting views on mental health: The consequences of traumatic events. In C. R. Figley (Ed.), *Trauma and its wake: The study and treatment of post traumatic stress disorder* (pp. 173–215). New York: Brunner/Mazel.

Winnik, H. J. (1979). The impact of persecution. In *Israel-Netherlands symposium on the impact of persecution* (Jerusalem, October 1977). Rijswijk, the Netherlands: Ministry of Cultural Affairs, Recreation and Social Welfare.

# 17

# *Breaking the Cycle of Genocidal Violence: Healing and Reconciliation*

***Ervin Staub***
*University of Massachusetts at Amherst*

## THE EFFECTS OF VIOLENCE ON GROUPS AND THEIR MEMBERS

Groups of people who have been victims of intense persecution, violence, mass killings, and genocide are deeply affected. This is true, of course, of individual survivors of mass killings or genocides, who were in camps or in territories where the violence occurred and who were personally targeted as victims. But it is also true of members of the victim group who were not in direct danger. They are also deeply affected by the persecution and the attempt to eliminate all or part of their group.

For most people, individual identity is deeply rooted in their group identity (Bar-Tal & Staub, 1997; Staub, 1997a), especially in the case of racial, ethnic, and to some extent religious groups, when membership in the group is not a matter of choice. The deaths of many others belonging to the group, the knowledge that, except for circumstances (often accidental ones like geography), one would have been killed, and the effects of the genocide on the whole group have deep impact on individuals, ranging from survivor guilt, to devaluation of oneself and one's group, to insecurity and the perception of the world as hostile.

Past victimization affects people's assumptions about the world (Janoff-Bulman, 1992). It deeply frustrates basic human needs like the need for security, for a positive identity, for a sense of effectiveness and control, for positive connections to others, and for a usable, meaningful comprehension of reality, including one's own place and role in the world (Staub, 1989, 1996b). It creates schemas or beliefs about what the world is like and what other people are like that make the constructive fulfillment of these needs more difficult. These include a negative view of human beings, of the world, and of one's ability to protect oneself and fulfill important goals in life (Staub, 1989).

This is a greatly expanded version of an article in the *Journal of Personal and Interpersonal Loss* (Staub, 1996a). The original article focused only on healing. Here, healing, reconciliation, and their relationship are discussed.

For these reasons members of a victim group have diminished capacity for leading satisfying, happy lives. In addition, a group that was the victim of violence has an increased potential for violence. The victims' intense insecurity in the world diminishes their capacity to consider others' perspective or needs, especially at a time of threat to the self. The capacity of groups of people to see their own role in hostile relations with other groups is limited even under the best circumstances and will be diminished by past victimization. People in the group may come to believe that violence is necessary to protect themselves and will respond with violence to conflict, threat, or hostility.

Victimization can also be part of a history that creates an "ideology of antagonism" (Staub, 1989; 1997b). This concept refers to a view of the other group as the enemy, bent on damaging or destroying one's own group, and a view or conception of one's group as an enemy of the other. Such ideologies are usually the result of a history of mutual hostility and violence. But in line with the limited perspective taken by groups of people already noted, even when harmdoing has been mutual and a victimized group has also victimized the other, groups and their individual members tend to focus on their own pain. They rarely take in the pain of the other or consider their own responsibility for it.

## HEALING FROM VIOLENCE AGAINST ONE'S GROUP

Healing deep-seated antagonism or changing ideologies of antagonism through various types of interactive conflict resolution procedures (Volkan, 1988; Rouhana & Kelman, 1994) can contribute to healing the self as well. In one such procedure, often referred to as a dialogue group, a few members of each group are brought together. People who are willing to enter such a situation usually feel less hostility or realize the destructive impact of the history of mutual violence on their own group. Members of each group can describe the pain and suffering of their group at the hands of the other. They can grieve for themselves in the company of the other, and as they open up to the pain of the other, they can begin to grieve for the other as well. Members of each group can acknowledge the role of their own group in harming the other. Mutual acknowledgment of responsibility can lead to mutual forgiving (Volkan, 1988).

Healing from trauma, which reduces pain, enables people to live constructive lives, and reduces the likelihood of violence by victims and thus a continuing cycle of violence, has several requirements. First, it is important for the world outside the group to acknowledge the group's suffering and to show caring and empathy. In the type of dialogue group I just described, when the process happens as planned, each group acknowledges the pain and suffering of the other and shows empathy.

In the case of the Holocaust, the world's acknowledgment of the victims' suffering has helped with the difficult process of healing. The absence of this acknowledgment by much of the world of the genocide of the Armenians has interfered with healing by Armenians. Turkey has denied that the genocide occurred. Turkish historians described the genocide as consisting mainly of the evacuation of Armenians from the war zone in World War I, where they lived, which was necessary because of Armenian hostility and rebellions that interfered with the war effort. In the course of this, some people died. Other nations, partly due to the difficulty individuals and nations have in taking in and responding to others' suffering, partly due to diplomatic efforts by Turkey, also have not acknowledged that the genocide has occurred (Smith, 1986).

Support and affirmation by the world can contribute to processes within the group that help members to grieve and to feel empathy with themselves. This is another important condition for healing. This, as well as psychological education, can help victims overcome the self-devaluation that is a natural result of victimization. Self-devaluation may be unarticulated, and outside conscious awareness. But victims often feel that something must be wrong with them or they would not have been treated so cruelly and violently. Self-devaluation is partly due to just-world thinking (Lerner, 1980), the belief that the world is a just place and therefore people who suffer must deserve their suffering, due either to their actions or to their character.

The behavior of bystander nations—both their punishment of perpetrators and their guarantees of active future response—can help victims feel innocent. It also has the potential of creating a feeling of security, based on confidence that the group will be protected and victimization will not be repeated. Unfortunately, bystander nations usually do not do what is required for this.

Tribunals and truth commissions have an important role. They accomplish many things. First, they clearly communicate to the victims that the world considers what was done to them as wrong, immoral, and unacceptable by the community of nations. They tell the victims that what was done to them was not their fault. The punishment of perpetrators can enhance the victims' feelings of security and satisfy, to some degree, their need for justice. It can lead victims to feel connected to, rather than isolated from, the rest of the world.

But truth commissions and tribunals also have another important function. Most members of perpetrator groups tend to feel innocent. Direct perpetrators, people involved in supporting roles, and the rest of the group, the bystanders, all tend to see the actions of their group as justified. They see it either as self-defense or as a way of dealing with a group that stood in the way of important, legitimate goals, possibly embodied in a "higher" ideological vision like communism, Nazism, or nationalism.

This was also evident to me as a host of a forum on "Healing and Reconciliation," which took place as part of a New York Times Internet "conference" called "Bosnia: Uncertain Path to Peace," a month-long series of forums in June and July 1996. Many members of the ethnic groups in Bosnia, mostly living now in the U.S., entered into the discussion. All of them pointed fingers at the other groups and claimed they were at fault. They were not able and willing to look at the role and responsibility of their own group, whether historical or current.

The public examination of what has happened can bring home to members of perpetrator groups what actually happened and the horrors of their groups' actions. Gunther Grass, the great German author who has written much about the culpability of Germans, was profoundly affected when as a young man the American troops marched him, together with other local Germans, through one of the concentrations camps.

It may be reasonable to regard the important process of public examination of the Hitler regime and the Holocaust in the Nuremberg trials as laying the groundwork for the democratic Germany of today. In the course of the Nuremberg trials the history and actions of Germany during the Hitler era were laid bare in great detail, using to a large extent materials created by the Nazis and the German bureaucracy. Without this, it is likely that the Germans, once again, would have felt like victims.

The way the perpetrator group behaves can help or hinder healing by victims. Truth commissions and tribunals, when they are conducted in a serious and lawful manner, can affect the awareness and consciousness of the perpetrators as well as their attitudes towards their actions and towards the victims. They make compensatory actions by the perpetrator group, like assuming responsibility, expressions of guilt and regret, and monetary compensation, more likely. A period of initial healing is probably required before victims can take in such compensatory actions, rather than reject them together with everything that has to do with the perpetrators. But once such actions are taken in and acquire psychological meaning, they can contribute to healing.

## SELF-HEALING

In the absence of support, concern, and empathy by much of the world, victims may remain deeply affected. This has been true, for example, of the Armenians. After the collapse of the Soviet Union they created a nation, which affirms their identity. They built a genocide museum. At the opening of the museum in April 1995, hundreds of thousands of people stood in line, waiting to go through the museum, with many children. One of the major political issues in Armenia, and one of the major psychological issues for the people is the need for and demand of Turkey's acknowledgment that the genocide has occurred.

While the role of the outside world is very important for healing victim groups, the Armenian experience points to the need for internal healing. Victimized groups always have to attend to their own healing. But if the group does not focus on self-healing and affirmation and support from others is not forthcoming, then the perpetrators and bystander nations, who by their passivity have often contributed to the evolution of mass killing or genocide against the group in the first place (Staub, 1989), continue to victimize the group.

Shared remembering, building a cohesive internal community, and rituals which bring the suffering to light and in which grief and empathy with oneself and others in the group can be felt and expressed are important elements in group healing. Calling on potentially responsive allies to help with this process seems valuable. Ideally, this process, and the strength gained through it, will also led to the creation of a constructive vision of the future.

Constructive visions are important. A victim group needs both to engage with the past, in the form of memorials, rituals, grieving, and empathy with themselves, and to look at and move towards the future. Garbarino, Dubrow, Kostelny, and Pardo (1992) describe the Cambodians as constructively engaged with building a positive future. They believe that this is made possible by a characteristic of

Cambodian culture, holding as a basic attitude towards life, a deeply held belief and vision, that the best revenge is creating a good life. A constructive vision of the future that is inclusive, that embraces all segments of society and points to goals around which people can unite, can fulfill basic needs and bring practical fruits.

The socialization of children in the group must also attend to healing the trauma, which is inevitably transmitted to children. The psychological impact on adults that I briefly noted, their pain, feelings of insecurity, mistrust, and other negative views of people and the world, impact children. This impact can be enhanced either by silence—adults not talking about what happened to them as individuals and to the group as a whole—or by incessant focus on the past trauma. Children need to learn about the past, partly to be able to make sense of their own experience of the adults around them. Their awareness of what has happened, of how their parents have been impacted, and how they themselves have been impacted in turn, is part of a process of becoming free. It can help children lead untraumatized lives.

The developmental level of children is essential to consider in choosing ways to expose them to this history and knowledge. Exposing young children to images of horror, especially involving people in their own group, can unnecessarily traumatize them. Sensitivity to the age and personality of children is essential.

## RECONCILIATION

So far, a connection between healing and reconciliation has been implicit, and at times explicit, as in the discussion of dialogue groups and of truth commissions and tribunals. This connection is especially significant when the victim group and the perpetrator group, or two groups that have mutually victimized each other, live together. When this is the case, as in Bosnia and Rwanda, genuine healing cannot take place without reconciliation. While circumstances can be created that make the victims somewhat safe, a feeling of safety must come from a combination of institutional arrangements and trust that develops through reconciliation. The danger of renewed victimization at the hands of former perpetrators interferes with healing. On the other hand, it is difficult for reconciliation to begin, when the violence is very recent, without some prior healing.

Some of the requirements for healing are also preconditions for reconciliation. The acknowledgment of responsibility by perpetrators, and mutual acknowledgment when there was a history of reciprocal harmdoing, is important. Expressions of regret and sorrow, grieving with the victims, and participation by members of the perpetrator group in shared memorials (when the victims allow this) make reconciliation more possible.

This exploration of the past is essential. It makes it possible to move beyond the past. The events in the former Yugoslavia would probably have enfolded very differently if, in the nearly 50 years of the country's existence, such exploration had taken place. In the course of it, the tremendous violence that the Croats inflicted on the Serbs during World War II, some violence by Serbs against Croats during that time, together with long standing historical antagonisms could have been aired, looked at, and discussed. Unfortunately, Tito did not allow this. Many

Serbs still blame the Muslims of the former Yugoslavia for converting to Islam hundreds of years ago, and look at them as stand-ins for the Turks who ruled Serbia for over 500 years.[1]

There is no established "technology" as yet for this kind of exploration, especially on a societal rather than a small group level. Truth commissions in a number of South American countries have attempted to establish the facts of violence against particular elements of society, mostly by military regimes (see, e.g., Nunca Mas, 1986). The process in South Africa, consisting of hearings, confessions, and the accompanying descriptions of deeds of violence, torture, and murder, combined with amnesty for the perpetrators who confess, is a brave and inspired attempt at healing and reconciliation.

This raises, and may to some extent answer, questions about the importance of the experience of justice for healing and reconciliation to occur. Some perpetrators who express no regret or offer no apology, may receive amnesty. Truth and memory may be served, even if not fully, but not justice. Acknowledgment of responsibility will be partial, expressed in terms of facts, but not in emotional or moral terms. Still, the exposure of actions and actors to the public, accompanied by institutional and political changes, may go a long way toward creating constructive engagement between groups.

When there has been a history of mutual violence, putting dialogue groups on television may help with reconciliation. Through their vicarious experiences, viewers can develop empathy for members of the other group, grieve for their own group, participate in the assumption of responsibility for the harm their group has caused, and hear and accept the regret for harm done to them expressed by members of the other group. This can only be done when there is already a public process of reconciliation, so that participation in such a process does not expose people to inordinate danger at the hands of members of their own group who consider them traitors.

An unusual kind of dialogue group is One by One, in which children of Jewish survivors and children of German perpetrators of the Holocaust talk to each other. The Germans talk about their own pain and suffering that was the result of what *their parents did.* They talk about their guilt and empathy with children of survivors. This process, that began as private dialogue, has expanded into public talks which may inspire reconciliation of many kinds.

"Understanding" the perpetrator can also help victims heal and open up to reconciliation. This does not mean forgetting, or even forgiving. It means understanding the psychological, cultural, and societal process that leads perpetrators to their violent actions. This helps victims understand how the horrible things that were done to them can and did come about and help to fulfill their need for comprehension of reality. By leading the victims to see that, horrible as it is, what the perpetrators did is a comprehensible, human process, they may also become more open to reconciliation. But even attempting such understanding can only take place after some time has passed and healing has begun.

Compensation by perpetrators can help with both healing and reconciliation.

[1]This was evident from conversations I had with people in Belgrade during a visit in October 1996.

Compensation is an acknowledgment of wrongdoing and can be a form of atonement. Compensation will work less well, however, if it creates or maintains some form of superiority by perpetrators in their relationship to victims, rather than express guilt, regret, and humility.

Reconciliation must take groups and their members into the future. Deep engagement with the "other" is important, to discover the other's humanity and to overcome a history of devaluation on the part of perpetrators, and fear, anger, and other negative emotions on the part of victims. Deep engagement can best occur when it is in the service of shared goals, whether economic, cultural, psychological (such as healing and reconciliation), or structural (such as building peaceful and peace-building institutions). For deep engagement to be successful in humanizing the other, certain requirements must be fulfilled. They include equality in relations (Allport, 1954: Cook, 1970) and learning about the other's culture and ways of being so that one can understand and relate to the behavior of the other (Staub, 1989). Individual relationships and friendships that are formed in this process will help overcome devaluation of the other group (Pettigrew, 1997).

Genuine reconciliation between groups is difficult to create but is possible. There has been a transformation in the relations of the French and the Germans following World War II, as a result of wise policies by leaders. The more avenues that are created for humanizing members of the other group, the better. The role of the media in this is extremely important. The media can create or maintain devaluation, prejudice, and enemy images or can show the humanity of members of other groups. In Macedonia, journalists belonging to the different ethnic groups formed teams, interviewing and writing stories about the everyday lives of members of the different ethnic groups.

## CONCLUSIONS

In summary, the healing of trauma can diminish self-focus, self-devaluation, fear, mistrust, and pain. It can open victims up to reconciliation. It can increase the capacity for empathy with others, effectiveness in pursuing goals, and the capacity for enjoying life. It can make violence by victim groups less likely.

Nations and the community of nations, which are often passive when violence occurs, are often passive bystanders again to the pain of victims. It requires, therefore, special effort to create a process of responding by bystanders—nations, nongovernmental institutions, and individuals. An important element of this is the strengthening of international institutions, possibly within the U.N., that have the task of both activating a machinery and actually providing help and support.

This should be part of a broader effort by bystander nations to prevent genocides (Staub, 1996c, 1997b). This effort should include the use of early warning that a group of people is the object of persecution and violence, and the *activation* of the community of nations to warn perpetrators and to take steps to stop them (by withholding aid, boycotts and sanctions, and by military actions, if necessary). Genocides frequently evolve, and the earlier such responses, the more effective can be the community of nations in inhibiting this evolution without the use of military force.

Effective international institutions are needed for all these purposes. The process of creating them can also be used to work on changing the way nations define their national interest and to promote values that might guide nations to respond to the suffering of people outside their border.

## REFERENCES


Allport, G. W. (1954). *The nature of prejudice.* Reading, MA: Addison-Wesley.

Bar-Tal, D., & Staub, E. (1997). Introduction: The nature and forms of patriotism. In D. Bar-Tal and E. Staub (Eds.), *Patriotism in the lives of individuals and groups.* Chicago: Nelson-Hall.

Cook, S. W. (1970). Motives in conceptual analysis of attitude-related behavior. In W. J. Arnold and D. Levine (Eds.), *Nebraska symposium on motivation.* Lincoln, NE: University of Nebraska Press.

Garbarino, J., Dubrow, N., Kostelny, K., & Pardo, C. (1992). *Children in danger: Coping with the consequences of community violence.* San Francisco: Jossey-Bass.

Janoff-Bulman, R. (1992). *Shattered assumptions.* New York: The Free Press.

Lerner, M. (1980). *The belief in a just world: A fundamental delusion.* New York: Plenum.

Nunca Mas. (1986). *The report of the Argentine national commission on the disappeared.* New York: Farrar, Straus, Giroux.

Pettigrew, T. F. (1997). Generalized intergroup contact effects on prejudice. *Personality and Social Psychology Bulletin, 23*(2), 173–185.

Rouhana, N. N., & Kelman, H. C. (1994). Promoting joint thinking in international conflicts: An Israeli-Palestinian Continuing Workshop. *Journal of Social Issues, 50,* 157–178.

Smith, R. W. (1986). *Denial and justification of genocide: The Armenian case and its implications.* Paper presented at the Annual Meetings of the American Political Science Association, Washington, D.C. August 28–31.

Staub, E. (1989). *The roots of evil: The origins of genocide and other group violence.* New York: Cambridge University Press.

Staub, E. (1996a). Breaking the cycle of violence: Helping victims of genocidal violence heal. *Journal of Personal and Interpersonal Loss, 1,* 191–197.

Staub, E. (1996b). Cultural-societal roots of violence: The examples of genocidal violence and of contemporary youth violence in the United States. *American Psychologist, 51,* 117–132.

Staub, E. (1996c). Preventing genocide: Activating bystanders, helping victims and the creation of caring. *Peace and Conflict: Journal of Peace Psychology, 2,* 189–201.

Staub, E. (1997a). Blind versus constructive patriotism: Moving from embeddedness in the group to critical loyalty and action. In D. Bar-Tal and E. Staub (Eds.), *Patriotism in the lives of individuals and groups.* Chicago: Nelson-Hall.

Staub, E. (1997b). *Halting and preventing collective violence: The role of bystanders.* Background paper for participants in Beyond Lamentation: A Symposium on the Prevention of Genocide, Stockholm, June 13–16.

Volkan, V. D. (1988). *The need to have enemies and allies.* Northvale, NY: Jason Aronson.

# IV

# *LOSSES RELATED TO SOCIAL IDENTITY*

# 18

# *The Experience of Loss in Sport*

***David Lavallee***
*Leeds Metropolitan University*

***J. Robert Grove, Sandy Gordon, and Ian W. Ford***
*University of Western Australia*

*In the beginning I went through months of self-searching. . . . I remember my sister had cancer and she said to my mother, "you know she [me] has got to realize that it [the injury] is not a life-threatening disease. . . . That really annoyed me because I felt she was undermining my injury just because hers was theoretically more severe. . . . I thought that is such a typical thing for a non-athlete to say because for lots of athletes their limbs are their life because that is what gives them their financial support and intrinsic motivation.*
(Elite-level volleyball player after suffering a severe injury; Ford & Gordon, 1995)

The sport-scientific community is becoming increasingly interested in the concept of loss. The losses experienced by competitive athletes have been analyzed by several theorists (e.g., Astle, 1986; Wehlage, 1980), and a number of recent studies have empirically examined the coping strategies employed by athletes who are confronted with different types of losses in their lives (e.g., Lavallee, Gordon, & Grove, 1997). However, as Wehlage (1980) has previously suggested, the notion of loss remains poorly understood, frequently overlooked, and generally mismanaged by coaches and other professionals responsible for the well-being of athletes.

In this chapter we examine the concept of loss as it applies to elite-level athletes, with a specific focus on symbolic losses experienced in competitive sport. Competitive sport is defined as an organized sporting activity in which training and participation are time-consuming, and in which the level of performance meets relatively high standards of expectations. A general discussion on the nature of coping with loss is initially presented, followed by an overview of the literature on sport-related losses. Empirical and theoretical research which has been directed at exploring symbolic losses associated with athletic injuries, performance slumps, and retirement from sport is then reviewed. The chapter concludes by examining the relationship between the degree to which an individual identifies with the athlete role and the experience of loss in competitive sport.

## COPING WITH LOSS

A loss has been broadly defined as a reduction in personal, material, and/or symbolic resources (Harvey, 1996). Research on this phenomenon, which has been conducted in a wide variety of academic disciplines, has focused primarily on the adverse consequences associated with the experience of loss. Harvey and colleagues (e.g., Harvey, 1996; Harvey, Orbuch, Chwalisz, & Garwood, 1991) have considered the conceptions and connotations of a spectrum of losses that people experience in their lives. A number of other researchers have also focused on identifying specific types of personal and interpersonal loss and their various consequences (e.g., Hobfoll, 1988; Staudacher, 1987). Whereas each loss event differs in its psychosocial characteristics and dynamics, the available literature suggests that there is significant commonality among different categories of loss (Harvey, 1996). It appears likely, therefore, that sport-related losses share common features with the other types of loss outlined in this handbook.

### Loss in Sport

Although research on symbolic losses experienced by athletes is a relatively recent line of inquiry, the reactions associated with competitive losses in sport have previously been delineated in the literature. For example, Goffman's (1956) concept of failure has been employed to describe how the most frequently experienced sporting loss is that of losing a competition (e.g., Ball, 1976; Harris & Eitzen, 1978). Wehlage (1980) has also outlined how the failure to obtain highly valued outcomes such as an important victory or a championship can stimulate a grief reaction in sport performers. In addition, a number of researchers have empirically examined the psychological effects of losing a competition by comparing pre-game and post-game anxiety levels among athletes (e.g., Sanderson & Ashton, 1981; Scanlan, 1977). For the most part, however, it appears that sport theorists have endorsed Peretz's (1970) classification of loss events when analyzing how symbolic losses manifest themselves in competitive sport.

Peretz (1970) has identified four different types of losses: (1) loss of significant or valued people; (2) loss of some aspect of the self; (3) loss of external objects or possessions; and (4) losses that occur in the process of human growth and development. In this chapter we consider an assortment of symbolic losses frequently encountered in sport that have implications extending across each of these categories. These loss events, which will be addressed in terms of aspects of our research programs that connect to the concept of loss, include alterations of self-definition due to sporting injuries, sustained decrements in performance due to slumps, and life changes which often accompany athletic retirement.

## ATHLETIC INJURY

*Life is absurd. Just when I begin to put it all together, I pull this muscle. I'm so depressed . . . Why me? Why now? I'll never be able to get to this place again. I'm so*

> *afraid I'll never fully recover. Is there any doctor who can help me to get going? The stress is unbearable, to say nothing of the physical pain itself. It's just not fair. I feel like dying. A terrible loss.* (Lynch, 1988, p. 161)

The above quote expresses the painful emotional reaction and perception of deprivation experienced by a distance runner following injury two weeks prior to an Olympic trial. Responses like this are not uncommon for athletes who consider participation in sport an integral part of their lives. Indeed, for anyone who derives significant amounts of self-esteem or personal competence from their ability to perform, the occurrence of injury can result in a symbolic loss that far outweighs any physical pain and discomfort (Petitpas & Danish, 1995). In acknowledgment of this, research investigating the psychological effects of sport injury has received increased attention as attempts to enhance the rehabilitation process have been initiated (Heil, 1993; Pargman, 1993).

Any physical impairment which prohibits active involvement in an elite-level athlete's sport, whether temporary or permanent, is cognitively, emotionally, and behaviorally challenging (Pedersen, 1986). In addition to the physical losses (e.g., agility, speed), decreases in physical conditioning, and changes in lifestyle as a result of an athletic injury, there is an abrupt cessation or deprivation of positive experiences acquired through participation in sport (Smith, Scott, & Wiese, 1990). Moreover, injury threatens a competitive athlete's self-concept, belief system, social and occupational functioning, values, commitments, and emotional equilibrium (Petitpas & Danish, 1995).

The experience of loss in injured athletes has previously been discussed in terms of Peretz's (1970) model (e.g., Astle, 1986; McDonald & Hardy, 1990). Whereas the most common form of symbolic loss suffered by injured athletes is perhaps the loss of some aspect of the self, such as the loss of identity or sense of importance (Brewer, 1994), it appears that this population is prone to suffer numerous other forms of loss. For example, the following experiences can be extinguished by an athletic injury: mobility; independence; sense of control; confidence; virility; daily routine; social ties; opportunities, income, or financial rewards; status; playing time; and attention (McDonald & Hardy, 1990; Petitpas & Danish, 1995).

Hobfoll's (1988) conservation of resources model also offers a viable conceptualization of the experience of loss and athletic injury. By emphasizing object definitions of person–environment transactions likely to result in psychological distress, this model suggests that the promotion of well-being and prevention of stress depends on the availability and successful management of resources. According to Hobfoll, resources are personal characteristics, energies, conditions, and objects which people strive to retain, protect, and/or build. *Personal characteristics* are resources to the extent that they generally aid stress resistance (e.g., self-efficacy, optimism). *Energies* aid in the acquisition of other kinds of resources (e.g., time, money, knowledge). *Conditions* are resources to the extent that they are valued and sought after (e.g., seniority), and *objects* are important because of some aspect of their physical nature and/or because of their acquiring secondary status value based on their rarity or expense (e.g., property). According to the model, when any of these resources are lost (or invested without consequent gain) people become vulnerable to psychological and physical disorder and debilitated functioning (Hobfoll, 1988). Thus, an athletic injury can be perceived as stressful because of the threat, potential or actual, it has on an athlete's resources.

In a sporting context various resources are "acquired" through participation. For example, personal characteristics may include self-esteem, self-confidence, virility, affection, and mastery. Energies may be competency, money/rewards, and group membership/ties. Regarding conditions, resources may be status (e.g., position in team/sport), leadership, team involvement, and attention. Object resources, although perhaps not directly linked with sport involvement, may also be achieved through successful participation at high levels. Consequently, if any of these resources are acquired through sport participation, then injury presents a threat, perceived or actual, to their availability and recruitment. Moreover, other resources not necessarily achieved through competitive sport may also be threatened or lost because of injury (viz., mobility, independence, sense of control, and daily routines).

### Research Findings

In an attempt to describe the experience of loss, response to injury rehabilitation, and assistance required to facilitate the recovery process, Ford and Gordon (1997) conducted in-depth interviews with both female and male elite and nonelite athletes recovering from surgery for a major sport-related injury. As outlined in Table 1, results indicate that a variety of resources are either lost or depleted during the early stages of recovery from injury (i.e., the first 4–6 weeks post-surgery). Further analyses also suggested that social support is an intervention that offers much promise in terms of its role as both a coping and motivational mechanism during recovery from injury-related losses. If resources are being lost or depleted as a consequence of injury, social support may assist in alleviating the resultant stress incurred by athletes.

Social support can cover lost resources (e.g., money can be provided to assist with treatment costs) and/or help recruit latent resources (e.g., bolstering self-esteem may help an athlete deal with rehabilitation by instilling confidence and a sense of mastery over their recovery). In this regard, social support acts as a valuable tool to provide or facilitate the preservation of basic resources. In the Ford and Gordon (1997) study it was interesting to note that several athletes indicated that post-operative improvement in communication and friendship between themselves and significant others (e.g., family, friends, coaching staff, teammates) assisted in their recovery from injury.

## PERFORMANCE SLUMPS

In many ways, performance is the bottom line in competitive sport. Contract details for high-level players typically include performance-related contingency clauses (Wilson, 1991); there is a strong, positive correlation between team performance and spectator attendance (Becker & Suls, 1983); and turnover among coaches has been linked to poor win/loss records (Boynton, 1995). Sophisticated training

*Table 1.* The recovery process in injured athletes: Qualitative descriptions of lost resources

| Description | Example |
|---|---|
| Personal characteristics | |
| Decreased sense of achievement in sport | All my goals have just gone [as a result of the injury]. |
| Decreased sense of optimism | I've lost some sparkle, simply from being depressed and angry. |
| Decreased independence | Having to rely on others makes me feel very unindependent [*sic*]. |
| Energies | |
| Decreased physical fitness | I feel very lethargic and slothful because I can't do anything. |
| Depletion of finance | I'm on a performance-based contract so I'm losing money, which just adds to the stress. |
| Decreased levels of productivity | I was just too tired all the time and I couldn't sit down for long to do any work. |
| Conditions | |
| Decreased role in sport | I'm slightly concerned what my standing [in the team] is going to be when I come back. |
| Others | |
| Decreased sense of control | You get a bit frustrated that you can't do everything and sometimes you let fly. |
| Decreased social and recreational activities | It's nice to go out and mix with friends but I haven't been able to do it. |

regimes are therefore implemented by individual athletes and teams in an attempt to produce consistent, high-level performances.

Despite the best efforts of those involved, however, prolonged periods of below-average performance sometimes occur. These extended periods of poor performance are known as *slumps* (Taylor, 1988), and they are recognized by players, coaches, and sport scientists as an inherent part of involvement in competitive sport (Ogilvie & Howe, 1984). Slumps are also a source of considerable frustration, self-doubt, and anxiety for competitive athletes (Prapavessis & Grove, 1995).

Do performance slumps in sport constitute a form of symbolic loss? We believe that they do, and we believe this conclusion can be defended on both philosophical and empirical grounds. From a philosophical perspective, an actual or perceived decline in performance levels for an extended period of time may result in a loss of identity for athletes (cf. Astle, 1986), because their self-concept often includes a strong belief in physical competence (Ryckman, Robbins, Thornton, & Cantrell, 1982). Fears of losing the respect of coaches or teammates, status within the team, fan support, playing time, and/or salary bonuses are also likely to exist.

To the extent that losses of matches or games accompany the decline in performance, threats of being branded a "loser," losing bargaining power in contract negotiations, and/or losing one's job may be present as well.

## Research Findings

From an empirical perspective, recent research conducted in our laboratory indicates that athletes do sometimes interpret performance slumps as a symbolic loss, and that this interpretation is positively related to perceived stress. These findings were obtained from a survey of more than 300 male and female athletes who had competed in a variety of team and individual sports at levels ranging from local to international competition (Grove & Heard, 1997). As part of this survey, athletes were asked to recall the last time they had experienced a performance slump, to provide information about how they had perceived it, and to estimate the degree of stress that it had created for them.

Table 2 provides a partial summary of the results. The table includes descriptive statistics for selected variables as well as inter-correlations and associated

*Table 2.* Perceived qualities of the slump experience: Descriptive statistics and correlations with selected athlete demographics

| | Descriptives | | Inter-correlations | | | | | |
|---|---|---|---|---|---|---|---|---|
| Variable | Mean | SD | YRS | EDU | CHL | THR | LOS | STR |
| Age | 22.11 | 5.07 | .37* | .17 | .04 | –.08 | .02 | .00 |
| Years of competition (YRS) | 8.99 | 4.94 | | .08 | .12 | .05 | .04 | .03 |
| Education level (EDU)[a] | 4.67 | 0.91 | | | –.03 | .03 | .12 | .12 |
| Perceived challenge (CHL)[b] | 7.01 | 2.00 | | | | .29* | .35* | .36* |
| Perceived threat (THR)[b] | 5.24 | 2.62 | | | | | .59** | .63** |
| Perceived loss (LOS)[b] | 5.98 | 2.25 | | | | | | .63** |
| Perceived stress (STR)[b] | 5.71 | 2.33 | | | | | | |

[a]1–6 ordinal scale.
[b]0–10 bipolar scale.
*$.60 < d < .80$. **$1.45 < d < 1.65$.

effect sizes. We prefer to rely on effect sizes rather than statistical significance when interpreting these data because of the large sample size and its strong influence on the significance level of correlations. In general, we consider the correlations meaningful if they reach .20 ($d > .40$), since this value represents a moderate effect size. Correlations of .40 or more ($d > .85$) are viewed as very meaningful because they indicate large effect sizes (cf. Cohen, 1988).

Examination of means in Table 2 reveals that these competitive athletes were more inclined to view slumps as a challenge than as a loss or a threat. At the same time, however, ratings for perceived loss and threat were both above the midpoint of the 0–10 response scale. Moreover, perceptions of slumps as a loss or a threat were unrelated to personal demographics, and strongly and positively related to the amount of perceived stress (both *r*s = .63, both *d*s = 1.62). These relationships were still evident when partial correlation procedures were used to control for the interrelations among the predictors, suggesting that loss and threat perceptions made independent contributions to slump-related stress. More specifically, loss perceptions correlated .37 ($d = .79$) with perceived stress after controlling for the challenge and threat, while threat perceptions correlated .41 ($d = .89$) with perceived stress after controlling for challenge and loss.

## RETIREMENT FROM SPORT

Over a period of 30 years, a significant amount of psychological and sociological literature on the issue of retirement from competitive sport has accumulated (for reviews, see Gordon, 1995; Murphy, 1995; Ogilvie & Taylor, 1993), yet there still exists considerable debate about the evidence, extent, and magnitude of the distress caused. On the one hand, several researchers have maintained that few athletes experience adjustment difficulties upon athletic career termination, and thus may consider retirement from sport as a form of "social rebirth" (e.g., Coakley, 1983; Greendorfer & Blinde, 1985). As Coakley (1983) has suggested, "the transition out of intercollegiate sport seems to go hand in hand with transitions from college to work careers, new friendships, marriage, parenthood, and other roles normally associated with early adulthood" (p. 4).

Other examinations of retirement from elite-amateur and professional sport have arrived at different conclusions. Anecdotally, for example, the dysfunctional and behavioral manifestations of loss associated with career termination have included financial difficulties and drug abuse (Newman, 1991), alcoholism and criminal activity (Ogilvie & Taylor, 1993), and suicide (Frith, 1990). At more scholarly levels, it has also been reported that retired athletes often experience a loss of status, social support, self-identity, and direction and focus (Astle, 1986; Messner, 1992; Werthner & Orlick, 1986). In Mihovilovic's (1968) study of professional Yugoslavian soccer players, representatives of management (including coaches) believed that retired players drank alcohol excessively, resorted to illegal activities, were in a serious psychic state, and had significant fears about the future. Curtis and Ennis (1988) have also reported that 50% of a sample of competitive hockey players in Canada reported difficulties with athletic retirement, and 75% experienced a sense of loss. Moreover, in their study of 28 former female professional tennis players, Allison and Meyer (1988) reported that 30% expressed feelings of isolation and loss of identity upon career termination.

In terms of which argument is most persuasive, we acknowledge that many athletes may experience few adjustment difficulties following their retirement from sport. At the same time, however, the literature seems replete with both ecologically valid and empirical evidence that retiring athletes are at-risk to experience a sense of loss both prior to and upon career termination. As Murphy (1995) has suggested, assisting athletes to make successful transitions to post-athletic careers may be one of the most frequently encountered issues for sport psychology practitioners. We strongly advocate, therefore, that increased attention be focused on the identification of athletes who experience feelings of loss following athletic retirement, as well as the effectiveness of specific strategies for working through any distress that arises.

### Research Findings

Fifteen athletes identified as having endured highly distressful reactions to retirement from sport were invited to write autobiographical accounts of their career termination experiences (Lavallee et al., 1997). This methodology was employed to investigate the dynamics of the athletic retirement process by focusing on the following issues: the degree of adjustment necessitated by retirement; overall success in coping with retirement; amount of account-making/confiding activity since retirement; the degree to which the reactions of the confidant(s) were perceived as helpful and empathic; and present negative affect about the retirement experience (cf. Harvey et al., 1991).

Results indicated that perceived success in coping was inversely related to present negative affect ($r = -.55$, $d = 1.32$), and directly related to both the degree of account-making/confiding activity since retirement ($r = .72$, $d = 2.08$) and perceived empathy of confidants ($r = .82$, $d = 2.87$). In addition, a significant positive relationship was evident between degree of account-making/confiding post-career end and perceived empathy of confidants ($r = .79$, $d = 2.58$), and present negative affect was highly negatively correlated with both the degree of account-making/confiding since retirement ($r = -.63$, $d = 1.62$) and extent to which confidant reactions were perceived as helpful/empathic ($r = -.72$, $d = 2.08$).

## ATHLETIC IDENTITY: A SYNTHESIZING CONSTRUCT

This chapter has attempted to provide an overview of the experience of loss in sport. Although the reported research findings may be generally applicable across other levels of sport participation, our specific focus has been on the losses experienced by competitive athletes. A review of the losses associated with sporting injuries, performance slumps, and athletic retirement has demonstrated that participants in competitive sport are often confronted with numerous loss events both during and after their playing careers. A closer examination of these losses also suggests that there exists considerable overlap across the many occurrences of sport-related loss. In this concluding section, we propose that athletic identity plays a central role in the experience of symbolic loss in competitive sport.

Athletic identity, which has been defined as the degree to which an individual defines herself or himself in terms of the athlete role, is a cognitive orientation that guides and organizes the processing of self-related information (Braun & Wicklund, 1988; Brewer, Van Raalte, & Linder, 1993). The development of an athletic identity often begins during the early stages of participation in sport and becomes stronger as athletes become more committed to their chosen sport(s). As Brewer et al. (1993) have suggested, individuals with strong athletic identities are more likely to interpret a given event in terms of its implications for their athletic functioning than individuals only weakly identified with the athlete role. Thus, individuals who derive their self-identity exclusively from their role in sport are prone to experience a symbolic loss following a sporting injury, performance slump, and/or athletic retirement.

For example, a strong athletic identity may be associated with depressed mood should injury impair an athlete's ability to perform (Brewer, 1993). When an athlete lacks other sources of self-worth outside their sport, there is an increased risk for the experience of loss when a sport-related injury is sustained. As outlined in our discussion of Hobfoll's (1988) model, the resources that contribute to the athletic role can be eroded or lost as a consequence of injury. Moreover, if these resources are unable to be replaced from other sources of self-identification, it appears that post-injury emotional difficulties may result.

Temporary declines in performance as a result of a slump may also be perceived as the loss of an essential self-attribute for an athlete with a strong and exclusive athletic identity. As Braun and Wicklund (1988) have suggested, a person's performances serve to underscore and manifest their striven-for identity (e.g., athletic) to which they are committed. Consequently, for an individual whose self-worth is entirely dependent on sport, performance slumps often disrupt the pursuit of her or his self-defining activity. The more narrowly focused the sense of self, the more threatened the athlete in the midst of a slump is to experience a symbolic loss of identity.

The notion of athletic identity has also received considerable attention in recent years due to its potential influence on retirement from sport. As with sporting injuries, the degree to which an individual identifies with the athlete role appears to influence an athlete's affective response to retirement. Moreover, individuals who highly value the athletic component of the self are less likely to pursue post-athletic career, education, and lifestyle options prior to retirement (Good, Brewer, Petitpas, Van Raalte, & Mahar, 1993). This premature "identity foreclosure" has been found to hinder an athlete's development and thus leads to difficulties encountered during a career transition from sport (Murphy, Petitpas, & Brewer, 1996).

The importance of athletic identity in determining these kinds of loss-related reactions was demonstrated in the Lavallee et al. (1997) study. Changes in athletic identity were assessed directly by having retired athletes complete standard (present tense) and retrospective (point of retirement) versions of the Athletic Identity Measurement Scale (AIMS; Brewer et al., 1993). The loss of athletic identity was subsequently correlated among self-reports of adjustment processes obtained from the micronarrative accounts. Results indicated that decreases in athletic identity since retirement (i.e., negative change scores) were associated with greater amounts of account-making activity since retirement ($r = -.84$, $d = 3.10$), greater perceived empathy from confidants ($r = -.90$, $d = 4.15$), and greater overall success in coping with retirement ($r = -.86$, $d = 3.37$). On the other hand, an increase (or minimal loss) in athletic identity was positively related to present negative affect ($r = .55$, $d = 1.32$).

Athletes as a group not only experience loss, but they are also likely to encounter certain types of losses more frequently than others (Astle, 1986). In particular, competitive athletes whose self-identity is dependent on sport are prone to experience a symbolic loss following an injury, performance slump, and/or retirement. Sport involvement is often an intense, important, and self-defining activity for serious athletes (Murphy, 1995; Werthner & Orlick, 1986). An appreciation of the experience of loss is therefore central to an understanding of the thoughts and behaviors of performers in competitive sport.

## REFERENCES


Allison, M. T., & Meyer, C. (1988). Career problems and retirement among athletes: The female tennis professional. *Sociology of Sport Journal, 5,* 212–222.

Astle, S. J. (1986). The experience of loss in athletes. *Journal of Sports Medicine and Physical Fitness, 26,* 279–284.

Ball, D. W. (1976). Failure in sport. *American Sociological Review, 41,* 726–739.

Becker, M. A., & Suls, J. (1983). Take me out to the ball game: The effects of objective, social, and temporal performance information on attendance at Major League Baseball games. *Journal of Sport Psychology, 5,* 302–313.

Boynton, B. (1995). Managers and close games. *The Baseball Research Journal, 24,* 81–87.

Braun, O. L., & Wickland, R. A. (1988). The identity-effort connection. *Journal of Experimental Social Psychology, 24,* 37–65.

Brewer, B. W. (1993). Self-identity and specific vulnerability to depressed mood. *Journal of Personality, 61,* 343–363.

Brewer, B. W. (1994). Review and critique of models of psychological adjustment to athletic injury. *Journal of Applied Sport Psychology, 6,* 87–100.

Brewer, B. W., Van Raalte, J. L., & Linder, D. E. (1993). Athletic identity: Hercules' muscles or Achilles' heel? *International Journal of Sport Psychology, 24,* 237–254.

Coakley, J. J. (1983). Leaving competitive sport: Retirement or rebirth? *Quest, 35,* 1–11.

Cohen, J. (1988). *Statistical power analysis for the behavioral sciences* (2nd ed.). Hillsdale, NJ: Lawrence Erlbaum.

Curtis, J., & Ennis, R. (1988). Negative consequences of leaving competitive sport? Comparative findings for former elite-level hockey players. *Sociology of Sport Journal, 5,* 87–106.

Ford, I. W., & Gordon, S. (1995, September). Coping with athletic injury: The role of social support. In S. Hanrahan (Chair), *Coping processes in sport.* Symposium conducted at the 30th Annual Conference of the Australian Psychological Society, Perth.

Ford, I. W., & Gordon, S. (1997). *Matching support with stress during rehabilitation: Case studies of injured athletes.* Unpublished manuscript, Department of Human Movement, The University of Western Australia, Nedlands.

Frith, D. (1990). *By his own hand: A study of cricket's suicides.* Crows Nest, NSW: Australian Broadcasting Company.

Goffman, E. (1956). Embarrassment and social organization. *American Journal of Sociology, 62,* 264–274.

Good, A. J., Brewer, B. W., Petitpas, A. J., Van Raalte, J. L., & Mahar, M. T. (1993, Spring). Identity foreclosure, athletic identity, and college sports participation. *The Academic Athletic Journal,* 1–12.

Gordon, S. (1995). Career transitions in competitive sport. In T. Morris & J. Summers (Eds.), *Sport psychology: Theory, applications and issues* (pp. 474–501). Brisbane: Wiley.

Greendorfer, S. L., & Blinde, E. M. (1985). Retirement from intercollegiate sports: Theoretical and empirical considerations. *Sociology of Sport Journal, 2,* 101–110.

Grove, J. R., & Heard, N. P. (1997). *Performance slumps in sport: Appraisal processes and perceived stress.* Unpublished manuscript, Department of Human Movement, The University of Western Australia, Nedlands.

Harris, D. S., & Eitzen, D. S. (1978). The consequences of failure in sport. *The Journal of Ethnographic Research, 7,* 177–188.

Harvey, J. H. (1996). *Embracing their memory: Loss and the social psychology of story-telling.* Needham Heights, MA: Allyn & Bacon.

Harvey, J. H., Orbuch, T. L., Chwalisz, K. D., & Garwood, G. (1991). Coping with sexual assault: The roles of account-making and confiding. *Journal of Traumatic Stress, 4,* 515–531.

Heil, J. (Ed.). (1993). *Psychology of sport injury.* Champaign, IL: Human Kinetics.

Hobfoll, S. E. (1988). *The ecology of stress.* New York: Hemisphere.

Lavallee, D., Gordon, S., & Grove, J. R. (1997). Retirement from sport and the loss of athletic identity. *Journal of Personal and Interpersonal Loss, 2,* 129–147.

Lynch, G. P. (1988). Athletic injuries and the practising sport psychologist: Practical guidelines for assisting athletes. *The Sport Psychologist, 2,* 161–167.

McDonald, S. A., & Hardy, C. J. (1990). Affective response patterns of the injured athlete: An exploratory analysis. *The Sport Psychologist, 4,* 261–274.

Messner, M. A. (1992). *Power at play: Sports and the problem of masculinity.* Boston: Beacon Press.

Mihovilovic, M. (1968). The status of former sportsmen. *International Review of Sport Sociology, 3,* 73–93.

Murphy, G. M., Petitpas, A. J., & Brewer, B. W. (1996). Identity foreclosure, athletic identity, and career maturity in intercollegiate athletes. *The Sport Psychologist, 10,* 239–246.

Murphy, S. M. (1995). Transitions in competitive sport: Maximizing individual potential. In S. M. Murphy (Ed.), *Sport psychology interventions* (pp. 331–346). Champaign, IL: Human Kinetics.

Newman, B. (1991, March 11). The last return. *Sports Illustrated,* pp. 38–42.

Ogilvie, B. C., & Howe, M. A. (1984, July). Beating slumps at their own game. *Psychology Today,* 28–32.

Ogilvie, B. C., & Taylor, J. (1993). Career termination in sports: When the dream dies. In J. M. Williams (Ed.), *Applied sport psychology: Personal growth to peak performance* (2nd ed., pp. 356–365). Mountain View, CA: Mayfield.

Pargman, D. (Ed.). (1993). *Psychological bases of sport injuries.* Morgantown, WV: Fitness Information Technology.

Pedersen, P. (1986). The grief response and injury: A special challenge for athletes and athletic trainers. *Athletic Training, 21,* 312–314.

Peretz, D. (1970). Development, object-relationships, and loss. In B. Schoenberg, A. C. Carr, D. Peretz, & A. H. Kutscher (Eds.), *Loss and grief: Psychological practice in medical practice* (pp. 3–19). New York: Columbia University Press.

Petitpas, A., & Danish, S. (1995). Psychological considerations in caring for injured athletes. In S. M. Murphy (Ed.), *Sport psychology interventions* (pp. 255–281). Champaign, IL: Human Kinetics.

Prapavessis, H., & Grove, J. R. (1995). Ending batting slumps in baseball: A qualitative investigation. *The Australian Journal of Science and Medicine in Sport, 27,* 14–19.

Ryckman, R. M., Robbins, M. A., Thornton, B., & Cantrell, P. (1982). Development and validation of a physical self-efficacy scale. *Journal of Personality and Social Psychology, 42,* 891–900.

Sanderson, F. H., & Ashton, M. K. (1981). Analysis of anxiety levels before and after competition. *International Journal of Sport Psychology, 12,* 23–28.

Scanlan, T. K. (1977). The effects of success-failure on the perception threat in a competitive situation. *Research Quarterly, 48,* 144–153.

Smith, A. M., Scott, S. G., & Wiese, D. M. (1990). The psychological effects of sports injuries: Coping. *Sports Medicine, 9,* 352–369.

Staudacher, C. (1987). *Beyond grief.* Oakland, CA: New Harbinger.

Taylor, J. (1988). Slumpbusting: A systematic analysis of slumps in sport. *The Sport Psychologist, 2,* 39–48.

Wehlage, D. F. (1980). Managing the emotional reaction to loss in athletics. *Athletic Training, 15,* 144–146.

Werthner, P., & Orlick, T. (1986). Retirement experiences of successful Olympic athletes. *International Journal of Sport Psychology, 17,* 337–363.

Wilson, J. (1991). Efficiency and power in professional baseball players' employment contracts. *Sociology of Sport Journal, 8,* 326–340.

# 19

# *What is Lost by Not Losing: Losses Related to Body Weight*

**Carol T. Miller**
*University of Vermont*

The one loss heavyweight people would most like to have is the one most commonly denied them: losing weight. Prevalent beliefs about body weight include the notion that being obese or overweight, or, less pejoratively, heavyweight or fat results from a failure. Fat people are thought to lack self-discipline and self-control, and consequently cannot control their weight. From this perceived loss of control stems a number of losses. Heavyweight people's efforts to control their weight through dieting can result in loss of control over eating and the development of eating disorders. Prejudice against heavyweight people causes a loss of regard from others and limits the ability of fat people to control life outcomes. There are lost opportunities in education, employment, access to good medical care, and interpersonal relationships. Finally, there may be a loss of psychological adjustment and loss of body-satisfaction and self-esteem. This chapter will summarize some of the research that documents the existence of these weight-related losses. It will also examine how some of these losses may be avoided by compensating for the effects of prejudice.

## BODY WEIGHT AND PERCEIVED CONTROL

Most people believe that weight can be controlled by diet and exercise. The medical, diet, and exercise industries promote (and profit from) this view. There can be little dispute about the relationship between being fat and some health problems, for example, heart disease and diabetes. There also can be little debate about the basic tenet of weight loss theory: that weight loss will occur when calories consumed drop below calories expended. However, there is considerable debate about whether there are any practically useful weight loss programs. Many programs produce temporary, sometimes quite substantial weight losses, but long-term weight loss is rare (Heatherton, Polivy, & Herman, 1991; Cogan & Rothblum, 1993; Wilson & Brownell, 1980). Weight loss is difficult because there may be a strong genetic contribution to body weight and because, however a person becomes fat, being fat is associated with physiological and metabolic changes that tend to preserve existing levels of fat (Rodin, 1981). In their review of weight loss treatment studies conducted during the past two decades, Cogan and Rothblum (1993) reported that, "In general, participants were obese before treatment, still obese after treatment, and continued to be obese as long as they were followed up" (p. 408).

The perceived controllability of weight makes being heavyweight so stigmatizing that Crandall (1991) has called it one of the last remaining socially acceptable prejudices. In modern times most people are careful to conceal their negative reactions to ethnic minority groups, women, and people with disabilities (Gaertner & Dovidio, 1986; Monteith, 1993). People feel little compunction about experiencing or expressing negative reactions toward stigmatizing conditions that are perceived as being the fault of the stigmatized person. In this respect, heavyweight people are perceived in the same class as child abusers and drug addicts (Weiner, Perry, & Magnusson, 1988).

In the United States and other Western societies, the loss of self-control runs counter to cherished cultural values related to the Protestant work-ethic (Crandall, 1994). Surveys of people in the United States and Mexico (where such values are less important) show that prejudice against heavyweight people is stronger among people who place a high value on individualism and self-control (Crandall & Martinez, 1996). Experimental studies have shown that others evaluate heavyweight individuals less harshly than usual if their weight is described as a result of a medical condition such as a thyroid condition (DeJong, 1980; Rodin, Price, Sanchez, & McElligot, 1989).

## LOSSES RELATED TO PERCEIVED CONTROL

### Dieting and Control Over Eating

The people most likely to lose control over eating are those who have a history of attempting to lose weight by dieting (Lowe, 1993; Polivy & Herman, 1985). Experimental studies indicate that restrained eaters eat more after consuming a diet-breaking snack than do nondieters. Dieters also eat more when they are anxious or after consuming alcohol, whereas nondieters do not increase eating in these conditions (see Polivy and Herman, 1985, for a review). This and other research suggests that one effect of trying to restrain eating through dieting is binge eating (Heatherton & Baumeister, 1991). Dieting to control weight severs the connection between hunger pangs and eating. Most people who perceive themselves as too heavy believe that past overeating is a major cause. The widespread belief that overeating causes fatness leads heavyweight people and other dieters to lose confidence in feelings of hunger or satiety to guide their intake of food (Lowe, 1993). Consequently, social cues and other aspects of situations, such as the salience of palatable foods, assume greater importance in the regulation of eating. Despite their best efforts, dieting can destroy the ability of heavyweight people to regulate food intake according to physiological need and to maintain control over food intake.

### Loss of Control Over Responsiveness to External Stimuli

People who diet to control their weight are not necessarily fat, but dieting is especially prevalent among heavyweight people (Lowe, 1993; Polivy & Herman,

1985). Before the effects of restrained eating were understood as well as they are at present, one influential theory about the causes of heavyweight is that people become fat because they eat in response to external cues, for example, whether foods are highly palatable or easy to eat and whether it is mealtime, rather than in response to internal cues such as gastric motility (a growling stomach; Schachter & Rodin, 1974; Rodin, 1981). Experiments conducted to test this externality hypothesis compared the responsiveness of fat and thin people to external food-related cues. This research showed, for example, that heavyweight people ate more when foods were easy to eat (e.g., shelled peanuts) than when they were hard to eat (e.g., unshelled peanuts). They also ate more when in the presence of a clock that was rigged to advance the hour closer to mealtime than it really was. Thin people tend to eat the same regardless of such changes in the situation (Schachter & Rodin, 1974).

Subsequent research showed that heavyweight people also may be highly responsive to external non-food-related cues. Thus, externality appeared to be a general trait of heavyweight people. For example, heavyweight people who were seated in a room devoid of any objects or cues to indicate the passing of time thought that more time had passed when they were exposed to an intense auditory cues (frequent, loud tones) than when exposed to less intense auditory cues (infrequent, softer tones; Pliner, 1973a). Moderate-weight people's time estimates were less affected by variations in the tones. Other research indicates that heavyweight people are more responsive than moderate-weight people to visual cues (Pliner, 1973b), social cues (Pliner, Meyer, & Blankstein, 1974), and distraction (Rodin & Singer, 1976).

Ultimately, the externality hypothesis proved to be insufficient to explain the origins of heavyweight largely because researchers discovered there was a great deal of overlap in the externality of heavyweight and moderate-weight people (Rodin, 1981). Moreover, it became apparent that the tendency to be responsive to external cues could be a *consequence* of two effects that being heavyweight has on people. First, it causes them to diet. We have already seen that dieting is associated with responsiveness to salient food-related cues (Heatherton & Baumeister, 1991). Second, several of the experiments testing the externality of heavyweight people in response to non-food-related cues used social cues. This suggests that heavyweight people may have been concerned about how others were evaluating them (Krantz, 1978; Miller & Myers, 1998).

For example, Rodin and Slowchower (1974) found that heavyweight students were more likely to do a favor for a moderate-weight confederate than a heavyweight confederate. They interpreted this as evidence of the greater externality of heavyweight people. However, it also is possible that heavyweight students assumed that they needed to ingratiate themselves with the moderate-weight person because of the stigma associated with their weight. In fact, postexperimental interviews indicated that heavyweight students overwhelmingly indicated that their weight had been a factor in how the confederate had treated them during the experiment. Similarly, interacting with (Rodin & Slowchower, 1974) or being observed by (Rodin & Singer, 1976) a confederate had a greater impact on task performance of fat students than thin students. These findings were interpreted as evidence that distracting, irrelevant cues monopolize the attention of fat people, thereby threatening task performance. However, Miller and Myers (1998) pointed out that the attention of a potentially evaluative person may be extremely relevant to stigmatized people who must carefully attend to details of situations that might warn them of an impending prejudiced response.

## LOST OPPORTUNITIES

### Higher Education

Among high school students, weight is not related to educational goals, grades, enjoyment of school, or self-rated intelligence and ability (Crandall, 1995). However, college students on average are thinner than national norms for their sex, age, and height (Crandall, 1995). This suggests that heavier high school students are less likely to attend college than other students. Crandall (1991, 1995) believes that fat discrimination is the reason. One source of the discrimination might be expected. Canning and Mayer (1966) found that heavyweight students were less likely than thin students to attend Ivy League colleges, despite equivalent high school grades, entrance exam scores, and high school activities. Canning and Mayer thought they had identified the culprit responsible for this under-representation of heavyweight people. Ivy League colleges typically require an interview of prospective students, during which the heavyweight students' stigmatizing condition would become apparent. However, fat people are also under-represented in colleges that do not require interviews (Pargman, 1969).

This raises an interesting question. Who or what is responsible for heavyweight people not attending college? Crandall (1991, 1995) believes that there is discrimination from an unexpected source: the parents of fat children. He found that heavyweight college students, especially women, provide a greater share of their own support for college than do thinner students. A much higher proportion of thin women (74%) are supported by their parents than heavyweight women (53%; Crandall, 1995). Moreover, these effects occur even after variables that might be expected to affect parents' ability to provide college support for their offspring are controlled. These include parents' income, ethnic status, family size, and number of children attending college.

Parental withholding of financial support for heavyweight daughters is related to the parents' political conservatism (Crandall, 1991, 1995). Being fat is an anathema to those who espouse conservative ideology because of the value it places on self-control. Crandall's findings suggest that this value is salient enough to conservative parents that they may be willing to sacrifice the education of their heavyweight offspring. Loss of educational opportunity is likely to have profound effects of the lives of heavyweight people. They may be less well qualified than others for employment as a result.

### Employment

Heavyweight people may need all the qualifications they can get, because for them the world of employment can be a hostile place (Rothblum, Brand, Miller, &

Oetjen, 1990). The common stereotype of heavyweight people as being lazy, weak-willed, and lacking in self-discipline is not conducive to employment opportunities. Fat people are perceived as less well qualified than thin people, even when their qualifications are identical. Jobs associated with heavyweight people are either low-status jobs (e.g., maid) or those that require little physical activity (e.g., librarian; Heatherton, Kiwan, & Hebl, 1995). These negative stereotypes may lead to discrimination in hiring (Larkin & Pines, 1979, Rothblum et al., 1990).

## SES

Given their lost opportunities in education and employment, it should come as no surprise that heavyweight people tend to occupy the lower rungs of the socio-economic (SES) ladder in Western societies (Rothblum, 1994; Sobal & Stunkard, 1989). Although poverty and the diet associated with it could promote weight gain, there also is evidence of downward mobility among heavyweight people (Moore, Stunkard, & Srole, 1962). This is partly because of reduced opportunities in education and employment. For women, marriage also plays a role. Attractive women are more likely than less attractive women to marry men with higher SES than their parents'. Fat women are not perceived as attractive (Singh, 1993) and thus are likely to lose out in the competition for affluent, well-educated men.

## Health Care

Health care providers share society's general aversion toward heavyweight people (Maddox & Liederman, 1969). They may not always be able to disguise or ignore their negative reactions when they treat heavyweight people. A survey of very heavyweight people showed that one common situation in which they experienced prejudiced responses from others was when they interacted with health professionals (Myers & Rosen, 1996). The quality of care received by heavyweight people may be compromised because obesity may be so salient to health care providers that medical conditions unrelated to weight may be misdiagnosed or ignored (Millman, 1980). These experiences may lead fat people to avoid medical care (Adams, Smith, Wilbur, & Grady, 1993).

## Social Interactions

Children dislike heavyweight children more than they dislike children with other potentially stigmatizing conditions (for example, being confined to a wheel-chair or having a visual impairment; DeJong & Kleck, 1986). Being ignored or disliked by others may limit opportunities to develop the social skills that are needed to develop and sustain relationships. In a test of this hypothesis, Miller, Rothblum, Barbour, Brand, and Felicio (1990) had heavyweight and thin women converse by telephone with another person who never saw them and thus was never aware of their weight. After the conversation concluded, the women were rated by their telephone partners and by naive raters who listened to an audiotape of what the women said without having any other information about them. Results showed that fat women created more negative impressions than thin women did on both the telephone partners and the naive raters. This finding suggests that prejudice may limit fat people's opportunities to develop social skills.

One mechanism by which fat prejudice might compromise the social skills of fat people is expectancy confirmation processes that give rise to self-fulfilling prophecies. These processes recently were demonstrated in studies in which male college students were first shown a photograph of a fat or thin woman (Snyder & Haugen, 1994; 1995). They were (falsely) told that this represented the woman with whom they were about to speak. They then conversed by telephone with a female college student, who was randomly assigned to speak with men who had seen a photograph of a fat or thin woman. Thus, there was no actual relationship between the women's weight and the men's beliefs about their weight.

Men's ratings of the women showed that prior to the conversation, they expected the supposedly fat woman to be consistent with traits associated with negative stereotypes about fat people. These prejudiced expectations set the stage for a self-fulfilling prophecy. Ratings made of the men by people who listened to recordings of what the men said during the conversation showed that the men behaved in a more positive manner toward supposedly thin women than toward fat women. After the conversation was over, men's ratings of the women showed that they thought their expectations had been confirmed. Men who thought they spoke to a heavyweight woman rated her less positively on traits such as sociable, happy, enthusiastic, interesting, and socially skilled than did men who thought they spoke to a thin woman. This shows that the men believed that the women had confirmed their expectations. Moreover, ratings made by people who listened to what the women said without knowing anything about how they had been depicted to the men showed the men's expectations had become a reality. The women believed to be fat actually behaved in a more stereotypically fat manner than did the women believed to be thin.

Self-fulfilling prophecies are important in the lives of fat people and other stigmatized people because they may produce short- and long-term effects on their behavior and characteristics. Fortunately, self-fulfilling prophecy effects occur only under certain conditions. In the experiments just described, for example, the men's prejudicial treatment of fat women occurred only when the men had been told to check out their impressions of the women, not when they were told to try to get along with them (Snyder & Haugen, 1994). Similarly, the supposedly fat women responded to the men's treatment of them in a stereotype-consistent manner only when the women had been told to try to get along with the men (Snyder & Haugen, 1995).

The fact that stigmatized people may have some control over whether they conform or do not conform to negative expectations suggests that all is not lost in the relationships of heavyweight people. In fact, in a study in which fat and thin women completed a battery of measures about their social relationships, fat and thin women did not differ in the social support they said they received from others, the size of their social networks, social self-esteem, or social skills (Miller, Rothblum, Brand, & Felicio, 1995). These reports could reflect wishful thinking on the part of fat women. However, a friend and co-worker of each study participant also rated the women in these areas. Their judgments about the social lives of the fat or thin women they knew corroborated what the women had said.

## PSYCHOLOGICAL OUTCOMES

### Psychopathology

Given the losses heavyweight people face, it seems reasonable to conclude that they must suffer some psychological consequences. However, the finding that there were no discernable differences between the social lives of heavyweight and moderate-weight women (Miller et al., 1995) demonstrates a common finding of research on psychological correlates of being fat. Evidence that fat people suffer poor psychological adjustment has been surprisingly elusive.

For many years clinical psychologists have suspected that weight is associated with anxiety and depression. In a recent review of research on the issue, Friedman and Brownell (1995) concluded that this is not so. Friedman and Brownell (1995) pointed out, however, that heavyweight people, especially women, do seek psychological counseling for problems associated with their weight. Eating disorders and depression are prevalent symptoms. Participants in weight-loss treatment therapies or programs also have been found to be more depressed than the general population (Friedman & Brownell, 1995).

Friedman and Brownell (1995) argued that even though comparisons of general populations of fat and thin people reveal that fat people do not suffer from psychopathology more than other people do, there may be subpopulations of fat people who are at risk for psychological problems connected to weight. Women, especially adolescents, may suffer because appearance plays a major role in how women are perceived and evaluated by others. Moreover, standards for female body weights are very demanding and, many believe, unrealistic given biological factors governing the accumulation and distribution of female body fat (Rodin, Silbertstein, & Striegel-Moore, 1985). This may explain why heavyweight people who seek psychological therapy for weight-related problems are overwhelmingly female (Friedman & Brownell, 1995).

People who are perceived as extremely fat may also be at greater risk for psychological dysfunction. This may be because they experience more prejudice from others. In a survey of people who had participated in a weight loss treatment program or were candidates for gastric by-pass surgery, Myers and Rosen (1996) found that even among these very fat people (most of whom, on average, weighed more than 300 pounds), the more fat they were, the more frequently they reported having encountered specific instances of prejudiced responses from others. People who perceive themselves as heavyweight also are likely to diet to lose weight. Dieting is associated with two undesirable outcomes: binge eating and weight cycling (Friedman & Brownell, 1995). Friedman and Brownell identified both as risk factors for the development of psychopathology.

### Body-Satisfaction

One area in which heavyweight people consistently express more concern than thin people is body-satisfaction (Friedman & Brownell, 1995). Because prevailing norms for what constitutes acceptable body weight are now very demanding for women, body-dissatisfaction is rampant even among thin women. Most girls and women want to be thinner than they are (Heatherton & Baumeister, 1991; Polivy, Herman, & Pliner, 1990). However, among heavyweight people, body-dissatisfaction is even more prevalent (Friedman & Brownell, 1995).

## Self-Esteem

People usually assume that fat people have low self-esteem. This turns out to be true (Miller & Downey, 1998; Friedman & Brownell, 1995), but the reasons are a little more complex than they are often assumed to be. People who are the targets of prejudice can develop low self-esteem in several ways. We have already seen how negative expectations, for example, men's beliefs about heavyweight women, can produce behavior that conforms to those expectations (Snyder & Haugen, 1994, 1995). Other research shows that once behavioral confirmation has occurred, it can change self-perceptions (Snyder, 1984). That is, people who have been induced to behave in a stereotype-consistent fashion by the treatment they receive from others may perceive their own behavior as a reflection of their personal characteristics. In this way self-fulfilling prophecies can result in the internalization of negative stereotypes. Internalization can also occur more directly. One major theory of self-esteem is the "looking-glass self" model, which proposes that self-esteem is derived from the esteem of others (Mead, 1934; Shrauger & Schoeneman, 1979).

Crocker and Major (1989) noticed that despite theory and research indicating that prejudice should result in low self-esteem, many studies of stigmatized people indicate that there are no self-esteem differences between them and nonstigmatized people. They suggested this is because there are ways in which stigmatized people protect self-esteem from prejudice. One important way is that negative events can be attributed to prejudice rather than to shortcomings of the individual (Major & Crocker, 1993). Thus, a fat person who fails to get a job might conclude that the potential employer is prejudiced against fat people rather than that he or she did not interview well. This attributional strategy appears to effectively protect the self-esteem of stigmatized groups such as women and African-Americans. When presented with negative feedback, both groups attributed the feedback to prejudice and showed no reduction in self-esteem (Crocker, Voelkl, Testa, & Major, 1991).

However, the attributional strategy is not so effective for people who blame themselves for their stigmatizing condition because they think they could control it. When heavyweight college women received negative feedback from a man, they attributed the feedback to prejudice, but this attribution did not protect their self-esteem, which went down after the feedback (Crocker, Cornwell, & Major, 1993). Other ratings the women made indicated that the fat women did not blame the men for being prejudiced against them. Crocker et al. (1993) suggested that the perception of being to blame for being fat destroyed the self-protective function that attributing feedback to prejudice could otherwise have served.

This reasoning suggests that perceived controllability of a stigma will be an important factor in whether stigmatized people have low self-esteem. To test this hypothesis, Miller and Downey (1998) statistically compared results of existing studies of the relationship of body-weight and self-esteem with results of a review of the literature on the relationship of physical attractiveness and self-esteem (Feingold, 1992). Being fat and being unattractive are both very stigmatizing conditions that are easily discernable by others. However, being fat is generally perceived as the result of a failure to exercise self-control, but being unattractive is not. The hypothesis that perceived controllability influences whether stigmatized people have low self-esteem was supported by this comparison. Heavy body weight was more highly correlated with low self-esteem than was a lack of physical attractiveness. Once again, the losses associated with being heavyweight seem to stem from the loss of self-control that most people assume is responsible for the failure to lose weight.

## FOR EVERY LOSS, IS THERE A GAIN?

### Compensation for Prejudice

Prejudice is usually thought of as a threat to the well-being of stigmatized people, but it can also function as a challenge. A challenge has the quality of requiring the full use of one's abilities, and may even require acquiring new abilities. Without denying the substantial negative impacts of stigma, Miller and Myers (1998) have proposed that stigmatized people develop and use skills that enable them to avoid some of the negative outcomes they would otherwise receive due to the prejudice of others. Stigmatized people may supplement defensive strategies, such as the attributional strategy described above, that buffer the adverse effects of negative outcomes that occur because of prejudice with skills and strategies that circumvent or compensate for the prejudice of others, thereby preventing the negative outcomes from occurring.

The inspiration for this view was a study of heavyweight and moderate-weight women (Miller, Rothblum, Felicio, & Brand, 1995). These women conversed by telephone with another person who actually could see them on a video monitor during the conversation or could not see them. Thus, the other person's prejudice against fat women was either activated (when the women could be seen) or not activated (when they could not be seen). So far, this study is similar to many others that have been conducted on self-fulfilling prophecies. However, there was an additional experimental manipulation. The women also were informed that the person to whom they spoke either could or could not see them. Whether or not this information was accurate depended, of course, on whether the other person really could see them.

Results of this experiment showed that heavyweight women were perceived more negatively by their telephone partners after the conversation was over only if the women actually were visible to their partners, but the women thought they were not visible. In other words, heavyweight women were able to overcome their partners' negative reaction to their appearance provided that they knew that their partners knew what they looked like. This suggests that heavyweight women may have been able to compensate for the effects of their partners' prejudice. Ratings made by the women who spoke to female (but not male) telephone partners showed that heavyweight women who thought they were visible rated themselves as more likable and socially skilled before and after the conversation than thin women did. There was no difference between fat and thin women's self-ratings when the women thought they were not visible. This suggests that fat women may have approached this social situation as a challenge—a situation that called for optimal employment of their social skills.

Results of this study appear to contradict the study described earlier (Miller et al., 1990) in which fat and thin women conversed by telephone with someone who never saw them. In that study fat women were perceived more negatively than thin women were. A critical difference between the two studies is whether there was a possibility that the heavyweight women's stigma was apparent to the other person. In the most recent study (Miller, Rothblum, Felicio, & Brand, 1995), there was the potential for prejudice to affect how the other reacted to the women, and the women knew this. In the earlier study (Miller et al., 1990) there was no possibility that prejudice might be important, and the women knew this.

## What is Lost by Compensation

This suggests that just as the losses associated with prejudice may be partly alleviated by gaining the ability to counteract them, so too might the ability to counteract prejudice be associated with a loss. This loss can be seen in the behavior of fat women who think they are not visible to others. Why do they make a more negative impression than thin women? They clearly have the ability to make impressions on others that are as positive as those made by thin women, even if the person to whom they are speaking is aware of their stigmatizing condition (Miller et al., 1995). What happens in the conditions in which they think they are not visible?

The answer may lie in the attributions that are required to successfully compensate for others' prejudice. In order to do so, the fat person must be aware that prejudice is a potential problem, have a strategy for dealing with the problem, and then carry out the strategy. Expectations about the influence of prejudice may lead to the possibly erroneous assumption that everything would proceed smoothly with minimal or no effort—if only the person were not fat or the other were not prejudiced. This "if only" thinking may lead fat people and other stigmatized people to develop unrealistic views about what level of skills people in general need to use in situations in which prejudice is not a potential threat.

Consequently, when they find themselves in a situation such as those investigated by Miller et al. (1990) in which the other person is not prejudiced (because the other cannot see their stigmatizing condition, and thus has no knowledge of it), they may use less effort and skill than a nonstigmatized person in the same situation would. Another example of the harm "if only" thinking may cause is that people who remedy a physical condition that they believe exposes them to the prejudice of others by, for example, cosmetic surgery or weight loss, may not enjoy the expected benefit to self-esteem. This is because life problems that they previously attributed to a particular aspect of appearance may continue even though the physical feature that was assumed to create the problems has now been remedied.

## What is Gained by Compensation

Although the tendency to "slack off" in the presumed absence of prejudice may be problematic in some situations, the skills and efforts that may enable fat people and other stigmatized people to overcome prejudice represent a real gain. Frable, Blackstone, & Scherbaum (1990) found, for example, that being deviant (including being heavyweight) was associated with better memory for details about a social interaction. Stigmatized people also are more accurate about the behaviors and characteristics of nonstigmatized people than vice versa (Ryan, 1996). This could be because stigmatized people need more information about others in order to deal with problems that can arise because of the others' prejudice (Miller & Myers, 1998). Being especially responsive to changes in situations helps stigmatized people negotiate the perils of interacting with possibly prejudiced people.

As we have already seen, the tendency for heavyweight people to be influenced by external cues was an important element of the externality hypothesis about the causes of being fat (Schachter & Rodin, 1974). At the time that research was conducted, externality was considered to be something of a defect. Externality was described as a loss of internal control over behavior and cognitions. An alternative way to think about externality is that it is a skill. In fact, another type of person who is extremely responsive to situations is one high in the characteristic of self-monitoring (Snyder, 1974). High self-monitoring people are attuned to situational cues that inform them about what behaviors are appropriate to meet the demands of the situation. Not only are they attentive to situational skills, but they also are skilled in fitting into diverse situations (see Snyder, 1979, for a review). Low self-monitoring individuals, in contrast, tend to behave in accord with internal standards and are infrequently willing or able to change their behavior to match the changing demands of different situations. It is interesting that the description of high self-monitoring people seems to embody some of the skills that stigmatized people may acquire to compensate for prejudice. It also is interesting that research on the externality of heavyweight people indicates that they may have many of the characteristics of high self-monitoring people. In fact, Younger and Pliner (1976) administered a measure of self-monitoring to fat and thin high school and college students. They found that heavyweight people were higher in self-monitoring.

## The Ultimate Weight-Related Loss

Research on how heavyweight women compensate for prejudice indicates that there may be factors that help prevent losses associated with the stigma of being fat. One of the most important may be the ability to reject or ignore society's dictates about acceptable body weight. One group of people who appear to have done just this are African-American women. African-American girls have a larger (and, many would argue, more realistic) ideal about body weight than white girls do (Collins, 1991). African-American women also have more favorable impressions of large women than white women do on dimensions such as happiness, popularity, and relationship satisfaction (Heatherton, Kiwan, & Hebl, 1995). They also appear to base their self-esteem less on body size than whites do (Kerr, Crocker, & Broadnax, 1995).

Heatherton et al. (1995) suggested that being fat is less stigmatizing for African-Americans because it is more prevalent than it is among whites, in part because of the relationship of SES to being fat. Being fat is not only less statistically deviant for African-Americans, but it also may have a different meaning. As was described above, fat prejudice is especially prevalent among people who hold conservative values (Crandall, 1994). African-Americans, on average, have less of a vested interest in maintaining the status quo than whites do, and thus are less likely to subscribe to conservative ideologies. Moreover, because African-Americans are stigmatized for their race, they tend to reject or disidentify with dominant cultural values (Steele & Aronson, 1995; Major & Schmader, 1998). This might include disidentification with the value of thinness (Heatherton et al., 1995).

Disidentification with mainstream culture is a powerful tool in the arsenal of stigmatized people. African-Americans, for example, have a strong group identity that supports in-group favoritism (Judd, Park, Ryan, Brauer, and Kraus, 1995; Ryan, 1996). Perhaps the ultimate loss for fat people is that they tend not to identify with other fat people (Crandall, 1994). One reason is that most fat people think of themselves as temporarily fat, a belief that discourages group cohesion. Unlike African-Americans and other stigmatized groups, heavyweight people exhibit prejudice toward their own group (Crandall, 1994). Fat people may therefore be denied the comfort and social support that strong group identification can provide.

## REFERENCES


Adams, C. H., Smith, N. J., Wilbur, D. C., & Grady, K. E. (1993). The relationship of obesity to the frequency of pelvic examinations: Do physician and patient attitudes make a difference? *Women and Health, 20,* 45–57.

Canning, H., & Mayer, J. (1966). Obesity—Its possible effect on college acceptance. *New England Journal of Medicine, 275,* 1172–1174.

Cogan, J. C., & Rothblum, E. D. (1993). Outcomes of weight-loss programs. *Genetic, Social, and General Psychology Monographs, 118,* 385–415.

Collins, M. E. (1991). Body figure perceptions and preferences among preadolescent children. *International Journal of Eating Disorders, 10,* 199–208.

Crandall, C. S. (1991). Do heavyweight students have more difficulty paying for college? *Personality and Social Psychology Bulletin, 17,* 601–611.

Crandall, C. S. (1994). Prejudice against fat people: Ideology and self-interest. *Journal of Personality and Social Psychology, 66,* 882–894.

Crandall, C. S. (1995). Do parents discriminate against their heavyweight daughters? *Personality and Social Psychology Bulletin, 21,* 724–735.

Crandall, C. S., & Martinez, R. (1996). Culture, ideology, and antifat attitudes. *Personality and Social Psychology Bulletin, 22,* 1165–1176.

Crocker, J., Cornwell, B., & Major, B. (1993). The affective consequences of attributional ambiguity: The case of overweight women. *Journal of Personality and Social Psychology, 64,* 60–70.

Crocker, J., & Major, B. (1989). Social stigma and self-esteem: The self-protective properties of stigma. *Psychological Review, 96,* 608–630.

Crocker, J., Voelkl, K., Testa, M., & Major, B. (1991). Social stigma: The affective consequences of attributional ambiguity. *Journal of Personality and Social Psychology, 60,* 218–228.

DeJong, W. (1980). The stigma of obesity: The consequences of naive assumptions concerning the causes of physical deviance. *Journal of Health and Social Behavior, 21,* 75–87.

DeJong, W., & Kleck, R. E. (1986). The social psychological effects of overweight. In C. P. Herman, M. P. Zanna, & E. T. Higgins (Eds.), *Physical appearance, stigma, and social behavior: The Ontario Symposium. Vol. 3* (pp. 65–88). Hillsdale, NJ: Lawrence Erlbaum.

Feingold, A. (1992). Good-looking people are not what we think. *Psychological Bulletin, 111,* 304–341.

Frable, D. E. E., Blackstone, T., & Scherbaum, C. (1990). Marginal and mindful: Deviants in social interaction. *Journal of Personality and Social Psychology, 59,* 140–149.

Friedman, M. A., & Brownell, D. D. (1995). Psychological correlates of obesity: Moving to the next research generation. *Psychological Bulletin, 117,* 3–20.

Gaertner, S. L., & Dovidio, J. F. (1986). The aversive form of racism. In J. F. Dovidio & S. L. Gaertner (Eds.), *Prejudice, discrimination, and racism* (pp. 61–89). San Diego, CA: Academic Press.

Heatherton, T. F., & Baumeister, R. F. (1991). Binge eating as escape from self-awareness. *Psychological Bulletin, 110,* 86–108.

Heatherton, T. F., Kiwan, D., & Hebl, M. R. (1995). *The stigma of obesity in women: The difference is Black and White.* Paper presented at the Annual Meeting of the American Psychological Association, August, New York.

Heatherton, T. F., Polivy, J., & Herman, C. P. (1991). Restraint, weight loss, and variability of body weight. *Journal of Abnormal Psychology, 100,* 78–83.

Judd, C. M., Park, N., Ryan, C. S., Brauer, M., & Kraus, S. (1995). Stereotypes and ethnocentrism: Diverging perceptions of African American and White American youth. *Journal of Personality and Social Psychology, 69,* 460–481.

Kerr, K., Crocker, J., & Broadnax, S. A. (1995). *Thinking you're fat and feeling depressed: Race differences.* Paper presented at the Annual Meeting of the American Psychological Association, August, New York.

Krantz, D. S. (1978). The social context of obesity research: Another perspective on its place in the field of social psychology. *Personality and Social Psychology Bulletin, 4,* 177–184.

Larkin, J. E., & Pines, H. A. (1979). No fat persons need apply. *Sociology of Work and Occupations, 6,* 312–327.

Lowe, M. R. (1993). The effects of dieting on eating behavior: A three-factor model. *Psychological Bulletin, 114,* 100–121.

Maddox, G. L., & Liederman, V. (1969). Overweight as a social disability with medical implications. *Journal of Medical Education, 44,* 210–220.

Major, B., & Crocker, J. (1993). Social stigma: The consequences of attributional ambiguity. In D. M. Mackie & D. L. Hamilton (Eds.), *Affect, cognition, and stereotyping: Interactive processes in group perception* (pp. 345–370). San Diego, CA: Academic Press.

Major, B., & Schmader, T. (1998). Coping with stigma: The role of psychological disengagement. In J. K. Swim & C. Stangor (Eds.), *Prejudice: The target's perspective* (pp. 219–241). San Diego, CA: Academic Press.

Mead, G. H. (1934). *Mind, self, and society.* Chicago, IL: University of Chicago Press.

Miller, C. T., & Downey, K. (1996). *A meta-analysis of heavyweight and self-esteem.* Unpublished manuscript, University of Vermont, Burlington, VT.

Miller, C. T., & Myers, A. (1998). Compensating for prejudice: How heavyweight people (and others) control outcomes despite prejudice. In J. K. Swim & C. Stangor (Eds.), *Prejudice: The target's perspective* (pp. 191–217). San Diego CA: Academic Press.

Miller, C. T., Rothblum, E. D., Barbour, L., Brand, P. A., & Felicio, D. (1990). Social interactions of obese and nonobese women. *Journal of Personality, 58,* 365–380.

Miller, C. T., Rothblum, E. D., Brand, P. A., & Felicio, D. M. (1995). Do obese women have poorer social relationships than nonobese women? Reports by self, friends, and co-workers. *Journal of Personality, 63,* 65–85.

Miller, C. T., Rothblum, E. D., Felicio, D., & Brand, P. (1995). Compensating for stigma: Obese and nonobese women's reactions to being visible. *Personality and Social Psychology Bulletin, 21,* 1193–1106.

Millman, M. (1980). *Such a pretty face.* New York: W. W. Norton.

Monteith, M. J. (1993). Self-regulation of prejudiced responses: Implications for progress in prejudice-reduction efforts. *Personality and Social Psychology Bulletin, 65,* 469–485.

Moore, M. E., Stunkard, A., & Srole, L. (1962). Obesity, social class, and mental illness. *Journal of the American Medical Association, 181,* 138–142.

Myers, A., & Rosen, J. (1996). *Obesity stigma and coping: Relationship with mental health symptoms, body-image, and self-esteem.* Unpublished manuscript, University of Vermont, Burlington, VT.

Pargman, D. (1969). The incidence of obesity among college students. *Journal of School Health, 39,* 621–627.

Pliner, P. (1973a). Effects of cue salience on the behavior of obese and normal subjects. *Journal of Abnormal Psychology, 82,* 226–232.

Pliner, P. (1973b). Effect of external cues on the thinking behavior of obese and normal subjects. *Journal of Abnormal Psychology, 82,* 233–238.

Pliner, P., Meyer, P., & Blankstein, K. (1974). Responsiveness to affective stimuli by obese and normal individuals. *Journal of Abnormal Psychology, 83,* 74–80.

Polivy, J., & Herman, C. P. (1985). Dieting and bingeing: A causal analysis. *American Psychologist, 40,* 193–201.

Polivy, J., Herman, C. P., & Pliner, P. (1990). Perceptions and evaluation of body image: The meaning of body shape and size. In J. M. Olson & M. P. Zanna (Eds.), *Self-inference processes: The Ontario Symposium, Volume 6* (pp. 87–114). Hillsdale, NJ: Lawrence Erlbaum.

Rodin, J. (1981). Current status of the internal-external hypothesis for obesity: What went wrong? *American Psychologist, 36,* 361–372.

Rodin, J., Silberstein, L. R., & Striegel-Moore, R. H. (1985). Women and weight: A normative discontent. In T. B. Sonderreger (Ed.), *Nebraska Symposium on Motivation: Vol. 32. Psychology and gender* (pp. 267–307). Lincoln, NE: University of Nebraska Press.

Rodin, J., & Singer, J. L. (1976). Eye-shift, thought, and obesity. *Journal of Personality, 44,* 594–610.

Rodin, J., & Slowchower, J. Fat chance for a favor: Obese-normal differences in compliance and incidental learning. *Journal of Personality and Social Psychology, 29,* 557–565.

Rodin, M., Price, J., Sanchez, F., & McElligot, S. (1989). Derogation, exclusion, and unfair treatment of persons with social flaws: Controllability of stigma and attribution of prejudice. *Personality and Social Psychology Bulletin, 15,* 439–451.

Rothblum, E. D. (1994). "I'll die for the revolution but don't ask me not to diet": Feminism and the continuing stigmatization of obesity. In P. Fallon, M. A. Katzman, & S. C. Wooley (Eds.), *Feminist perspectives on eating disorders* (pp. 53–76). New York: Guilford Press.

Rothblum, E. D., Brand, P. A., Miller, C. T., & Oetjen, H. (1990). The relationship between obesity, employment discrimination, and employment-related victimization. *Journal of Vocational Behavior, 37,* 251–266.

Ryan, C. S. (1996) Accuracy of Black and White college students' in-group and out-group stereotypes. *Personality and Social Psychology Bulletin, 22,* 1114–1127.

Schachter, S., & Rodin, J. (1974). *Obese humans and rats.* Washington, D.C.: Erlbaum/Halsted.

Shrauger, J., & Schoeneman, T. (1979). Symbolic interactionist view of self-concept: Through the looking glass darkly. *Psychological Bulletin, 86,* 549–573.

Singh, D. (1993). Adaptive significance of female physical attractiveness: Role of waist-to-hip ratio. *Journal of Personality and Social Psychology, 65,* 293–307.

Snyder, M. (1974). Self-monitoring of expressive behavior. *Journal of Personality and Social Psychology, 30,* 526–537.

Snyder, M. (1979). Self-monitoring processes. In L. Berkowitz (Ed.), *Advances in experimental social psychology. Vol. 12* (pp. 85–128). New York: Academic Press.

Snyder, M. (1984). When belief creates reality. In L. Berkowitz (Ed.), *Advances in experimental social psychology. Vol. 18* (pp. 247–305). San Diego, CA: Academic Press.

Snyder, M., & Haugen, J. A. (1994). Why does behavioral confirmation occur? A functional perspective on the role of the perceiver. *Journal of Experimental Social Psychology, 30,* 218–246.

Snyder, M., & Haugen, J. A. (1995). Why does behavioral confirmation occur? A functional perspective on the role of the target. *Personality and Social Psychology Bulletin, 21,* 963–974.

Sobal, J., & Stunkard, A. J. (1989). Socioeconomic status and obesity: A review of the literature. *Psychological Bulletin, 105,* 260–275.

Steele, C. M., & Aronson, J. (1995). Stereotype threat and the intellectual performance of African Americans. *Journal of Personality and Social Psychology, 69,* 797–811.

Weiner, B., Perry, R. P., & Magnusson, J. (1988). An attributional analysis of reactions to stigmas. *Journal of Personality and Social Psychology, 55,* 738–748.

Wilson, G. T., & Brownell, K. D. (1980). Behavior therapy for obesity: An evaluation of treatment outcome. *Advances in Behavior Research and Therapy, 3,* 49–86.

Younger, J. C., & Pliner, P. (1976). Obese-normal differences in the self-monitoring of expressive behavior. *Journal of Research in Personality, 10,* 112–115.

# 20

# *Homelessness and Loss: Conceptual and Research Considerations*

**Gary A. Morse**
*University of Missouri–St. Louis*

*Home is the sanctuary where the healing is. . . . Nothing brings as quickly to mind the horror of natural upheaval, civil strife or war as the picture of the "homeless." The deprivation of the security of the home is the worst of the mass tragedies.*
—Walter Cronkite (*Reader's Digest,* August 1970).

Evidence from divergent sources—research publications, mass media reports, a casual drive through the downtowns of most large cities—points to the sad fact that many people reside without a home. Since the early 1980s, homelessness has constituted a major social problem in the United States. As others have observed, the problem has continued to grow despite increasing attention (Rossi, 1989).

Estimates of the extent of homelessness in the United States have ranged widely and triggered scientific and political controversy. The estimates have varied in part due to different definitions of homelessness (especially whether the count was limited to literally homeless or included people who were living in overcrowded housing situations). The term homeless is used here to include people who are sleeping in shelters, the streets, parks, abandoned buildings, or other public or private places not normally used for residency. It does not include the millions of people who are "doubled up," staying with family or friends, nor living in substandard housing; these individuals, who also experience significant difficulties, represent the "near-homeless" and the problem of a shortage of affordable housing, rather than the "literally homeless" (Rossi, 1989) Estimates have also varied significantly because of varying methodological approaches. Recent research by Link and colleagues (1994) corrected for some of the earlier methodological deficiencies in a study that examined five-year and lifetime prevalence rates of homelessness in a national random-digit dialing telephone study. Results from Link's study, which is the most methodologically sophisticated study yet conducted, indicated a prevalence rate of literal homelessness of 7.4% or 13.5 million people in the United States who had been homeless at some point in their lives. The prevalence rate for those people who had been literally homeless for the five-year period of 1985 through 1990 was 3.1% or 5.7 million people.

Just as the number of people who are homeless has increased dramatically, so too has there been an explosion of social science and health research on homelessness. In particular, researchers have directed their attention to counting the number of homeless people, describing their demographic and social characteristics, and identifying the common needs and problems of the homeless, especially within the domains of mental health, health, and social services (e.g., Robertson & Greenblatt, 1992). More recently, greater thought has also been given to service and treatment approaches (e.g., Dixon, Krauss, Kernan, Lehman, & DeForge, 1995; Morse et al., 1996). Despite the exponential growth in research, it is striking how little thought or research has focused on understanding the phenomena of loss and homelessness. There is also a corresponding paucity of work on the process of recovery from homelessness and its associated losses. This appears to be a critical gap in our current knowledge, given that loss appears to be intensely and invariably involved in homelessness.

The goal of this chapter is to provide a preliminary conceptualization and review of loss and homelessness. A key premise of this chapter is that loss is not only intimately intertwined with homelessness, but that it is a complex phenomena involving multiple types and layers of losses. The paper provides a conceptualization of the major factors related to homelessness and loss. In describing these factors, an effort is made to synthesize relevant research, where it is available, and to offer preliminary thoughts about the nature of the phenomena of loss as related to homelessness and the need for additional research. The next section of this chapter focuses on the experience of becoming and being homeless.

## BECOMING AND BEING HOMELESS

In lectures about homelessness to students and the general public I have often asked participants to engage in a visualization exercise. The exercise calls for the audience to close their eyes, let go of extraneous thoughts, and then imagine their own homes. People are asked to visualize home in some detail, and then to be aware of the emotions they are feeling. After a minute or two, participants are instructed to imagine that they had lost their home for some reason such as finances, unemployment, or disability, and to visualize themselves walking on the sidewalk of downtown, thinking about where they might spend the night. Individuals are again asked to be aware of the emotions they are feeling. After a couple of minutes, the audience is instructed to let the image go and to slowly open their eyes. The group is then invited to share their feelings from both scenarios, imagining home and imagining themselves walking the streets without a place of their own.

Individuals invariably share that home is associated with a range of positive emotions, including warmth, comfort, security, peace. There is often a feeling of belonging reported, and a sense of support from loved ones. These feelings are in stark contrast to people's perceptions of what it would feel like to lose one's home. In this scenario, a sense of fear is predominant, along with feelings of a loss of security, belonging, identity, and well-being.

We cannot, of course, extrapolate perfectly from the imagined responses of the general public in a visualization exercise to the actual experience of becoming homeless. However, the responses do remind us that a home connotes far more than physical shelter, and that becoming homeless is likely to involve a complex set of emotions laden with emotional, social, and material loss. It is a popular adage that "home is where the heart is." The saying itself implies the fundamental and deep sense of emotional loss that is inherent in becoming homeless.

My own observations in the field (drawing at the moment more from clinical experience and case studies than quantitative data) suggest that the immediate experience of people who become homeless is similar to the imagined responses of students and lay citizens. People who first enter homeless shelters or the streets often typically experience the event as traumatic. Like with other traumatic events, individual responses vary widely, but across people there appear to be common emotional reactions, or phases, to becoming homeless. The initial phase of this trauma or loss is often characterized by heightened fear, anxiety, and insecurity. Within this first phase, however, the emotions and feelings of loss are multiple and diverse. There are often strong feelings of loss, including the loss of belonging, and the loss of the companionship and the support of loved ones. There is also a sense of loss of physical comfort, as one has to sleep on cots or out "rough" on the streets or within a large warehouse shelter rather than a family or individual home. Typically, there are also feelings of loss of material possessions, not only of apartments per se but of treasured furniture, clothing, and personal belongings. This loss often deepens over time, since the longer a person stays homeless, the less likely he or she is able to keep personal belongings without their becoming lost or stolen. Not suprisingly, throughout this phase of being homeless, which typically involves a constellation of disturbing feelings, the individual feels overwhelmed and unable to cope.

Anger is another emotion that is often present initially, but it sometimes becomes more pronounced and may indicate a second phase of being homeless for some people. The anger is often directed at someone else who may have abused, stolen, taken advantage of, or in some way "let down" the homeless individual. Over time, however, the intensity and type of angry feelings seem to shift. Feelings of personal anger seem to fade somewhat, but a number of homeless people speak increasingly with a sense of injustice, a bitterness which is more diffuse but which implicates service systems, which have failed to help, and society at large, which had promised "the good life," a life which is tremendously discrepant with the extreme poverty of living continuously in shelters or on the streets. People during this phase grow increasingly alienated from society and mistrustful of others, including human service workers.

As homelessness persists, a number of individuals develop a susbequent phase, one of despair. During this period, people who are homeless often seem to grow more demoralized. One of the greatest losses occurs during this phase, the loss of hope. Many people who are homeless lose hope and develop a sense of helplessness. These two feelings undoubtedly relate to the finding in one large study that more than one in five homeless people were contemplating suicide within the prior week (Morse et al., 1985). The despair often continues, at least until effective outreach and resources are offered to help people end homelessness.

Becoming and being homeless is the most central aspect of loss for this group of individuals. It is, however, not the only common experience of loss. People who are homeless typically have suffered multiple and repeated losses. These losses sometimes begin with early childhood experiences; they often also include losses that immediately precede homelessness, as well as co-occuring and pre-existing conditions. The next section explores these three associated facets of loss commonly involved in homelessness.

## ASSOCIATED ASPECTS OF LOSS

### Early and Developmental Losses

Relatively little research has been conducted on the developmental and early experiences of people who are homeless. It is striking, however, that the limited available research has tended to find that people who are currently homeless were likely as children to have experienced a major disruption or loss of normal family and home arrangements, such as being placed in institutional or foster care settings (e.g., Piliavin, Sosin, & Westerfelt, 1989; Sosin, Colson, & Grossman, 1988).

Case study reports (e.g., Morse et al., 1996; Spencer, Zawier, Tempelhoff, Morse, & Calsyn, 1994) are also noteworthy for the extent to which they describe childhoods replete with losses for many people who become homeless as adults. In particular, the stories of these individuals are often colored by frequent, premature, and sometimes traumatic losses of parents and other key family members. Another significant trend in many childhood case histories of homeless persons is the high frequency with which a parent or other significant family member suffered from severe mental illness or substance abuse. In this way, normal parent-child relationships were lost for many people who later became homeless.

The research is lacking at present to make definitive conclusions, especially of a causal nature. This is an important area for further investigation, but it seems likely that people who became homeless as adults suffered disproportionately a major loss of home or family members as children. It may well be that people who are homeless not only experienced excessive losses at an early age, but that these experiences created a vulnerability that contributed to homelessness in adulthood.

### Stressful Life Events

A second associated facet of loss involved in homelessness concerns stressful life events in the year prior to first becoming homeless. For many, this appears to be a critical period of life filled with important losses. In prior research we examined the extent to which men and women had experienced stressful life events in the year prior to first becoming homeless; the research focus previously was on the extent to which these stressful life events predicted current problems for homeless people, such as mental health symptoms and alcohol use (Calsyn & Morse, 1991, 1992). However, the nature and extent of the stressful life events themselves have been largely overlooked, and it appears that they include important experiences which relate to loss and homelessness.

In one study, we randomly selected and interviewed 248 homeless men and women who were representative of the adult shelter population in St. Louis (Morse et al., 1985). We assessed the frequency of life crises in the year prior to first becoming homeless using a 15-item scale of stressful life events used in other research studies with the general population and psychiatric patients (Moos, Cronkite, Billings, & Finney, 1982). Most of these stressful life event items involve some sort of major loss (death of a close friend, death of immediate family member, loss of job, etc. see Table 1). We found that the mean number of life crises for homeless people was 4.45; this was 3.3 times greater than the number of crises for the general population, and 1.9 times greater than the mean number for depressed psychiatric patients (comparative data from Moos et al., 1982). Thus, in the year preceding initial homelessness, people staying in shelters experienced far more life crises than either normal or depressed people do in one year's time. These crises not only diminished homeless people's social resources but they undoubtedly also left considerable grief even prior to the loss of home.

## Co-Occuring and Pre-Existing Conditions

Finally, the third associated facet of loss involves co-occuring and pre-existing conditions. One of the clear conclusions that has emerged from needs assessment and epidemiological research is that people who are homeless struggle not only with a lack of housing but with a plethora of other needs and problems as well (Ball & Havassy, 1984; Morse & Calsyn, 1986). It is particularly well documented that a majority of people who are homeless also experience a major, disabling health condition (Morse, 1986; Robertson & Greenblatt, 1992). Serious psychiatric

*Table 1.* Life crisis events

| Life event | Frequency |
|---|---|
| You lost something of sentimental value | 41.9 |
| A close friend died | 32.3 |
| You had trouble with friends and neighbors | 29.8 |
| You got separated from your spouse | 16.9 |
| Your got divorced | 3.2 |
| You had trouble with your in-laws | 16.1 |
| Your spouse died | 2.0 |
| An immediate family member other than your spouse died | 26.2 |
| Your had trouble with a boss | 23.1 |
| You got laid off or fired from a job | 35.9 |
| You were unemployed for a month or more | 78.9 |
| Your income decreased a lot | 58.5 |
| You went deeply into debt | 45.6 |
| Legal problems (arrest; other) | 31.3 |
| Assaulted or robbed | 28.7 |

Note. Frequencies are in percentages; they are independent for each life event, and therefore are not cumulative. (Adapted from Morse et al., 1985.)

disorders are common, with approximately one-third of people who are homeless having a serious mental illness (Dennis et al., 1991). In most cases, mental illness preceded homelessness (Morse et al., 1985). In addition to one-third of the homeless population having a major mental illness, about another one-third experience acute psychiatric distress (Morse & Calsyn, 1986).

A sizable subgroup of the homeless population also has a substance abuse disorder involving alcoholism or street drugs. Prevalence rates have been estimated to be between 30% and 45% percent (Schutt & Garrett, 1992). Psychiatric and substance abuse problems are often co-morbid among the homeless, with about 50% of those with major mental illness also having a co-occuring substance abuse disorder (Drake, Osher, & Wallach, 1991). General health problems are also extremely common, although a relatively small percentage have disabling physical conditions (Morse, 1986).

These disabling mental health and health conditions pose a number of challenges for individuals. The important implication for the present discussion is that they invariably involve loss and compound the experience of loss inherent in homelessness. The types of losses stemming from disabling conditions are multiple, but they include a loss of functioning. People with serious psychiatric disorders often suffer a loss of functioning in important roles, including as student, worker, spouse, and family member. Often, their functioning not only deteriorates, but they lose their social role altogether, becoming unemployed or estranged from family. People who are homeless often first began to experience significant psychiatric and substance abuse problems as teenagers. The early onset of these disorders typically affects the person's emotional and social development. In particular, there is a loss (or arrestment) of normal development. Many adults with long-standing disorders clinically appear to have delayed emotional maturity and diminished coping skills.

These disabilities and their associated losses affect the person's perspectives and mood. People with serious mental illness or long-term substance abuse disorders often feel a pervasive sense of lost opportunity in their own lives. They are often painfully aware of the major discrepancy between their long-held aspirations for educational attainment, successful careers, material success, and their current realities of disability and poverty. The losses often affect their inner world in a fundamental, nefarious manner. People who struggle with serious mental illness, chronic substance abuse, and homelessness often feel as if they have lost themselves. There is a loss of personal identity and personhood (Davidson, 1992). The stigma that surrounds psychiatric and substance abuse disorders chips away not only at the individual's self-esteem but at the underlying sense of self. Too often, people with serious psychiatric disability are treated as cases or "schizophrenics." These social pressures, in interaction with the distressing symptoms and emotions of their disorders, tend to rob individuals of their own sense of self, their basic humanity, and a sense of joy and pleasure in life.

Serious mental and substance abuse disorders are only one set of the commonly occurring phenomena that further laden the person who is homeless with loss. All too frequently, people who are homeless have also suffered sexual abuse and violence. In an early, cross-sectional study in St. Louis (Morse et al., 1985), we found that nearly 15% of the women who were homeless had been raped or otherwise sexually abused *while* they were homeless. Similarly, more than one in four (28.3%) of both men and women who were homeless had been beaten, robbed, or assaulted while they were homeless. Recent longitudinal research in Boston with homeless women found even much higher rates of total violence (Bassuk et al., 1996). The study found that 91.6% of homeless women suffered some form of violence during their lifetime. Not surprisingly, given the history of abuse and the high level of life crises, the prevalence of post traumatic stress disorder (PTSD) is exceedingly high; approximately 18% of homeless men and 34% of homeless women in one study were found to have a lifetime PTSD (North & Smith, 1992). These abuses add still another layer of loss to the lives of many homeless people.

Perhaps more pervasive but less extensively studied among the homeless are the effects of long-term poverty. From prior research (Morse et al., 1985), we know that most homeless people came from and remained in low socioeconomic status backgrounds. From case reports, it seems clear that some people experience the loss of disillusionment with the stereotypic American dream and a sense of loss for their own personal aspirations for an improved economic existence.

Up to this point, the chapter has focused on the experiences of loss and homelessness that occur for individuals. It is also important, however, to consider the loss related to homelessness that is occurring at a cultural level.

## SECONDARY LOSS

As others have discussed (Ferguson, 1990; Uzelac, 1990), the growing public sympathy toward homeless people began to fade by the late 1980s and early 1990s. In the early 1980s, helping the homeless was becoming a *crise celibrae* (Hopper, 1984). However, despite increasing government funding for services and resources and considerable volunteerism, homelessness did not cease. This is not surprising for two primary reasons. One, relatively little activity was directed at correcting the underlying societal and institutional causes creating homelessness (see Morse, 1992). Two, despite exponential growth in funding, the level of services and resources dedicated to helping homeless people remained woefully inadequate compared to the overall level of need. However, rather than recognizing and correcting the societal response, there has been some shift in public and governmental response toward the people who are homeless. There has been an increase in localities enacting tougher, more punitive measures toward homeless people, such as ordinances forbidding panhandling or sleeping in public places (Ferguson, 1990; Uzelac, 1990).

More insidious, however, is that there has been diminished interest in homelessness altogether. It appears that we have desensitized ourselves to the knowledge that hundreds of thousands of people must sleep in temporary shelters or the streets or abandoned buildings. As a culture we have come to act as if homelessness is an acceptable scene within the urban landscape. It no longer "shocks our moral sensibilities" (Hopper, Mauch, & Morse, 1990). Others have described the phenomena as "compassion fatigue" (see Ferguson, 1990; Uzelac, 1990). It can also be appropriately classified as a "secondary loss" (see Harvey, 1996, p. iv). As Harvey (1996) described in another context, this type of secondary loss involves putting up *barriers to grim news or to horrific realities. They are too much to bear, or we simply do not want to deal with them in their stark particulars. In a major way, these barrier-building or dismissive reactions are losses, too. They are losses of feeling and wisdom that cohere with diligent effort to understand the plight of others.*

In this way, the losses involved in homelessness affect more than those staying on the streets and in shelters. Unfortunately, it is clear that in our passive acceptance of homelessness we have lost an element of compassion and awareness as a people.

## RECOVERY

Given its inherent hardships and losses, it is a rather remarkable tribute to the durability of humankind that people do survive homelessness. Kim Hopper and his colleagues (Baxter & Hopper, 1981) were one of the first groups of researchers to carefully observe and describe the multifarious coping techniques that homeless people use for basic survival in adapting to homelessness. Over time, however, it has become clear that homeless people do more than simply survive homelessness. From outcome research, we know that people who are homeless and mentally ill improve significantly over time in such important domains as becoming stably housed, experiencing fewer psychiatric symptoms, and increasing in income (Dixon et al., 1995; Morse, Calsyn, Allen, Tempelhoff, & Smith, 1992; Morse et al., 1997). However, clinical experience and case studies (e.g., Morse, Calsyn, & Wolff, 1996) suggest that many people who were homeless change in important ways that are not captured by statistically significant differences in the means of quantitative outcome measures. The nature of this change is difficult to articulate, but it has to do with a qualitative and fundamental shift in the development of the person. There appears to be not only improved functioning, but a person who is stronger, more at peace, and more centered. The type of change that occurs in many people who were homeless seems to overlap significantly with the concept of recovery from severe mental illness (e.g., Anthony, 1993; Davidson, 1992). Anthony describes recovery as:

*a deeply personal, unique process of changing one's attitudes, values, feelings, goals, skills, and/or roles. It is a way of living a satisfying, hopeful, and contributing life even with limitations caused by illness. Recovery involves the development of new meaning and purpose in one's life as one grows beyond the catastrophic effects of mental illness. . . . Successful recovery from a catastrophe does not change the fact that the experience has occurred. . . . Successful recovery does mean that the person has changed, and the meaning of these facts to the person has therefore changed.* (p. 15)

The aspect of new meaning and purpose is central to most discussions of recovery among people with severe mental illness. Another important facet emphasized by other recovery researchers is the person's sense of self (Davidson, 1992). In particular, the rediscovery and reconstruction of "an enduring sense of the self as an active and responsible agent separate from the illness" is seen as a critical element (Davidson, 1992, p. 7).

People who experience homelessness (especially prolonged homelessness), whether or not they have a severe mental illness, sometimes seem to undergo a significant, qualitative change over time as they become stably housed. The process, for many, overlaps with overcoming severe mental illness or substance abuse, but there also seems to be an element related to recovering from homelessness itself, an experience which is unique for each individual but which all too often involves hardships, degradation, and multiple losses. At present, we know little about the experience or process of recovery from homelessness. It is an important area for further thought and research. Future workers would do well to describe the nature and process of recovery from homelessness, to delineate its similarities from recovery from severe mental illness, trauma, and substance abuse among non-homeless people, and to relate the experience to the universal aspects of loss and recovery inherent in life (Campbell,1988). Such research also needs to be longitudinal, bearing in mind T. S. Eliot's words (as cited in Davidson, 1992): "There is only the fight to recover what has been lost/ And found and lost again and again."

## CONCLUSION

Relatively little thought or research has been directed to the topic but it is clear that homelessness is an area imbued with loss. The losses involved in homelessness are multidetermined. As discussed, becoming and being homeless is a fundamental, significant experience of loss. It invariably involves serious and multiple social, material, and psychological losses. The loss of home is traumatic and appears to involve painful emotional phases characterized initially by fear and insecurity, followed by anger and alienation, and, subsequently, by despair and loss of hope. Unfortunately, we have little systematic thought or research in this area. Moreover, it is clear that becoming and being homeless is only one facet of the phenomena of loss for these individuals. For many, homelessness is one station on a long journey of lifetime losses. Many people who are homeless as adults experienced significant disturbances as children, including the loss of the childhood home or a parent. The year before first becoming homeless also seems to be a highly stressful time, and one marked by significant losses such as the death of a close family member, the loss of employment, separation, or divorce. Meanwhile, the majority of people who are homeless are also facing a severe psychiatric or substance abuse disorder (or both); these disabilities also create losses of functioning, roles, social status, and even sometimes personal identity.

As homelessness has continued as a major social problem (as we have failed as a society to take the necessary corrective actions to end this problem), we have also numbed ourselves to the plight of people who are homeless. Punitive responses are proposed and implemented by some locales, while indifference appears to mount; as a culture, we have developed "compassion fatigue," a secondary loss of our own humane response. Perhaps in part because of this compassion fatigue, we have all too often failed to recognize that many individuals successfully recover from being homeless and its associated problems and losses.

As noted earlier, it is striking how little thought and research has been conducted on homelessness and loss. Considerably more effort is needed to develop a more thorough and better understanding of the phenomena. The field will benefit from additional, well-designed quantitative research on each topic described previously. Our understanding will also be greatly deepened by qualitative methods, particularly the use of personal narrative and accounts that will bring to light the experiences and stories of people who have become homeless and those who are in the process of recovery. While much additional research is needed, it is also imperative that we renew our current efforts to intervene to prevent homelessness and to assist those who have suffered the loss of home.

## REFERENCES

Anthony, W. A. (1993). Recovery from mental illness: The guiding vision of the mental health service system in the 1990s. *Psychosocial Rehabilitation Journal, 16*(4), 11–23.

Ball, F. L. J., & Havassy, B. E. (1984). A survey of the problems and needs of homeless consumers of acute psychiatric services. *Hospital and Community Psychiatry, 35,* 917–921.

Bassuk, E. L., Weinreb, L. F., Buckner, J. C., Browne, A., Salomon, A., & Bassuk, S. S. (1996). The characteristics and needs of sheltered homeless and low-income housed mothers. *Journal of American Medical Association, 276,* 640–646.

Baxter, E., & Hopper, K. 1981. *Private lives/public spaces: Homeless adults on the streets of New York City.* New York: Community Service Society.

Calsyn, R. J., & Morse, G. A. 1991. Correlates of problem drinking among homeless men. *Hospital and Community Psychiatry, 42,* 721–725.

Calsyn, R. J., & Morse, G. A. 1992. Predicting psychiatric symptoms among homeless people. *Community Mental Health Journal, 28,* 385–395.

Campbell, J. 1988. *The power of myth.* New York: Doubleday.

Davidson, L. (1992). Developing an empirical-phenomenological approach to schizophrenia research. *Journal of Phenomenological Psychology, 23*(1), 3–15.

Dennis, D. L., Buckner, J. C., Lipton, F. R., & Levine, I. S. (1991). A decade of research and services for homeless mentally ill persons. *American Psychologist, 46,* 1129–1138.

Dixon, L. B., Krauss, N., Kernan, E., Lehhman, A. F., & DeForge, B. R. (1995). Modifying the PACT model to serve homeless persons with severe mental illness. *Psychiatric Services, 46,* 684–688.

Drake, R. E., Osher, F. C., & Wallach, M. A. (1991). Homelessness and dual diagnosis. *American Psychologist, 46,* 1149–1158.

Ferguson, S. (1990, Sept./Oct.). Us vs. them: America's growing frustration with the homeless. *Utne Reader,* 50–55.

Harvey, J. H. (1996). Editorial and commentary: On creating the "Journal of Personal and Interpersonal Loss" and the nature of loss. *Journal of Personal and Interpersonal Loss, 1*(1), iii–ix.

Hopper, K. (1984). Whose lives are these, anyway? *Urban and Social Change Review. 17*(2), 12–13.

Hopper, K., Mauch, D., & Morse, G. (1990). *The 1986-1987 NIMH-funded CSP demonstration projects to serve homeless mentally ill persons: A preliminary assessment.* Rockville, MD: National Institutes of Mental Health.

Link, B. G., Susser, E., Stueve, A., Phelan, J., Moore, R. E., & Struening, E. (1994). Lifetime and five-year prevalence of homelessness in the United States. *American Journal of Public Health, 84,* 1907–1912.

Moos, R., Cronkite, R. C., Billings, A. G., & Finney, J. W. (1982). *The health and daily living form manual.* Department of Psychiatry and Behavioral Sciences, Stanford University, Stanford, CA.

Morse, G. A. (1986). *A contemporary assessment of urban homelessness: Implications for social change.* Center for Metropolitan Studies, University of Missouri-St. Louis.

Morse, G. A. (1992). Causes of homelessness. In M. J. Robertson, & M. Greenblatt, (Eds.), *Homelessness: A national perspective.* New York: Plenum Press.

Morse, G., & Calsyn, R. J. (1986). Mentally disturbed homeless people in St. Louis: Needy, willing, but underserved. *International Journal of Mental Health, 14,* 74–94.

Morse, G. A., Calsyn, R. J., Allen, G., Tempelhoff, B., & Smith, R. (1992). Experimental comparison of the effects of three treatment programs for homeless mentally ill people. *Hosptial and Community Psychiatry, 43,* 1005–1010.

Morse, G. A., Calsyn, R. J., Klinkenberg, W. D., Trusty, M. L., Gerber, F., Smith, R., Tempelhoff, B., & Ahmad, L. (1997). An experimental comparison of three types of case management for homeless mentally ill persons. *Psychiatric Services, 48,* 497–503.

Morse, G. A., Calsyn, R. J., Miller, J., Rosenberg, P., West, L., & Gilliland, J. (1996). Outreach to homeless mentally ill people: Conceptual and clinical considerations. *Community Mental Health Journal, 33,* 261–274.

Morse, G., Calsyn, R. J., & Wolff, N. (1996, March). *Final report: Cost effectiveness of case management for the homeless.* Gerontology Program, University of Missouri-St. Louis.

Morse, G., Shields, N. M., Hanneke, C. R., Calsyn, R. J., Burger, G. K., & Nelson, B. (1985). *Homeless people in St. Louis: A mental health program evaluation, field study, and followup investigation.* St. Louis: State of Missouri, Department of Mental Health.

North, C. S., & Smith, E. S. (1992). Posttraumatic stress disorder among homeless men and women. *Hospital and Community Psychiatry, 43,* 1010–1016.

Piliavin, I., Sosin, M., & Westerfelt, H. (1989). *Conditions contributing to long-term homelessness: An exploratory study.* Institute for Research on Poverty, University of Wisconsin-Madison.

Robertson, M. J., & Greenblatt, M. (Eds.). (1992). *Homelessness: A national perspective.* New York: Plenum Press.

Rossi, P. H. (1989). *Down and out in America: The origins of homelessness.* Chicago: University of Chicago Press.

Schutt, R. K., & Garrett, G. R. (1992). The homeless alcoholic: Past and present. In Robertson, M. J., & Greenblatt, M. (Eds.), *Homelessness: A national perspective.* New York: Plenum Press.

Sosin, M. R., Colson, P., & Grossman, S. (1988). *Homelessness in Chicago: Poverty and pathology, social institutions and social change.* School of Social Service Administration, University of Chicago, IL.

Spencer, R., Zawier, B., Tempelhoff, B., Morse, G., & Calsyn, R. J. (1994). *Incorporating integrated treatment approaches in the continuous treatment team model: A manual for working with dually-diagnosed homeless individuals.* Gerontology Program, University of Missouri-St. Louis.

Uzelac, E. (1990). Turning cold. *Miami Sun-Sentinel,* December 9, pp. 1G, 6G.

# 21

# *Coping with Threat from Intimate Sources: How Self-Protection Relates to Loss for Women*

**Paula S. Nurius and Jan E. Gaylord**
*University of Washington*

This chapter considers the ways through which women's emotional, cognitive, and behavioral efforts to grapple with threat from intimate sources relates to various forms of personal and interpersonal loss. This analysis highlights loss-related factors that have heretofore remained relatively overlooked in practice and prevention literatures and that, if incorporated, should serve to render health promotion and protection interventions in these arenas more effective.

## WHAT ARE WE TALKING ABOUT AND WHY IS IT IMPORTANT?

Much of the decision-making research and public education related to health assumes an epidemiological approach to risk perception and response. If one does not want to experience heart disease, then one takes steps expected to reduce that risk, such as lifelong low-fat dietary habits, regular exercise, low stress, and no smoking. Simple as that, right? This is one of the most common and broadly applicable adult health issues we could think of. Even though this example carries little of the emotionality and internal conflict associated with the health risks we will discuss in this chapter, it well illustrates that the way individuals approach risk in their daily lives is seldom a cut and dry phenomenon (Mark Twain is credited with a view that life without his beloved whisky and cigars hardly seemed life worth living!). There are a host of social, cognitive, and emotional variables that are part of the complex interplay between risk perception and response in the context of individuals' lives, relationships, and futures. Gaining increased benefit or safety in one domain of life very often carries a price of loss in another life domain. And, sometimes, that price can feel very costly.

Examination of women's self-protection against threats from intimate sources is one arena in which this complexity is both poignant and essential to understand if prevention efforts are to be effective. We use the term "intimate sources" to

This work was supported in part by a grant from the National Institute of Mental Health (NIMH; MH53702).

indicate sources that directly or symbolically relate to women's intimate relationships or sense of self. The possibility of encountering psychological, physical, or sexual violence or disease (e.g., sexually transmitted diseases, HIV/AIDS) from a man that a woman trusts and cares about are relational examples. The possibility of developing breast cancer is a more symbolic form. A diagnosis of breast cancer involves not solely a life-threatening malady, and potentially the loss of one or both breasts, but for many women it also represents the irrevocable loss of powerful symbols of themselves as healthy, feminine, or intimately appealing beings. Based on our own work and the work of others, we are hypothesizing that threats of this intimate nature pose special challenges for women in acknowledging that these risks apply to them, in detecting personal threats, and in privileging self-protection and health promotion over other goals or priorities.

We maintain that the intimate nature of some threats represent possible and/or realized losses that impede a woman's acknowledgment and recognition of risk, and present personal conflicts that may complicate and compromise her ability to cope with that risk. We draw upon literature that indicates that the processes underlying these impediments are largely explainable through normative social psychological phenomena. Thus, consideration of these phenomena provides important alternatives to pathological explanations (e.g., of irrationality, self-defeating personality, neuroticism) of individual responses to intimate sources of threat. Threat of loss and normative social cognitive factors that come into play in the face of possible loss have received attention as factors in some health promotion and prevention interventions, e.g., those that look at costs-benefits that people gauge and psychological difficulties associated with fear and acknowledging vulnerability (Weinstein, 1993, provides some comparisons). However, distinctions related to threatened losses that are associated with more deeply personal aspects of our lives and identities have not yet been well investigated. We believe this will add an important dimension.

However, we must note a caveat at the onset. In linking intimate threats to women, we run the risk of reinforcing stereotypes of women, victim blaming, or suggesting that males are not vulnerable to intimacy-related concerns, none of which is our intent. Clearly, individuals differ in how they approach and experience intimate threats and losses. Further, we expect individuals and groups to be affected differentially by varying forms of personal loss; for example, see Icard & Nurius (1996) for a discussion of special risk of loss in coming out for African-American gays and lesbians. Our expertise in the area of women's health and safety inclines us to examine how loss relates to self-protection for women, but many of the phenomena we will discuss here are part of the human experience.

This book is explicitly integrative in the theory bases it draws upon and provides a valuable opportunity to focus on relatively neglected aspects and applications of loss that may prove to advance progress across diverse areas of work. In this vein, we draw upon social cognitive formulations of risk perception, self-concept and assumptive worlds, and coping. Together, we believe these concepts help us better understand the various points at which loss comes into play when women confront intimate threats, and how such losses affect women's perceptions and decision-making. We will devote the bulk of the chapter to summarizing the social psychological concepts and findings involved in women's acknowledgment of, perception of, cost-benefit analysis of, and coping response to intimate sources of threat. Within these summaries, we will include examples of how we and others have observed these phenomena in arenas such as acquaintance sexual aggression, partner transmission of HIV/AIDS, and breast cancer. We will conclude the chapter with implications that we see for future research and for designing health promotion and prevention outreach and programs.

## ASSUMPTIVE WORLDS AND SELF-CONCEPT: COGNITIVE MECHANISMS LINKING THREAT TO LOSS

As Ogden (1995) recently noted, health psychology theories have increasingly shifted toward a person-in-environment perspective. This includes attention to ways that people are contextually "situated" in their current life circumstances, to the interactions between people and their environments, and to intra-action (the self dealing with and controlling the self). The following section illustrates some of the ways through which social cognitive processes come into play and influence, both positively and negatively, the perception of personal risk. Within an everflowing stream of environmental, perceptual, and emotional factors, to interpret risk, individuals must continually draw upon their fund of knowledge and understanding (irrespective of their objective accuracy) about themselves and their world. The beliefs, values, and expectancies we amass during our lives strongly influence what we seek out, recognize, and interpret in the panoply of information and experiences we encounter. As we develop scripts and assumptions about who we are, how the world works, and what to expect, we come to heavily rely on these as fact rather than as cognitive constructions of reality as we understand it (Langer, 1989; Nurius, 1993). By and large, these psychological processes serve us well, but they also contribute challenges to coping with unexpected threats.

An extensive literature review of these topics is beyond the scope of this paper. Attention to selected factors, however, will help illuminate ways in which the experience or fear of loss relates to coping with threat from intimate sources. A compelling body of work has examined the adverse effects of traumatic life events (e.g., loss of loved one, victimization, debilitating injury or accident) on one's assumptive worlds, that is, on the fundamental beliefs individuals hold about their own worth, power, and luck and about the benevolence and meaningfulness of the world around them (summarized in Janoff-Bulman, 1992). In addition to a range of tangible losses that can accompany these injurious experiences, the violation or loss of one's core assumptions (e.g., that bad things happen to bad people, not to me; that I am in control of myself and my life) holds serious implications for subsequent intrapsychic and interpersonal coping and well-being (Gordon & Benishek, 1996; Janoff-Bulman & Frantz, 1996; Nurius, 1994 illustrates the positive function of supported assumptive worlds in relation to goal striving). In addition to the physical and material aspects of recovery, individuals must rebuild their understanding of and assumptions about the world and redesign a life course that takes into account the negative fallout from the personal threat that was encountered.

Although positive outcomes can be, and for some people are, derived from personal trauma (e.g., Taylor, 1983), damage to one's positive core assumptions about oneself and one's world carries the threat of impairment to subsequent optimism, confidence, trust, and positive self-concept (Janoff-Bulman, 1989). Findings that have focused on the consequences of challenges to core self-conceptions and world assumptions provide insight into the strength of inherent motivations to protect oneself from such psychological affronts. For example, normative biases toward anticipating, seeking out, and interpreting positive, expectancy-confirming information and overlooking or minimizing discrepant information have been robustly demonstrated (see Kunda, 1990; Scheier & Carver, 1985; Taylor, 1989; Weinstein & Klein, 1995 for overviews). Such positive biases are associated with increased levels of prosocial and well-being factors such as motivation, contentment, confidence, self-esteem, and greater use of effective coping strategies.

Conversely, positive biases in one's core assumptions may also work against perceptions of vulnerability that are necessary for self-protective action and thus impede adoption of precautionary practices. For example, when socializing in familiar circumstances with friends and acquaintances, women tend to anticipate normative and affiliation-related behavior. Behaviors that, in a different context, may be interpreted as cautionary cues will tend to be interpreted in a manner consistent with positive expectations and goals, e.g., that his behavior is flirtatious or that he is attempting to foster intimacy, rather than as cues that he could become aggressive and she could lose control of the situation (Nurius & Norris, 1996). Similarly, when gauging personal risk related to HIV/AIDS, Thompson, Anderson, Freedman, and Swan (1996) found that women's perceptions of low risk were based on unrealistic estimations of their ability "to tell" if a man was HIV positive and on characteristics about him that are unrelated to HIV status. In both cases, such optimistic biases may hamper recognition of personal risk and thus impede effective self-protective action.

Our self-concept includes not only the person we see ourselves currently to be, but also the memories of the person we were in the past (e.g., our childhood, or before we underwent various changes) and the person we imagine ourselves becoming in the future—both hoped for and feared (Markus & Nurius, 1986). Possible selves are not passing worries and whimsies, but rather represent the possible futures we care about and have given considerable thought to. These possible futures include the goals we hope to achieve (love, happiness, attractiveness, vigor, success) as well as outcomes we fear and hope to avoid or escape (rejection, sadness, ugliness, illness or injury, failure). Possible selves closely reflect how we feel about ourselves and our futures and how we behave to affect that future (Cross & Markus, 1994; Hart, Fegley, & Brengelman, 1993; Hooker & Kaus, 1994).

Snyder (1996) illustrates the importance of hope and goals in people's lives and how people are affected by goal loss—the most profound sense of loss involving truly cherished goals. Our conceptualization adds to this the importance of the carrier or source of the threatened loss of cherished goals and aspects of self. We may be able to conceive of the possibility of becoming seriously ill, becoming injured, or losing something precious to us. But, it is far more difficult to conceive of someone we care about being the person who injures us in these ways (e.g., assaults us, gives us AIDS, hurts something or someone we care about, betrays us in any number of other ways; see Barbee, Cunningham, Druen, and Yankeelov,

1996, for an interesting discussion regarding loss as an organizing principle to clarify many dynamics of close relationships). Once we lose the security of our positive illusions that we can trust people, that we have control over our lives, and that the world is the place we understand it to be, we have lost part of our very foundation as individuals. Once we have lost positive possible selves that we cared about and counted on, we have lost treasured parts of our futures.

To summarize, while people acknowledge that bad things happen, they hold the illusion that these bad things happen to others, not themselves. The assumptions, predispositions, and motivations that we have described here are not unique to women, but are common across people. Finding oneself in a potentially threatening situation is not a result of being dumb or careless. Rather, it is an unfortunate and often unavoidable consequence of participating in everyday activities under circumstances we have good reason to believe are normative and safe. It is, however, an illustration of the tension women experience between the need to stay safe and the need to believe one does not have to worry about staying safe (i.e., that one has a safe world and future and the capacity or luck to escape dangers that may befall others). In the next section, we look at some of the experiential binds women encounter in the contemplation process and potential losses that must be weighed prior to action.

## BETWEEN A ROCK AND A HARD PLACE: THE BIND OF CHOOSING AMONG LOSSES?

What we have been striving to depict thusfar are some of the balances and tensions that are important to understanding what women realistically grapple with in undertaking defense of themselves against threats from intimate sources. Part of the "rock and hard place" that we refer to involves trade-offs associated with, on the one hand, sustaining positive assumptive worlds, possible selves, and coping practices consistent with these expectations while, on the other hand, simultaneously maintaining an awareness of harm from intimate sources and a preparedness to do what it takes to protect oneself.

Consider, for example, the compounded risks that one undertakes when anticipating, perceiving, and responding to personal risk from an intimate source. Most obviously, one must acknowledge the physical harm itself, such as harm from an act of aggression or jeopardy to health and life from disease such as HIV/AIDS or breast cancer, and thereby cope with the emotional fallout of that loss of presumed safety and well-being. While this is also true of threats from nonintimate sources, such as the possibility of an auto accident, threats from intimate sources carry with them potential losses of additional forms.

In relation to intimate threats, for example, there is the possible loss of positive social standing. This loss takes form through public stigmatization, distancing, and rejection such as that associated with sexual assault victimization, contraction of HIV/AIDS, and the physically altering and debilitating effects of breast cancer treatment. There is also possible relational loss. For example, women express hesitancy about moving to decisively protect themselves from sexually aggressive acts out of fear that they may be misjudging the man's intentions, may make him feel badly by their rejection, or that he may choose to terminate the relationship if she does not acquiesce (Norris, Nurius, & Dimeff, 1996). Similarly, women have included fears that a male partner will become angry, hurt, suspicious, or turned off, as reasons for not asking or insisting that their sex partners use condoms (Pinkerton & Abramson, 1992). And women diagnosed with breast cancer often fear that the disease or its treatment will negatively affect their intimate relationships (Berger & Bostowick, 1994). Further, there is the loss of emotional well-being that accompanies the dissonance between trust and betrayal, and between pursuit of intimacy and pursuit of safety. Finally, as previously discussed, there are psychological costs that accompany shattered illusions and the recognition that the world is not the benevolent, just, meaningful place one thought it to be, and a diminished self-concept or notion that one is not who she thought herself to be.

Thus, trying to imagine, identify, and cope with potential threat from intimate sources places one squarely at the crossroads of these psychological and social phenomena. Rather than focusing solely on appraisals related to safety, when encountering threats from intimate sources, women must weigh safety risks alongside potential threats and losses related to other goals (such as feeling wanted and loved, having a trusting relationship, seeing oneself as healthy and strong, and exercising freedom in one's choices and activities). There are multiple and sometimes contradictory pros and cons associated with each course of action. If a woman insists that her partner use a condom, for example, she has increased her health safety but potentially decreased her "relationship safety" (e.g., through offending him, making him suspicious of her, diluting the sense of passion and intimacy), and thus increased her risk of rejection, abandonment, hurt, and loneliness. If a woman tries to assess the assaultive potential of her partner, using factors that make sense to her but are actually unreliable, she may be protecting her psychological sense of safety and her relationship with that partner, but potentially jeopardizing her physical health (cf. Williams et al., 1992).

Our emphasis thusfar has been on normative psychological processes that have adaptive functions, but which can also complicate women's coping when threats from intimate sources are involved. In the next section we will examine in more detail how these factors, in addition to variations across situations and individuals, impact women's coping response to sources of intimate threat.

## COMPLICATIONS IN COPING WHEN THREAT IS FROM INTIMATE SOURCES

In the previous sections we examined how an individual's assumptions, expectancies, goals, and self-concept influence their appraisals of personal risk, and some of the ways that normative psychological biases and process can be double-edged for women when it comes to potential threats from intimate sources. We now consider how coping with intimate threats differs from more general forms of threat, how individual variability influences the way women enter the process of coping with intimate threats, and ways that coping alternatives and actions are complicated by ambiguity and the limitations of how many things we can worry about at one time.

Part of what makes coping with threats from intimate sources especially difficult is their deeply personal nature. Family, friends, and partners are closely related to a woman's identity, goals, and visions of the future. Coping with threats from intimate sources typically requires us to contend with conflicting valued goals. For example, should I try hardest to protect myself, regardless of the consequences this may have on my relationship with a man (safeguard physical well-being but risk rejection, loss of affection and trust)? Should I trust my perceptions that this is a trustworthy person who is not a threat to me (protect the relationship and intimacy-related possible selves, but potentially put health and safety on the line)? Should I have regular mammograms and do self-exams, even though I know that doing them makes me more anxious about cancer than not doing them (protect one's health and intimacy-related possible selves, but compromise early detection and greater likelihood of survival)? The contemplation process illustrated by these examples requires significant effort and is not something that can be sustained indefinitely.

To further complicate the situation, not all threats are obvious or straightforward. In our daily lives we frequently encounter information and situations that are ambiguous in nature. Ambiguous sources of threat pose unique challenges to individuals attempting to appraise and evaluate available information (cf. Hock, Krohne, & Kaiser, 1996). Many of the situations women are likely to encounter, in relation to intimate threats in particular, may lack the saliency necessary for them to be expediently identified as potentially threatening or personally relevant. Even if potentially threatening cues are noticed, their ambiguity leaves considerable room for alternative appraisals and evaluations and for interpretation consistent with more anticipated, familiar, or preferred conclusions (Lazarus & Folkman, 1984).

Moreover, a person's behavior and conditions that constitute risk are very often embedded within the same circumstances within which women are pursuing common goals related to friendship, intimacy, entertainment, group membership, and self-definition. The mindset, expectancies, and preparedness needed for risk perception, safety orientation, and a priority of self-protection are inconsistent with those needed for (and far more likely to be activated by) social situations in which goals such as entertainment, friendship, and intimacy predominate (Nurius, in press; see also Benthin, Slovic, & Severson, 1993, for comment on familiarity effects and past experience influences on risk perception).

Individual differences among women also play a role in coping with intimate sources of threat. One example of an individual difference that would likely come into play in a potentially threatening situation involves the different types of attentional strategies people use for selecting and processing threat cues. Some individuals devote tremendous cognitive energy scanning for and attending to information about possible threats and stressors (a monitoring style characterized by an information sensitivity or vigilance), whereas others are more inclined to ignore or blunt threat-related cues (a style whereby one tends to overlook or actively avoid threat information; see Miller, Shoda, & Hurley, 1996).

In general, the more vigilant a person's attentional style the more likely she or he is to notice early and subtle signs of threat. The greater the threat an individual perceives, the more likely he or she is to think and worry about the threat as well as seek out further information about it. The opposite is true for those with blunting attentional styles. Those with high blunting tendencies generally have a high sense of invulnerability, being either unwilling or unable to attend to or assimilate information discrepant with this belief. While a monitoring style may seem to be an advantage, at high levels this vigilance becomes a preoccupation, entailing exaggerated overestimation of threat, negativistic expectations, interpretation of ambiguous cues as threats, intrusive ideation, views of oneself as fragile, and distancing (e.g., relying on others to take care of the problem) or avoidant coping styles (Miller, Rodeletz, Schroeder, Mangan, & Sedlacek, 1996 and Miller, Shoda, & Hurley, 1996 provide good overviews of research). Thus, becoming more vigilant per se about the possibility of threat is not necessarily healthy or advantageous. On the other hand, in order to launch an effective defense against a threat, should it materialize, one needs to be able to know where to look for the signs, to see it coming, and to tolerate the accompanying distress in order to plan and implement protective action.

These attentional style differences may be of particular significance in intimately threatening situations where there are likely to be high levels of ambiguity, uncertainty, and goal conflicts for many women. When we think about the familiar contexts in which women are most likely to experience threat from intimate sources, we realize that the mindset women are likely to have in these situations does not enable or ready them to be "on guard" or vigilant. Thus women's attentional style is likely to play a key role in their ability to perceive and effectively cope in already difficult-to-discern situations. Particularly when threat stems from the behavior of others, such as partner or acquaintance aggression, it is important that we not confuse assisting women through a better understanding of naturally occurring impediments with assigning women responsibility for the inappropriate behavior of others. We are suggesting, however, that the attentional style of a woman is one of many factors that might differentially influence her ability to cope with intimate sources of threat. Identifying and examining such differences should inform prevention efforts designed to teach women to more effectively protect themselves from a variety of intimate forms of threat.

Finally, the options a woman views as really doable in countering intimate threats may be considerably more limited relative to the repertoire of coping responses she can envision or perhaps has demonstrated ability for. Women have been found, for example, to understand that acquaintance aggression is a social problem, to be able to generate a range of actions to take in defending themselves, and to report instances in which they have undertaken such actions to protect others that they see in risky situations (Norris et al., 1996). When it comes to defending themselves against sexual aggression by dates, boyfriends, and other acquaintances, however, the range of what they are prepared to undertake is more truncated (Furby, Fischhoff, & Morgan, 1990) and intertwined with concerns such as physically or emotionally injuring the man or being negatively judged by others. Research on coping with domestically violent men suggests that women can simultaneously feel concern for the abuser as well as anger and fear toward him, and that women may be better able to take immediate protective action in the defense of others (such as children) than of themselves (Nurius, Furrey, & Berliner, 1992).

## CONCLUSION

Aspects of personal loss clearly play a significant role in influencing women's ability to cope with intimate sources of threat. In this chapter we have attempted to highlight some of the reasons why loss related to threat from intimate sources operates differently for many of us than does loss from more generic, less personal, forms of threat. Better understanding the ways in which individuals think about and approach intimate risks on a daily basis is essential to the creation and development of better risk prevention and health promotion programs across a wide range of health issues, not just in the areas of sexual assault, HIV prevention, and breast cancer.

We readily acknowledge that women as a group are quite diverse and that there is unquestionably a range of ways women think about and respond to various forms of loss in relation to the examples we used to illustrate our points. However, in our own struggle to better understand and explain these phenomena in relation to intimate sources of threat, we have come to accept that, while we might not always agree or like it, social and cultural influences play a significant role in defining for many women the relative weight of a particular loss. For example, how might societal messages about the importance of beauty and stereotypes about what constitutes feminine beauty relate to fears of loss associated with breast removal? Similarly, research related to female socialization raises concerns that pressures to fulfill norms of the "good woman" foster intimacy-related schemas (such as securing attachments by putting the needs of others before the self; inhibiting self-expression and action to avoid conflict and possible loss of relationship) that put women at risk of depression and exploitation (Jack & Dill, 1992).

This is by no means to argue that social and cultural influences are inherently negative nor that loss is inherently problematic. Hope and fear of loss of that which is cherished are powerful forces and reflect values, commitments, and virtues that are profoundly meaningful to both the individual and the society. These hopes and fears are forces that play an important role in the way people measure personal risk and vulnerability (regardless of how realistic, rational, or sensible others judge them to be), and ultimately in people's decisions about what to do in the face of threatened loss. Moreover, fear of loss can have a productive galvanizing effect, particularly related to detection behaviors. Loss-framed messages to persuade women to engage in detection actions such as self-exams and mammography screening, for example, have been found significantly more effective than gain-framed messages (Banks et al., 1995; Meyerowitz & Chaiken, 1987).

The examples we selected as illustrations have similarities as well as differences in exactly how they relate to the social psychological phenomenon we have discussed as well as how they relate to women's lives. Educators, practitioners, and researchers in each arena could identify factors that are relatively unique or importantly distinctive to that issue. Our goal was to highlight the similarities among these different forms of intimate threat, in an attempt to begin building a foundation of understanding upon which theory in this area can be built and programs and prevention efforts can be based. What makes some kinds of threat simply harder to face and cope with than other kinds? We have theorized here that one essential root answer to this question, regardless of whom the question is posed to, has to do with loss. We argue that greater consideration of loss as well as the beliefs and values and the hopes and fears associated with loss will better enable us to appreciate the stakes involved with threat from intimate sources, and thus better enable us to support self-protective coping.

## REFERENCES


Banks, S. M., Salovey, P., Greener, S., Rothman, A. J., Moyer, A., Beauvais, J., & Epel, E. (1995). The effects of message framing on mammography utilization. *Health Psychology, 14,* 178–184.

Barbee, A. P., Cunningham, M. R., Druen, P. B., & Yankeellov, P. A. (1996). Loss of passion, intimacy, and commitment: A conceptual framework for relationship researchers. *Journal of Personal and Interpersonal Loss, 1,* 93–108.

Benthin, A., Slovic, P., & Severson, H. (1993). A psychometric study of adolescent risk perception. *Journal of Adolescence, 16,* 153–168.

Berger, K., & Bostowick, J. (1994). *A woman's decision: Breast care, treatment, and reconstruction* (2nd. ed). St. Louis, MO: Quality Medical Publishing.

Cross, S. E., & Markus, H. R. (1994). Self-schemas, possible selves, and competent performance. *Journal of Educational Psychology, 86,* 423–438.

Furby, L., Fischhoff, B., & Morgan, M. (1990). Preventing rape: How people perceive the options for assault prevention. In E. Viano (Ed.), *The victimology research handbook* (pp. 227–259). New York: Garland.

Gordon, P. A., & Benishek, L. A. (1996). The experience of chronic illness: Issues of loss and adjustment. *Journal of Personal and Interpersonal Loss, 1,* 299–307.

Hart, D., Fegley, S., & Brengelman, D. (1993). Perceptions of past, present, and future selves among children and adolescents. *British Journal of Developmental Psychology, 11,* 265–282.

Hock, M., Krohne, H. W., & Kaiser, J. (1996). Coping dispositions and the processing of ambiguous stimuli. *Journal of Personality and Social Psychology, 70,* 1052–1066.

Hooker, K., & Kaus, C. R. (1994). Health-related possible selves in young and middle adulthood. *Psychology and Aging, 9,* 126–133.

Icard, L. D., & Nurius, P. S. (1996). Loss of self in coming out: Special risks for African American Gays and Lesbians. *Journal of Personal and Interpersonal Loss, 1,* 29–47.

Jack, D. C., & Dill, D. (1992). The Silencing the Self Scale: Schemas associated with depression in women. *Psychology of Women Quarterly, 16,* 97–106.

Janoff-Bulman, R. (1989). Assumptive worlds and the stress of traumatic events: Applications of the schema construct. *Social Cognition, 7,* 113–136.

Janoff-Bulman, R. (1992). *Shattered assumptions: Towards a new psychology of trauma.* New York: Free Press.

Janoff-Bulman, R., & Frantz, C. M. (1996). The loss of illusions: The potent legacy of trauma. *Journal of Personal & Interpersonal Loss, 1,* 133–150.

Kunda, Z. (1990). The case for motivated reasoning. *Psychological Bulletin, 108,* 480–498.

Langer, E. J. (1989). *Mindfulness.* Reading, MA: Addison-Wesley.

Lazarus, R., & Folkman, S. (1984). *Stress, appraisal, and coping.* New York: Springer-Verlag.

Markus, H., & Nurius, P. S. (1986). Possible selves. *American Psychologist, 41,* 954–969.

Meyerowitz, B. E., & Chaiken, S. (1987). The efffect of message framing on breast self-examination attitudes, intentions, and behavior. *Journal of Personality and Social Psychology, 52,* 500–510.

Miller, S. M., Rodoletz, M., Schroeder, C. M., Mangan, C. E., & Sedlacek, T. V. (1996). Applications of the monitoring process model to coping with severe long-term medical threats. *Health Psychology, 15,* 216–225.

Miller, S. M., Shoda, Y., & Hurley, K. (1996). Applying cognitive-social theory to health-protective behavior: Breast self-examination in cancer screening. *Psychological Bulletin, 119,* 70–94.

Norris, J., Nurius, P. S., & Dimeff, L. A. (1996). Through her eyes: Factors affecting women's perception of and resistance to acquaintance sexual aggression threat. *Psychology of Women Quarterly, 20,* 123–145.

Nurius, P. S. (1993). Human memory: A basis for better understanding the elusive self-concept. *Social Service Review, 67,* 261–278.

Nurius, P. S. (1994). Assumptive worlds, self-definition, and striving among women. *Basic and Applied Social Psychology, 15,* 311–327.

Nurius, P. S. (in press). Risk perception of acquaintance sexual aggression: A social-cognitive perspective. *Aggression and Violent Behavior.*

Nurius, P. S., Furrey, J., & Berliner, L. (1992). Coping capacity among women with abusive partners. *Violence and Victims, 7,* 229–243.

Nurius, P. S., & Norris, J. (1996). A cognitive-ecological model of women's response to male sexual coercion in dating. *Journal of Psychology and Human Sexuality, 8,* 117–139.

Ogden, J. (1995). Changing the subject of health psychology. *Psychology & Health, 10,* 257–265.

Pinkerton, S. D., & Abramson, P. R. (1992). Is risky sex rational? *Journal of Sex Research, 29,* 561–568.

Scheier, M. F., & Carver, C. S. (1985). Optimism, coping and health: Assessment and implications of generalized outcome expectancies. *Health Psychology, 4,* 219–247.

Snyder, C. R. (1996). To hope, to lose, and to hope again. *Journal of Personal and Interpersonal Loss, 1,* 1–16.

Taylor, S. E. (1983). Adjustment to threatening events: A theory of cognitive adaptation. *American Psychologist, 38,* 1161–1173.

Taylor, S. E. (1989). *Positive illusions: Creative self-deception and the healthy mind.* New York: Basic Books.

Thompson, S. C., Anderson, K., Freedman, D., & Swan, J. (1996). Illusions of safety in a risky world: A study of college students' condom use. *Journal of Applied Social Psychology, 26,* 189–210.

Weinstein, N. D. (1993). Testing four competing theories of health protective behavior. *Health Psychology, 14,* 132–140.

Weinstein, N. D., & Klein, W. M. (1995). Resistance of personal risk perceptions to debiasing interventions. *Health Psychology, 14,* 132–140.

Williams, S. S., Kimble, D. L., Covell, N. H., Weiss, L. H., Newton, K. J., Fisher, J. D., & Fisher, W. A., (1992). College students use implicit personality theory instead of safer sex. *Journal of Applied Social Psychology, 22,* 921–933.

# 22

# *Loss of Collective Identity: Self-Sacrifice, Beauty Contests, and Magical Practices*

**Aurora Liiceanu**
*Institute of Psychology, Bucharest*

In his "Editorial and Commentary: On Creating the 'Journal of Personal and Interpersonal Loss' and the Nature of Loss," Harvey (1966) provides a personal view on the nature of loss. Loss is made of real events, personal and interpersonal, and most people are likely to experience a loss at some time in their lives. Harvey's assertion that "in the 1990s, we are constantly bombarded by media with images of loss" is correct. Indeed, it seems that loss is quite normal, that certain necessary losses are experienced by everyone, and that, naturally, collective losses have higher prestige when they do occur. In the personal sense, loss could be that of self-esteem or of a close relationship that no longer exists or is in danger. In a larger sense, loss could be that of collective identity such as the case of Romanian women. This is the case presented in the chapter, in which it will be described how, at the beginning of the century, the female identity was built, how it supported changes during the totalitarian years, and how it was promoted in recent years after Romanian society moved towards a democratic life. My presentation will eventually show the continuity of gender stereotypes and the importance of personal solutions in solving individual losses.

To understand the Romania of today, one cannot underestimate the importance of the enduring and deeply entrenched patriarchal culture and the consequences of the communist ideology and praxis in gender relations. In the community's daily life, the traditions, values, and moral standards deriving from the significance of the village and Christian Orthodoxism play a crucial role. Men's domination and women's submissiveness are seen as rooted in a natural and religious order beyond the rational mind. The smooth functioning of the household and the peace/well-being/welfare of the home depend largely on women. Committing themselves physically and emotionally to the home, women leave men room for participation and decision-making in the social space, where they act as the interface between community and family.

Although communist policies have made Romania an industrial country striving toward modernism, gender relations have not changed. The roles of women are still similar to those of the traditional household, and the patriarchal family was embodied in working-class culture. Families have maintained strong bonds with relatives living in villages regardless of their status, and the family has remained the basic social unit. Marriage is an integral part of Romanian society.

Wives make meals, offer love, and provide a stable, secure home base for married men. There is no better guarantor of long life, health, and happiness for a man than a wife well socialized to perform the "duties of a wife"—the kind of wife willing to devote her life to taking care of him and providing a well-ordered home for both him and the children.

As a former communist country, Romania benefitted for a long time from a social model whereby women were almost forcibly attracted into economic-social activity. At the same time, and mainly after 1973, when the communist party decided to promote women into leading positions, explicitly criticizing the precommunist period, women were pushed towards top managerial positions of high responsibility at various decision-making levels. The compulsory quotas were sustained by the rhetoric of equal access and of egalitarianism; the submissive role of women was strongly questioned; and a new identity was supposed to be proposed and reinforced: women as partners in social and political life and women as reproductive bodies. In fact, women striving for the top of the hierarchy were usually ending a step or two below it, and reality never approached equality of rights of all citizens, especially with respect to women's participation in sharing the power and decision-making responsibility at all levels.

The evolution, with both its positive and its negative results, was interrupted by the events of December 1989, which brought about political changes, economic restructuring, recession, and instability. The artificially planned process of involving women in all facets of social life was brought to an end, and women came to be affected to a greater extent by social exclusion and poverty. After having made significant political inroads (for example, in 1987, 34.4% of members of Parliament were women and there were 2–3 women ambassadors), in 1992, their participation decreased, so that less than 4% of members of Parliament were women, with no remaining women ambassadors. After the 1996 elections, women represented less than 5% of Parliament members. Romanian society is proving to be more and more machismo, seen and felt by women as a world where men attribute themselves the lion's share. The present government is composed only of men and the newspapers allocate little space for women's issues and complaints; however, one of them is ironically entitled "Women in the Men's World."

In the first years after 1989, the Romanian female audience exhibited a strong tendency toward romance and psychologically erotic availability. This was expressed by "falling in love" with the charismatic new Prime Minister, for according to a slogan, "No need for any money and hard currency for us [Romanian women]. We only need for Roman [the Prime Minister] to 'fuck us'." The same interest was shown in Barbara Cartland's and Sandra Brown's novels. Women could read such fiction in buses or in parks. The communist regime left Romanian women frustrated and open to any kind of substitution for reducing the dissatisfaction created by gender relations. As years passed, the phenomenon started to decrease in importance: some women discovered the newly introduced South American soap operas on TV and were seduced by more and more media messages promoting beauty as the supreme currency. Preadolescent and young girls compete for "Miss contests," and the female voice changes into that of a mermaid. The irony resides in the fact that women experiencing the consequences of the failure of patriarchal marriages turn to stories and realities that tell again and again about patriarchal marriages. The paradox of the romance is, thus obviously, that women use traditional female prescriptions to resist their situation as women. The reading of the romance, controversial as it may be, is a way of securing privacy and, at the same time, of procuring companionship and conversation. The ultimate route towards the fulfillment of a mature feminine subjectivity remains patriarchal marriage, which is no longer patriarchal, since women's wages are added to men's.

## ELENA CEAUSESCU SYNDROME

Nowadays, there is a fixation on "beauty" as a direct consequence of abolishing the "Elena Ceausescu" syndrome. This syndrome describes the dissatisfaction of public opinion with the image of "the leading woman" due to the negative personality of the Romanian communist leader's wife, considered, more than him, responsible for the Romanian communist nightmare. Women themselves had little courage to cope with the association between woman and evil, and the late prima donna's image is still vivid in people's memories. Paradoxically, the compulsive entry of women into formally powerful positions during the communist regime has as a direct consequence the triumph of "ugliness" ideologies: a beautiful woman was not supposed to be easily promoted regardless of her political involvement and devotion to the party cause.

Now, under the "feminine mystique," virtually all middle-class women are compelled to choose either domesticity or beauty, defined as a legitimate and necessary qualification for a woman's rise in power. As for domesticity, it was acquired mainly by women as a consequence of the totalitarian regime. The image of the businessman accompanied by two bodyguards and a very young, slender woman with heavy make-up is slowly becoming the paradigm of the relationship between men and women and the very expression of social success. With youth and beauty, the working woman is visible, able to have a job, to be promoted, and to be eligible on the marital market. All marriage demands emphasize the importance of age, and "beauties" reach the peak of the possibilities open to them in the economy in their early youth. Culture stereotypes women by flattening the feminine into beauty-without-intelligence or intelligence-without-beauty. Women are allowed a mind or a body but not both. According to a joke, when someone has both, then it is surely a man. Women are bombarded with definitions of beauty coming from outside but conveyed by women's voices, and adhering to that standard is felt to be a must.

To return to the topic of the rise of Romanian feminism, it should be noted that in 1918, the League of the Women Emancipation in Romania was already founded. One can say that the feminine identity proposed at that time did not include self-sacrifice as a definition of womanhood but, on the contrary, the cooperation of both sexes for the benefit of society. After about 50 years of communism, the female identity was lost at the social level, and was resisted only at the personal level thanks to traditions and patriarchal values. Today, on the whole, societal depictions of women are dissonant in multiple ways from socialized images of healthy, happy, normal, and successful males and females. Romanian women adopt individual strategies to achieve higher status individually according to their natural propensity to possess a relational self.

## RITUALS AND BELIEFS

Traditional values endure despite the influence of modern ideas, and the villages are rich repositories of traditions, rituals, and beliefs that have survived for the most part unchanged. Old customs are highly valued and viewed as worth continuing. In most families, young girls are trained in magical cures that are aimed at improving physical health and family well-being and that are embodied in rules such as the following: one must not comb one's hair on Thursday evening, spin or work hard on Thursday, or bake on Friday. A specific evil is associated with each interdiction. Such rules of conduct are frequently found in everyday urban life as well.

My field research in rural areas (Liiceanu, 1966) recorded the role of the witch in dealing with the evil perceived to be threatening women's and the family's well-being. A housekeeper consults a witch only when she finds herself unable to deal with the evil and is afraid that her personal identity is in danger. A major loss or a suspicion of the "evil-generalized" is believed to be a result of maledictions or envy. The evil-generalized is defined as an evil having the power to invade the whole household, and the witch must perform a complete ritual of driving it away. The witch is fully competent; it is her responsibility to acquire as much magical knowledge as necessary to meet the wide range of needs in the community's daily life.

Myths about the powers, motives, and special qualities of women occur in myriad forms; certain themes have been observed to have continuity with the present. The myth of the woman who enchants a man with her magic charms and seduces him away from his spouse or potential spouse is persistent and is expressed by stories, simple or epic, about men rendered powerless. He has no choice but to surrender to the woman, who has only the frail weapons of her body, her eyes, and certainly, her connections with potent forces in the occult dimension that defy the rational mind. Magical techniques are used to recover from any kind of loss or from being a victim of envy. In Surani, a village in southern Romania, a couple asked a witch to heal the husband, after many visits to physicians gave them no success. The witch told them that an envious woman had put some magical objects in their courtyard in order to inflict harm on the wife, but fortunately it was the husband who touched the malignant traces and became subject to the evil. Had the wife touched the object, she would have died, the witch said. In Vadu Izei, a village in northern Romania, the complaints of women—because women are the witch's clients even if the evil subject is a man or a child—were solved by a famous witch, called Anuta. She enjoyed the fruits of her magical knowledge until her death and was known for her ability to heal the sick. To adjust the energy fields in and around the body, she offered prayers and chants to the divine forces that have the power to restore harmony and to increase the life force of the diseased person. As a rural witch, she expressed deep concern for the public image of witches in terms of fame and authority. She was a medicine woman, healer and repository of rituals, myths, and secret lore, a specialist in the human soul, and a generalist whose sacred and social functions covered a wide range of responsibilities. She could be viewed as a technician of magic.

In the villages, the household and its members are confronted with a variety of problems ranging from economic losses following the sickness and death of animals, to loss of health or well-being of family members to diseases contracted by children. Pennebaker (1990) wrote of the many psychological and physical consequences of the failure to confront one's "devils," be they pain, despair, sadness, or sorrows resulting from vital losses. In the Romanian village, it is the witch who is supposed to help one deal effectively with loss. Her magical methods are positively related to coping with loss and its consequences on personal identity. Regardless of the sex of the victim, a woman (it may be the victim herself, a relative, a spouse, or the victim's mother) usually seeks out a witch and carries out what the witch determines will be an effective path to recovery. Traditional village inhabitants who suffer major losses always seek the help of a witch.

The witch's work entails maintaining balance in the human community at the individual level. When the various domains of existence are out of balance, it is she who takes the responsibility for restoring harmony and well-being. In Surani, a mother lost two sons. They climbed on the wires used for electric connections—one of them to play and the other to help the first—and were electrocuted. After a year of terrible grief, she asked a witch to help her to survive, and the witch told her that "both boys were destined to die in their early age." The mother convinced herself that fate was stronger than her love and adopted a personal strategy to cope with the loss: visiting the cemetery almost daily to talk to the boys.

The crisis of a powerful illness can be the central experience of the magical repertory. It involves an encounter with forces that decay and destroy. It may be the malignant influence of others or a malediction acted out by others. The Romanian people believe the influence of others covers a wide range of negative effects. However, effects can be positive, as in the case of Palaguta's marriage. Her husband's account of their marriage is that Palaguta, who otherwise was powerless, got what she wanted, marriage (much more important in rural areas than in urban ones) and, thus, a man, by using devious, cunning means. Her sexual attractiveness was a strong element in bringing about the downfall of her prey, the man. The following words capture Mahai's belief that he was to be her husband not by his choice.

> *Long time ago, when I was a young and inexperienced lad, while bypassing in a wagon, near a glade, I saw several dancing naked women. The sky was cloudless and the night was so clear that one could believe that it was daytime. The young women [had] long, undone hair and they picked up flowers and they seemed to be happily interacting with one another. Surely, they were enchantresses, witches. My Palaguta danced with them. She enchanted and seduced me as to be her husband. It was a time for charm-making. As I was coming back home, I found that I was naked, too, without my shirt. Then I was sure of something: she will marry me.*

According to Mihai and to various village sources, the loss of a shirt symbolizes a loss of freedom, namely, the loss of male freedom insofar as marriage is a kind of prison. Moreover, the seeming perversity of Palaguta's behavior, the wonderment she excited with her strange powers, and the ways she was different from the man gave rise to the idea that she was made up of a feminine essence that was beyond Mihai's capacity to understand. He deems Palaguta important for the services she performed and has ascribed to her a special status. But, at the same time and deeper in his mind, she is viewed as a different order of being to whom the laws and rules by which behavior is normally understood do not always apply. By defining Palaguta as a mysterious other, Mihai is hinting at her power. While listening to him, Palaguta displayed an ambiguous smile, looking ironically at him in mild satisfaction and self-content.

To the Romanian people, woman is an ambiguous person: a comforter, a nurse, a teacher, an inculcator of collective values, industrious, and productive, but also an evil agent. She is a necessary evil. As the most important developmental task, marriage is highly valued among women: remaining single and/or childless is considered senseless. Sexuality is by no means a life dimension in itself, and it can be expressed only in marriage and in motherhood. Girls who say that they are not interested in marrying are not credible at all, and both mothers and fathers teach their sons about girls' hidden intentions. Therefore, the major losses are the loss of vital force, which in a woman's case includes loss of sexual desire, and the loss of potency in men. A popular song expresses the concern very well:

*My dearest daughter, what a husband could I give you?*
*A driver, maybe, will suit to you!*
*No, no, my dear mother, no!*
*All the day missing the house*
*Hunting the women and drinking!*
*A shepherd, maybe, will suit to you!*
*Yes, yes, my dear mother, yes!*
*All the day looking after the sheep.*
*But potent in bed!*

When there is a loss of vital force, the recovery is effected through a witch's intervention because the loss is usually ascribed to the intrusion of malign spirits activated by rivals and enemies. Thus, the statement "she bewitched me and caused me to do something which I would otherwise never have done or to leave my beloved" is quite frequently mentioned when a relationship is broken up or a woman is abandoned without any clear reason.

It is common for people to become severely depressed when an intimate relationship comes to an end, especially if they wanted the relationship to change into a marital bond and the ending was a surprise, or when they are rejected by someone who previously fully accepted them. In such cases, a confidant is often sought, and particularly the advice of a witch. Sorensen, Russell, Harkness, and Harvey (1995) found that men tend to do less account-making and confiding when coping with their losses as compared to women. The witch may use magical cures and systematic and scripted techniques to try to restore the individual's well-being and personal identity. The witch is both the confidant looked to most often and a decision-maker regarding the most effective procedure for dealing with evils. Pennebaker (1990) argued and found that confiding is positively related to coping. The person experiencing a loss examines carefully his or her motives and selects the most reliable confidant among those possible. Then, usually in rural areas but also in urban ones, it is the witch to whom he or she carries out extended confiding. Harvey (1995) placed greater emphasis on the contents of confiding and the value of private reflection that form a foundation for the confiding acts. Confiding in Anuta to ask for recovery of sexual potency was one of the most frequent demands in her magical performances. For example, a mother complained that her son lost his "maleness." Another young, newly wedded woman felt that her vital force was diminishing and lacking due to the malediction of her husband's former sweetheart. Similarly, a wife suddenly felt an unexplained physical repugnance towards her husband. In the last case, the following spells were used by Anuta: "Who did 'the done'/Nevermind what kind of evil is/Sadness, sorrows, hurt, pain, harm, disagreement, hatred; Between this woman and this man; Injuring the marriage bond. . . ." To change a powerless man into a sexually active husband, Anuta used different magical methods, which the wife was expected to participate in. Often, Anuta asked the wife to stand naked in the middle of her courtyard, on the night of a full moon, and recite the following magical discourse:

*Stars, my sisters,*
*Only you know what I am going to do,*
*Only you and the God.*
*What I tie, I never untie.*
*I tie the husband's name.*
*And his mind,*
*And his thoughts,*
*And his ears,*
*And his eyes,*
*And his mouth,*
*And his hands,*
*And his legs,*
*And the drive of his love toward*
*All the girls, all the women,*
*All the disreputable women,*
*To be dumb in front of them,*
*To be blind when stands by them,*
*With powerless hands and legs,*
*With powerless back,*
*To be cheated by his love making power,*
*To not feel as a man.*

The wife/girl must have a linen string and must tie a knot while saying each interdiction to the wrongdoer. Then, the string must be hidden at a house entrance so that the man will pass over it, and then be placed in a bottle. Finally, the bottle is buried in the grave of a man with the same Christian name as the husband. On the road home, the wife must offer candies to a small child who is unable to answer "Thanks" and remains voiceless: "As the child does not know to say 'Thanks,' so he would not be able to have relationship with other women."

On the basis of accounts of both women and men, I have found in both rural and urban communities that the close relationships impacted by evils attributed to magical practices can evolve into complex feelings of loss, both personal and interpersonal. Only rarely does the loss concern the social space and, consequently, social identities.

Most modern Romanian women now commonly face age discrimination. Job hunters can see the following type of advertisement: "We employ girls for fast food," "We hire young girls for saloon, and women for kitchen." Obviously, the girls are supposed to perform on the front stage, and the women on the back stage.

By 1990, accusations of loss of femininity during the communist regime justified the invasions of all types of messages in which beauty and femininity were being discussed but not separated. Now, notions of femininity are in flux. The distinction between the public and the private spheres has changed since 1990. Women had escaped from the privacy of the family into the social public domain, not in political life, but in business. Age and gender became the most significant variables used in the job market; distinctions between jobs for women and jobs for men, jobs for young people and jobs for adults, are frequently mentioned in newspapers. New dividing lines between male and female territories have appeared. The job market is explicitly sexist. Freshly escaped from planned, artificial promotion to top positions, women came back willingly to the past, finding again the satisfaction given by motherhood and marriage bonds. Even highly educated women give priority to their extra-occupational roles and to their husbands' careers. At least, this is the message conveyed by tradition and by the culture that these women belong to.

## LOST IN MODELS

The result of nongendered education during the communist years was supposed to be the creation of a sexless creature. The traditional patterns of masculinity and femininity seem to be infinitely more human than the loss of identity promoted as a general rule, and disseminated by the official discourse. This life provided stances of stronger self-sacrifice than that usually attached to female stereotypes.

By the turn of the century, rivalry marked the rise of feminism in Romania. It was a special form of rivalry among educated women who thought about what it meant to be a woman. It was a time of literary and artistic groups when women breached the privacy of family life and brought "society" into their houses. If the men were supposed to act in society at large, women reacted by acting in "small societies," mounted in their private spaces. The newspapers mentioned their names and achievements so that the ridiculous joke "long hair, narrow mind" became questionable. In the present day, feminine rivalry is again found, but as an implicit message aimed at physical appearance rather than the mind. In advertising, the use of women's bodies is frequent, and women are depicted in their position of virtual love-makers. The dominant visual theme in magazines targeting teenagers and women is the female body as a tool for seducing men. During the communist years, demands that women be depicted in a wide range of social and work-related roles were met only in the form of "politically correct" tasks. Now these images have disappeared, leaving room only for images of women as mothers, wives, and sexual partners. Love magic is in fashion, and prescriptions and "musts" are proposed to women in magazines. Hot-lines function instead of witches without excluding them; witches overtly offer their services without being afraid of punishment; morning TV shows begin with astrological information. Pluralism of voices is everywhere present, and critics of the irrationality of present day society are overtly sustained by science defenders. TV is a multi-headed witch in the service of a client who has broken the silence.

Prejudice against women is acquired, used, or changed in social situations, and as a function of structures of social dominance. The concrete manifestations of the generalized group prejudice, for instance, in social acts of discrimination, are, however, controlled by so-called "models" (Van Dijk & Kintsch, 1983). These models are mental representations of personal and social experiences, for instance, interactions with group members. Under the biasing influence of group representations, members of the dominant group thus build or update situational models. This may happen in everyday perception or interaction, but also indirectly, through discourse and communication about women. Miroiu (1994) notices that women are deliberately excluded from political and decision-making positions: they are mostly unemployed, socially unprotected, poor, and fighting to survive. The number of abortions is still high and women's public image is in great part pejorative. Women suffer from the Elena Ceausescu complex but, the author asks herself, why do men not suffer from a Nicolae Ceausescu complex? As a social reality, abandonment of children is surely associated with a government attitude fostered by the previous regime. This situation is also an expression of the loss of identity at a personal level. Romanian women have experienced many kinds of losses that are unusual in nature and magnitude, but the most important indignity is that they once exercised a high level of social control over their bodies. Now, they do not realize that they are being taken over by a discourse of disconsideration, that their bodies are again being used, and nobody is reacting.

However, despite rhetorical equality between the sexes, social realities and women's issues have begun to be research topics and a preoccupation of the civil society, which is interested in developing a new kind of gender awareness in coming to terms with this loss of identity. Returning to the model of the early women's emancipation movement is not a solution, since the new reality provides new specificities concerning gender relations and power structures. It is not too bold to venture that representation and identity are the most revealing arenas in which to observe the complex process by which whole sets of given and inherited values have been fundamentally altered.

## REFERENCES

Harvey, J. H. (1995). *Odyssey to the heart: The search for closeness, intimacy, and love.* New York: Freeman.

Harvey, J. H. (1996). Editorial and commentary: On creating the "Journal of Personal and Interpersonal Loss" and the nature of loss. *The Journal of Personal and Interpersonal Loss*, *1,* iii–ix.

Liiceanu, A. (1996). *Povestea unei vrajitoare (The story of a witch).* Bucharest: All.

Lorint, F.-E., & Bernabe, J. (1977). *La sorcellerie paysanne.* Brussels, Belgium: Editions A. de Boeck.

Miroiu, M. (1994). Iesirea din vraja (Breaking the spell). *Revista de Cercetari Sociale, 2,* 144–157.

Pennebaker, J. W. (1990). *Opening up.* New York: Morrow.

Sorenson, K. A., Russell, S. M., Harkness, D. J., & Harvey, J. H. (1995). Account-making, confiding, and coping with the ending of a close relationship. *Journal of Social Behavior and Personality, 8,* 73–86.

Van Dijk, T. A., & Kintsch, W. (1983). *Strategies of discourse comprehension.* New York: Academic Press.

# 23

# *Job Loss: Hard Times and Eroded Identity*

***Richard H. Price, Daniel S. Friedland, and Amiram D. Vinokur***
*University of Michigan*

Freud (1961) argued that the two great wellsprings of mental health are love and work. If Freud is correct, then job loss—the loss of one's work—may entail human disruption and pain worthy of our attention and understanding. In what follows we review research and theory on job loss, especially as it influences well-being, and in so doing, consider the evidence available concerning Freud's assertion about the importance of work for mental health. We begin by identifying three orienting assumptions that inform our review of job loss.

First, we consider job loss to mark a *transition in the life course.* Life transitions are not discrete events. They are processes marked by a beginning or entry and an ending or exit. As people attempt to negotiate life transitions, their sense of purpose and agency becomes closely tied to their social context (Elder & O'Rand, 1995). Therefore, an analysis of the transition sparked by job loss must pay close attention to both the individual and the social context.

Second, we regard job loss as a *network event,* rather than as a loss with consequences only for the individual. For example, we expect that family ties, friendship networks, and other aspects of the job loser's social network are critically implicated in the job loss and its consequences. Job loss and the many other events it triggers reverberate through the social network and family relationships of the person, sometimes producing a cascade of subsequent strains in personal and family relationships.

Third, and building from the last point, we assume that the impact of job loss will differ for the individual depending on the type and quantity of *personal and social resources* available and how those resources are *mobilized* to cope with the loss. In line with this assumption, we suggest that intentionally designed organizational efforts to aid the individual in mobilizing their resources to make the transition back to employment can be of real benefit.

In the remainder of the chapter we will try to assess the validity of Freud's observation and offer suggestions for how the loss of work may be related to the

This chapter was supported by National Institute of Mental Health grant #5P30MH8330 to the Michigan Prevention Research Center, Institute for Social Research, University of Michigan. A small portion of this chapter was originally developed for the Proceedings of the National Institute of Health workshop on Social Conditions, Stress, Resources and Health held in Bethesda, Maryland, August 1995.

loss of mental health. We will begin with a brief review of what is known about the impact of job loss. While a number of reviews have documented an extremely wide range of impacts of job loss, ranging from increased risk for traffic accidents to increased crime (Leigh & Waldon, 1991; Catalano, Dooley, Novaco, & Wilson, 1993), we will confine our review primarily to physical health, mental health, and economic impacts on individuals and families. Then, we will briefly examine two of the important early theoretical interpretations of people's reaction to job loss. These early accounts foreshadow two of the recent research streams that have linked the economic and identity implications of job loss to the health of job losers. The next section of the paper will examine these two separate streams of research. After reviewing that research, we will consider some ways in which these two streams may be combined to provide us with a fuller and more detailed account of the impact of job loss. Finally, we will consider how this synthesis of theory and research illuminates how people may make the transition back to employment or into other life trajectories.

## DOCUMENTING THE IMPACT OF JOB LOSS ON INDIVIDUALS AND FAMILIES

In the modern economy, job loss is a pervasive phenomenon. As economic changes trigger workplace shutdowns and reductions in the workforce, large numbers of workers who would never have thought themselves vulnerable in the past are experiencing job loss (Price, 1990). According to a report by the Organization for Economic Cooperation and Development for the year of 1994, approximately 8 million people were unemployed in the United States (OECD, 1995). Of those 8 million people, between fifty and sixty-five percent of them were unemployed because they lost their jobs (U.S. Department of Labor, 1995).

Findings from the Great Depression to the present have documented the psychological and social costs of job loss for the unemployed person, for individual members of the person's family, and for the family as a whole (for a recent review, see Dew, Penkower, & Bromet, 1991). Though it is clear that some people may lose their jobs because of previous mental health problems, several studies have demonstrated that job loss produces mental health problems that extend significantly beyond any prior problems (Dooley, Catalano, & Wilson, 1994; Kessler, Turner, & House, 1987).

Job loss has adverse effects on the job seeker's social and psychological functioning (Vinokur, Caplan, & Williams, 1987). Research indicates that job loss leads to increased depressive symptoms (Catalano, 1991; Catalano & Dooley, 1977; Kessler, Turner & House, 1988; 1989), increased anxiety (Catalano, 1991), decreased subjective perceptions of competence (Warr, Jackson, & Banks, 1988), and decreased self-esteem (Jackson & Warr, 1984). Job loss is also associated with increased risk of suicide attempts (Platt & Kreitman, 1985), increased risk of alcohol abuse (Catalano, Dooley, Wilson, & Hough, 1993), and increased propensity for violent behavior (Catalano, Dooley, Novaco, & Wilson, 1993).

The effects of job loss are not limited to the lives of the individuals who lose their jobs. Job loss also affects members of the job seeker's family (Dew et al., 1991; Elder & Caspi, 1988). For example, the job seeker's increased propensity for aggressive, even violent, behavior often manifests itself in the context of the family. Positive correlations have been found between job loss and both spousal abuse (Windschuttle, 1980) and child abuse (Gil, 1970; Parke & Collmer, 1975). Also, research indicates that the wives of job losers have a higher prevalence of psychiatric disorders than wives of people who remain employed (Bebbington, Hurry, Tennant, Stuart, & Wing, 1981). Finally, job loss has been linked to marital and family dissolution (Liem & Liem, 1988).

Even this brief summary makes it clear that job loss can have a range of adverse effects on the lives of individuals and their families. The evidence seems to support Freud's claim that the absence of work has adverse effects on mental health. To better understand the processes by which job loss is linked to these outcomes, we now turn to a review of theory and research on the nature and consequences of job loss.

## HISTORICAL PERSPECTIVES ON JOB LOSS: JAHODA AND BAKKE

Some of the earliest and most insightful theoretical work on the impact of job loss on well-being was done by Jahoda, Lazarsfeld, and Zeisel (1933) and Bakke (1933, 1940a, 1940b). Jahoda and Bakke based their writings on intensive case studies of job loss and community during the Great Depression. Marie Jahoda focused on job loss as the loss of psychological and social functions of work (Jahoda, 1979, 1981, 1982). Jahoda's work began with her research on a community she called Marienthal that was devastated by unemployment during the Great Depression (Jahoda et al., 1933). Much of her theoretical work on the psychological and social impact of unemployment was based on her observations in this community.

Jahoda believed that there were a number of *social and psychological functions* served by work that are critical to the well-being of the individual. When people lost their jobs, she argued, these social and psychological functions were also lost. Critical "manifest functions," such as the capacity to earn money, and other "latent functions" were lost to the individual. Among these latent functions were a required and regular set of activities and time structures in one's life, the status and identity conferred by employment, the sense of participation in a collective effort and purpose, and the opportunity to carry on social activities with coworkers. Thus, for Jahoda, it was these manifest and latent psychosocial functions that constituted the crucial losses in the job loss experience.

Jahoda also argued that the psychological impact of job loss was largely due to the loss of these critical functions. She observed that in other societies, where formal employment as an institution did not exist, these same psychological functions were fulfilled through community activities, rituals, and religious practices that provided a sense of shared purpose and identity to those who participated in them (Jahoda, 1982; Feather, 1982). Thus, for Jahoda, the psychological needs met by employment were central to an understanding of the psychological impact of job loss. Warr's (1987) more recent theoretical work provides an insightful extension of Jahoda's functional interpretation of various critical features of work.

Before proceeding to discuss the work of Bakke, we would like to draw out several of Jahoda's ideas that have foreshadowed the course of research on job loss. First, her attention to the manifest function of work—earning money—parallels more recent trends that focus on job loss and economic hardship. Second, her discussion of the latent functions of work highlight the issues of personal and social identity and their relation to loss that more recent research has emphasized (Kelvin & Jarrett, 1985). Jahoda makes the point that work provides people with a sense of personal identity which may be tied to the particular work role or the more general social role of breadwinner in a family. She also documents how paid employment can provide people with a sense of social identity or shared purpose. People identify with the organization they work for or the profession they work in. When people lose their jobs, their claims on the financial and identity resources provided by work become more tenuous.

The early contributions of Bakke (1933, 1940a, 1940b) illuminated additional dimensions of the job loss experience. Bakke observed that loss of income and the fear of poverty were profound influences on the lives of the unskilled Greenwich workers and their families that he studied. This focus on perceived and anticipated economic problems is closely tied both to Jahoda's description of the manifest functions of work and to more recent work on economic hardship. In addition to highlighting the issue of economic hardship, Bakke observed how the previous work experience of the unemployed has a powerful effect upon the experience of unemployment. Bakke's work primarily focused on how unskilled workers experienced unemployment. He observed that unemployed unskilled workers generally believed that they had little control over their lives. Bakke traced these control beliefs to the content of the workers' jobs before they became unemployed. The content of unskilled work provided little opportunity to make decisions, plan, or control their work. Working under those conditions over time fostered the belief that they were relatively powerless to shape their world and that their fate was largely controlled by others. One of the great strengths of Bakke's work is that it reminds us that the experience of unemployment is shaped not only by the experience of job loss but by the lingering effects that previous employment has on people's lives.

## MOVING FROM THE PAST TO THE PRESENT: FOCUSING IN ON ECONOMIC HARDSHIP AND IDENTITY IN JOB LOSS RESEARCH

Both Jahoda and Bakke were prescient in their early theoretical work on the nature of job loss. Their recognition that economic hardship and personal identity were critical features of the job loss experience foreshadowed much of the later research and theory on job loss. Their insights have held up after further case study analysis as well as large-scale quantitative longitudinal research. In this next section of the chapter, we move on to discuss the pathways through which economic hardship and identity are linked to job loss and mental health.

### Economic Hardship and the Impacts of Job Loss

Job loss has also been described as a stressful life event that influences health and mental health (Pearlin, 1989; Pearlin, Lieberman, Menaghan, & Mullan, 1981). This perspective suggests that job loss is a *primary stressor* that can lead to an array of *secondary stressors,* most notably economic hardship. In this view, the health and mental health consequences of job loss depend not only upon the event of job loss itself, but also on the number and strength of secondary stressors, such as increased debt and family conflict, triggered by the event. From the perspective of understanding human loss, this framework also recognizes that job loss events unfold over time and may be causally linked to one another, and that some features of the loss experience may be much more consequential for well-being than others.

**Economic hardship.** A number of studies have identified *economic hardship* as a key influence mediating between job loss and depressive symptomatology (e.g., Kessler et al., 1987; Vinokur, Price, & Caplan, 1996; Vinokur & Schul, 1997). When conceptualizing economic hardship, it is important to recognize that it is both objective and subjective. Objective economic hardship occurs when people are experiencing a reduction in financial status and have to cope with that by cutting back on their expenses. Subjective economic hardship, often referred to as financial strain, occurs when people perceive that they are under financial constraint or are anticipating future financial problems. Both objective and subjective economic hardship are critically important for understanding the relationship between job loss and mental health. Furthermore, there is evidence that suggests that the relationship between economic hardship and health outcomes is more general than job loss and is critical in understanding the impact of widowhood for some women, for example (Umberson, Wortman, & Kessler, 1992).

The deprivation that results from economic hardship may affect physical health and general well-being both because of its impact on basic needs such as nutrition (Beasley, 1991; Pollitt, 1994) and because of loss of access to health care. Price (1990) has observed that families experiencing job loss will often reallocate limited health benefits among family members. For example, a family may seek treatment for children while neglecting acute conditions among parents. Individuals may fail to either seek preventive services or care for acute and chronic conditions. In these circumstances, acute conditions can become chronic, and chronic conditions may deteriorate still further.

**Cascade of secondary stressors.** Economic hardships can produce a cascade of stressful economic life events that challenge the coping capacities of families and individuals both in the short and long term. In the short term, economic hardship forces people to worry about facets of life that had been previously taken for granted (Conger et al., 1990). Inability to meet payments for housing may lead to the threat of or actual foreclosure of mortgages or eviction. Loss of an automobile means not only the loss of family transportation, but also a key resource which helps to sustain an effective job search. Economic hardship can also have delayed effects on health and mental health. People may cope with their financial difficulties by drawing heavily on savings and taking on additional debt, and create a spiral of financial problems that will continue even after employment is regained.

Still another set of mechanisms reflecting the interplay of economic hardship and family dynamics can influence the job loss experience. Several studies suggest that the distress displayed by job losers affects the well-being of their spouses (Liem & Liem, 1988; Penkower, Bromet, & Dew, 1988) as well as their children (Elder & Caspi, 1988; Justice & Duncan, 1977; Steinberg, Catalano, & Dooley, 1981). Recent results reported by Vinokur, Price, and Caplan (1996) implicate couple dynamics in influencing the mental health of the unemployed person. Their analyses suggest that economic hardship can increase depressive symptoms in both job losers and their spouses. Depressed spouses or partners may then withdraw social support and undermine the job loser, producing even greater distress.

## Identity and the Impacts of Job Loss

Research and theory have examined many facets of the relationship between identity and job loss. In this section of the chapter, we focus on three ways in which identity is related to mental health as a result of job loss. The first perspective concerns identity during transition between role states. The second perspective concerns job loss and perceptions of control or mastery. The third perspective concerns job loss and social stigma.

**Difficulty maintaining a sense of personal identity.** Job loss involves the loss of a social role. Because roles are used to construct the self (Callero, 1992, 1994; Turner, 1978) the loss of the central role of worker represents a major challenge to a person's identity. Ezzy (1993) argues that job loss is a form of *status passage* that directly disrupts an individual's attempt to sustain consistent and positive self-images and therefore increases the risk of mental health problems. This image of job loss as a status passage is critical for several reasons. Viewing it as a status passage highlights that job loss marks the beginning of a transition cycle or passage from one position in the life course to another. The transition presents challenges to a person's identity by making it more difficult to sustain consistent self-evaluations. Furthermore, because multiple life domains are interrelated, role loss in one domain has radiating effects on other domains. Thus, loss of an occupational role also presents identity challenges to the individual in their role as a friend, spouse, or parent.

Job loss may also present a challenge to identity and self esteem by altering an individual's network of *friendships and social support.* The loss of a job may result in the loss of a primary source of contact with friends (Bolton & Oatley, 1987). Since friendships often arise and are maintained by proximity (Whyte, 1956), the bonds of friendship are more difficult to maintain when people are no longer employed by the same organization. Over time, the frequency of contact with friends from the previous job decreases (Atkinson, Liem, & Liem, 1986). There is some evidence that loss of friendship networks can erode mental health. Kessler et al. (1988) found that being integrated into an affiliative network reduced the impact of unemployment on anxiety, depression, somatization, and physical illness of job losers. Their findings underline the importance of supportive friendships for identity and well-being.

One's identity and sense of mastery and competence are normally sustained in *valued social roles* as provider, spouse, and parent within the family (Thoits, 1991).

Job loss disrupts these roles and the sense of personal identity and mastery they provide. Job loss introduces new and pressing agendas into the family that can disrupt previously stable household role allocations and relationships, including coping with financial hardship and mobilizing to find reemployment (Conger et al., 1990; Menaghan, 1991).

When role reallocation due to job loss involves shifts in authority and status in the family, the resulting shift in power dynamics can lead to conflicts that threaten the short-term stability of the couple relationship (Atkinson et al., 1986). Such a realignment can undermine the self-confidence of the job seeker and partner in coping with job loss individually, and as a couple (Howe, Caplan, Foster, Lockshin, & McGrath, 1995; Vinokur & Caplan, 1987). It can also reduce the likelihood that the couple will develop workable solutions to the concrete demand of the crisis and, consequently, increase the risk of depression for both partners (e.g., Kowalik & Gotlib, 1987; Vinokur et al., 1996). This destabilizing process can result in a downward trajectory in the marital relationship that may end in separation and divorce (Gottman, 1993).

Job loss and economic hardship can also place strains on parent-child relationships (Conger et al., 1990; Elder & Caspi, 1988). These strains not only undermine the parent's sense of identity and mastery in the parental role, but often increase the likelihood of parental irritability, conflictual interactions between parent and child, harsh punishment, and family violence and child abuse (Broman, Hamilton, & Hoffman, 1990).

In a real sense, job loss marks an interruption in the natural process of reaffirming identity that is essential to maintaining mental health (Burke, 1991; Thoits, 1991). These identity interruptions are stressful, and the key to preventing their negative consequences is to allow a new identity to be affirmed. If people are able to negotiate new identities that are satisfactory, the negative effects of job loss may be minimized.

**Perceptions of mastery or control and mental health following loss.** Research on well-being and mental health suggests that perceptions of mastery or control are critical to sustaining mental health. Some authors view perceptions of mastery explicitly as components of well-being (Ryff & Keyes, 1995). Others view mastery as a critical mediator between stress and mental health (Vinokur & Schul, 1997). Research suggests that stress erodes perceptions of mastery and control in the roles where stress occurs (Krause, 1994). This erosion of mastery is most evident in roles that are valued by the individual (Krause, 1994; Thoits, 1991). Thus, much research on identity and stress has posited that stress in salient social roles is more detrimental to health than stressors in less valued social roles.

While stress erodes perceptions of mastery, people with low levels of mastery are more vulnerable to the stressors they encounter in their lives. The work of Bakke (1933, 1940a, 1940b), O'Brien (1986), and Kohn and Schooler (1983) reminds us that the content of work in a person's previous occupation can influence their perceptions of mastery and control. People who work in jobs that do not afford opportunities for self-direction exhibit lower levels of mastery and control. Combining the message of this research with the research that links mastery to health and well-being provide a vivid image of risk. Workers with low levels of mastery before job loss are likely to be especially vulnerable to the stresses they encounter as a result of job loss.

**Social stigma and mental health.** Job loss may also influence an individual's sense of personal and social identity because unemployment is a *stigmatized* social status. Though some jobs are low in status, few are as stigmatized as unemployment. The fact that unemployment status represents a form of "spoiled identity" (Goffman, 1968) is nicely illustrated by the fact that job losers will often construct an alternative work identity such as "consultant" or "student" rather than describe themselves as unemployed. This tactic avoids the erosion of self-esteem and demoralization often associated with socially devalued roles and statuses (Hughes, 1945).

Kelvin and Jarrett's work (1985) raises the important point that the degree to which the unemployed feel stigma from their social status depends heavily on the social context they occupy. In eras such as the Great Depression, when levels of unemployment were very high, being unemployed was less stigmatized than it would be in periods where fewer people were unemployed. This notion that the social context shapes and guides the judgments people make about themselves and others is critical to understanding how people respond to and experience unemployment.

## RISK GROUPS AND EVENT RESOLUTION

Our review of the literature makes it clear that job loss has its impact through two distinctly different pathways. One pathway is material; the other is symbolic. The loss of these material and symbolic resources results in both short- and long-term problems for individuals and their families. As detailed earlier, the consequences of job loss include mental health problems, increased risk of family disruption, divorce, and conflict. However, not all individuals and their families are equally affected by these two influences on well-being. It also follows that loss of a job that offers little material reward, is of low status, and provides little sense of control or satisfying relationships may even have a positive impact on mental health. For some individuals and their families, material loss will be paramount, and many of the negative impacts of job loss may be due largely to loss of material resources. On the other hand, even when material losses are not threatened, for other individuals and their families, job loss may represent a significant loss of identity and self-esteem and a diminished sense of mastery (Kaufman, 1982).

### Risk Groups

A recent study by Turner (1995) drawn from a national probability sample of unemployed persons supports and extends this argument. Turner found that negative mental health consequences of unemployment were associated with both identity strains and economic hardship. However, these two types of strains were differentially important for different groups of job losers. More highly educated and affluent job losers suffered more from the loss of identity than from the loss of material resources. On the other hand, less affluent and less well educated job losers suffered more from increases in financial strain associated with unemployment.

These differences have implications for the tactics and strategies most appropriate for job seeking and reentry into the labor force. A job loss resulting in only mild economic and identity loss may require only minor adjustments over a long period of time, and may even provide the opportunity for new career exploration. On the other hand, job losses where the economic loss is severe may place heavy demands on the job loser and his or her family to find sources of income replacement. Over the last decade the United States has experienced large numbers of job losses of this type, particularly in the industrial sector, where work was relatively high in pay relative to its status (Reich, 1991).

## Event Resolution

We argued earlier that job loss marks a transition in the life course. An implication is that the mental health outcomes of the transition triggered will depend on whether the economic and personal identity consequences of the job loss can be successfully resolved. Research conducted by Turner and Avison (1992) has shown that whether a life event has an enduring mental health impact depends on the degree to which the individual is able to resolve the consequences of the event. In a national study of social factors in health and mental health, Turner and Avison (1992) showed that when negative life events such as loss of a close relationship or a job, or onset of illness were successfully resolved, they had no enduring effects on mental health. On the other hand, when the consequences were not resolved, the individual continued to experience poor mental health.

We have seen that economic hardship is a key consequence of job loss that influences mental health. Resolution of the economic consequences of job loss may vary dramatically, with predictable effects on long-term mental health. A new source of income from reemployment or some other source such as marriage will help resolve the financial strain to the degree that it restores a previous level of income. On the other hand, eroded savings, a foreclosed mortgage, or foregone opportunities may be restored only slowly or not at all. Furthermore, if the new source of income, whether from a job or elsewhere, is inadequate, the person will continue to experience a stream of secondary stressors that produce continuing turmoil and distress for the person and his or her family. Danziger and Gottschalk (1995) have documented the growing disparity of income among individuals at the top and the bottom of the income distribution in the United States. We may expect that for those unable to adequately resolve the economic hardship brought on by job loss, continuing economic strain will produce chronic individual and family distress and poor mental health.

The personal identity aspects of job loss including the inability to maintain a clear sense of personal identity, lost feelings of control and mastery, and a stigmatized status may involve different social and psychological mechanisms. For those who have to accept a less prestigious job, stigma may be difficult to overcome. Loss of income and status may lead to a devaluing of work and career goals to maintain a sense of identity. Still other people may cope with threats to personal identity by reframing their sense of self, pursuing a simpler life, retiring, and seeking other sources of life satisfaction. Finally, even if reemployment is successfully achieved, the individual's sense of mastery and control may be shaken if the new job is markedly less secure.

Organized social efforts to help individuals gain new employment or otherwise successfully make the transition from job loss to a new life trajectory must address both the coping challenges presented by economic hardship and the assault on identity and the sense of mastery that job loss produces. Recent research (Caplan, Vinokur, Price, & van Ryn, 1989; Price, van Ryn, & Vinokur, 1992; Vinokur, Price, & Schul, 1995; Vinokur, van Ryn, Gramlich, & Price, 1991) has shown that such organized efforts can be successful and can prevent depression and produce better paying jobs for those who participate and economic benefits to society as well. Ultimately, such programmatic efforts must address the impact of job loss on family life and on economic well-being while at the same time helping individuals take up a new life course trajectory.

Freud (1961) argued that work is essential to mental health because it helps to maintain benefits for individuals that they could not obtain in isolation and because it helps establish and maintain vital identity-affirming social relationships. The research reviewed here amply confirms Freud's observations and helps us to understand why work that provides adequate material resources and a sense of personal identity is essential to mental health.

## REFERENCES

Atkinson, T., Liem, R., & Liem, J. (1986). The social costs of unemployment: Implications for social support. *Journal of Health and Social Behavior, 27,* 317–331.

Bakke, E. W. (1933). *The unemployed man.* London: Nisbet.

Bakke, E. W. (1940a). *Citizens without work.* New Haven, CT: Yale University Press.

Bakke, E. W. (1940b). *The unemployed worker.* New Haven, CT: Yale University Press.

Beasley, J. D. (1991). *The betrayal of health: The impact of nutrition, environment, and lifestyle on illness in America.* New York: Times Books.

Bebbington, P., Hurry, J., Tennant, C., Stuart, E. Y., & Wing, J. K. (1981). Epidemiology of mental disorders in Camberwell. *Psychological Medicine, 11,* 561–579.

Bolton, W., & Oatley, K. (1987). A longitudinal study of social support and depression in unemployed men. *Psychological Medicine, 17,* 453–460.

Broman, C. L., Hamilton, V. L., & Hoffman, W. S. (1990). Unemployment and its effect on families: Evidence from a plant closing study. *American Journal of Community Psychology, 18,* 643–659.

Burke, P. J. (1991). Identity processes and social stress. *American Sociological Review, 56,* 836–849.

Callero, P. L. (1992). The meaning of self-in-role: A modified measure of role-identity. *Social Forces, 71*(2), 485–501.

Callero, P. L. (1994). From role-playing to role-using: Understanding role as resource. *Social Psychology Quarterly, 57*(3), 228–243.

Caplan, R. D., Vinokur, A. D., Price, R. H., & van Ryn, M. (1989). Job seeking, reemployment, and mental health: A randomized field experiment in coping with job loss. *Journal of Applied Psychology, 74*(5), 759–769.

Catalano, R. (1991). The health effects of economic insecurity. *American Journal of Public Health, 81,* 1148–1152.

Catalano, R., & Dooley, D. (1977). Economic predictor of depressed mood and stressful life events in a metropolitan community. *Journal of Health and Social Behavior, 18,* 292–307.

Catalano, R., Dooley, D., Novaco, R., & Wilson, G. (1993). Using ECA survey data to examine the effect of job layoffs on violent behavior. *Hospital and Community Psychiatry, 44*(9), 874–879.

Catalano, R., Dooley, D., Wilson, G., & Hough, R. (1993). Job loss and alcohol abuse: A test using data from the Epidemiologic Catchment Area project. *Journal of Health and Social Behavior, 34*(3), 215–225.

Conger, R. D., Elder, G. H., Lorenz, F. O., Conger, K. J., Simons, R. L., Whitbeck, L. B., Huck, S., & Melby, J. N. (1990). Linking economic hardship to marital quality and instability. *Journal of Marriage and the Family, 52,* 643–656.

Danziger, S., & Gottschalk, P. (1995). *America unequal.* Cambridge, MA: Russell Sage Foundation, Harvard University Press.

Dew, M. A., Penkower, L., & Bromet, E. J. (1991). Effects of unemployment on mental health in the contemporary family. *Behavior Modification, 15,* 501–544.

Dooley, D., Catalano, R., & Wilson, G. (1994). Depression and unemployment: Panel findings from the epidemiologic catchment area study. *American Journal of Community Psychology, 22*(6), 745–765.

Elder, G. H. Jr., & Caspi, A. (1988). Economic stress in lives: Developmental perspectives. *Journal of Social Issues, 44*(4), 25–45.

Elder, G. H., & O'Rand, A. M. (1995). Adult lives in a changing society. In K. S. Cook, G. A. Fine, & J. S. House (Eds.), *Sociological perspectives on social psychology* (pp. 452–475). Needham Heights, MA: Allyn and Bacon.

Ezzy, D. (1993). Unemployment and mental health: A critical review. *Social Science & Medicine, 37*(1), 41–52.

Feather, N. (1982 ). Unemployment and its psychological correlates: A study of depressive symptoms, self-esteem, protestant ethic values, attributional style, and apathy. *Australian Journal of Psychology, 34,* 309–323.

Freud, S. (1961). *Civilization and its discontents.* New York: Norton (original work in 1930).

Gil, D. G. (1970). *Violence against children: Physical abuse in the United States.* Cambridge, MA: Harvard University Press.

Goffman, E. (1968). *Stigman: Notes on the management of spoiled identity.* Harmondsworth: Penguin.

Gottman, J. M. (1993). A theory of marital dissolution and stability. *Journal of Family Psychology, 7*(1), 57–75.

Howe, G. W., Caplan, R., Foster, D., Lockshin, M., & McGrath, C. (1995). When couples cope with job loss: A research strategy for developing preventive intervention. In L. R. Murphy, J. J. Hurrell Jr., S. L. Sauter, & G. P. Keita (Eds.), *Job stress interventions* (pp. 139–158). Washington, D.C.: American Psychological Association.

Hughes, E. C. (1945). Dilemmas and contradictions of status. *American Journal of Sociology, 1,* 353–359.

Jackson, P. R., & Warr, P. B. (1984). Unemployment and psychological ill-health: The moderating role of duration and age. *Psychological Medicine, 14,* 605–614.

Jahoda, M. (1979). The impact of unemployment in the 1930s and 1970s. *Bulletin of the British Psychological Society, 32,* 309–314.

Jahoda, M. (1981). Work, employment and unemployment: Values, theories, and approaches in social research. *American Psychology, 36,* 184–191.

Jahoda, M. (1982). *Employment and unemployment: A social psychological analysis.* Cambridge, UK: Cambridge University Press.

Jahoda, M., Lazarsfeld, P. F., & Zeisel, H. (1933). *Marienthal: The sociography of an unemployed community* (English translation, 1971). Chicago: Aldine.

Justice, B., & Duncan, D. F. (1977). Child abuse as a work-related problem. *Corrective and Social Psychiatry and Journal of Behavior Technology, Methods and Therapy*, *23,* 53–55.

Kaufman, H. G. (1982). *Professionals in search of work.* New York: Wiley.

Kelvin, P., & Jarrett, J. E. (1985). *Unemployment: Its social psychological effects.* Cambridge, UK: Cambridge University Press.

Kessler, R., Turner, J., & House, J. (1987). Intervening processes in the relationship between unemployment and health. *Psychological Medicine, 17,* 949–961.

Kessler, R. C., Turner, J. B., & House, J. S. (1988). The effects of unemployment on health in a community survey: Main, modifying, and mediating effects. *Journal of Social Issues, 44*(4), 69–86.

Kessler, R. C., Turner, J. B., & House, J. S. (1989). Unemployment, reemployment and emotional functioning in a community sample. *American Sociological Review, 54,* 648–657.

Kohn, M. L., & Schooler, C. (1983). *Work and personality: An inquiry into the effect of social stratification.* Norwood, NJ: Ablex.

Kowalik, D. L., & Gotlib, I. H. (1987). Depression and marital interaction: Concordance between intent and perception of communication. *Journal of Abnormal Psychology, 96*(2), 127–134.

Krause, N. (1994). Stressors in salient social roles and well-being in later life. *Journal of Gerontology: Psychological Sciences, 49*(3), 137–148.

Leigh, J. P., & Waldon, H. M. (1991). Unemployment and highway fatalities. *Journal of Health Policy, 16,* 135–156.

Liem, R., & Liem, J. H. (1988). The psychological effects of unemployment on workers and their families. *Journal of Social Issues, 44,* 87–105.

Menaghan, E. G. (1991). Work experiences and family interaction processes: The long reach of the job. *Annual Review of Sociology, 17,* 419–444.

O'Brien, G. E. (1986). *Psychology of work and unemployment.* New York: Wiley.

Organization for Economic Cooperation and Development (OECD). (1995). *OECD Economic Outlook, 57,* June, 1995.

Parke, R., & Collmer, C. (1975). Review of child development research. *Child Abuse: An interdisciplinary review.* Chicago: University of Chicago Press.

Pearlin, L. I. (1989). The sociological study of stress. *Journal of Health and Social Behavior, 30,* 241–256.

Pearlin, L. I., Lieberman, A., Menaghan, E. G., & Mullan, J. T. (1981). The stress process. *Journal of Health and Social Behavior, 22,* 337–356.

Penkower, L., Bromet, E., & Dew, M. (1988). Husbands' layoff and wives' mental health: A prospective analysis. *Archive of General Psychiatry, 45,* 994–1000.

Platt, S., & Kreitman, N. (1985). Parasuicide and unemployment among men in Edinburgh, 1968-1982. *Psychological Medicine, 15,* 113–123.

Pollitt, E. (1994). Poverty and child development: Relevance of research in developing countries to the United States. Special Issue: Children and poverty. *Child Development, 65*(2), 283–295.

Price, R. H. (1990). Strategies for managing plant closings and downsizing. In D. Fishman & C. Cherniss (Eds.), *The human side of corporate competitiveness* (pp. 127–151). Beverly Hills, CA: Sage.

Price, R. H., van Ryn, M., & Vinokur, A. (1992). Impact of a preventive job search intervention on the likelihood of depression among the unemployed. *Journal of Health and Social Behavior, 33,* 158–167.

Reich, R. B. (1991). *The work of nations: Preparing ourselves for 21st century capitalism.* New York: Knopf.

Ryff, C. D., & Keyes, C. L. M. (1995). The structure of psychological well-being revisited. *Journal of Personality and Social Psychology, 69*(4), 719–727.

Steinberg, L. D., Catalano, R., & Dooley, D. (1981). Economic antecedents of child abuse and neglect. *Child Development, 52*(3), 975–985.

Thoits, P. A. (1991). On merging identity theory and stress research. *Social Psychology Quarterly, 54*(2), 101–112.

Turner, J. B. (1995). Economic context and the health effects of unemployment. *Journal of Health and Social Behavior, 36,* 213–229.

Turner, R. (1978). Role and the person. *American Journal of Sociology, 84,* 1–23.

Turner, R. J., & Avison, W. R. (1992). Innovations in the measurement of life stress: Crisis theory and the significance of event resolution. *Journal of Health and Social Behavior, 33,* 36–50.

Umberson, D., Wortman, C., & Kessler, R. (1992). Widowhood and depression: Explaining long-term gender differences in vulnerability. *Journal of Health and Social Behavior, 33*(1), 10–24.

U. S. Department of Labor (1995). *Monthly Labor Review, 118*(7), 98–99.

Vinokur, A., Caplan, R. D., & Williams, C. C. (1987). Attitudes and social support: Determinants of job-seeking behavior and well-being among the unemployed. *Journal of Applied Social Psychology, 17*(12), 1007–1024.

Vinokur, A. D., Price, R. H., & Caplan, R. D. (1996). Hard times and hurtful partners: How financial strain affects depression and relationship satisfaction of unemployed persons and their spouses. *Journal of Personality and Social Psychology, 71*(1), 166–179.

Vinokur, A. D., Price, R. H., & Schul, Y. (1995). Impact of the JOBS intervention on unemployed workers varying in risk for depression. *American Journal of Community Psychology, 23*(1), 39–74.

Vinokur, A., & Schul, Y. (1997). Mastery and inoculation against setbacks as active ingredients in the Jobs intervention for the unemployed. *Journal of Consulting and Clinical Psychology, 65,* 867–877.

Vinokur, A. D., van Ryn, M., Gramlich, E., & Price, R. H. (1991). Long-term

follow-up and benefit-cost analysis of the JOBS program: A preventive intervention for the unemployed. *Journal of Applied Psychology, 76*(2), 213–219.
Warr, P. (1987). *Work, unemployment, and mental health.* Oxford, UK: Clarendon Press.
Warr, P. B., Jackson, P., & Banks, M. (1988). Unemployment and mental health: Some British studies. *Journal of Social Issues, 44*, 47–68.
Whyte, W. H., Jr. (1956). *The organization man.* New York: Simon & Schuster.
Windschuttle, K. (1980). *Unemployment: A social and political analysis of the economic crisis in Australia.* Ringwood, Victoria, Australia: Penguin.

# V

# *SYNTHESIZING COMMENTARIES ON LOSS THEORY AND RESEARCH*

# 24

# *Why There Must Be a Psychology of Loss*

***John H. Harvey***
*University of Iowa*

***Ann L. Weber***
*University of North Carolina at Asheville*

*As many as 25 percent of the people exposed to the traumatic events that are becoming endemic to modern life can be expected to develop full-blown PTSD as a consequence.*
—(Wylie, 1996, p. 22)

## THE CASE FOR A PSYCHOLOGY OF LOSS

The above statistic is rather staggering given the frequency with which people in our world encounter traumatic events in their lives or the lives of close others. Closer to 100% of the population at one time or another experience multiple events constituting major losses in their lives and producing significant stress for them and their loved ones. Loss is pervasive in our lives. Whether we are directly impacted by horrorific trauma such as airplane disasters, or we experience more subtle losses due to homelessness, prejudice and stigmatization, or disabling disease, we all in due time will learn the dread and struggle that major loss brings to our lives.

So many national losses have occurred in the last few years in the United States (e.g., the Oklahoma City Federal Building bombing, the TWA 800 disaster, the Atlanta Olympic Park bombing) that media pundits have discussed a "culture of loss" that is pervasive in the late 1990s in the United States. At one time in mid-1996, President Bill Clinton had represented the nation so often at memorial services such as the one for Commerce Secretary Ron Brown, who died in an airline crash in Bosnia, that political strategists suggested this association between loss and Clinton would work in his favor in the 1996 Presidential Election. Presumably, this association made the President seem more human and drew sympathy from the general population.

In this context, ironically, psychology has had little to say explicitly about the psychology of loss. What is the psychology of loss? What are the psychological implications of major loss? How is the psychology of loss similar to or different from similar fields such as traumatology or thanatology? This volume in part is

The authors thank Eric Miller and Julia Omarzu for comments on earlier drafts of this chapter.

directed toward that gap in research and theory, both for psychology and for several related fields that are concerned with loss experiences. Important assumptions in this study of loss are that there are unique contributions that can represent a psychology of loss and that such a study will tell us as much about people's courage and resiliency as it will their susceptibility to stress and breakdown due to serious losses.

## AN IMPLICIT ASSUMPTIVE BASE

Examination of dictionaries and encyclopedia of psychology will reveal little explicit consideration or definition of the concept of loss (e.g., Reber, 1995). Yet, this concept forms the undergirding for significant fields of work in contemporary psychology. We define a major loss as involving a reduction in a person's resources, whether personal, material, or symbolic, to which the person was emotionally attached (Harvey, 1996). It may involve the more subtle types of loss such as the loss of virginity and childhood friends that Viorst (1986) discussed in her analysis entitled *Necessary Losses.* It may involve losses occurring in the midlife turmoil of divorce or occupational uncertainty and financial difficulty. It may involve the sudden and devastating death of a loved one. It may involve a major disability of the body and mind that may occur at any time to anyone. It may involve a host of experiences that typically may not be considered when the topic arises, including: being homeless, being the victim of violence, being the target of racial or ethnic prejudice and discrimination. It always involves the survivors, all of whom must grieve, be reduced in many both clear and unclear ways, and then try to adapt to the new meanings created by the loss.

It is our contention that the concept of loss forms an often implict assumptive base for other concepts in the literature of psychology, including those of stress and coping, death and dying, trauma, and psychopathology. To a considerable degree, the stress and coping and trauma literatures are concerned with how people cope with major stressors such as life-threatening injury and illness (e.g., Lazarus & Folkman, 1984; Wilson & Raphael, 1993). Typically, the emphasis is upon various cognitive, emotional, and behavioral strategies that the individual may use in maintaining morale and finding meaning in the situation. Sensitivity to the construct of loss and its meaning to the individual in this situation would lead to greater understanding of the individual's sense of loss that is connected to the stressor, resulting stress, and other experiences.

In areas of fundamental work in extant psychology such as psychopathology (e.g., Dowson & Grounds, 1995), the various dimensions of a person's loss are often implied in a dilineation of the case particulars. However, typically there is little explicit analysis of the circumstances as constituting a perceived loss of such-and-such nature and magnitude. Beyond that, there usually is no detailed inquiry into the implications of the felt losses in the individual's life. Sophisticated treatments of clinical phenomena and treatment approaches exist for students that involve only veiled reference to the human loss experience that so often nurtured the phenomena. Clinical, counseling, and school psychology all are distinctive helping professions, but seldom are these fields defined with reference to humans' experience of loss. For example, in a well-known clinical psychology textbook, Nietzel, Bernstein, and Milich (1994) indicate that one major aspect of clinical psychology is to "help people who are psychologically distressed" (p. 2). No mention is made of the common experience of loss as a highly probable, at least partial, basis for psychological distress.

In the field of death and dying, loss is the central topic. Interestingly, though, the intellectual emphasis most often does not pertain to the many ways people feel reduced by events not connected to death, per se. Sociologist Carolyn Ellis (1995) makes this point wonderfully in her autobiographical memoir and sociological analysis *Final Negotiations,* which tells the story of her nine-year relationship with sociologist Eugene Weinstein. During their relationship, Weinstein was in the process of slowly succumbing to emphysema. Ellis tells of the many types of loss each of them experienced as Weinstein's condition worsened to the point that he no longer could teach, had little mobility, and had great difficulty doing anything "normal" on a day-to-day basis. These losses included: losses in their careers and ability to make scholarly accomplishments; losses in their sexual interaction and in their love life; losses of self-esteem associated with his debilitated condition (including her own perceived stigma in being with a chronically ill person) and problems with presenting themselves as a couple in public; losses in the abilities to do normal chores together and to travel and experience fun as they had previously; and various losses in identity, including when medical personnel would "look through" Weinstein in talking about him and sometimes would not listen to Ellis as an "official relative" in making medical decisions, because Ellis and Weinstein were not married.

How can a recognition of issues of loss help us understand people's reactions to major stressors and traumatic circumstances, including those surrounding death and dying? Perhaps the most telling observation about how people often deal with stress and trauma is that they do so through a process of expending energy and resources. The act of coping itself becomes a loss in many instances. For example, a family may drain their financial resources in battling a long-term cancer situation on the part of one member. The person with cancer may survive, but in so doing may be debilitated by the treatment as well as the disease. Employment may be terminated for a lengthy period. Self-esteem and social activity may plummet. While grateful to survive, the survivor as well as the family may become cynical about the medical establishment and its treatment of them. As Janoff-Bulman (1992) eloquently describes, this family's assumptions about the world may take a major hit through this stressful period. They may no longer believe that the world is a benign place and that good things happen to good people. Although Janoff-Bulman appropriately sees this greater reality-orientation as positive for these individuals, it is nonetheless a secondary loss experience for them. Thus, it is important to focus on the pervasive nature of loss when major losses ripple into secondary losses, resulting eventually in a cumulative loss experience. Further, what the individuals involved must process and deal with in coping and adapting to the changes wrought is far greater in scope and detail than dealing with the primary loss, per se, whether cancer or some other circumstance.

## REVERBERATING LOSSES, SELF-SCHEMAS, AND SELF-IDENTITY

Perhaps one of the most daunting aspects of reveberating losses through a lifespan are the recurrent memories associated with the losses. Emotionally wrenching events invite memories that are more permanently encoded in our minds (Everly & Lating, 1994). Beginning in infancy we build a unique mountain of experience upon which the person we are today perches. Included in that experience are many losses, whether deaths or other events that in some way reduce us. Warm and welcome, or haunting and troubling, we can no more separate the self from memory than, in the poet Yeats' image, "the dancer from the dance." These haunting memories often affect us as we attempt to sleep when our minds size up our lives and focus in on the unresolved and troubling areas. A build-up in major losses as we progress over time means there will be a build-up in associated memories, some of which are positive in that we feel that we have grown or reacted to situations in ways consistent with our values. We seldom have time, however, to work through all of our losses. Hence, these memories very likely will lie dormant in our mind and periodically be triggered by cues we encounter in daily life.

This line of reasoning about reverberating losses suggests that the self-identity is greatly influenced by losses and our efforts to process them. In some significant way, we essentially become what we feel that we have treasured and lost in our lives. As Horowitz (1976) emphasizes, we develop schemas that represent themselves and the most important relationships in our lives. Severe stressors often lead to a necessary reconfiguring of these self-schemas. But how does a series of different kinds of losses affect self-schemas? We have only vague knowledge relevant to this question. From neuropsychology, we know that people who suffer severe brain injuries or diseases may show short-term (or possibly long-term) memory debilitation. Their self-schemas are likewise impaired.

We theorize that the concept of self-schema deserves greater elaboration than exists in the literature in light of the phenomenology that many people report in connection with their most daunting losses. For example, when a spouse dies, a person must learn to not expect further images and experiences of interaction with the loved one. Plans of togetherness must change. Wondrously human qualities such as that of physical touch and of seeing with one's eyes the smile or joy of the loved one can no longer be anticipated. All that the lost other meant to the survivor must be mentally rearranged. From making a phone call to the loved one while he or she is at work to opening the door upon arrival at home expecting to see the loved one with open arms, all of the habits of daily life that have centered around interaction with the loved one must be dashed. As C. S. Lewis (1961) commented in reference to his recently deceased wife, a voice that evokes the intonations of a lost loved one's voice may send the survivor into immediate anguish. The same may be true if the survivor is looking through the loved one's clothing or jewelry. Such personal belongings may be symbolic of interactions with the loved one and in general of the loved one's personality and dynamism; they now stand in stark contrast to a life being lived and the remembered occurrence of joyful activity.

These schemas of interaction, sights, sounds, and smells elicit periods of angst, sadness, and grief in the survivor. Such periods occur at anniversaries. They occur at holidays. They occur when visiting places that were special to the relationship.

They occur at any moment when the person is reviewing the big picture of his or her life. Related types of mental, emotional, behavioral correlates of loss may just as readily ensue from the dissolution of a close relationship as from a loved one's death. Further, they may derive from many other types of trauma, including violence, predudice, and stigmatization. Knowledge is quite limited regarding the power of such schemas to influence all types of behavior from eating and sleeping to motivation and the will and motivation to become close to others.

After such colossal mental and behavioral revisions, the survivor may wonder "who am I anyway?" That question may occupy the survivor for years—even to one's dying day. The first author of this chapter knew a woman in her eighties who for 30 years had told and then reminded all who would listen that her 25-year-old son had died in a tragic automobile accident. She did not want anyone to forget who he was. That became part of who she was: the memory, for all who cared, that her son who meant so much to her and who had such great potential in all areas had died much too soon. Of course, schema change is likely to be highly individualized after major loss. Other mothers may have found it possible to more readily "forget," or put away their memories of their deceased sons, at least for major periods of time. The whys of these differences in who people become after great loss deserve the study of psychologists and other social scientists.

What value does such reasoning about the rippling and cumulative nature of loss have for the overall health of the individual? We believe that this reasoning has value both for the person who is the primary survivor and for those who relate to the survivor, whether a close other or a health care providers. Each must realize the extent of what must be addressed in time. The relevant literatures are too quick to use terms such as "recovery," "closure," and "healing" when the loss experience is very much still in process for the individual. Given the frequent wave of loss experiences in everyone's life, Rando (1993) argues that the term "adjustment" makes more sense to use in considering the struggle to deal with major loss than do other, more falsely positive terms, that seem to be preferred in the literature.

## A LANGUAGE, RHETORIC, AND CULTURE OF LOSS

*2:04:09: Takeoff*
*2:09:02: (Sound of click)*
. . .
*2:10:07: Pilot: "What was that?"*
*2:10"08: Co-Pilot: "I don't know."*
. . .
*2:10:20: Pilot: "We're losing everything."*
. . .
*2:10:22: Co-Pilot: "We need to go back to Miami."*
*2:10:23: (Sounds of shouting from passenger cabin.)*
*2:10:25: Female voices in cabin: "Fire, fire, fire, fire."*
. . .
*2:14:00: Valujet Flight 592 crashes into the Everglades*
[May 11, 1996]

Cockpit transcript reported in *Dallas Morning News,* November 19, 1996, p. 16A.

It was also reported that during the confusion in the five minutes of terror aboard this Valujet flight, an unidentified man apparently used his cellular phone to make a final, good-bye call to his wife.

Media reports such as the transcript of the Valujet's final minutes are not unusal. We who pay attention to the news hear them with some frequency. Our pain in hearing such reports pales in comparison to the pain of survivors' families, who often, via prolonged court cases, must endure years of scrutiny of such records. Yet all of us are increasingly privy to others' final moments of life. Because of the media, we also know a lot more about the terror that many airline crash victims experience. Because of this media attention, are we more sensitized to their losses and those of their survivors? Or, are we more inured to their losses and grief? While we do not know the answers to these questions, we suggest that media has an extraordinary impact on our sense of loss—our own and others' losses—in contemporary society. The media further influence whether or not we feel empathy for victims and survivors.

The December 5, 1996 issue of *USA TODAY* was headlined with "Putting Grief to Work: Survivors of Tragedies Find Peace in Activism." This article discussed how the great degree of media coverage of tragedies such as the TWA 800 Disaster or 12-year-old Polly Klaas' cruel abduction, rape, and killing had produced public sympathy for victims. Writer Andrea Stone said:

> *In a nation intrigued with victimhood, they share a need to make their senseless loss somehow meaningful for others. Candy Lightner founded Mothers Against Drunk Driving, John Walsh hosts a popular TV crime show, Carolyn McCarthy soon will be sworn into Congress. It's a mirror of the victim's rights movement, people striking back to turn tragedy into action and rage into reform. Some experts question whether a few are crossing the line from do-gooder to self-promoter, but others say these family members have created healthy outlets for their grief.* (p. 1)

Stone continues by suggesting that while most people want to keep their tragedies private, others go public and seek media attention. She quotes Fred Thompson, an image consultant, who says: "It is a new phenomenon. People are increasingly very media-savvy, and they see opportunities to take their victimization and use it as a means of obtaining attention" (p. 2).

Stone notes that Marc Klaas became an effective, zealous campaigner against the early release from prison of persons convicted of sexual abuse against children and for the "three strikes and you're out" legislation in California designed to imprison habitual criminals for life if they have been convicted of felonies three times. Klaas is quoted as saying that his life changed in the "blink of an eye" when Polly was killed. He quit his job as a franchise holder for a rental car agency and became a full-time crusader for tougher sentencing. He said in the interview: "My purpose before was to insure a future for my child, but my child is gone" (p. 2).

There is virtually a "loss-speak" that has emerged in our language to reflect the sense of a culture of loss. It includes terms invented to represent especially difficult times for a people, such as: "grapes of wrath," "summer of sorrow," "winter of despair," "season of darkness," "journey of doom," and, to borrow further from

Dickens, the "epoch of incredulity and unbelievability." Despite the frequency of such phrases in the media and the frequency of events that they portray, ironically enough we, especially in the media-sophisticated Western cultures, may be becoming increasingly desensitized to loss-speak and accompanying pictures of tragedy and loss.

In very recent years, several nonfiction memoirs telling stories of loss have become bestsellers. They include: Mary Pipher's *Reviviing Ophelia* that focuses on the everyday dangers that beset teen-age girls; Kay Redfield Jamison's *An Unquiet Mind* which chronicles a psychiatrist's struggle with her own manic depression; and, perhaps the most controversial, *The Kiss* by Kathryn Harrison, who tells of her affair with her father starting in her late teens; she starkly narrates how a seductive kiss by her father was the prelude to a dark passage of obsessed love that she finally found the strength to end when her mother died. Critics have suggested that this wave of popularity is partially due to many readers' own experience with and interest in diverse types of major loss. The memoirs show how human and hence frail we all are, but they may also provide rays of hope and meaning if we are struggling with personal demons.

We are bombarded by these words and pictures on television, in movies, and in the newspapers and other media. They become abstractions removed from our lives; or if they elicit a personal note of anguish, that note may quickly be lost amidst the clutter of our practical lines of action and daily chores. Gergen (1991) spoke of the modern person as often a "saturated self," given the abundance of demands on time and attention from the many sources of modern technology at our disposal—from television to cellular phones to faxes to email to junk mail. This saturated self may only infrequently take the time to reach out in mind or action to strangers in their times of great loss.

In addition to the frequent reference to loss in the popular media, the great literatures of all cultures have always looked to loss as an experience that binds all humans and that so often rivets our minds to images and memories. Consider book critic Sharman Stein's (1996) comment on the focus on grief in literature:

> *In many ways, all literature is about some kind of grief. And when it is done well, you never forget it. I still feel utter misery when I think about the death of the beloved dog in Milan Kundera's "The Unbearable Lightness of Being," how his owner gave him his last roll to eat, and how she and her husband dug his grave and wept.* (p. 5)

## THE DIALECTIC OF LOSS AND GROWTH: THE VALUE OF CONFRONTING LOSS

> *He has seen but half the universe who has not seen the house of pain.*
>
> —Ralph Waldo Emerson

In the context of arguing that the field of psychology needs to explicitly focus on loss as a concept and research topic, it may seem strange to also contend that such a focus lends itself to enhancement of the field regarding human growth and potential. Loss and growth form a remarkable dialectic for all of us to try to appreciate. As Hemingway suggested, we are "strongest at the broken places." When people come through the "dark wood" of personal loss, to use Dante's term about the period of midlife, they often grow and become much more deeply attuned to losses in humanity in general. After our own humbling and devastating experiences, one direction for change is for our antennae for empathy with others who suffer to become like "giant rabbit ears." Our losses become, in a sense, a lesson and a gift. Psychology needs to give much more attention to this pattern of thought, feeling, and behavior accompanying major losses.

Scholars who have studied human change over decades emphasize the importance of watershed-type events, often centering around some type of major loss, such as the death of a parent or a divorce, in having dramatic impacts on a survivor's subsequent behavior (Levinson, 1978, 1996). Certainly the behavior of the survivors' organization that formed after the 1998 terrorist bombing of Pan Am 103 over Scotland is representative of this logic. This group has lobbied U.S. and world officials to hunt down terrorists and to make airlines safer against terrorists' acts. They also have created a program of giving annual scholarships to Syracuse University students in memory of the many Syracuse students who died in this tragedy. Further, Sarah Lowenstein, one of the mothers in the group, has created at Syracuse University a memory garden entitled "Dark Elegy," which involves sculptured human forms of women kneeling and weeping. These women represent the mothers of Syracuse students upon hearing of their sons' or daughters' death.

At both the group and individual levels, the type of growth and change that may emerge from great loss and grief can be linked to Erikson's (1963) powerful concept of generativity. This concept refers to the "giving back of values and acts of caring to future generations" by the present generation. It is a concept that either explicitly or implicitly may be found in hallmark contributions such as Frankl's (1959) testimony to human courage and quest for meaning.

Joining a growing corpus of scholarship in the social and behavioral sciences, many approaches to dealing with major loss emphasize the value of confrontation with the loss (e.g., Neeld, 1990; Pennebaker, 1990; Rando, 1993). Presumably after some period of grieving or a "time out" in which people do not actively confront their loss (Aldwin, 1994), people can best begin to achieve resolution by conscious work aimed at processing the meaning and implications of the loss and taking the next steps for the survivor in light of the loss. Weber (1992) has provided evidence and discussed how widows and widowers sometimes work diligently on mental accounts of their prior relationships with their late spouses as a way of grieving, developing new identities, and giving greater meaning to the major events that constituted their relationships. They may then confide aspects of these accounts to close others in still another form of adapting to their losses (Harvey, Weber, & Orbuch, 1990). There is a cogent saying that the more we deny death, the more we get tangled up in it; the same is true for our other great losses as well.

Beyond the foregoing focus on the value of expression, scholars and nonscholars alike are giving greater credence to people's stories and narratives, which often are addressed to daunting dilemmas of living that involve losses of parts of themselves. Health professionals are finally learning the power of listening to patients' stories of illness. Sick persons are finally insisting on being heard—by doctors, family members, legislators, and other officials. The work of scholars such as Coles (1989), Bruner (1990), and Ellis (1993) has been particularly important in this movement.

In the 1990s, personal stories of loss are pervasive in all forms of popular writing. Rohan B. Preston made such a point in the *Chicago Tribune,* in commenting on the work of the 1997 Pulitzer Prize poetry winner Lisel Mueller:

> *[P]oet Lisel Mueller, 73, winner of this year's Pulitzer Prize for poetry, is the kind of writer who does art to save herself and her world. And like fellow prize-winning poets Gwendolyn Brooks, Louise Gluck, Andrienne Rich and Yusef Koniunyakaa, who spin life's ragged threads into luminous gold and give witness to unspeakable cruelties, Mueller seeks salvation, not through religion-clad spirituality but soulful and engaged probing. . . .* (p. 1)

## CAN WE EVER REALLY ACHIEVE RESOLUTION?

While the foregoing reasoning about the restorative power of various forms of story-telling and confiding is congenial to us, we also want to emphasize that people can never totally achieve resolution for some major losses. As Langer (1991, 1995) has argued regarding contemporary peoples' cognizance of the Holocaust, some events, because of their extraordinary personal devastation, may defy cognitive and emotional work. In such cases, people have survived, even if reduced in ways that are not imaginable to others. They have every right to avoid as best they can those images of unspeakable horror.

As suggested by Weiss (1988), we can have a sense that we adapted to major loss when the following criteria are met:

1. We show the ability to give energy to everyday life.
2. We show psychological comfort, as demonstrated by freedom from psychic pain and distress.
3. We show the ability to experience gratification—to feel pleasure when desirable, hoped-for, or enriching events occur.
4. We show hopefulness regarding the future, being able to plan and care about plans.
5. We show the ability to function with reasonable adequacy in social roles as spouse, parent, and member of the community.

These criteria devolve to our commitment to go on, and in so doing endorse a set of values and beliefs in our lives and interactions with others. As noted by Hollis (1996), the word "grief" derives from the Latin *gravis*, "heavy, burdensome," from which also derives the word "gravity." Thus, to experience grief is to bear a heaviness of our loss. We only grieve that which we value very much and then lose. In going on and working for what we believe in, we may also recognize the truth of the maxim suggested by Frankl (1959) that people can become wiser by becoming sadder.

## CONCLUSION

The main conclusion of this paper is that psychology and related fields in the social and behavioral sciences must explicitly treat the topic of loss in a much more thorough way than has been true in the past. Psychology must do so to be true to its putative breadth of inquiry into the human condition. It must do so to better understand currently studied topics for which loss is a central, but neglected, dimension.

Korte (1996) argues that as we approach the 21st century, the prolongation of individual lives delays the time when people ordinarily receive reminders of death. Such reasoning, however, may overlook the extensiveness of reminders of mortality and death that surround the living (as in the foregoing argument about media influences). Even the young sometimes lose friends and loved ones to traffic accidents and a variety of other types of death. Beyond that point, a principal argument of this chapter is that major loss is pervasive in all people's lives.

So what is new about how we have conceived loss in this paper? We believe that it is somewhat new to advocate not only studying the consequences of loss, but indeed to suggest the value of major loss in leading people to become more passionate, more compassionate, more humane, and more attuned to the grief passages of others and of nature. Great loss and its attendant grief may be the greatest teacher of how to be empathic and available to humans. It beckons with compelling force and obsession. It sits us in a perch overlooking an ocean of feelings of despair, regrets, dashed hopes and plans, lost and never possessed innocence, and tears of pain, fear, and loneliness. We do not readily take our eyes off this ocean, its waves and currents and countless forms.

Most appropriately, great loss keeps us awake at night. It hammers at the brain cells and moves the pen, sometimes in miraculous ways. It haunts. It releases. It reappears again and again. It is relentless. But so is its charge to do, act, be our best selves more powerfully than ever before. For Dante, the greatest losses were those of loss of hope and connection with others. Each human is faced with the dilemma of trying to find his or her own antidotes to losing hope and connection. The final thrust of our argument resonates with Camus' compelling admonitions: "I shall tell you a great secret, my friend. Do not wait on the last judgment. It takes place every day," and "There can be no happiness if the things we believe in are different from the things we do."

## REFERENCES

Aldwin, C. M. (1994). *Stress, coping, and development.* New York: Guilford.

Bruner, J. (1990). *Acts of meaning.* Cambridge, MA: Harvard University Press.

Coles, R. (1989). *The call of stories.* Boston: Houghton Mifflin.

Dowson, J. H., & Grounds, A. T. (1995). *Personality disorders: Recognition and clinical management.* New York: Cambridge University Press.

Ellis, C. (1993). There are survivors: Telling a story of sudden death. *The Sociological Quarterly, 34,* 711–730.

Ellis, C. (1995). *Final negotiations: A story of love, loss and chronic illness.* Philadelphia: Temple University Press.

Erikson, E. (1963). *Childhood and society* (2nd ed.). New York: Norton.
Everly, G. S. Jr., & Lating, J. M. (1994). *Psychotraumatology: Key papers and core concepts in post-traumatic stress.* New York: Plenum.
Frankl, V. E. (1959). *Man's search for meaning.* New York: Washington Square Press.
Gergen, K. (1991). *The saturated self: Dilemnas of identity in contemporary life.* New York: Basic Books.
Harvey, J. H. (1996). *Embracing their memory: Loss and the social psychology of story-telling.* Needham Heights, MA: Allyn & Bacon.
Harvey, J. H., Weber, A. L., & Orbuch, T. L. (1990). *Interpersonal accounts: A social psychological perspective.* Oxford, UK: Blackwell.
Hollis, J. (1996). *Swamplands of the soul: New life in dismal places.* Toronto: Inner City Books.
Horowitz, M. J. (1976) *Stress response syndromes* (2nd ed.). Northvale, NJ: Jason Aronson.
Janoff-Bulman, R. (1992). *Shattered assumptions.* New York: Free Press.
Korte, J. (1996). *Outliving the self: How we live on in future generations.* New York: Norton.
Langer, L. L. (1991). *Holocaust testimonies: The ruins of memory.* New Haven, CT: Yale University Press.
Langer, L. L. (1995). *Admitting the Holocaust.* New York: Oxford University Press.
Lazarus, R. S., & Folkman, S. (1984). *Stress, appraisal, and coping.* New York: Springer-Verlag.
Levinson, D. J. (1978). *The seasons of a man's life.* New York: Knopf.
Levinson, D. J. (1996). *The seasons of a woman's life.* New York: Knopf.
Lewis, C. S. (1961). *A grief observed.* New York: Farrar, Straus & Giroux.
Neeld, E. (1990). *Seven choices: Taking the steps to a new life after losing someone you love.* New York: Delta.
Nietzel, M. T., Bernstein, D. A., & Milich, R. (1994). *Introduction to clinical psychology* (4th ed.). New York: Prentice-Hall.
Pennebaker, J. (1990). *Opening up.* New York: Morrow.
Preston, R. B. (1997). *Chicago Tribune, Tempo Section,* April 11, p. 1.
Rando, T. A. (1993). *Treatment of complicated mourning.* Champaign, IL: Research Press.
Reber, A. S. (1995, new ed.) *The Penguin dictionary of psychology.* New York: Penguin.
Stein, S. (1996). *The Chicago Tribune Books Section,* November 17, p. 5.
Stone, A. (1996). Putting Grief to Work: Survivors of Tragedies Find Peace in Activism. *USA Today,* December 5, pp. 1–2.
Viorst, J. (1986). *Necessary losses.* New York: Fawcett.
Weber, A. L. (1992). The account-making process: A phenomenological approach. In T. L. Orbuch (Ed.), *Close relationship loss: Theoretical approaches* (pp. 174–191). New York: Springer-Verlag.
Weiss, R. S. (1988). Loss and recovery. *Journal of Social Issues, 44,* 37–52.
Wilson, J. P., & Raphael, B. (Eds.) (1993). *International handbook of traumatic stress syndromes.* New York: Plenum.
Wylie, M. S. (1996, July/August). Going for the cure. *Networker,* pp. 20–37.

# 25

# *Can There Be a Psychology of Loss?*

**Robert A. Neimeyer**
*University of Memphis*

The reader of this volume cannot fail to be impressed by the remarkable—indeed, almost bewildering—variety of topics, theories, methods, and disciplinary matrices being brought to bear on the human encounter with loss. If nothing else, this recent burgeoning of interest in the subject speaks to the often bold pioneering efforts of the contributors to this sourcebook, to say nothing of the breadth of vision of its editor! But this same diversity also raises a fundamental question that represents something of a linguistic counterpart to the implied assertion in the title of Harvey and Weber's contribution (Chapter 24):[1] "Can There Be a Psychology of Loss?"

Granted, psychology and related disciplines can *attend* to loss, and loss in its many forms is a compelling part of the human experience. But does a "psychology of loss" implicitly presume some level of integration in the resulting field of study, whether at the level of theory, content, or method? My goal in the present chapter is not to review the substantive contributions made by the various authors, but to reflect on this central question, and in so doing, to raise a set of related issues that have relevance for the emerging field of "loss studies" as a whole. I will conclude by drawing attention to a few thematic emphases that emerge across chapters, despite their diversity of content, and make some recommendations regarding the progressive extension or refinement of the research programs on which they are based.

## A BRIDGE TOO FAR?

To open a consideration of whether there can indeed be a "psychology of loss," it is conceptually clarifying to deconstruct the question by posing its opposite: "Can there be a psychology of *gain*?" To flesh out this question, is it tempting to consider whether any psychology, theory, or field would retain sufficient coherence if it were to attempt to encompass birth (vs. death), marriage (vs. divorce), friendship formation (vs. decline), fitness (vs. overweight), performance enhancement (vs. performance slumps), apartment rental (vs. loss of home), wellness (vs.

[1]Unless otherwise noted, my citation of the work of particular authors refers to their contributions to the present volume.

injury and illness), confirmation of expectations (vs. shattering of assumptions), optimism (vs. loss of hope), stability (vs. change) in gender identity, and peaceable coexistence (vs. ethnic genocide). If the prospect of accommodating such diverse events, conditions, and processes in a single field of study strains the imagination, this might serve as an appropriate caution about the feasibility of constructing a coherent "psychology of loss" as well.

But on closer inspection, what might be meant by a "psychology of loss" is open to alternative interpretations, which vary considerably in their ambitiousness. Thus, I will briefly consider four possible meanings of the term as reflected in the work of the contributors to this volume: (a) the development of a "grand unifying theory," (b) the discovery of common factors, (c) the application of more general psychosocial theories, and (d) the enhancement of multidisciplinary cross-fertilization. Because each of these approaches to cultivating a psychology of loss encounters problems as well as prospects, I will comment on the apparent aspirations of advocates of each program, and draw attention to some of the obstacles they are likely to confront.

## GRAND UNIFYING THEORY

Proponents of an encompassing theory of loss in its many aspects are the inheritors of a dream that has motivated scientists and philosophers since the Enlightenment: the prospect of subsuming all (justified) knowledge under a single coherent theory or set of propositions. In psychology, advocates of such a grand unifying theory (GUT) are dismayed by the fragmentary state of psychological "science," and tend to favor a logical positivist approach to theory building that (a) maintains close contact with "objective" observations, and (b) encourages formulations that are compatible with the presumably more "basic" sciences of biology, and ultimately physics (Staats, 1991).

While more modest in their aspirations, loss theorists like Miller and Omarzu (Chapter 1) appear to view themselves as working toward a general model through their advocacy of a taxonomy of various types of loss as an "essential" step toward greater theoretical unity. More subtly, broad definitions of loss in terms of "reductions in a person's resources, whether personal, material, or symbolic" (Harvey and Weber; cf. Lavallee, Grove, Gordon, and Ford, Chapter 18) or the "removal of hoped-for goals" (Snyder, Chapter 5) may also reinforce the aspirations of GUT theorists, to the extent that they imply that "losses" can be subsumed under a single definitional, and by extension, explanatory framework.[2]

Despite its appeal in some quarters, the quest for a grand unifying theory in psychology has encountered serious conceptual problems. Not only is psychology

[2]In contending that highly abstract definitions of loss encourage the quest for theoretical unification, I am not claiming that the authors of such definitions necessarily hold this view. Rather, I am suggesting that such definitions can rhetorically reinforce the "reasonableness" of a unified program, much as the (re)definition of psychology as "the science of human behavior" tantalized generations of psychologists with the vision of a unified, rigorous study of virtually all human functioning configured along behavioristic lines.

partitioned into quite different "language communities," each with its own preferred way of parsing, abstracting, and explaining human experience (Koch, 1976), but contemporary philosophers (Feyerabend, 1978; Kvale, 1992) and psychologists of science (Gholson, Shadish, Neimeyer & Houts, 1989) question whether such unificationism and reductionism are desirable in the first place. To draw a parallel to the field of psychotherapy integration (Norcross & Goldfried, 1992), critics have cautioned that attempts at the synthesis of distinctive models can contribute to a thinly veiled discouragement of divergent thinking and an ironic reduction in the internal coherence of the presumably more "unified" theory (Messer, 1986; Neimeyer, 1993). Thus, on intellectual grounds alone, pursuit of a singular general theory of "loss" seems unlikely to succeed.

If the field of loss studies is unlikely to formulate a grand unifying theory, does this mean that only highly specific mini-theories of particular losses are feasible? Not at all. Indeed, some of the models advanced in the present volume hold promise of shedding useful light on a range of loss experiences, as I will outline below. But ultimately, this generality may be purchased at a price, insofar as more abstract models tend to lose focus on the idiosyncrasy of the phenomena they subsume. This limitation also applies to a second approach to the psychology of loss, one predicated on a "common factors" model.

## COMMON FACTORS MODEL

Only slightly less ambitious than the pursuit of a unifying theory of loss would be the attempt to identify common factors or processes that characterize all or most losses, irrespective of their origin or form. For example, Miller and Omarzu imply that some form of grieving may accompany all loss, and that the identification of such responses and the personality factors that affect their "staging" is a legitimate goal of loss theory. Snyder's conceptualization of suffering as a blockage in goal-directed activity, while specifically relevant to an understanding of physical pain, may also be generalizable to many other forms of loss that undermine one's sense of agency, energy, or the habitual pathways that lead to goal attainment. Likewise, Janoff-Bulman and Berg's (Chapter 3) analysis of shattered illusions suggests yet another core process triggered by various losses, at least those of a traumatic nature.

While the extension and empirical validation of such models seem feasible, it is important to bear in mind the intrinsic limitations of common factors models, whether in the area of loss or elsewhere. Again drawing on the field of psychotherapy integration, models that emphasize the core variables responsible for therapeutic change (e.g., the provision of hope through the enactment of a credible ritual) have been criticized for their tendency to gloss over differences in the way these common factors are realized in different therapies, as well as their tendency to ignore potentially quite important factors that characterize particular forms of therapy, but are minimal or absent in others (e.g., explicit use of the therapeutic relationship). Such concerns are equally pertinent to the area of loss studies. For example, Stroebe, Schut, and Stroebe (Chapter 6) take pains to tease out both the common and distinctive features of adjustment to trauma and bereavement, two related forms of loss that certainly have more shared features than, say, retiring from sports and failing to lose weight. When one considers that many of the essential features that attend some profound forms of loss (e.g., of cognitive and personality functions in brain injury) are wholly absent in others (e.g., divorce or nonneurological disability), it seems likely that a common factors model of loss will be necessarily limited in its exhaustiveness and range of application.[3]

Ultimately, the pertinence of common factors models may depend ironically on *restricting* the range of experiences considered to represent relevant forms of loss in terms of the model being proposed. For example, focusing on an identifiable stress response may be fruitful for a range of morphologically dissimilar losses (e.g., of employment, health, or loved ones through genocide or suicide), but it will be less relevant to other less "personal" losses (e.g., of collective identity) or those to which one has habituated (e.g., chronic overweight). Moreover, it is important to critically examine the assumption of common factors even where they seem most obvious. For instance, even such "core" responses as grief in response to bereavement are by no means universal, and the very assumption that grieving can be associated with predictable stages or features has been called radically into question by contemporary grief theorists (Attig, 1996; Neimeyer, 1997). Thus, it is likely that the identification of common factors will (a) prove feasible for only circumscribed forms of loss, and (b) leave much of the "variance" in responses to even these forms of loss to be accounted for by specific personal, social, and situational factors not subsumed within the model.

## APPLICATION OF GENERAL THEORIES

A third strategy for promoting greater integration in loss research would be to draw on or extend existing psychosocial theories to encompass loss phenomena, in the recognition that the losses studied will be highly specific in character. In this sense the application of more general theories to various forms of loss represents a less ambitious attempt to produce a coherent field of loss studies than the previously discussed approaches, although it pursues the more modest goal of linking loss research with larger literatures in the parent discipline. Research that focuses on the role of equity or account-making in relationship loss would exemplify this approach.

One potential advantage of general theories is that they promote empirical assessment and refinement through the fairly precise identification of variables implicated in loss. This is well illustrated by those loss theories in the present volume that have a strong social psychological base. Thus, Williamson and Shaffer (Chapter 12) have studied differences in high and low "communal" relationships

[3]Despite this guarded assessment of the prospects for developing a satisfying common factors model of loss, it seems likely that some common processes can be identified that have a high degree of relevance to many, if not most, of the forms of loss described in this book. One set of such factors concerned with the critical process of meaning reconstruction is highlighted below. My point is simply that an attention to what is *shared* in different forms of loss must necessarily be supplemented by the study of what is *unique* across different forms of loss, and that the domain of noncommon factors will grow substantial to the extent that the losses being studied differ in logical type.

affected by the increasing disability and dependency of one partner, and Felmlee (Chapter 8) has isolated a number of factors (e.g., attraction to dissimilar others, extreme descriptions) that heighten the likelihood of "fatal attractions" in which partners are ultimately rejected for the very reasons they were considered attractive in the first place. More generally, Sprecher and Fehr (Chapter 7) summarize the broad literature on the dissolution of personal relationships, which has drawn on a variety of experimental and correlational designs to establish common factors influencing relationship breakdown. The success of such research programs suggests that efforts to extend well-developed existing theories to the new domain of loss studies are likely to prove fruitful.

Still, it is worth noting, along with Miller and Omarzu, that the majority of current research in loss studies is *issue-driven*, rather than *theory-driven* in nature. By extension, much of the current work is essentially descriptive rather than inferential; the attempt to test theory-driven hypotheses seems at best premature when investigators are trying to understand the scope and effects of such phenomena as homelessness, brain injury, multiracial marriage, suicidal bereavement, chronic pain, job loss, genocide, or holocaust survivorship. Moreover, several of these losses may be better accommodated by forms of (nonexperimental) social theory that lie outside psychology altogether, such as economic theories bearing on the cycle of poverty, or sociological theories of labeling or stigmatization. While the application of such theories may be revealing in its own right, it will not necessarily promote the goal of establishing a *psychology* of loss, *per se.*

## MULTIDISCIPLINARY CROSS-FERTILIZATION

While the above three approaches to advancing a psychology of loss share a concern with the development of more comprehensive theory, the final approach considered in this chapter is more pragmatic in its intent, namely, to foster conceptual exchange among investigators who would otherwise be isolated in their respective specializations, whether the social psychology of personal relationships, behavioral medicine, sports psychology, death studies, or vocational behavior. The synergy of such exchange is an explicit theme in several of the chapters (e.g., Lavallee et al. and Nurius & Gaylord, Chapter 21), and in a more general sense, characterizes the book as a whole.

The advantages of blurring the boundaries between traditionally distinct specialties or disciplines are both conceptual and methodological. At a conceptual level, Stroebe and her colleagues demonstrate the utility of importing a concern with traumatic stress responses into models of bereavement, as well as considering the grief responses that attend many forms of trauma. At a methodological level, Ellis (Chapter 4) illustrates the fertility of transgressing the frontiers that usually separate science and literature in her moving and evocative autoethnographic studies of losses in her own life and the lives of her associates. Indeed, one could even argue that this openness to cross-fertilization among traditionally distinct fields is essential to the full understanding of many forms of loss (e.g., job loss, homelessness, disability), which inevitably require analysis in economic and sociological, as well as strictly psychological terms.

What challenges confront proponents of this form of (inter)disciplinary integration? Like the motivation for pursuing cross-fertilization, the obstacles to it may be more pragmatic than theoretical. Specifically, difficulties may arise at the level of the *sociology* of science, rather than its *content* per se. For example, most existing institutions for the dissemination of research findings (e.g., conferences, organizations, journals) promote communication with others within the same discipline, while fewer promote cross-fertilization with those in quite different areas. Moreover, even in cases where well-established interdisciplinary organizations, conferences, and journals exist (as in the Association for Death Education and Counseling, the annual meetings of the American Association for Suicidology, or the peer-reviewed journal *Death Studies*), identification with these multispecialty entities tends to be purchased at the cost of a certain degree of marginality within one's parent discipline (Wass & Neimeyer, 1995). Thus, it remains to be seen whether the success of volumes like the present one, or high-quality journals like the *Journal of Personal and Interpersonal Loss* can bring about a measure of useful cross-fertilization in the field of loss studies without also contributing inadvertently to the insularity of the field from psychology as a whole.

In summary, the prospects for establishing a "psychology of loss" vary depending on the form that such a psychology might take. In general, the most ambitious of these programs (e.g., the pursuit of the GUT model) are likely to encounter the most severe problems, while those with more modest aspirations for conceptual coherence, topical reach, and disciplinary range are more likely to succeed, at least in part. In the hopes of further promoting the progressive expansion of the field of loss studies, I will close by signaling three issues that deserve more explicit attention by investigators, whatever their specific focus of interest. These include (a) the social embeddedness of loss, (b) the process of meaning reconstruction, and (c) the therapeutic and caregiving implications of this research.

## THE SOCIAL EMBEDDEDNESS OF LOSS

Of all the themes that underpin this sourcebook, the social dimension of loss is perhaps the most pervasive. Lyons and Sullivan (Chapter 10) argue explicitly for the adoption of a "relationship perspective" on illness and disability, viewing these as a breach in the unwritten contract with family members. Sprecher and Fehr, Femlee, Rosenblatt and Tubbs (Chapter 9), and Williamson and Shaffer are all necessarily focused on the interpersonal causes and consequences of various forms of disruption in intimate relationships, and Price, Friedland, and Vinokur (Chapter 23) stress the extent to which job loss is a "network event," rather than merely an individual one. The emphasis of each of these authors could be construed as *molecular*, insofar as each considers the context of close relationships that defines, mediates, or supports experiences of interpersonal loss.

In contrast to this attention to relatively intimate dyadic or familial relationships, several other authors consider extensively or in passing the more *molar* social field and its relevance for various loss experiences. Thus, Harvey and Weber note the impact of media coverage on the degree of empathy accorded bereaved individuals, and Stroebe and her colleagues draw attention to the way in which grief can be considered pathological to the extent that it deviates from broader cultural norms. At a societal level, Rosenblatt and Tubbs speculate about the losses to multiracial couples resulting from racisim, Liiceanu (Chapter 22) analyzes the restructuring of women's identity with the advent of the Communist and post-Communist Romania, and Solomon, Ram, and Neria (Chapter 16) critically dissect the prevailing social and historical factors responsible for Israel's ironic neglect of the losses of Holocaust survivors. Finally, Staub (Chapter 17) adopts an international perspective in arguing for the role of "bystander nations" in validating and investigating the suffering engendered by ethnic genocide. Such molar analyses stretch beyond the "psychology of loss" per se to foreshadow a "politics of loss" that is even less developed in the emerging field of loss studies.

What additional steps might be taken to study these more social dimensions of the loss experience? At the molecular level, a fuller understanding of relational factors in loss would be gained through (a) systematic attention to social factors in *all* forms of loss, (b) longitudinal studies to identify changes in relationship processes over time, from pre-loss, through acute loss and readjustment phases of the relationship, and (c) greater use of experimental and quasi-experimental methods, where appropriate, to more clearly identify factors associated with favorable and less favorable outcomes. These recommendations have less relevance at the molar level, however, in view of the larger time scale and the societal, rather than individual or dyadic impact of such losses. In this case, greater rigor might be introduced by using various forms of discourse analysis (Edwards & Potter, 1992) to study the structure and strategy of public rhetoric, debates, reporting, or legal proceedings bearing on broad societal losses. To take but a single example, a careful analysis of the discourse in and surrounding the Eichmann trial could yield a systematic and fascinating account of such factors as changes in Israeli society's depiction of Holocaust survivors from the early to mid-1960s, rhetorical devices used both by state prosecutors to indict Eichmann for Nazi war crimes and by Eichmann in his own defense, and the differential response of the media in various countries (e.g., Germany vs. the U.S.) to the events of this highly publicized tribunal. While these more qualitative methods are unlikely to yield the degree of precision and replicability of experimental or even correlational studies conducted on a molecular level, they could nonetheless move studies of social and cultural responses to loss to a greater level of sophistication, going beyond the more informal or intuitive analysis of events that characterizes the current literature.

## MEANING RECONSTRUCTION

Popular models of grief and mourning depict a stagic progression through the emotional sequelae of loss, typically beginning with some form of shock or denial, and progressing through phases of yearning and searching, anger and anxiety, and depression and disorganization, before eventuating in acceptance, recovery, and the like. Likewise, professional systems for diagnosing and assessing bereavement responses focus on psychiatric symptomatology (e.g., anxiety, sleep disruption, social upheaval) that besets the survivor, and which, if prolonged or intense, can point to "complications" in the course of grieving that require treatment.

While useful in providing a general framework for conceptualizing the loss experience, these models share many deficiencies. Among them are their tendencies to (a) ignore individual and cultural variations in the response to loss, (b) cast grievers in a passive role, as persons who must negotiate a sequence of stages and symptoms forced upon them by external events, (c) implicitly prescribe some forms of grieving as "normal," while pathologizing others, (d) assign primacy to emotional responses, while minimizing the role assigned to meanings and actions, and (e) individualize the experience of grieving, treating it as a private act outside the context of human relatedness (Neimeyer, 1997). In response to this critique, a "new wave" in grief theory is emerging, which argues that *meaning reconstruction in response to a loss is the central process in grieving* (Neimeyer, 1997; Neimeyer, Keesee, & Fortner, 1997; Neimeyer & Stewart, 1996). Founded on a constructivist approach to psychology and psychotherapy (Kelly, 1955; Neimeyer & Mahoney, 1995), the meaning reconstruction approach strives to reveal the individuality of loss for different persons and cultures, while viewing grievers as active agents attempting to assimilate events into personal and shared systems of belief that may be challenged by the loss experience. Moreover, it strips the varied human responses to loss of their pathological implications, and instead seeks to provide a richer description of the passionately held meanings that shape our emotional, behavioral, and physical responses. Finally, it draws attention to the delicate interplay of self and social context, and the way in which both are renegotiated in the aftermath of significant loss. Stated succinctly, grieving is reconstrued as a process of relearning the self, and relearning the world (Attig, 1996).

Several of the contributors to this sourcebook are clearly participating in this emerging paradigm for understanding loss. For example, Miller and Omarzu note the high degree of individuality in the words, images, and thoughts associated with loss, and Chwalisz (Chapter 13) and Range (Chapter 15) both emphasize the persistent "search for meaning" that attends traumatic losses, whether in the form of brain injury or the suicide of a loved one. Importantly, Chwalisz, along with Sprecher and Fehr, recognize that this effort after meaning has a social as well as private dimension, as survivors attempt to formulate and secure validation for a coherent account of their experience. The picture that emerges from these considerations depicts significant loss as a profound challenge to the narrative constructions that sustain life, a challenge that requires a reauthoring of one's (inter)personal world of meaning in order to allow the survivor to once again participate in a life that is both comprehensible and significant.

Of the authors to address these themes in the present volume, Janoff-Bulman and Berg offer the most detailed account of the process of meaning reconstruction. In their view, survivors of trauma confront the terror of a shattered, malevolent world, one that calls into question their fundamental illusions of security, predictability, and justice. But in keeping with a constructivist epistemology, they acknowledge that "the ontological status of any belief is unknowable," so that no simple objective criterion of "truth" or "rationality" exists to guide survivors toward a more adequate assumptive world. Instead, they are confronted with the task of finding a deeply personal meaning and value in the face of their loss, while nonetheless rebuilding a belief system that accommodates the tragic dimensions of human existence.

Several additional authors amplify this basic theme by stressing the extent to which loss disrupts one central domain of personal assumptions, namely, those that define one's sense of self. Accordingly, Harvey and Weber argue that our self-schemas are greatly affected not only by the losses we sustain, but also by our efforts to process them. Kelley (Chapter 14) notes that one's sense of self is undermined by the experience of chronic pain, and that those who suffer from it are validated by both professional and lay acknowledgment of the reality of their condition. Likewise, Nurius and Gaylord underscore the degree to which breast cancer and other "intimate threats" to women threaten not only their life, but also their gender identity. Liiceanu shifts this theme of loss of gender role to a sociological level in her analysis of the deconstruction and reconstruction of women's identities in Romanian culture. And finally, Ellis subtly captures the poignant multiplicity of self, the sense of inner contradiction, that attends life-changing losses and transitions. Taken together, these contributions extend our appreciation of the challenges to our assumptive world posed by loss, which often require deep-going revisions in our sense of identity as well as the world external to us.

But despite the consistency with which themes of meaning reconstruction and self-transformation are sounded by the contributors to this volume, one is tempted to conclude that such themes are more commonly acknowledged than they are studied. As a consequence, the process of rebuilding a shattered assumptive world remains underspecified, with few investigators other than Janoff-Bulman and her colleagues systematically studying the process. In the view of Stroebe, Schut, and Stroebe, this general inattention may be due to intrinsic difficulties in measuring "the fundamental but elusive 'meaning of loss' factor, which is so intricately bound up with measures of adjustment that assessment is almost precluded." However, the social scientific methods of Janoff-Bulman and her collaborators, the more narrative and literary approaches of Ellis, and the hybrid qualitative and quantitative methods espoused by constructivist investigators of loss (Neimeyer, 1997; Neimeyer et al., 1997; Sewell, 1996) suggest that meaning reconstruction, while often subtle and idiosyncratic, is nonetheless open to empirical and clinical study. The further refinement and application of such methods clearly deserves more widespread attention among loss researchers.

## THERAPEUTIC IMPLICATIONS

A final theme relevant to this collection of chapters merits attention not because of its salience, but because of its virtual absence, namely, the astonishingly underdeveloped therapeutic implications of the theory and research reported throughout the sourcebook. Williamson and Shaffer briefly note the differential forms of support that might be extended to high- versus low-communal spouse caregivers, grounding their recommendations in their empirical study of both groups. More extensively, Snyder carefully teases out the various forms of goal, pathway, and agency "work" that might inform a model of therapy guided by a theory of hope for those who suffer chronic pain. But for the most part, the contributors to this volume fall curiously silent when it comes to the implications of their work for ameliorating the human suffering that attends loss, for healing disrupted intimate relationships, or for promoting the reconstruction of meaning and restoration of a viable sense of identity.

This neglect of the healing dimensions of loss studies may be explained by several factors, including the intention of the editor to develop a text of basic rather than applied research on the many facets of loss, the recruitment of predominantly social psychological rather than clinical contributors, the need to first develop a conceptual frame to guide subsequent therapeutic interventions, the wish to underscore the universality of loss, rather than cast it as a special clinical problem to be solved, and so on. But clearly there is room for further work that would extend the implications of this literature for helpful forms of support, counseling, and caregiving to those whose lives have been torn apart by loss, whether these clinical extensions take the form of idiographic case studies, nomothetic investigations of processes of "recovery," or controlled outcome trials that attempt to evaluate the utility of various interventions. The varied conceptual and methodological frameworks offered by the present contributors could provide useful points of departure for this effort.

## CONCLUSION

As an identifiable field of scholarship, loss studies is in its infancy. While some of the traditions on which it draws and which it in some measure subsumes (e.g., thanatology, traumatology) are better institutionalized as specialties in their own right, even these constituent fields are only now beginning to evolve into mature (sub)disciplines with clear focus and direction. Thus, loss researchers face problems as well as prospects as they attempt to define their collective, as opposed to individual goals: To what degree do they seek unifying theories, common factors that cut across different forms of loss, general theories that tether them securely to their parent disciplines, or forums for cross-fertilization with others pursuing quite different research programs? In this chapter I have tried to sketch some of the challenges posed to each of these forms of integration, as well as to draw attention to a few possible themes—the social embeddedness of loss, meaning reconstruction, and the therapeutic implications of current research—that might provide foci for future studies. If such challenges can be surmounted and such themes can be addressed, there may yet emerge a "psychology of loss" that enriches our understanding of this essential facet of the human experience.

## REFERENCES

Attig, T. (1996). *How we grieve: Relearning the world.* New York: Oxford University Press.

Edwards, D., & Potter, J. (Eds.). (1992). *Discursive psychology.* London: Sage.

Feyerabend, P. (1978). *Against method.* London: Verso.

Gholson, B., Shadish, W., Neimeyer, R., & Houts, A. (Eds.). (1989). *Psychology of science: Contributions to metascience.* New York: Cambridge University Press.

Kelly, G. A. (1955). *The psychology of personal constructs.* New York: Norton.

Koch, S. (1976). Language communities, search cells, and the psychological studies. In W. J. Arnold (Ed.), *Nebraska Symposium on Motivation 1975* (pp. 477–559). Lincoln, NE: University of Nebraska Press.

Kvale, S. (Ed.). (1992). *Psychology and postmodernism.* London: Sage.

Messer, S. (1986). Eclecticism in psychotherapy: Underlying assumptions, problems, and trade-offs. In J. C. Norcross (Ed.), *Handbook of eclectic psychotherapy* (pp. 379–397). New York: Brunner/Mazel.

Neimeyer, R. A. (1993). Constructivism and the problem of psychotherapy integration. *Journal of Psychotherapy Integration, 3,* pp. 133–157.

Neimeyer, R. A. (1997). Meaning reconstruction and the experience of chronic loss. In K. J. Doka (Ed.), *Living with grief* (pp. 159–176). Washington, D.C.: Taylor & Francis.

Neimeyer, R. A., Keesee, N. J., & Fortner, B. V. (1998). Loss and meaning reconstruction: Propositions and procedures. In S. Rubin, R. Malkinson, & E. Wiztum (Eds.), *Traumatic and non-traumatic loss and bereavement.* Madison, CT: Psychosocial Press.

Neimeyer, R. A., & Mahoney, M. J. (1995). *Constructivism in Psychotherapy.* Washington, D.C.: American Psychological Association.

Neimeyer, R. A., & Stewart, A. E. (1996). Trauma, healing, and the narrative emplotment of loss. *Families in Society, 77,* 360–375.

Norcross, J., & Goldfried, M. (Eds.). (1992). *Handbook of psychotherapy integration.* New York: Basic.

Sewell, K. W. (1996). Constructional risk factors for a post-traumatic stress response after a mass murder. *Journal of Constructivist Psychology, 9,* 97–108.

Staats, A. W. (1991). Unified positivism and unification psychology. *American Psychologist, 46,* 899–912.

Wass, H., & Neimeyer, R. A. (1995). Closing reflections. In H. N. Wass & R. A. Neimeyer (Eds.), *Dying: Facing the Facts. Vol. 3* (pp. 435–446). Washington, D.C.: Taylor & Francis.

# 26

# *Issues in the Study of Loss and Grief*

**Robert S. Weiss**
*University of Massachusetts, Boston*

## THE CONCEPTUALIZATION OF LOSS AND CONSEQUENT DISTRESS

Losses are of various sorts, differing in their nature and their impact. Some losses don't matter that much: we've lost a small possession, or an unimportant opportunity. Other losses matter a great deal: we've lost a job, a home, or a spouse. Some of the losses that matter a lot give rise to grief; others make for a kind of distress that may be no less painful, but that is different.

If we classify losses by the nature of the distress to which they give rise, we can recognize at least three categories. In the first are the losses that produce grief. These include losses of critically important relationships, including especially the deaths of partners in pair-bonds or of children. In the second category are the losses that damage self-esteem, foster self-doubt, and produce a sense of diminished social worth. These include losses of social position, of place in a community, as through being fired from a job. In the third category are the losses that occur as a result of victimization. These include loss of money or possessions through criminal victimization and loss of self-respect through social humiliation. Losses of this sort damage the capacity both to trust others and to trust a self that has proven vulnerable to misuse.

Each of the losses can be expected to give rise to sadness and anger. However, losses of different kinds will differ in the feelings and ideations—the thoughts and images—that are associated with the sadness and anger. The grief that is the usual response to relational loss includes as a central element a wish for the return of the lost figure. The damaged self-esteem stemming from loss of social position is likely to be organized around desire once again to have social value comparable to that which was lost. Whereas a new widower or widow will want again to be with the spouse, even while acknowledging that this is impossible, someone who has been fired from a job will not want to rejoin former coworkers so much as to once again have work that would elicit the respect of others. In the first instance it is a relationship with a particular figure that was lost; in the second, what is lost is a social place that had sustained a particular sense of self. Diminished self-esteem

I am indebted to Marie Killilea for helpful comments on an earlier draft of this chapter.

may occur in grief, but is not central to the grief syndrome; it is, to the distress that follows loss of social place.

Diminished self-esteem is also central to the distress following victimization. Loss of social place and victimization each produce narcissistic damage, i.e., damage to the person's self-valuing. But the syndrome that follows loss of social place has as a central element a sense of imposed marginality, of having been rejected by significant communities. The syndrome that follows victimization has as a central element a sense of a self that is untrustworthy. In the first instance one has been rejected by others and continues to be excluded; in the second instance one rejects oneself.

The way loss would be undone would be different in each of the three forms of loss. For the griever who has lost a relationship, it would be through the return of the lost figure; for the person experiencing narcissistic damage associated with loss of social place, it would be through social acceptance; and for the person experiencing narcissistic damage as a consequence of victimization, it would be through restoration of self-respect and self-confidence.

Insofar as the loss cannot be undone, it seems likely that in every instance of loss some sort of emotional and cognitive reorganization becomes necessary for restoration of well-being. In the case of grief, this is called "grief work," although the reorganization may in some instances occur through another process. (I say more about this below.) In the case of narcissistic damage, reorganization may require learning to reframe experience, so that self-respect and self-confidence are restored.

I believe we are less advanced in our understanding of narcissistic damage and its management than we are in our understanding of grief. With further understanding of the processes that give rise to distress among those who have lost social position or been victimized, we may be able to develop theories that parallel those we have for grief and for processes of recovery from grief. We may then be able to describe for these other losses how normal recovery processes differ from those that have gone awry, and to suggest how treatment may make a difference.

We now understand the grieving that follows loss of loved figures well enough to describe its usual course and the impediments to recovery. Nevertheless, controversial issues remain. In the remainder of this chapter, the most important of these issues will be discussed. Resolution of these issues in our understanding of grief may suggest how they might be resolved in our understanding of responses to other losses.

## FREUD, LINDEMANN, BOWLBY, AND FUNDAMENTAL ISSUES IN THE STUDY OF GRIEF

Grief is among the emotional states that seems always to have been recognized. The phenomena of grief are described in our earliest stories and myths. The Iliad, for example, includes detailed descriptions of Achilles' grief for his friend Patroclus, and Priam's for his son Hector. But it was not until Freud's paper, "Mourning and Melancholia," (1917) that it was asked, as an issue for examination, what processes lead from loss to grief and how it is that grief finally abates.

Freud in his paper proposed that the phenomena of grief expressed painful awareness of the permanent removal of a figure to whom there was emotional linkage. He further proposed that the processes through which grief was resolved, which he called "the work of mourning," required that "each single one of the memories and expectations" that linked the mourner to the lost figure be considered and its potential for pain neutralized. However, he noted, this process of "hypercathexis" could fail, in which event grief, instead of abating, would give rise to persisting melancholia.

Erich Lindemann's paper, "Psychopathology and Management of Acute Grief" (1944), subjected loss and grieving to systematic examination. Lindemann accepted entirely Freud's idea that grief work was necessary to loosen the griever's emotional investment in the lost figure. He added the thought that therapeutic intervention could facilitate grief work where it was impeded. Lindemann's paper provided an extraordinarily vivid and evocative description of grief as well as a view of grief as a disabling condition whose resolution could be facilitated by therapeutic intervention. It made grieving an issue of psychiatric interest.

Two elements of Lindemann's paper which we can now recognize as oversights suggest the distance research has covered since the paper appeared. Lindemann significantly understated the length of time required for grief to abate. He wrote, "With eight to ten interviews in which the psychiatrist shares the grief work, it was ordinarily possible to settle an uncomplicated and undistorted grief reaction." We now know that widows and widowers require two to four years before they are capable of giving full energy to ongoing life (Parkes & Weiss, 1983). Lindemann also failed to recognize the importance of the specific relationship that had existed between the griever and the lost figure. He did not distinguish between people who had lost partners with whom they shared a pair-bond and people who had lost friends and relatives for whom they cared, whom they may have cherished, but who were not essential to their emotional stability. It now seems evident that protracted grieving follows the loss of someone with whom there had existed a relationship of attachment (Weiss & Richards, 1997) and follows only this sort of loss (Weiss, 1993).

John Bowlby (1961, 1980, 1982) provided the first sound theoretical basis for understanding the phenomena of grief. He proposed that grief in adults is caused by interruption of the same socio-emotional system (called by him the "attachment" system) whose interruption produces separation distress in children. As evidence, he pointed to the similarities between grief in adults and separation distress in children. In each there is a focussing of attention on the absence of the lost figure, vigilance regarding that figure's return, restlessness, intense distress, protest at the separation, and inconsolability. Feelings of security are diminished. In Bowlby's view, both children who believe themselves abandoned and adults whose partners have died express in their grief a striving to regain the lost figure together with a sense of vulnerability in that figure's absence. (C. S. Lewis, in *A Grief Observed,* said that he was surprised by how much grief resembled fear.)

Implicit in the work of Lindemann and explicit in Bowlby's work was the idea that grieving occurred in stages. For Lindemann and Bowlby, grief displayed first an acute phase marked by agitation, tears, and preoccupation with the image of the deceased, and then a more persisting, chronic, phase in which there was withdrawal and depression. (Hofer, 1984, summarizes phase theories of grieving.) Bowlby reported that in some instances the acute phase was preceded by a brief self-protective interval of shock and denial in which feelings were held in abeyance and the reality of the loss refused.

More recent work has much advanced our understanding of grief as a response to relational loss. The issues considered by Freud, Lindemann, and Bowlby have been further explored, and their appraisals both developed and qualified. (Stroebe & Stroebe, 1987, and Schuchter & Zisook, 1993, provide reviews.) In addition, research is exploring topics unimagined by the early investigators, such as the consequences of bereavement for the functioning of the immune system (Irwin & Pike, 1993).

Some of the proposals made by the pioneer investigators have been questioned, and their status at this point seems uncertain. Chief among the unresolved issues are whether relational loss regularly gives rise to grief, whether grief appears in phases, and whether grief work is necessary to the resolution of grief. (See the influential paper by Wortman & Silver, 1989, in which these proposals are criticized, and the response to the Wortman & Silver criticisms in Stroebe, Hansson, & Stroebe, 1993, and Fraley & Shaver, in press.)

## IS GRIEF UNIVERSAL?

The question "Is grief universal?" can be taken in at least three ways. A first is that the question asks whether in *every* society grief is the normal response to loss of a loved figure. A second is that it asks whether in our society grief is the normal response to loss of *any* important relationship. A third way of taking the question is that it asks whether in our society grief is *invariably* the response to loss of a *loved* figure.

Stroebe and Stroebe (1987) examined the cross-cultural literature on the occurrence after bereavement of crying, which they assume is a reliable indicator of grief. They report that in every culture but one, among those about which information was available, people cried after the loss of someone to whom they were close. The one exception was the Balinese. And among the Balinese the absence of tears seemed better ascribed to stoic suppression of grief than to grief's absence. Mourning customs, on the other hand, varied greatly from society to society. It seems fair to conclude that grieving is biological, whereas mourning is cultural, and that in every society grief is a normal reaction to loss. (See also Darwin, 1892.)

This does not mean that loss is always, everywhere, reacted to by grieving. It is likely that in every society some losses do not give rise to grief, and also likely that among those losses that normally give rise to grief, some proportion of the bereaved do not grieve. It seems most likely that grieving is in every society a response normally, but not always, made to certain kinds of losses.

From studies in our society it appears that grief follows the ending of relationships of attachment. Such relationships include pair-bond relationships and also the relationships of parents and small children. With much more variability, relationships of attachment seem sometimes to include adult children's relationships with parents and people's relationships with figures they revere (Weiss, 1993). Loss of any of these relationships can give rise to grief. Grief seems unlikely on loss of ordinary friendships or work relationships; although these may be relationships of genuine warmth and loyalty, their loss, while it may make for sadness, does not usually lead to the deep distress of grief. Indeed, the loss of work relationships through retirement may not give rise to distress at all, even when the retirement ends relationships that for years had been of emotional importance (Weiss, in press).

The third question of universality is whether in our society everyone experiences grief on loss of a figure with whom there was a bond of attachment. Quite regularly, research finds that although the great majority of people display grief symptoms on loss of a husband or wife, some do not. In studies of marital bereavement, perhaps 10% seem not to display "depressed mood" and 70% or more do not report symptoms of depression sufficient to justify the psychiatric diagnosis of depression. (Wortman & Silver, 1989).

How should we interpret the finding of occasional absence of indications of grief and frequent absence of clinically significant depression? There are several possibilities.

1. The bond whose interruption gives rise to grief did not exist in the relationships in which grief was absent. It may be that in a small proportion of marriages the bond of attachment was absent.
2. Depression is not the same as grieving, nor does its absence mean there is no grief. Grief can express itself in a state of sadness that is without depression's self-reproach, and in a sense of desolation that is not accompanied by depression's withdrawal and emotional inaccessibility.
3. Some people may not grieve the loss of a loved figure because they deny the reality of the loss. They may enlist themselves in the completion of the loved figure's work and so, through identification with the loved figure, keep that figure alive in themselves. Or they may wholeheartedly believe in an afterlife in which they will rejoin the lost figure, and so believe that their separation from the lost figure is temporary.
4. Grief may exist but be dissimulated. There may be people who respond to loss with grief, but by suppressing their grief or compartmentalizing it, they remain unaware of it. There may be still others who are aware of their grief but refuse to acknowledge it to anyone else. Inquiry would mistakenly classify people of both kinds as nongrievers.
5. There may indeed be people who were attached to someone whom they lost to death, who fully acknowledge that loss, and yet do not grieve. Their absence of grief is not defensive; they simply do not grieve. I cannot, myself, understand how a relationship of attachment is consistent with an absence of separation distress on interruption of that relationship, and an absence of grief on loss of the relationship, but perhaps it is. There may, perhaps, be people so fully autonomous that they can establish attachments and, on loss of those attachments, experience only brief distress, after which they go on as before. Or there may be some other emotional constellation that permits attachment without loss giving rise to grief.

Except for the last, each of the five alternatives permits us to view grieving as a universal response to the loss of an attachment figure. Should there be instances of the last alternative, I believe that we would have to revise our understanding of how attachments function. In particular, we would have to accept that some people can form attachments without experiencing more than minimal separation distress should the attachments be interrupted.

## DO RESPONSES TO LOSS ASSUME THE FORM OF A PROGRESSION OF STAGES?

There are two stage models that have currency today. In addition to Bowlby's, there is Kübler-Ross's (1969) five-stage reaction to learning that one has a terminal illness. Kübler-Ross's model was not actually intended as a description of reactions to loss, although it has been used in this way. Rather, it was intended to capture reactions to a threat that cannot be averted. However, my comments on Bowlby's stage theory also apply to hers.

Bowlby proposed that loss is followed by three phases of response. First may be a brief interval of shock or denial, a phase most likely when loss has not been anticipated. This phase, when it occurs, is likely to last no more than a few days. The second phase is one of searching and protest. Energy is given in this phase to undoing the loss. The bereaved person may understand that the loss is irreversible, but is nevertheless emotionally driven to reverse it. The third phase is then one of reaction. In this phase the hopelessness of the loss is recognized and the agitated searching and yearning of the second phase is replaced by sad withdrawal.

Bowlby's proposal of three phases of response following bereavement implies two hypotheses that can be considered separately. The first is that bereaved people experience three distinct emotional organizations corresponding to the phases. The second is that the occurrence of the three emotional organizations is structured in time, with denial preceding protest, which in turn precedes reaction.

We might note about these three emotional organizations that they seem as much to be logical constructs as empirical generalizations. The phase of denial is, essentially, a refusal or inability to grasp that loss has occurred, the phase of protest is one of acceptance that loss has occurred together with effort to undo it, and the phase of reaction is one of recognition that the loss is irreversible. The three underlying assumptions are mutually exclusive and exhaustive of possibilities. Logically, one and only one of the phases should characterize the state of the griever at any particular time.

Do these logical categories actually map onto empirical reality? So far as I know, we have only qualitative materials to draw on. These suggest strongly that the state of the bereaved at any particular time can be recognized as expressing one or another of the underlying phase-assumptions. (See, for discussion, Schuchter & Zisook, 1993; Stroebe et al., 1993). Beyond this, I know of no evidence for the empirical reality of the phases as characterizations of the emotional organization of the bereaved.

The second implication of the "phase" proposal is that the emotional organizations suggested by the phases are structured in time. Most investigators, I believe, now hold that far from the phases describing a sequence of stages through which the bereaved must pass, the phases may alternate in time (see, for example, Schuchter & Zisook, 1993.)

What many investigators might agree to, though, is a weak form of the proposal of invariable sequence, in which denial is most likely on first awareness of the loss, protest most likely early in bereavement, and reaction most likely later on. But just how much more likely one phase is than another at any particular time, and when in the course of grieving it is most likely that denial or protest or reaction dominate, are matters not yet examined by research.

## IS GRIEF WORK NECESSARY IF PEOPLE ARE TO RETURN TO NORMAL FUNCTIONING AFTER LOSS?

Loss makes people vulnerable to invasion of their thoughts and feelings by memories or awareness that flood them with distress. "Grief work" is generally taken to mean a cognitive and emotional review of such memories or awareness which will neutralize them, so that their recall will no longer trigger distress. Belief in the necessity of grief work often plays a role in responses made by caregivers to ordinary grief and often underlies therapists' treatment of pathological grief.

"Pathological grief" can be defined as grief that is excessively prolonged or that in some other way interferes with functioning (Horowitz, Wilner, Marmar, & Krupnick, 1980). "Ordinary grief" moves toward resolution; pathological grief does not. There have been several reviews of the evidence for and against the idea that grief work is necessary if grief is not to become pathological (Stroebe, 1992–1993; Bonanno, Keltner, Holen, & Horowitz, 1995; Fraley & Shaver, in press). The conclusion that seems on its way to becoming a consensus is that although many, perhaps most, among the bereaved find grief work to be valuable, some among the bereaved seem not to engage in grief work yet seem also to exhibit no indications at all of pathological grief.

Apparently there are other ways besides grief work of dealing with the distress associated with loss. Some among the bereaved seem to do well by suppressing their grieving or by distracting themselves from grieving. In the short run the strategies of suppression and distraction appear stressful, but in the longer run, for some people at least, they may be beneficial (Bonanno et al., 1995).

Grief work may even be inadvisable for some among the bereaved. People who have survived traumatic experiences, and whose memories of their losses are so searing that they are unintegratable, may do best to "seal off" their experiences, rather than attend to them and risk retraumatization. Their best approach to returning to effective functioning may be to learn techniques for continuing the suppression of painful thoughts and memories (Flannery, 1992).

These observations suggest that fostering grief work among the bereaved is likely to benefit some, but not all. Some among the bereaved may well do better if they act on the advice to get on with their lives—advice that is often disparaged by therapists and investigators who know how difficult it is to put grief aside (Fraley & Shaver, in press.)

Still, many among the bereaved do find grief work of value. Investigators who argue that attending to loss early on in grieving is associated with poorer outcomes seem to confuse rumination with grief work. But rumination is repetitive and unbudging, whereas grief work changes thoughts and feelings about the loss, making them less insistent and, when they occur, more tolerable. Indeed, rumination indicates a failure of grief work.

It may be that grief work, rather than being necessary if those who have experienced emotional reverse are to move toward recovery, is only one among several possible coping strategies. What may be needed at this point is research investigation that could make evident the different coping strategies grievers use. Such research would almost surely have to be in frequent close contact with people dealing with loss in different ways. To be sure, research of this sort could constitute an intervention, affecting the emotional state of those being studied. But the intervention would very likely be benign (Pennebaker, Kiecolt-Glaser, & Glaser, 1990) and its effects should not be so great that they would overwhelm the individual's own coping strategies.

One question that might be examined is whether a process like grief work, which achieves neutralization of memory, can occur in the absence of conscious attention to the loss. Is it possible for people to immerse themselves in work or family or distraction, and yet somehow experience amelioration of the pain of their loss? Or is it usually the case that without conscious grief work distress remains, encapsulated, ready to emerge if given a chance?

Acknowledging the possibility of achieving the effects of grief work through other processes suggests that we do not really understand the process of grief work. Might it be that grief work helps return people to functioning not by neutralizing painful memory so much as by fostering techniques for mastering painful memory should such memory recur? If this is the case, those who accomplish the tasks of grief work would not so much be free of distressing thoughts and memories as they would be prepared to cope with them when they occurred.

In any event, we must change our thinking about what is accomplished by grief work from the idea proposed by Freud. Freud seems to have been mistaken in his idea that grief work loosens bonds to the lost figure. We know now that, to some degree at least, the bonds of attachment persist after the loss of the attachment figure. Long after the loss, the attachment figure continues to be thought of with affection and a sense of closeness; indeed, it may not go too far to say that the attachment figure continues to be loved (Klass, Silverman, & Nickman, 1996). The result of grief work, when it is successful, seems not to be that the lost figure no longer plays a role in emotional life, but rather that there is acceptance of the present and future absence of that figure.

## RESEARCH ON LOSS

I believe there is value in research that would consider together, as well as separately, losses that give rise to grief and losses whose consequences, though perhaps equally distressing, are different. Understanding the processes involved in one sort of loss may help us understand the processes involved in another. It may turn out that in narcissistic damage, and the associated loss of trust in the self, there is the same loss of feelings of security, and the same responses to insecurity, as occur in loss of loved figures; that there is a kind of grieving for a lost self. It may turn out that treatment issues are similar in the different kinds of loss, and that something like grief work may be valuable for at least some among the narcissisticly damaged, and that some sort of reframing of the image of the self may be valuable for at least some among the grief-stricken. We may, indeed, be able to work toward a general theory of loss and its management.

In any event, the study of loss means that we must consider the consequences of the withdrawal from our lives of a basis for our emotional organization. In any instance, there will be in the withdrawal both an injury to our emotional organization and a subsequent deficit in our lives, in that the withdrawn element is now absent.

Both injury and deficit must be considered in treatment, but it may be worth noting the contribution that study of deficit can also make to our understanding of human functioning. A principle of research that has gained deserved respect is that to learn what something does for people, it's useful to see what happens to those who don't have it. We can learn the provisions of a particular vitamin by seeing what happens to people deprived of that vitamin. In the same way we can learn the provisions of a social bond by seeing what happens to people without it, and so come to understand more about loneliness, social isolation, feelings of marginality, and feelings of meaninglessness. And we can learn the provisions of social place by seeing what happens to the marginal and excluded, and the provisions of a sense of reasonable invulnerability by seeing what happens when it is shattered, and so come to understand more about the motivations for self-protective withdrawal.

By studying the consequences of the deficits that follow loss, we can learn more about the way in which our functioning depends on our relationships to others and on our sense of ourselves as relational figures. In this way we can learn more about what it means to be human.

## REFERENCES

Bonanno, G. A., Keltner, D. Holen, A., & Horowitz, M. J. (1995). When avoiding unpleasant emotions might not be such a bad thing: Verbal-autonomic response dissociation and midlife conjugal bereavement. *Journal of Personality and Social Psychology, 69,* 975–989.

Bowlby, J. (1961). Processes of mourning. *International Journal of Psychoanalysis, 42,* 317–340.

Bowlby, J. (1980). *Attachment and loss. Vol. 3. Loss: Sadness and depression.* New York: Basic Books.

Bowlby, J. (1982). Attachment and loss: Retrospect and prospect. *American Journal of Orthopsychiatry, 52,* 664–678.

Darwin, C. (1892). *The expression of the emotions in man and animals.* New York: Appleton. (First published 1872.)

Flannery, R. B., Jr. (1992). *Post-traumatic stress disorder: The victim's guide to healing and recovery.* New York: Crossroad Publishing.

Fraley, R. C., & Shaver, P. R. (in press). Loss and bereavement: Attachment theory and recent controversies concerning "grief work" and the nature of detachment. In J. Cassidy and P. R. Shaver (Eds.), *Handbook of attachment theory and research,* New York: Guilford.

Freud, S. (1917). Mourning and melancholia. In J. Strachey (Trans. & Ed.), *Complete psychological works. Vol. 14* (standard ed.). London: Hogarth Press, 1957.

Horowitz, M. J., Wilner, N., Marmar, C., & Krupnick, J. (1980). Pathological grief and the activation of latent self-images, *American Journal of Psychiatry, 137*(10), 1157–1162.

Irwin, M., & Pike, J. (1993). Bereavement, depressive symptoms, and immune function. In M. Stroebe, W. Stroebe, and R. O. Hansson (Eds.), *Handbook of bereavement* (pp. 160–171). New York: Cambridge University Press.

Klass, D., Silverman, P. R., & Nickman, S. L. (Eds.). (1996). *Continuing bonds: new understandings of grief.* Washington, D.C.: Taylor & Francis.

Kübler-Ross, E. (1969). *On death and dying.* New York: Springer-Verlag.

Lindemann, E. (1944). Symptomatology and management of acute grief, *American Journal of Psychiatry, 101*, 141–148.

Parkes, C. M., & Weiss, R. S. (1983). *Recovery from Bereavement.* New York, Basic Books.

Pennebaker, J., Kiecolt-Glaser, J. K., & Glaser, R. (1988). Disclosure of traumas and immune function: Health implications for psychotherapy, *Journal of Consulting and Clinical Psychology, 56,* 239–245.

Schuchter, S. R., & Zisook, S. (1993) The course of normal grief. In M. Stroebe, W. Stroebe, and R. O. Hansson, *Handbook of Bereavement* (pp. 23–43). New York: Cambridge University Press.

Stroebe, M. S., Hansson, R. O., & Stroebe, W. (1993). Contemporary themes and controversies in bereavement research. In M. Stroebe, W. Stroebe, and R. O. Hansson (Eds.), *Handbook of Bereavement* (pp. 457–475). New York: Cambridge University Press.

Stroebe, M. S. (1992–93). Coping with bereavement: A review of the grief work hypothesis. *Omega: Journal of Death and Dying, 26,* 19–42.

Stroebe, W., & Stroebe, M. S. (1987). *Bereavement and health: The psychological and physical consequences of partner loss.* New York, Cambridge University Press.

Weiss, R. S. (1993). Loss and recovery. *Journal of Social Issues, 44*(3), 37–52.

Weiss, R. S. (1997). Adaptation to retirement. In I. Gotlib and B. Wheaton (Eds.), *Stress and adversity over the life course: Trajectories and turning point* (pp. 232–245). New York: Cambridge University Press.

Weiss, R. S., & Richards, A. (1997). A scale for predicting quality of recovery following the death of a partner. *Journal of Personality and Social Psychology, 72,* 885–891.

Wortman, C. B., & Silver, R. C. (1989). The myths of coping with loss. *Journal of Consulting and Clinical Psychology, 57*(3), 349–357.

# Index


abortion, 56
adversity, growth from, 207–208, 261–263, 325–327, 328
African-American
  heavyweight women, 263–264
  homosexuals, 282
anger, homelessness and, 271
anxiety
  athletes, 242, 245
  chronic illness, 205
  job loss and, 304
Armenian genocide, 232, 234
attachment theory, 8–9, 90
autoethnography, 335
  chronic illness and, 52–55
  definition, 49
  impact on identity, 58
autonomy, 119
avoidance, 84, 86, 88, 91

bereavement. *See also* grief; grieving
  coping with, 89–90
  definition, 83
  pathology, 87
  stage reaction to, 348
  suicidal, 213–218
  *vs.* trauma, 81–84, 86–87, 94
blame
  Holocaust survivor and, 226
  suicidal bereavement, 214
  survivor's self-, 40
body weight
  African-American women and, 263–264
  employment and, 256–257
  external stimuli and, 254–256, 263
  higher education and, 256
  loss control, 253–254
  psychopathology, 259
  SES and, 257
Bowlby, John, 345–346, 348
brain injury
  characterological alterations from, 193
  loss issues after, 193–194, 197
  sequelae, 190–191
breast cancer, 282, 339
  threat to relationship, 286
bulimia, 57

caregiver. *See also* chronic illness; communal relationships
  emotional health, 173–174
  perceived burden, 181–182
  person with brain injury, 192, 198. *See also* support group
  relationships with care recipient, 174–175, 180–181, 205
  support to, 183–184
children
  with cancer, 28
  early development and homelessness, 272
  heavyweight, 257
  impact of victimization on, 235
  job loss and, 308, 309
  loss and, 8–9
  parent's chronic illness and, 140
  racism and multiracial families, 130
  world view and early care, 38
chronic illness, 52. *See also* fibromyalgia
  autoethnography and, 52–55
  commitment and, 148–149
  community and, 148. *See also* health care system
  education, 147
  employment and, 145–146
  family and, 137–138, 141, 145, 147. *See also* commitment

chronic illness (*cont.*)
  loss of relationships and, 139–140
  patient communication challenge, 143–144, 147
  patients and children, 140
  patient's stress, 140–141
  personal identity and, 141–142, 202–203
  relationships adjustment, 144–145, 147–148. *See also* communal relationships
  sexual activity and, 145, 204–205
  society adjustment to, 137
  support groups and, 146
chronic pain, 339
  theory of hope and, 68–70
co-constructed narrative, 55–56
cognitive behavior therapy, 73, 74, 208–209
commitment
  chronic illness and, 148–149
  passion and, 154, 161
communal relationships, 335
  description, 176
  theory of, 175–179
communication
  challenge for chronically-ill patient, 143–144, 147
  chronic pain and, 70
community
  chronic illness and, 148. *See also* health care system
  interracial couples and, 131
companionship
  homelessness and loss of, 271
  support group, 196
compensation
  healing and, 236–237
  prejudice and heavyweight people, 261–263
computer-mediated relationship, 107
concentration camp syndrome, 222
conflict resolution procedures, 232
connection, 119
conservation of resorce models, 243–250
control, sense of
  body weight and, 254–256
  cognitive approaches to restoration of, 25–27, 29, 208–209
  job loss and, 306
  loss and, 21
  pursuit of goals and, 29–30
  restoration of, 23–25, 40–41
coping
  with brain injury, 191, 196
  with breakup of relationships, 107–108
  with economic hardship, 307
  with Fm, 207–208
  with grief, 88–91
  grief work and, 350
  with homelessness, 276
  with loss, 90–92
  with loss of passion, 162–164
  as a loss process, 321
  perspective on the loss and, 28
  with racism, 125
  strategies and autoethnographic stories, 51–55
  with stress, 10, 88
  with threat from intimate sources, 283–284, 287–288
countertransference, 226–228

death
  psychology of loss and, 321
  *vs.* loss, 4, 6
deception, suicidal bereavement, 215
denial, 84–85, 88–89, 207
  brain injury and, 195
  phase of bereavement, 348
depression, 85
  caregiver, 178–179
  grief symptoms and, 347
  heavyweight people, 259
  job loss and, 304
  spouses of persons with brain injury, 194
despair, homelessness and, 271

Diagnostic and Statistical Manual (DSM-IV)
  bereavement definition, 83
  PSTD definition, 82–83
dialogue groups, 232
  reconciliation and, 235–236
dieting, weight control and, 254
discrimination
  age, 300
  interracial couples and police, 129–130
disillusionment, 333
  fatal attraction and, 115, 122
  trauma and, 35–36, 39
dissolution of relationships, 335
  causes of, 104–105
  coping with, 107–108
  distress after, 106–107
  fibromyalgia sufferers and, 205–206
  partner's cognitive reframing and, 116
  process models of, 105–106
  social psychological models, 103
  strategies for, 106
dissonance theory, 116, 118
distress
  conceptualization of loss and, 343–344
  dissolution of relationships, 106–107
  element of loss in psychological, 321
  holocaust survivors emotional, 222
  retirement from sport, 247
divorce, 101
  demographic studies, 104
  distress after, 106–107
  illness and disability's impact on, 139–140
Dual Process Model for Coping with Loss, 90–91, 94

economic hardship. *See also* income
  job loss and, 307
  mental health and, 311
education
  body weight and, 256
  chronic illness, 147
Elena Ceausescu Syndrome, 295
emotions. *See also* feelings
  caregivers of person with brain injury, 196
  loss and communication of, 26–27
  suicidal bereavement, 215
employment. *See also* job loss
  body weight and, 256–257
  chronic illness and, 145–146, 206
energy
  coping with pain and mental, 76
  pain and loss of, 70–71
equity theory, dissolution of relationships and, 103
Erikson, Erik, 157
exercise
  pain and, 74
  progressive relaxation, 75
Existentialism, 42
expectations, fatal attraction, 121–122
externality, 255, 263

family
  chronic illness and, 137–138, 141, 145, 147. *See also* commitment
  chronic pain sufferer and, 75, 204
  heavyweight children and, 256
  interracial couples and, 128
  job loss and, 304, 307–309
  loss and, 336
  person with brain injury and, 198
  Rumanian patriarchal, 293
  suicidal bereavement, 214, 217
fatal attraction
  contradictory forces in, 114–115, 119–122, 335
  definition, 113, 117
  object of, 158
  over-time process, 115–116
  prevalence of, 117
  process, 118
  role of differences in, 116–118

feelings. *See also* emotions
autoethnographic description of, 52–55
homelessness, 270–271
recounting and co-constructed narrative, 55–56
feminism, 300
fibromyalgia, 201–202
loss of normal functions and, 203–204
financial loss. *See also* job loss
chronic illness impact, 180–182
heavyweight students and, 256
Freud, Sigmund, 81, 303, 312, 344–345, 350
friendship, 308
fun, 119

gender
coping with loss, 92
intimacy-related concerns and, 282
passion and, 159, 161
relations in Rumania, 293–294
role, 339
generativity, 326
genocide, 337
Armenians, 234
healing, 232–233
goals identification
high-hope people and, 72
hope theory and, 65–67
life and importance of, 284
life purpose and, 29–30
no-pain, 68
pathway thinking and, 73
grief, 327
coping with, 88–91
Freud and, 344–345, 350
literature on, 344–346
loss and, 343
pathological, 349
reactions to, 85–86
research, 134, 350–351
universality of, 346–348
grieving. *See also* bereavement; memories
brain injury and, 193
dialogue group and, 232–233
grief work and, 349–350
mourning customs and, 346
stages of, 9, 15, 89, 326, 337
guilt. *See also* compensation; countertransference
survivor, 225–226

habituation, passion and, 155
healing, 232–233. *See also* reconciliation
psychology of loss and, 339–340
health, 64. *See also* mental health
caregiver emotional, 173–174
homelessness and, 273–275
job loss and, 307
psychology and person-in-environment, 283
trauma/bereavement and, 87, 93
health care system
chronic illness and, 149–150
heavyweight people and, 257
health professionals
chronically ill and, 142, 205
countertransference, 226–228
holocaust survivor and, 222–223, 226–228
listening skills, 326–327
suicidally bereaved people and, 217
helplessness, 23–24
HIV/AIDS
patients' sense of control, 23, 24
risk related to, 284
Holocaust survivors, 327. *See also* genocide
children of, 236
emotional distress, 222
Israeli society and, 224–226, 337
homelessness, 335
feelings triggered by, 270–271
statistics, 269–270
stressful life events and, 272–273
hope, psychology of, 65–76

homosexual relationships, 102, 104
human nature, perception of loss, 7

idealization, passion and, 157, 161
identity. *See also* personality
  athletic, 248–250
  chronic illness and personal, 141–142, 202–204
  decline in sport performance and loss of, 245
  group *vs.* individual, 231
  homelessness and personal, 274
  interracial couples and loss of, 129
  job loss and personal, 306, 308–309, 311
  losses' influence on personal, 322
  retirement from sport and loss of, 247–249
  sport injury and loss of, 243
  witch and personal, 297
illness, as a loss event, 11
illusion
  loss of. *See* disillusionment; trauma
  loss of positive, 285
  nature of, 38
  *vs.* reality, 39
incentive relationships, 30
incest, 22
income. *See also* economic hardship
  loss of, 206, 306
independence, loss of, 203–204
information, 196
  threat from intimate sources and, 287–288
injury, sport, 243–244. *See also* resources
interactive interview, 56–57
interdependence theory, dissolution of relationships and, 103
interracial couples
  family support for, 128
  identity loss and, 129
  police discrimination, 129–130
  racism research, 126
  status in community, 131
  white partner's loss feeling in, 132–134
intimacy
  passion and, 154, 161
  threat from intimate sources and, 287
intrusion, 84–85, 86, 88
invulnerability, 37

jealousy, 161
job loss, 335, 343
  adverse effects, 304–305
  historical perspective, 305–306
justice, as a fundamental assumption, 37

life purpose and meaning
  Cambodian vision of, 234–235
  cognitive approaches to restoration of, 25–27, 29, 208–209
  loss and, 21–22, 327
  pursuit of goals and, 29–30, 337–339
  recovery from homelessness and, 276–277
  restoration of, 22–25
  survivor's reevaluation of, 41–44
Lindemann, Erich, 345
loss
  as an academic discipline, 7–8
  application of general theories to, 334–335
  bereavement as, 89–90
  brain injury and, 190–191
  college students' definition of, 4–6
  common factors to, 333–334
  conceptualization deficiencies, 338
  creation of account of, 50
  cross cultural perspectives, 294–301
  definition, 12, 202, 242, 320, 332
  issues in studying loss and grief, 343–351
  multiple, 13
  origin of the word, 3

loss (*cont.*)
- physical *vs.* symbolic, 10
- psychology of, 319–328, 331–340
- theory of stage reaction to, 348
- types of, 4, 6, 350–351

loss-orientation, 91
love, *vs.* passion, 154

media, victimhood and, 324–325
medication, pain, 76
memories, loss and, 322–323, 349–350
mental health
- homelessness and, 274
- job loss and, 309, 311
- work and, 312

misunderstanding, suicidal bereavement, 215–216
myths, Rumanian women and, 296

narcissistic damage, 344
narrative approach, 49
- coping with Fm and, 208

novelty, 120

occupation. *See* employment
oscillation, 92–93

pain
- agency blocks, 70–71
- cognitive behavior therapy, 73, 74–75
- cycle and hope, 65–67
- definition, 63–64
- health awareness and, 64
- management and pathway thinking, 73
- response to, 67–68
- *vs.* suffering, 64

passion. *See also* fatal attraction
- decline and restoration, 162–164
- definition, 154
- evolution of, 155–156
- lack of reciprocity, 161
- maintenance, 160

pathway thinking, 65
- chronic pain and, 68–70
- theory of hope and, 73

performance levels, slumps in, 245–247, 249
personality. *See also* identity
- brain injury and change in, 193
- loss and change in, 16

positive thinking, 27–28
Post Traumatic Stress Disorder (PTSD), 82–86, 92, 319
- concentration camp syndrome and, 223
- homelessness and, 275

poverty
- homelessness and, 275
- job loss and, 306

predictability, 120
prejudice
- body weight and, 259–260
- heavyweight people compensation for, 261–263
- against women, 301

psychiatric disorders, homelessness and, 274
psychoanalytic approach, concentration camp syndrome and, 223
psychology of loss, 319
- multidisciplinary aspects, 335–336
- therapeutic implications, 339–340
- validity of unifying theory, 332–333
- *vs.* psychology of gain, 331–332

racism, 337
- categorization of, 126–127
- definition, 125
- losses resulting from, 125, 134–135

rape, 226
reconciliation, 235–237
rehabilitation process, 207
- Holocaust survivor, 224

relationships. *See also* divorce; fatal attraction; passion
- active *vs.* passive, 101
- adjustment with chronically-ill patient, 144–145, 147–148

beginnings and endings, 114, 346–347
black-white heterosexual, 127
breakup and types of, 107
breast cancer and, 286
caregiver/care recipient, 174–175, 180–181
communal. *See* communal relationships
dissolution of. *See* dissolution of relationships
exchange, 176
health professionals/chronically-ill patient, 142, 205
illness and disability's impact on, 139–141, 335
longevity, 104–105
precursors to breakup of, 100
redefinition of, 101
types of, 99–100
religion, suicidal bereavement and, 218
research. *See also* communal relationships; theories
autoethnographic approach to, 50–51
caregiver emotional well-being, 173
categories of loss, 350–351
dissolution of relationships, 104–105
fatal attraction, 117–118, 122–123
general psychosocial theories and loss, 334–335
grief process, 15
interracial couples and racism, 126
loss definition and, 12
models of loss, 8–9
multiple losses and, 13
personality change and loss, 16
post-loss psychological variables, 16
pre-loss variables and post-loss functioning, 14–15
social dimension of psychology of loss, 337
sport injury, 243–244
stress, 10–11
suicidal bereavement, 216–217
taxonomic *vs.* theoretical approach to loss, 13–14
resources
conservation of, 243–244
definition, 244
loss of, 245
restoration-orientation, 92
retirement, from sport, 247–248
risk group, 310–311
rituals, 224
loss and, 7

search for meaning, 21–30
in suicidal bereavement, 214–215, 218
self-concept, 284
self-delusion, positive interpretation and, 28
self-devaluation/evaluation, 233
view of the world and, 36–37
self-esteem
African-American women, 263
chronically-ill patient, 141, 144
heavyweight people, 260–261
job loss and, 304, 308
loss and, 343–344
passion and, 157, 161
self-image, 28–29, 259
Holocaust survivor, 224
self-monitoring/self-monitors (SMs), 263
passion and, 158–159
seriousness, 119
sexual abuse, 22, 285, 288
homelessness and, 274–275
sexual activity
chronic illness and, 145, 204–205
loss of vital force and, 298
use of condom and, 286
sexual attraction, 120, 145
passion and, 154–155, 159
shattered assumptions, 36–41
social psychology
job loss and, 305–306
loss and, 10
study of stress and, 10–11

society
  Holocaust survivors and Israeli, 224–226
  homelessness and, 275
  loss and, 7, 336
  stigmatization of heavyweight people, 254, 257–258
  support, 244
  victimhood and, 324–325
sport, competitive
  definition, 241
  injury, 243–244
  loss in, 242
  retirement from, 247–248
stereotype
  gender, 293, 295
  heavyweight people, 258, 260
stigmatization
  heavyweight people, 254, 257–258, 260–261
  job loss and social, 310, 311
  suicidal bereavement and, 213
storytelling, exploration of loss through, 50, 326–327
strength, 120
stress
  bereavement and, 82–83
  chronic-illness patient's, 140–141
  coping and, 10
  decline in sport performance, 246
  homelessness and life events, 272–273
  job loss and, 307
  mastery and, 309–310
  treatment of traumatic, 87
  types of, 11
stroke, 22
  sense of control and, 24
substance abuse
  homelessness and, 274
  job loss and, 304
suffering, definition, 64
suicidality, 215, 217
suicide, 213–218
  homelessness and, 271
  job loss and, 304
support, social, 244
support groups. *See also* friendship
  caregivers of person with brain injury, 196–198
  chronic illness and, 146
  communication and, 27
  heavyweight people and, 264
  loss and, 7
  suicidally bereaved people, 217
  survivor's interaction with, 41
syndrome, 84
  survivor, 222

terms/images, association with loss, 4–6
theories
  loss and general psychosocial, 334–335
  pathological *vs.* feeling of loss, 9
  social psychology and loss, 9–11
theory of hope, 65–67
  definition, 66
  goals identification and, 72
  impediments to, 67
transitions, 339
  life, 303, 308
trauma. *See also* Holocaust survivors
  bereavement *vs.,* 81–84, 86–87, 94
  definition, 82–83
  healing from, 232
  reactions to, 84
  rehabilitation process after, 207
  response to, 35
  role in value creation and appreciation, 43–44
  sense of control and, 21–22
  survivor's vulnerability, 39–40

victimization
  disillusionment and, 36–37
  loss and, 343–344
  survivor's existential crisis, 40–41
  victims and nations' behavior, 233–234
  world view after, 231–232

violence
homelessness and, 274–275
job loss and, 304
vulnerability, 120

witches
evil and, 296–297
role of, 298
women
coping with risk, 282
heavyweight African-American, 263–264
intimate sources' threats, 285–286, 288
perception of HIV/AIDS risk, 284
Rumanian, 293–295, 337
social and cultural influences on, 289
widowhood, 307
world, view of the, 338. *See also* illusion
self-devaluation and, 233
self-evaluation and, 36–37, 39
trauma survivor's, 40–41, 283–284